Solutions Manual for

Recursive Methods in Economic Dynamics

Solutions Manual for *Recursive Methods in Economic Dynamics*

Claudio Irigoyen

Esteban Rossi-Hansberg

Mark L. J. Wright

Harvard University Press
Cambridge, Massachusetts, and London, England

Printed in the United States of America

Second printing, 2004
ISBN 0-674-00888-X

To Marta, Santiago, and Federico
–C.I.

To María José
–E.R.H.

To Christine
–M.L.J.W.

Contents

Foreword

Over the years we have received many requests for an answer book for the exercises in *Recursive Methods in Economic Dynamics*. These requests have come not from inept teachers or lazy students, but from serious readers who have wanted to make sure their time was being well spent.

For a student trying to master the material in *Recursive Methods*, the exercises are critical, and some of them are quite hard. Thus it is useful for the reader to be reassured along the way that he or she is on the right track, and to have misconceptions corrected quickly when they occur. In addition, some of the problems need more specific guidelines or sharper formulations, and a few (not too many, we like to think) contain errors–commands to prove assertions that, under the stated assumptions, are just not true.

Consequently, when three of our best graduate students proposed to write a solutions manual, we were delighted. While we firmly believe in the value of working out problems for oneself, in learning by doing, it is clear that the present book will be an invaluable aid for students engaged in this enterprise.

The exercises in *Recursive Methods* are of two types, reflecting the organization of the book. Some chapters in the book are self-contained expositions of theoretical tools that are essential to modern practitioners of dynamic stochastic economics. These "core" chapters contain dozens of problems that are basically mathematical: exercises to help a reader make sure that an abstract definition or theorem has been grasped, or to provide a proof (some of them quite important) that was omitted from the text. This solutions manual contains solutions for most of the exercises of this sort. In particular, proofs are provided for results that are fundamental in the subsequent development of the theory.

Other chapters of *Recursive Methods* contain applications of those theoretical tools, organized by the kind of mathematics they require. The exercises in these chapters are quite different in character. Many of them guide the reader through classic papers drawn from various substantive areas of economics: growth, macroeconomics, monetary theory, labor, information economics, and so on. These papers, which appeared in leading journals over the last couple of decades, represented the cutting edge, both technically and substantively. Turning a paper of this sort into an exercise meant providing enough structure to keep the reader on course, while leaving enough undone to challenge even the best students. The present book provides answers for only a modest proportion of these problems. (Of course, for many of the rest the journal article on which the problem is based provides a solution!)

We hope that readers will think of this solutions manual as a trio of especially helpful classmates. Claudio, Esteban, and Mark are people you might look for in the library when you are stuck on a problem and need some help, or with whom you want to compare notes when you have hit on an especially clever argument. This is the way a generation of University of Chicago students have thought of them, and we hope that this book will let many more students, in a wide variety of places, benefit from their company as well.

Nancy L. Stokey
Robert E. Lucas, Jr.

Solutions Manual for

Recursive Methods in Economic Dynamics

1 *Introduction*

In the preface to *Recursive Methods in Economic Dynamics*, the authors stated that their aim was to make recursive methods accessible to the wider economics profession. They succeeded. Since *RMED* appeared in 1989, the use of recursive methods in economics has boomed. And what was once as much a research monograph as a textbook has now been adopted in first-year graduate courses around the world.

The best way for students to learn these techniques is to work problems. And toward this end, *RMED* contains over two hundred problems, many with multiple parts. The present book aims to assist students in this process by providing answers and hints to a large subset of these questions.

At an early stage, we were urged to leave some of the questions in the book unanswered, so as to be available as a "test bank" for instructors. This raises the question of which answers to include and which to leave out. As a guiding principle, we have tried to include answers to those questions that are the most instructive, in the sense that the techniques involved in their solution are the most useful later on in the book. We have also tried to answer all of the questions whose results are integral to the presentation of the core methods of the book. Exercises that involve particularly difficult reasoning or mathematics have also been solved, although no doubt our specific choices in this regard are subject to criticism.

As a result, the reader will find that we have provided an answer to almost every question in the core "method" chapters (that is, Chapters 4, 6, 9, 15, 17, and 18), as well as to most of the questions in the chapters on mathematical background (Chapters 3, 7, 8, 11, 12, and 14). However, only a subset of the questions in the "application" chapters (2, 5, 10, 13, and 16) have been answered.

It is our hope that this selection will make the assimilation of the material easier for students. At the same time, instructors should be comforted to find that they still have a relatively rich set of questions to assign from the application chapters. Instructors should also find that, because much of the material in the method and mathematical background chapters appears repeatedly, there are many opportunities to assign this material to their students.

Despite our best efforts, errors no doubt remain. Furthermore, it is to be expected (and hoped) that readers will uncover more elegant, and perhaps more instructive, approaches to answering the questions than those provided here. The authors would appreciate being notified of any errors and, as an aid to readers, commit to maintaining a website where readers can post corrections, comments and alternative answers. This website is currently hosted at:

http://www.stanford.edu/~mlwright/RMEDSolutions

In the process of completing this project we have incurred various debts. A number of people provided us with their own solutions to problems in the text, including Xavier Gine, Ivan Werning and Rui Zhao. Others, including Vadym Lepetyuk and Joon Hyuk Song, pointed out sins of commission and omission in earlier drafts. Christine Groeger provided extensive comments, and lent her LaTeX expertise to the production of the manuscript. At Harvard University Press, Elizabeth Gilbert and Benno Weisberg made substantial improvements to the manuscript's style and logic. We thank all of these people, together with Robert E. Lucas, Jr., and reserve a special thanks for Nancy Stokey, whose insight and enthusiasm were invaluable in seeing the project through to its conclusion.

2 An Overview

Exercise 2.1

The fact that $f : \mathbf{R}_+ \rightarrow \mathbf{R}_+$ is continuously differentiable, strictly increasing and strictly concave comes directly from the definition of f as

$$f(k) = F(k, 1) + (1 - \delta)k,$$

with $0 < \delta < 1$, and F satisfying the properties mentioned above. In particular, the sum of two strictly increasing functions is strictly increasing, and continuous differentiability is preserved under summation. Finally, the sum of a strictly concave and a linear function is strictly concave.

Also,

$$\begin{aligned} f(0) &= F(0, 1) = 0, \\ f'(k) &= F_k(k, 1) + (1 - \delta) > 0, \\ \lim_{k \to 0} f'(k) &= \lim_{k \to 0} F_k(k, 1) + \lim_{k \to 0}(1 - \delta) = \infty, \\ \lim_{k \to \infty} f'(k) &= \lim_{k \to \infty} F_k(k, 1) + \lim_{k \to \infty}(1 - \delta) = (1 - \delta). \end{aligned}$$

Exercise 2.2

a. With the given functional forms for the production and utility function we can write (5) as

note $U(c) = \ln(c)$, $f(k) = k^\alpha$, $f'(k) = \alpha k^{\alpha-1}$

$$\frac{\alpha\beta k_t^{\alpha-1}}{k_t^\alpha - k_{t+1}} = \frac{1}{k_{t-1}^\alpha - k_t},$$

which can be rearranged as

$$\alpha\beta k_t^{\alpha-1}(k_{t-1}^\alpha - k_t) = (k_t^\alpha - k_{t+1}).$$

Dividing both sides by k_t^α and using the change of variable $z_t = k_t / k_{t-1}^\alpha$ we obtain

$$\alpha\beta(\frac{1}{z_t} - 1) = 1 - z_{t+1},$$

or

$$z_{t+1} = 1 + \alpha\beta - \frac{\alpha\beta}{z_t},$$

which is the equation represented in Figure 2.1.

As can be seen in the figure, the first-order difference equation has two steady states (that is, z's such that $z_{t+1} = z_t = z$), which are the two solutions to the characteristic equation

$$z^2 - (1 + \alpha\beta)z + \alpha\beta = 0.$$

These are given by $z = 1$ and $\alpha\beta$.

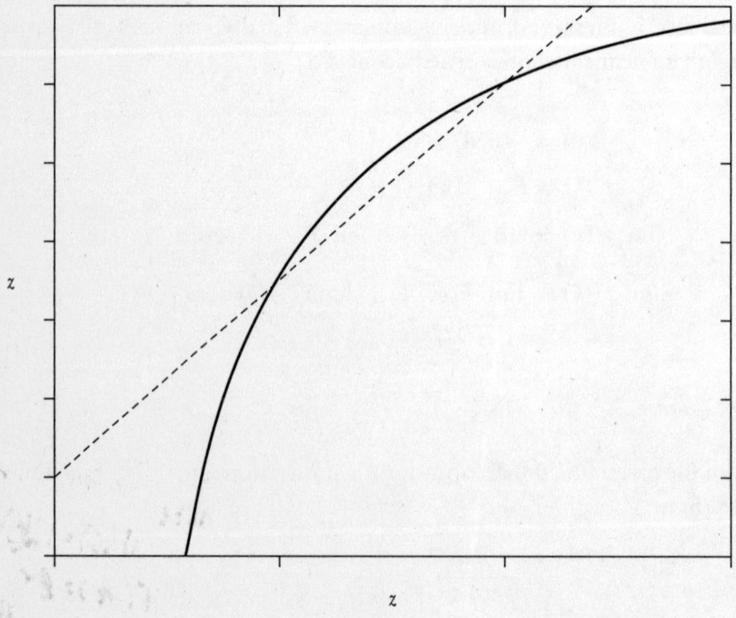

Figure 2.1

b. Using the boundary condition $z_{T+1} = 0$ we can solve for z_T as

$$z_T = \frac{\alpha\beta}{1+\alpha\beta}.$$

Substituting recursively into the law of motion for z_t derived above we can solve for z_{T-1} as

$$\begin{aligned} z_{T-1} &= \frac{\alpha\beta}{1+\alpha\beta - z_T} \\ &= \frac{\alpha\beta}{1+\alpha\beta - \frac{\alpha\beta}{1+\alpha\beta}} \\ &= \frac{\alpha\beta(1+\alpha\beta)}{1+\alpha\beta+(\alpha\beta)^2}, \end{aligned}$$

and in general,

$$z_{T-j} = \frac{\alpha\beta[1+\alpha\beta+\ldots+(\alpha\beta)^j]}{1+\alpha\beta+\ldots+(\alpha\beta)^{j+1}}.$$

Hence for $t = T - j$,

$$\begin{aligned} z_t &= \frac{\alpha\beta[1+\alpha\beta+\ldots+(\alpha\beta)^{T-t}]}{1+\alpha\beta+\ldots+(\alpha\beta)^{T-t+1}} \\ &= \frac{\alpha\beta s_{T-t}}{s_{T-t+1}} \end{aligned}$$

where $s_i = 1+\alpha\beta+\ldots+(\alpha\beta)^i$. In order to solve for the series, take for instance the one in the numerator,

$$s_{T-t} = 1+\alpha\beta+\ldots+(\alpha\beta)^{T-t},$$

multiply both sides by $\alpha\beta$ to get

$$\alpha\beta s_{T-t} = \alpha\beta+\ldots+(\alpha\beta)^{T-t+1},$$

and substract this new expression from the previous one to obtain

$$(1-\alpha\beta)s_{T-t} = 1-(\alpha\beta)^{T-t+1}.$$

Hence

$$s_{T-t} = \frac{1-(\alpha\beta)^{T-t+1}}{1-\alpha\beta},$$

$$s_{T-t+1} = \frac{1-(\alpha\beta)^{T-t+2}}{1-\alpha\beta},$$

and therefore

$$z_t = \alpha\beta\frac{1-(\alpha\beta)^{T-t+1}}{1-(\alpha\beta)^{T-t+2}},$$

for $t = 1, 2, \ldots, T+1$, as in the text. Notice also that

$$\begin{aligned} z_{T+1} &= \alpha\beta\frac{1-(\alpha\beta)^{T-(T+1)+1}}{1-(\alpha\beta)^{T-(T+1)+2}} \\ &= 0. \end{aligned}$$

c. Plugging (7) into the right-hand side of (5) we get

$$\left(k_{t-1}^{\alpha} - \alpha\beta\frac{\left[1-(\alpha\beta)^{T-t+1}\right]}{\left[1-(\alpha\beta)^{T-t+2}\right]}k_{t-1}^{\alpha}\right)^{-1} = \frac{\left[1-(\alpha\beta)^{T-t+2}\right]}{k_{t-1}^{\alpha}(1-\alpha\beta)}.$$

Similarly, by plugging (7) into the left-hand side of (5) we obtain

$$\begin{aligned} &\frac{\alpha\beta\left[\alpha\beta\frac{\left[1-(\alpha\beta)^{T-t+1}\right]}{\left[1-(\alpha\beta)^{T-t+2}\right]}k_{t-1}^{\alpha}\right]^{\alpha-1}}{\left[\alpha\beta\frac{\left[1-(\alpha\beta)^{T-t+1}\right]}{\left[1-(\alpha\beta)^{T-t+2}\right]}k_{t-1}^{\alpha}\right]^{\alpha}\left(1-\alpha\beta\frac{\left[1-(\alpha\beta)^{T-t}\right]}{\left[1-(\alpha\beta)^{T-t+1}\right]}\right)} \\ &= \frac{1}{k_{t-1}^{\alpha}}\left(\frac{\left[1-(\alpha\beta)^{T-t+1}\right]-\alpha\beta\left[1-(\alpha\beta)^{T-t}\right]}{\left[1-(\alpha\beta)^{T-t+2}\right]}\right)^{-1} \\ &= \frac{\left[1-(\alpha\beta)^{T-t+2}\right]}{k_{t-1}^{\alpha}(1-\alpha\beta)}. \end{aligned}$$

Hence, the law of motion for capital given by (7) satisfies (5).

Evaluating (7) for $t = T$ yields

$$k_{T+1} = \alpha\beta\frac{1-(\alpha\beta)^{T-T}}{1-(\alpha\beta)^{T-T+1}}k_T^{\alpha}$$
$$= 0,$$

so (7) satisfies (6) too.

Exercise 2.3

a. We can write the value function using the optimal path for capital given by (8) as

$$\begin{aligned} v(k_0) &= \sum_{t=0}^{\infty} \beta^t \log(k_t^{\alpha} - \alpha\beta k_t^{\alpha}) \\ &= \frac{\log(1-\alpha\beta)}{(1-\beta)} + \alpha \sum_{t=0}^{\infty} \beta^t \log(k_t). \end{aligned}$$

The optimal policy function, written (by recursive substitution) as a function of the initial capital stock is (in logs)

$$\log k_t = \left(\sum_{i=0}^{t-1} \alpha^i\right) \log(\alpha\beta) + \alpha^t \log k_0.$$

Using the optimal policy function we can break up the last summation to get

$$\begin{aligned} \sum_{t=0}^{\infty} \beta^t \log(k_t) &= \frac{\log(k_0)}{(1-\alpha\beta)} + \log(\alpha\beta)\sum_{t=1}^{\infty}\beta^t\left(\sum_{i=0}^{t-1}\alpha^i\right) \\ &= \frac{\log(k_0)}{(1-\alpha\beta)} + \beta\frac{\log(\alpha\beta)}{[(1-\beta)(1-\alpha\beta)]}, \end{aligned}$$

where we have used the fact that the solution to a series of the form $s_t = \sum_{i=0}^{t}\lambda^i$ is $\left(1-\lambda^{t+1}\right)/(1-\lambda)$, as shown in Exercise 2.2b. Hence, we obtain a log linear expression for the value function

$$v(k_0) = A + B\log(k_0),$$

where

$$A = \left[\log(1-\alpha\beta) + \frac{\alpha\beta\log(\alpha\beta)}{(1-\alpha\beta)}\right](1-\beta)^{-1},$$

and

$$B = \frac{\alpha}{1 - \alpha\beta}.$$

b. We want to verify that

$$v(k) = A + B\log(k)$$

satisfies (11). For this functional form, the first-order condition of the maximization problem in the right-hand side of (11) is given by

$$g(k) = \frac{\beta B}{1 + \beta B} k^{\alpha}.$$

Plugging this policy function into the right-hand side of (11) we obtain

$$\begin{aligned} v(k) &= \log\left(k^{\alpha} - \frac{\beta B}{1+\beta B}k^{\alpha}\right) + \beta\left[A + B\log\left(\frac{\beta B}{1+\beta B}k^{\alpha}\right)\right] \\ &= \alpha\log(k) - \log(1+\beta B) + \beta A \\ &\quad + \beta B\left[\log(\beta B) + \alpha\log(k) - \log(1+\beta B)\right] \\ &= (1+\beta B)\,\alpha\log(k) - (1+\beta B)\log(1+\beta B) \\ &\quad + \beta A + \beta B\log(\beta B). \end{aligned}$$

Using the expressions for A and B obtained in part a., we get that $(1 + \beta B)\,\alpha = B$ and

$$\beta B\log(\beta B) - (1+\beta B)\log(1+\beta B) + \beta A = A,$$

and hence $v(k) = A + B\log(k)$ satisfies (11).

Exercise 2.4

a. The graph of $g(k) = sf(k)$, with $0 < s < 1$, is found in Figure 2.2.

Since f is strictly concave and continuously differentiable, g will inherit those properties. Also, $g(0) = sf(0) = 0$. In addition,

$$\begin{aligned} \lim_{k\to 0} g'(k) &= \lim_{k\to 0} sf'(k) \\ &= \lim_{k\to 0} sF_k(k, 1) + \lim_{k\to 0} s(1-\delta) = \infty, \end{aligned}$$

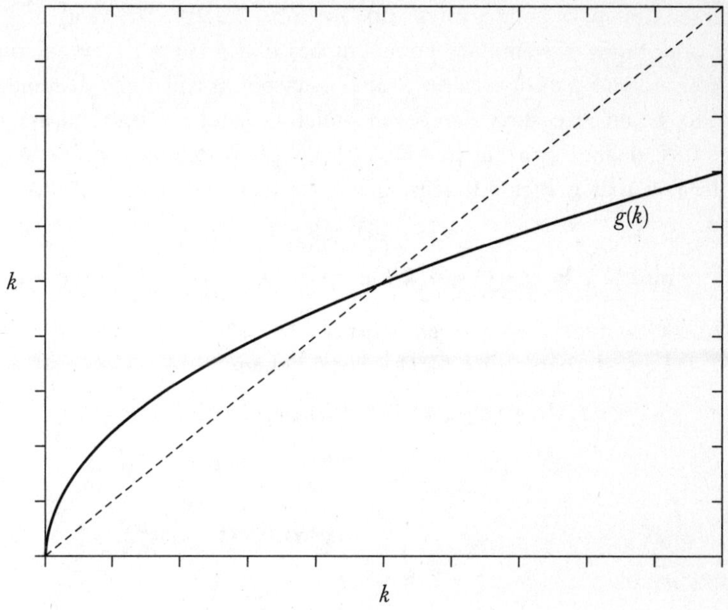

Figure 2.2

and

$$\lim_{k\to\infty} g'(k) = \lim_{k\to\infty} sf'(k)$$
$$= \lim_{k\to\infty} sF_k(k, 1) + \lim_{k\to\infty} s(1-\delta) = s(1-\delta) < 1.$$

First, we will prove existence of a nonzero stationary point. Combining the first limit condition (the one for $k \to 0$) and $g(0) = 0$, we have that for an arbitrary small positive perturbation,

$$0 < \frac{g(0+h) - g(0)}{h}.$$

This term tends to $+\infty$ as $h \to 0$, and hence $g(h)/h \to \infty$. Therefore, there exist an h such that $g(h)/h > 1$, and hence $g(k) > k$ for some k small enough. Similarly, the fact that $g(k) < k$ for k large enough is a direct implication of the second limit condition. Next, define $q(k) = g(k) - k$. By the arguments outlined above, $q(k) > 0$ for k small enough and $q(k) < 0$ for k large enough. By continuity of f, q is also continuous and hence by the Intermediate Value Theorem there exist a k^* such that $g(k^*) = k^*$.

That the stationary point is unique follows from the strict concavity of g. Note that a continuum of stationary points implies that $g'(k) = 1$ contradicting the strict concavity of g. A discrete set of stationary points will imply that one of the stationary points is reached from below, violating again the strict concavity of g. To see this, define $k^* = \min \{k \in \mathbf{R}_+ : q(k) = 0\}$. The limit conditions above, and the fact that g is nondecreasing implies that $g(k^* - \varepsilon) > k^*$, for $\varepsilon > 0$. Define

$$k^m = \min \{k \in \mathbf{R}_+ : q(k) = 0,\ k > k^* \text{ and } g(k - \varepsilon) - k > 0 \text{ for } \varepsilon > 0\}.$$

Then, by continuity of g, there exist $k \in (k^*, k^m)$ such that $g(k) < k$. Let $\alpha \in (0, 1)$ be such that $k = \alpha k^* + (1 - \alpha)k^m$. Then,

$$\begin{aligned} \alpha g(k^*) + (1 - \alpha) g(k^m) &= \alpha k^* + (1 - \alpha)k^m \\ &= k \\ &> g(k) \\ &= g(\alpha k^* + (1 - \alpha)k^m), \end{aligned}$$

a contradiction.

b. In Figure 2.3, we can see how for any $k_0 > 0$, the sequence $\{k_t\}_{t=0}^{\infty}$ converges to k^* as $t \to \infty$. As can be seen too, this convergence is monotonic, and it does not occur in a finite number of periods if $k_0 \neq k^*$.

Exercise 2.5

Some notation is needed. Let z^t denote the history of shocks up to time t. Equivalently, $z^t = (z^{t-1}, z_t)$, where z_t is the shock in period t.

Consumption and capital are indexed by the history of shocks. They are chosen given the information available at the time the decision is taken, so we represent them by finite sequences of random variables $c = \{c_t(z^t)\}_{t=0}^{T}$ and $k = \{k_t(z^t)\}_{t=0}^{T}$.

The pair (k_t, z^t) determines the set of feasible pairs (c_t, k_{t+1}) of current consumption and the beginning of next period capital stock. We can define this set as

$$B(k_t, z^t) = \left\{(c_t, k_{t+1}) \in R_+^2 : c_t(z^t) + k_{t+1}(z^t) \leq z_t f[k_t(z^{t-1})]\right\}$$

Because the budget constraint should be satisfied for each t and for every possible state, Lagrange multipliers are also random variables at the time the

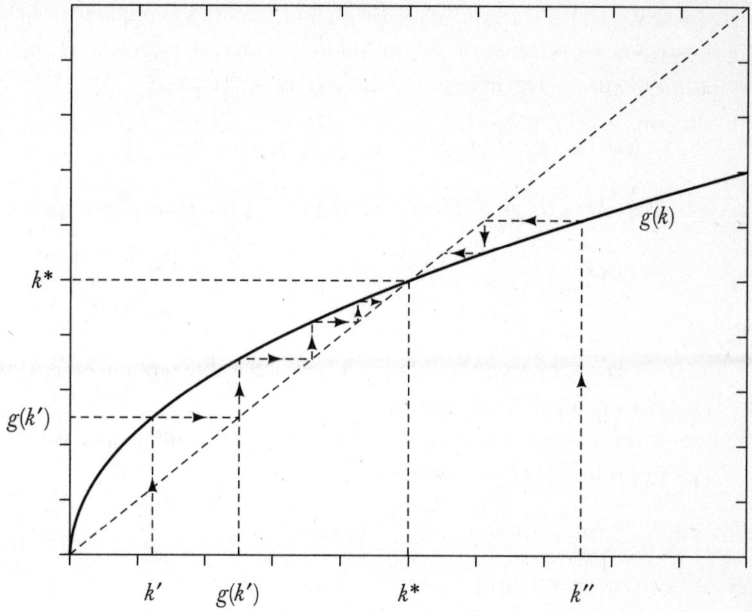

Figure 2.3

decisions are taken, and they should also be indexed by the history of shocks, so $\lambda_t(z^{t-1}, z_t)$ is a random variable representing the Lagrange multiplier for the time t constraint.

The objective function

$$U(c_0, c_1, \ldots) = E\left\{\sum_{t=0}^{\infty} \beta^t u[c_t(z^t)]\right\}$$

can be written as a nested sequence,

$$u(c_0) + \beta \sum_{i=1}^{n} \pi_i \left\{u[c_1(a_i)] + \beta \sum_{j=1}^{n} \pi_j [u(c_2(a_i, a_j) + \beta[\ldots]]\right\},$$

where π_i stands for the probability that state a_i occurs.

The objects of choice are then the contingent sequences c and k. For instance

$$c = \left\{c_0, c_1(z^1), c_2(z^2), \ldots, c_t(z^t), \ldots, c_T(z^T)\right\}.$$

We can see that $c_0 \in \mathbf{R}_+$, $c_1 \in \mathbf{R}_+^n$, $c_2 \in \mathbf{R}_+^{2n}$, and so on, so the sequence c belongs to the obvious cross product of the commodity spaces for each time period t. Similar analysis can be carried out for the capital sequence

$$k = \left\{k_0,\ k_1(z^1),\ k_2(z^2),\ \ldots,\ k_t(z^t),\ \ldots,\ k_T(z^T)\right\}.$$

Define this cross product as S. Hence we can define the consumption set as

$$C(k_0, z_0) = \{c \in S : [c_t(z^t),\ k_{t+1}(z^t)] \in B(k_t, z^t),$$
$$t = 0, 1, \ldots, \quad \text{for some } k \in S,\ k_0 \text{ given.} \}$$

(Notice that the consumption set, that is, the set of feasible sequences, is a subset of the Euclidean space defined above.)

The first-order conditions for consumption and capital are, respectively (after cancelling out probabilities on both sides):

$$u'[c_t(z_t, z^{t-1})] = \lambda_t(z_t, z^{t-1})$$

for all (z^{t-1}, z_t) and all t, and

$$\lambda_t(z_t, z^{t-1}) = \sum_{i=1}^{n} \pi_i \lambda_t(a_i, z_j^t) f'[k_t(a_i, z^{t-1})]$$

for all (z^{t-1}, z_t) and all t.

Exercise 2.6

As we did before in the deterministic case, we can use the budget constraint to solve for consumption along the optimal path and then write the value function as

$$\begin{aligned} v(k_0, z_0) &= E_0\left[\sum_{t=0}^{\infty} \beta^t \log(z_t k_t^\alpha - \alpha\beta z_t k_t^\alpha)\right] \\ &= \frac{\log(1-\alpha\beta)}{(1-\beta)} + E_0\left[\sum_{t=0}^{\infty} \beta^t \log(z_t)\right] \\ &\quad + \alpha E_0\left[\sum_{t=0}^{\infty} \beta^t \log(k_t)\right]. \end{aligned}$$

To obtain an expression in terms of the initial capital stock and the initial shock we need to solve for the second and third term above. Denoting $E_0(\log z_t) = \mu$, the second term can be written as

$$E_0\left[\sum_{t=0}^{\infty} \beta^t \log(z_t)\right] = \log z_0 + \sum_{t=0}^{\infty} \beta^t E_0(\log z_t)$$
$$= \log z_0 + \frac{\beta\mu}{1-\beta}.$$

In order to solve for the third term, we use the fact that the optimal path for the log of the capital stock can be written as

$$\log k_t = \left(\sum_{i=0}^{t-1} \alpha^i\right) \log(\alpha\beta) + \left(\sum_{i=0}^{t-1} \alpha^{t-1-i}\right) \log(z_i) + \alpha^t \log k_0.$$

Hence

$$\alpha E_0\left[\sum_{t=0}^{\infty} \beta^t \log(k_t)\right] = \alpha E_0\left[\sum_{t=1}^{\infty} \beta^t \left(\sum_{i=0}^{t-1} \alpha^i\right) \log(\alpha\beta)\right]$$
$$+ \alpha E_0\left[\sum_{t=1}^{\infty} \beta^t \left(\textstyle\sum_{i=0}^{t-1} \alpha^{t-1-i} \log(z_i)\right)\right]$$
$$+ \alpha E_0\left[\sum_{t=1}^{\infty} (\alpha\beta)^t \log(k_0)\right] + \alpha \log k_0.$$

Therefore, the next step is to solve for each of the terms above. The first term can be written as

$$\alpha E_0\left[\sum_{t=1}^{\infty} \beta^t \left(\sum_{i=0}^{t-1} \alpha^i\right) \log(\alpha\beta)\right] = \alpha \log(\alpha\beta) \sum_{t=1}^{\infty} \beta^t \left(\frac{1-\alpha^t}{1-\alpha}\right)$$
$$= \frac{\alpha \log(\alpha\beta)}{(1-\alpha)} \left[\frac{\beta}{(1-\beta)} - \frac{\alpha\beta}{(1-\alpha\beta)}\right]$$
$$= \frac{\alpha\beta \log(\alpha\beta)}{(1-\beta)(1-\alpha\beta)},$$

the second term as

$$
\begin{aligned}
&\alpha E_0 \left[\sum_{t=1}^{\infty} \beta^t \left(\sum_{i=0}^{t-1} \alpha^{t-1-i} \log(z_i) \right) \right] \\
&= \alpha E_0 \left[\beta \log(z_0) + \sum_{t=2}^{\infty} \beta^t \left(\sum_{i=0}^{t-1} \alpha^{t-1-i} \log(z_i) \right) \right] \\
&= \alpha E_0 \left[\beta \log(z_0) + \sum_{t=2}^{\infty} \beta^t \left(\alpha^{t-1} \log(z_0) + \sum_{i=1}^{t-1} \alpha^{t-1-i} \log(z_i) \right) \right] \\
&= \frac{\alpha\beta \log(z_0)}{(1-\alpha\beta)} + \alpha \sum_{t=2}^{\infty} \beta^t \left(\sum_{i=1}^{t-1} \alpha^{t-1-i} \mu \right) \\
&= \frac{\alpha\beta \log(z_0)}{(1-\alpha\beta)} + \frac{\alpha\mu}{(1-\alpha)} \sum_{t=2}^{\infty} \beta^t (1-\alpha^{t-1}) \\
&= \frac{\alpha\beta \log(z_0)}{(1-\alpha\beta)} + \frac{\alpha\beta^2\mu}{(1-\beta)(1-\alpha\beta)},
\end{aligned}
$$

and finally, the last two terms as

$$
\alpha E_0 \left[\sum_{t=1}^{\infty} (\alpha\beta)^t \log(k_0) \right] + \alpha \log k_0 = \frac{\alpha \log k_0}{(1-\alpha\beta)}.
$$

Hence,

$$
\begin{aligned}
\alpha E_0 \left[\sum_{t=0}^{\infty} \beta^t \log(k_t) \right] &= \frac{\alpha\beta \log(\alpha\beta)}{(1-\beta)(1-\alpha\beta)} + \frac{\alpha\beta \log(z_0)}{(1-\alpha\beta)} \\
&\quad + \frac{\alpha\beta^2\mu}{(1-\beta)(1-\alpha\beta)} + \frac{\alpha \log k_0}{(1-\alpha\beta)},
\end{aligned}
$$

and

$$
v(k_0, z_0) = A + B \log(k_0) + C \log(z_0)
$$

where

$$A = \left[\log(1-\alpha\beta) + \frac{\alpha\beta\log(\alpha\beta)}{(1-\alpha\beta)} + \frac{\beta\mu}{(1-\alpha\beta)}\right](1-\beta)^{-1},$$

$$B = \frac{\alpha}{(1-\alpha\beta)}, \text{ and}$$

$$C = \frac{1}{(1-\alpha\beta)}.$$

Following the same procedure outlined in Exercise 2.3, it can be checked that v satisfies (3) .

Exercise 2.7

a. The sequence of means and variances of the sequence of logs of the capital stocks have a recursive structure. Define μ_t as the mean at time zero of the log of the capital stock in period t. Then

$$\begin{aligned}
\mu_t &= E_0[\log k_t] \\
&= E_0[\log(\alpha\beta) + \alpha\log(k_{t-1}) + \log(z_{t-1})] \\
&= \log(\alpha\beta) + \mu + \alpha\mu_{t-1} \\
&= \log(\alpha\beta) + \mu + \alpha\left[\log(\alpha\beta) + \mu\right] + \alpha^2\mu_{t-2} \\
&= \left[\log(\alpha\beta) + \mu\right] + \left[1 + \alpha + \ldots + \alpha^{t-1}\right] + \alpha^t\mu_0 \\
&= \left[\mu_0 - \frac{\log(\alpha\beta) + \mu}{1-\alpha}\right]\alpha^t + \frac{\log(\alpha\beta) + \mu}{1-\alpha}.
\end{aligned}$$

Since $0 < \alpha < 1$,

$$\mu_\infty \equiv \lim_{t\to\infty} \mu_t = \frac{\log(\alpha\beta) + \mu}{1-\alpha}.$$

Similarly, define σ_t as the variance at time zero of the log of the capital stock in period t. Then

$$\begin{aligned}
\sigma_t &= Var_0[\log k_t] \\
&= Var_0[\log(\alpha\beta) + \alpha\log(k_{t-1}) + \log(z_{t-1})] \\
&= \alpha^2\sigma_{t-1} + \sigma,
\end{aligned}$$

which is also an ordinary differential equation with solution given by

$$\sigma_t = \left[\sigma_0 - \frac{\sigma}{1-\alpha^2}\right]\alpha^{2t} + \frac{\sigma}{1-\alpha^2}.$$

Hence, since $0 < \alpha < 1$,

$$\sigma_\infty \equiv \lim_{t\to\infty} \sigma_t = \frac{\sigma}{1-\alpha^2}.$$

Exercise 2.8

First, we will show that $\{c_t^*, k_{t+1}^*\}_{t=0}^T$, $k_{T+1}^* = 0$ satisfies the consumer's intertemporal budget constraint. By (19) and the definition of f,

$$f(k_t^*) = F(k_t^*, 1) + (1-\delta)k_t^*.$$

Since F is homogeneous of degree one, using (20)–(22) we have that

$$f(k_t^*) = (r_t^* + 1 - \delta)k_t^* + w_t^* = c_t^* + k_{t+1}^*,$$

and hence the present value budget constraint (12) is satisfied for the proposed allocation when prices are given by (20)–(22).

The feasibility constraint (16) is satisfied by construction. Hence, in equilibrium, the first-order conditions for the representative household are (for $k_{t+1}^e > 0$)

$$\beta^t U'[f(k_t^e) - k_{t+1}^e] = \lambda p_t,$$
$$\lambda[(r_{t+1} + 1 - \delta)p_t - p_t] = 0,$$
$$f(k_t^e) - c_t^e - k_{t+1}^e = 0,$$

for $t = 0, 1, \ldots, T$. Combining them and using (20)–(22) we obtain

$$U'\left[f(k_t^e) - k_{t+1}^e\right] = \beta U'\left[f(k_{t+1}^e) - k_{t+2}^e\right] f'(k_t^e),$$
$$f(k_t^e) - c_t^e - k_{t+1}^e = 0,$$

for $t = 0, 1, \ldots, T$, which by construction is satisfied by the proposed sequence $\{k_{t+1}^*\}_{t=0}^T$. Hence $\{(c_t^*, k_{t+1}^*)\}_{t=0}^T$, with $k_{T+1}^* = 0$, and $k_0^* = x_0$ solves the consumer's problem.

Finally, we need to show that $\{k_t^*, n_t^* = 1\}_{t=0}^T$ is a maximizing allocation for the firm. Replacing (21) and (22) in (9) and (10) together with the definition of $f(k)$ and the assumed homogeneity of degree 1 of F, we verify that the proposed sequence of prices and allocations indeed satisfy the first-order conditions of the firm, and that $\pi = 0$.

Exercise 2.9

Under the new setup, the household's decision problem is

$$\max_{\{(c_t,n_t)\}_{t=0}^{T}} \sum_{t=0}^{T} \beta^t U(c_t)$$

subject to

$$\sum_{t=0}^{T} p_t c_t \leq \sum_{t=0}^{T} p_t w_t n_t + \pi,$$

and

$$0 \leq n_t \leq 1, \quad c_t \geq 0, \quad t = 0, 1, \ldots, T.$$

Similarly, the firm's problem is

$$\max_{\{(k_t,i_t,n_t)\}_{t=0}^{T}} \quad \pi = p_0(x_0 - k_0) + \sum_{t=0}^{T} p_t[y_t - w_t n_t - i_t]$$

subject to

$$\begin{aligned} &i_t = k_{t+1} - (1-\delta)k_t, \quad t = 0, 1, \ldots, T, \\ &y_t \leq F(k_t, n_t), \quad t = 0, 1, \ldots, T, \\ &k_t \geq 0, \quad t = 0, 1, \ldots, T, \\ &k_0 \leq x_0, \quad x_0 \text{ given.} \end{aligned}$$

Hence, x_0 can be interpreted as the initial stock of capital and k_0 the stock of capital that is effectively put into production, while k_t for $t \geq 1$ is the capital stock that is chosen one period in advance to be the effective capital allocated into production in period t.

As stated in the text, labor is inelastically supplied by households, prices are strictly positive, and the nonnegativity constraints for consumption are never binding, so equation (14) in the text is the first-order condition for the household.

The first-order conditions for the firm's problem are (after substituting both constraints into the objective function)

$$\begin{aligned} w_t - F_n(k_t, n_t) &= 0, \\ -p_t + p_{t+1}[F_k(k_t, n_t) + (1-\delta)] &\leq 0, \end{aligned}$$

for $t = 0, 1, \ldots, T$, where the latter holds with equality if $k_{t+1} > 0$.

Evaluating the objective function of the firm's problem using the optimal path for capital and labor, we find that first-order conditions are satisfied, and $\pi = p_0 x_0$ so the profits of the firm are given by the value of the initial capital stock.

Next, it is left to verify that the quantities given by (17)–(19) and the prices defined by (20)–(22) constitute a competitive equilibrium. The procedure is exactly as in Exercise 2.8. In equilibrium, combining the first-order conditions for periods t and $t+1$ in the household's problem we obtain

$$U'[f(k_t) - k_{t+1}] = \beta U'[f(k_{t+1}) - k_{t+2}]f'(k_{t+1}),$$
$$f(k_t) - c_t - k_{t+1} = 0,$$

for $t = 1, 2, \ldots, T$, as before. Hence the proposed sequences constitute a competitive equilibrium.

Exercise 2.10

The firm's decision problem remains as stated in (8) (that is, as a series of one-period maximization problems). Let s_t be the quantity of one-period bonds held by the representative household. Its decision problem now is

$$\max_{\{(c_t, k_{t+1}, s_{t+1}, n_t)\}_{t=0}^{T}} \sum_{t=0}^{T} \beta^t U(c_t)$$

subject to

$$c_t + q_t s_{t+1} + k_{t+1} \leq r_t k_k + (1-\delta)k_t + w_t n_t, \quad t = 0, 1, \ldots, T,$$
$$0 \leq n_t \leq 1, \quad c_t \geq 0, \qquad t = 0, 1, \ldots, T,$$

and k_0 given.

We assume, as in the text, that the whole stock of capital is supplied to the market. Now, instead of having one present value budget constraint, we have a sequence of budget constraint, one for each period, and we will denote by $\beta^t \lambda_t$ the corresponding Lagrange multipliers.

In addition, we need to add an additional market clearing condition for the bond market that must be satisfied in the competitive equilibrium. This says that bonds are in zero net supply at the stated prices.

Hence, the first-order conditions that characterize the household's problem are

$$U'(c_t) - \lambda_t = 0,$$

$$-\lambda_t q_t + \beta\lambda_{t+1} = 0,$$

$$-\lambda_t + \beta\lambda_{t+1}[r_{t+1} + 1 - \delta] \leq 0,$$

$$\text{with equality for } k_{t+1} \geq 0,$$

and the budget constraints, for $t = 0, 1, \ldots, T$.

We show next that the proposed allocations $\{(c_t^*, k_{t+1}^*)\}_{t=0}^{T}$ together with the sequence of prices given by (21)–(22) and the pricing equation for the bond, constitute a competitive equilibrium. Combining the first and second equations evaluated at the proposed allocation, we obtain the pricing equation

$$q_t = \beta\frac{U'(c_{t+1}^*)}{U'(c_t^*)}.$$

From the first-order conditions of the firm's problem, and after imposing the equilibrium conditions, $r_t = F_k(k_t^*, 1)$. Combining the first-order conditions for consumption and capital for the household's problem, we obtain

$$f'(k_{t+1}^*)^{-1} = \beta\frac{U'(c_{t+1}^*)}{U'(c_t^*)}.$$

The rest is analogous to the procedure followed in Exercise 2.9. Hence, the sequence of quantities defined by (17)–(19), and the prices defined by (21)–(22) plus the bond price defined in the text indeed define a competitive equilibrium.

3 *Mathematical Preliminaries*

Exercise 3.1

Given $k_0 = k$, the lifetime utility given by the sequence $\{k_t\}_{t=1}^{\infty}$ in which $k_{t+1} = g_0(k_t)$ is

$$\begin{aligned} w_0(k) &= \sum_{t=0}^{\infty} \beta^t u[f(k_t) - g_0(k_t)] \\ &= u[f(k) - g_0(k)] + \beta \sum_{t=1}^{\infty} \beta^{t-1} u[f(k_t) - g_0(k_t)]. \end{aligned}$$

But

$$\begin{aligned} \sum_{t=1}^{\infty} \beta^{t-1} u[f(k_t) - g_0(k_t)] &= \sum_{t=0}^{\infty} \beta^t u[f(k_{t+1}) - g_0(k_{t+1})] \\ &= w_0(k_1) \\ &= w_0[g_0(k)]. \end{aligned}$$

Hence

$$w_0(k) = u[f(k) - g_0(k)] + \beta w_0[g_0(k)]$$

for all $k \geq 0$.

Exercise 3.2

a. The idea of the proof is to show that any finite dimensional Euclidean space $\mathbf{R}^l$ satisfies the definition of a real vector space, using the fact that the real numbers form a field.

Take any three arbitrary vectors $x = (x_1, \ldots, x_l)$, $y = (y_1, \ldots, y_l)$ and $z = (z_1, \ldots, z_l)$ in $\mathbf{R}^l$ and any two real numbers α and $\beta \in \mathbf{R}$. Define a zero vector $\theta = (0, \ldots, 0) \in \mathbf{R}^l$.

Define the addition of two vectors as the element by element sum, and a scalar multiplication by the multiplication of each element of the vector by a scalar. That any finite $\mathbf{R}^l$ space satisfies those properties is trivial.

$a:$

$$\begin{aligned} x + y &= (x_1 + y_1, x_2 + y_2, \ldots, x_l + y_l) \\ &= (y_1 + x_1, y_2 + x_2, \ldots, y_l + x_l) = y + x \in \mathbf{R}^l. \end{aligned}$$

$b:$

$$\begin{aligned} (x + y) + z &= (x_1 + y_1, \ldots, x_l + y_l) + (z_1, \ldots, z_l) \\ &= (x_1 + y_1 + z_1, \ldots, x_l + y_l + z_l) \\ &= (x_1, \ldots, x_l) + (y_1 + z_1, \ldots, y_l + z_l) \\ &= x + (y + z) \in \mathbf{R}^l. \end{aligned}$$

$c:$

$$\begin{aligned} \alpha(x + y) &= \alpha(x_1 + y_1, \ldots, x_l + y_l) \\ &= (\alpha x_1 + \alpha y_1, \ldots, \alpha x_l + \alpha y_l) \\ &= (\alpha x_1, \ldots, \alpha x_l) + (\alpha y_1, \ldots, \alpha y_l) = \alpha x + \alpha y \in \mathbf{R}^l. \end{aligned}$$

$d:$

$$\begin{aligned} (\alpha + \beta)x &= ((\alpha + \beta)x_1, \ldots, (\alpha + \beta)x_l) \\ &= (\alpha x_1 + \beta x_1, \ldots, \alpha x_l + \beta x_l) \\ &= \alpha x + \beta x \in \mathbf{R}^l. \end{aligned}$$

$e:$

$$\begin{aligned} (\alpha\beta)x &= (\alpha\beta x_1, \ldots, \alpha\beta x_l) \\ &= \alpha(\beta x_1, \ldots, \beta x_l) = \alpha(\beta x) \in \mathbf{R}^l. \end{aligned}$$

$f:$

$$\begin{aligned} x + \theta &= (x_1 + 0, \ldots, x_l + 0) \\ &= (x_1, \ldots, x_l) = x \in \mathbf{R}^l. \end{aligned}$$

g :

$$\begin{aligned} 0x &= (0x_1, \ldots, 0x_l) \\ &= (0, \ldots, 0) = \theta \in \mathbf{R}^l. \end{aligned}$$

h :

$$\begin{aligned} 1x &= (1x_1, \ldots, 1x_l) \\ &= (x_1, \ldots, x_l) = x \in \mathbf{R}^l. \end{aligned}$$

b. Straightforward extension of the result in part a.

c. Define the addition of two sequences as the element by element addition, and scalar multiplication as the multiplication of each element of the sequence by a real number. Then proceed as in part a. with the element by element operations. For example, take property c. Consider a pair of sequences $x = (x_0, x_1, x_2, \ldots) \in X = \mathbf{R} \times \mathbf{R} \times \mathbf{R} \ldots$ and $y = (y_0, y_1, y_2, \ldots) \in X = \mathbf{R} \times \mathbf{R} \times \mathbf{R} \ldots$ and $\alpha \in \mathbf{R}$, we just add and multiply element by element, so

$$\begin{aligned} \alpha(x + y) &= (\alpha(x_0 + y_0), \alpha(x_1 + y_1), \alpha(x_2 + y_2), \ldots) \\ &= (\alpha x_0 + \alpha y_0, \alpha x_1 + \alpha y_1, \alpha x_2 + \alpha y_2, \ldots) \\ &= \alpha x + \alpha y \in X. \end{aligned}$$

The proof of the remaining properties is analogous.

d. Take $f, g : [a, b] \rightarrow \mathbf{R}$ and $\alpha \in \mathbf{R}$. Let $\theta(x) = 0$. Define the addition of functions by $(f + g)(x) = f(x) + g(x)$, and scalar multiplication by $(\alpha f)(x) = \alpha f(x)$. A function f is continuous if $x_n \rightarrow x$ implies that $f(x_n) \rightarrow f(x)$. To see that $f + g$ is continuous, take a sequence $x_n \rightarrow x$ in $[a, b]$. Then

$$\begin{aligned} \lim_{x_n \rightarrow x} (f + g)(x_n) &= \lim_{x_x \rightarrow x} \left[f(x_x) + g(x_n) \right] \\ &= \lim_{x_n \rightarrow x} f(x_n) + \lim_{x_n \rightarrow x} g(x_n) \\ &= f(x) + g(x) \\ &= (f + g)(x). \end{aligned}$$

Note that a function defines an infinite sequence of real numbers, so we can proceed as in part c. to check that each of the properties is satisfied.

e. Take the vectors (0, 1) and (1, 0). Then (1, 0) + (0, 1) = (1, 1), which is not an element of the unit circle.

f. Choose $\alpha \in (0, 1)$. Then $1 \in I$ but $\alpha 1 \notin I$, which violates the definition of a real vector space.

g. Let $f : [a, b] \rightarrow \mathbf{R}_{+}$, and $\alpha < 0$, then $\alpha f \leq 0$, which does not belong to the set of nonnegative functions on $[a, b]$.

Exercise 3.3

a. Clearly, the absolute value is real valued and well defined on $S \times S$. Take three different arbitrary integers x, y, z. The non-negativity property holds trivially by the definition of absolute value. Also,

$$\rho(x, y) = |x - y| = |y - x| = \rho(y, x)$$

by the properties of the absolute value, so the commutative property holds.

Finally,

$$\begin{aligned} \rho(x, z) &= |x - z| \\ &= |x - y + y - z| \\ &\leq |x - y| + |y - z| \\ &= \rho(x, y) + \rho(y, z), \end{aligned}$$

so the triangle inequality holds.

c. Take three arbitrary functions $x, y, z \in S$. As before, the first two properties are immediate from the definition of absolute value. Note also that as x and y are continuous on $[a, b]$, they are bounded, and the proposed metric is real valued (and not extended real valued). To prove that the triangle inequality holds, notice that

$$\begin{aligned} \rho(x, z) &= \max_{a \leq t \leq b} |x(t) - z(t)| \\ &= \max_{a \leq t \leq b} |x(t) - y(t) + y(t) - z(t)| \\ &\leq \max_{a \leq t \leq b} (|x(t) - y(t)| + |y(t) - z(t)|) \\ &\leq \max_{a \leq t \leq b} |x(t) - y(t)| + \max_{a \leq t \leq b} |y(t) - z(t)| \\ &= \rho(x, y) + \rho(y, z). \end{aligned}$$

f. The first two properties follow by definition of absolute value as before, plus the fact that $f(0) = 0$, so $x = y$ implies $\rho(x, y) = 0$. In order to prove the last property, notice that

$$\begin{aligned}\rho(x, y) &= f(|x - y|) = f(|x - z + z - y|) \\ &\leq f(|x - z| + |z - y|) \\ &\leq f(|x - z|) + f(|z - y|) \\ &= \rho(x, z) + \rho(z, y),\end{aligned}$$

where the first inequality comes from the fact that f is strictly increasing and the second one from the concavity of f. To see the last point, without loss of generality, define $|x - z| = a$ and $|z - y| = b$, with $a < b$ and let $\mu = a/b$. By the strict concavity of f,

$$f(b) > \mu f(a) + (1 - \mu) f(a + b),$$

and hence

$$\begin{aligned}f(a + b) &< \frac{b}{(b - a)} f(b) - \frac{a}{(b - a)} f(a) \\ &< f(b) + f(a).\end{aligned}$$

Exercise 3.4

a. The first property in the definition of a normed vector space is evidently satisfied for the standard Euclidean norm, given that it is just the sum of squared numbers, where each component of the sum is an element of an arbitrary vector $x \in \mathbf{R}^l$. It is zero if and only if each component is zero. To prove the second property, notice that

$$\|\alpha x\|^2 = \sum_{i=1}^{l} (\alpha x_i)^2 = \alpha^2 \sum_{i=1}^{l} x_i^{\,2} = \alpha^2 \, \|x\|^2 \, ,$$

which implies that

$$\|\alpha x\| = |\alpha| \, \|x\| \, ,$$

by property a. To prove the triangle inequality, we make use of the Cauchy-Schwarz inequality, which says that given two arbitrary vectors x and y,

$$\left(\sum_{i=1}^{l} x_i y_i\right)^2 \leq \sum_{i=1}^{l} x_i^2 \sum_{i=1}^{l} y_i^2.$$

Hence,

$$
\begin{aligned}
\|x+y\|^2 &= \sum_{i=1}^{l}(x_i+y_i)^2 \\
&\le \sum_{i=1}^{l} x_i^2 + 2\sum_{i=1}^{l} x_i y_i + \sum_{i=1}^{l} y_i^2 \\
&\le \sum_{i=1}^{l} x_i^2 + 2\left(\sum_{i=1}^{l} x_i^2\right)^{\frac{1}{2}}\left(\sum_{i=1}^{l} y_i^2\right)^{\frac{1}{2}} + \sum_{i=1}^{l} y_i^2 \\
&= \|x\|^2 + 2\,\|x\|\,\|y\| + \|y\|^2 \\
&= (\|x\| + \|y\|)^2 .
\end{aligned}
$$

d. As we consider only bounded sequences, the proposed norm is real valued (and not extended real valued). To see that the first property holds, note that since $|x_k| \ge 0$, all k, $\|x\| = \sup_k |x_k| \ge 0$, and if $x_k = 0$, all k, $\|x\| = \sup_k |x_k| = 0$. The second property holds because

$$
\begin{aligned}
\|\alpha x\| &= \sup_k |\alpha x_k| \\
&= \sup_k |\alpha|\,|x_k| \\
&= |\alpha| \sup_k |x_k| \\
&= |\alpha|\,\|x\| .
\end{aligned}
$$

To see that the triangle inequality holds notice that

$$
\begin{aligned}
\|x+y\| &= \sup_k |x_k + y_k| \\
&\le \sup_k (|x_k| + |y_k|) \\
&\le \sup_k |x_k| + \sup_k |y_k| \\
&= \|x\| + \|y\| .
\end{aligned}
$$

e. We prove already that $C\,[a, b]$ is a vector space (see Exercise 3.2d.). To see that property *a.* is satisfied, let $x \in C\,[a, b]$. Then $|x\,(t)| \ge 0$ for all $t \in [a, b]$. Hence $\sup_{a \le t \le b} |x\,(t)| \ge 0$, and if $x\,(t) = 0$ for all $t \in [a, b]$, then $\sup_{a \le t \le b} |x\,(t)| = 0$. To check that the remaining properties are satisfied, we proceed as in part d.

Exercise 3.5

a. If $x_n \to x$, for each $\varepsilon_x > 0$, there exist N_{ε_x} such that $\rho(x_n, x) < \varepsilon_x$, for all $n \geq N_{\varepsilon_x}$. Similarly, if $x_n \to y$, for each $\varepsilon_y > 0$, there exist N_{ε_y} such that $\rho(x_n, y) < \varepsilon_y$, for all $n \geq N_{\varepsilon_y}$. Choose $\varepsilon_x = \varepsilon_y = \varepsilon/2$. Then, by the triangle inequality,

$$\rho(x, y) \leq \rho(x_n, x) + \rho(x_n, y) < \varepsilon$$

for all $n \geq \max\left\{N_{\varepsilon_x}, N_{\varepsilon_y}\right\}$. As ε was arbitrary, this implies $\rho\,(x, y) = 0$ which implies, since ρ is a metric, that $x = y$.

b. Suppose $\{x_n\}$ converges to a limit x. Then, given any $\varepsilon > 0$, there exists an integer N_ε such that $\rho(x_n, x) < \varepsilon/2$ for all $n > N_\varepsilon$. But then $\rho(x_n, x_m) \leq \rho(x_n, x) + \rho(x_m, x) < \varepsilon$ for all $n, m > N_\varepsilon$.

c. Let $\{x_n\}$ be a Cauchy sequence and let $\varepsilon = 1$. Then, $\exists\, N$ such that for all $n, m \geq N$,

$$\rho(x_m, x_n) < 1.$$

Hence, by the triangle inequality,

$$\begin{aligned}\rho(x_n, 0) &\leq \rho(x_m, x_n) + \rho(x_m, 0)\\ &< 1 + \rho(x_m, 0),\end{aligned}$$

and therefore $\rho(x_n, 0) \leq 1 + \rho(x_N, 0)$ for $n \geq N$. Let

$$M = 1 + \max\left\{\rho(x_m, 0),\ m = 1, 2, \ldots, N\right\} + 1,$$

then $\rho(x_m, 0) \leq M$ for all n, so the Cauchy sequence $\{x_n\}$ is bounded.

d. Suppose that every subsequence of $\{x_n\}$ converges to x. We will prove the contrapositive. That is, if x_n does not converge to x, there exists a subsequence that does not converge. If x_n does not converge to x, there exist $\varepsilon > 0$ such that for all N, there exist $n > N$ with $|x_n - x| > \varepsilon$. Using this repeatedly, we can construct a sequence $\left\{x_{n_k}\right\}$ such that $\left|x_{n_k} - x\right| > \varepsilon$ for all n_k.

Conversely, suppose $x_n \to x$. Let $\left\{x_{n_i}\right\}$ be a subsequence of $\{x_n\}$ with $n_1 < n_2 < n_3 < \ldots$. Then, since $\rho(x_n, x) < \varepsilon$ for all $n \geq N_\varepsilon$, it holds that $\rho\left(x_{n_i}, x\right) < \varepsilon$ for all $n_i \geq N_\varepsilon$.

Exercise 3.6

a. The metric space in 3.3a. is complete. Let $\{x_n\}$ be a Cauchy sequence, with $x_n \in S$ for all n. Choose $0 < \varepsilon < 1$, then there exist N_ε such that $|x_m - x_n| < \varepsilon < 1$ for all n, $m \geq N_\varepsilon$. Hence, $x_m = x_n \equiv x \in S$ for all n, $m \geq N_\varepsilon$.

The metric space in 3.3b. is complete. Let $\{x_n\}$ be a Cauchy sequence, with $x_n \in S$ for all n. Choose $0 < \varepsilon < 1$, then there exist N_ε such that $\rho(x_m, x_n) < \varepsilon < 1$ for all n, $m \geq N_\varepsilon$. By the functional form of the metric used $\rho(x_m, x_n) < 1$ implies that $x_m = x_n \equiv x \in S$ for all n, $m \geq N_\varepsilon$.

The normed vector space in 3.4a. is complete. Let $\{x_n\}$ be a Cauchy sequence, with $x_n \in S$ for all n, and let x_n^k be the kth entry of the nth element of the sequence. Then

$$\begin{aligned}
\|x_m - x_n\| &= \left(\sum_{k=1}^{l}(x_m^k - x_n^k)^2\right)^{\frac{1}{2}} \\
&\leq \left(l \max_k (x_m^k - x_n^k)^2\right)^{\frac{1}{2}} \\
&\leq l \max_k \left|x_m^k - x_n^k\right|
\end{aligned}$$

for $k = 1, \ldots, l$, and hence $\{x_n^k\}$ is a Cauchy sequence for all k. As shown in Exercise 3.5b., $\{x_n^k\}$ is bounded for all k, and by the Bolzano-Weierstrass Theorem, every bounded sequence in **R** has a convergent subsequence. Hence, using the result proved in Exercise 3.5d., we can conclude that a sequence in **R** converges if and only if it is a Cauchy sequence. Define $x^k = \lim_{n\to\infty} x_n^k$, for all k. Since **R** is a closed set, clearly $x = (x^1, \ldots, x^l) \in S$. To show that $\|x_n - x\| \to 0$ as $n \to \infty$, note that $\|x_m - x\| \leq l \max_k |x_n^k - x^k| \to 0$, which completes the proof.

The normed vector spaces in 3.4b. and 3.4c. are complete. The proof is the same as that outlined in the paragraph above, with the obvious modifications to the norm.

The normed vector space in 3.4d. is complete. Let $\{x_n\}$ be a Cauchy sequence, with $x_n \in S$ for all n. Note that x_n is a bounded sequence and hence $\{x_n\}$ is a sequence of bounded sequences. Denote by x_n^k the kth element of the bounded sequence x_n. Then $\|x_m - x_n\| = \sup_k |x_m^k - x_n^k| \geq |x_m^k - x_n^k|$ for all k. Hence $\|x_m - x_n\| \to 0$ implies $|x_m^k - x_n^k| \to 0$ for all k and so the sequences of real numbers $\{x_n^k\}$ are Cauchy sequences. Then, by the completeness of the real numbers, for each k there exists a real number x^k such that $x_n^k \to x^k$. Since $\{x_n\}$ is bounded, so is $\{x_n^k\}$ for all k. Hence $x = (x^1, x^2, \ldots) \in S$. To show that $x_n \to x$, by the triangle inequality, $|x_n^k - x^k| \leq |x_n^k - x_m^k| + |x_m^k - x^k|$ for all k. Pick N_ε such that for all $n, m \geq N$, $|x_n^k - x_m^k| < \varepsilon/2$ for all k. Hence for m large enough $|x_m^k - x^k| < \varepsilon/2$ and so $|x_n^k - x^k| < \varepsilon$ implies $\sup_k |x_n^k - x^k| < \varepsilon$.

The normed vector space in 3.4e. is complete. Let $\{x_n\}$ be a Cauchy sequence of continuous functions in $C[a, b]$ and fix $t \in [a, b]$. Then

$$\begin{aligned}|x_n(t) - x_m(t)| &\leq \sup_{a \leq t \leq b} |x_n(t) - x_m(t)| \\ &= \|x_n - x_m\|\end{aligned}$$

and therefore the sequence of real numbers $\{x_n(t)\}$ satisfies the Cauchy criterion. By the completeness of the real numbers $x_n(t) \to x(t) \in \mathbf{R}$. The limiting values define a function $x : [a, b] \to \mathbf{R}$, which is taken as our candidate function.

To show that $x_n \to x$, pick an arbitrary t, then

$$\begin{aligned}|x_n(t) - x(t)| &\leq |x_n(t) - x_m(t)| + |x_m(t) - x(t)| \\ &\leq \|x_n - x_m\| + |x_m(t) - x(t)|\,.\end{aligned}$$

Since $\{x_n\}$ is a Cauchy sequence, there exists N such that for all $n, m \geq N$, $\|x_n - x_m\| < \varepsilon/2$ and $|x_m(t) - x(t)| < \varepsilon/2$. Therefore, $|x_n(t) - x(t)| < \varepsilon$. Because t was arbitrary, it holds for all $t \in [a, b]$. Hence $\sup_{a \leq t \leq b} |x_n(t) - x(t)| < \varepsilon$ and so $x_n \to x$.

It remains to be shown that x is a continuous function. A function $x(t)$ is continuous in t if for all ε, there exists a δ such that $|t - t'| < \delta$ implies $|x(t) - x(t')| < \varepsilon$. By the triangle inequality,

$$|x(t) - x(t')| \leq |x(t) - x_n(t)| + |x_n(t) - x_n(t')| + |x_n(t') - x(t')|$$

for any $t, t' \in [a, b]$. Fix $\varepsilon > 0$, since $x_n \to x$ there exist N such that

$$|x(t) - x_n(t)| < \varepsilon/3$$

for all $n \geq N$, and N' such that

$$|x(t') - x_n(t')| < \varepsilon/3$$

for all $n \geq N'$. Since x_n is continuous, there exist δ such that for all t, t', $|t - t'| < \delta$,

$$|x_n(t) - x_n(t')| < \varepsilon/3.$$

Hence $|x(t) - x(t')| < \varepsilon$.

The metric space in 3.3c. is not complete. To prove this, it is enough to find a sequence of continuous, strictly increasing functions that converges to a function that is not in S. Consider the sequence of functions

$$x_n(t) = 1 + \frac{t}{n},$$

for $t \in [a, b]$. Pick any arbitrary m. Then

$$\begin{aligned}\rho(x_n, x_m) &= \max_{a \le t \le b} \left| \frac{t}{n} - \frac{t}{m} \right| \\ &= \max_{a \le t \le b} \left| \frac{t(m-n)}{nm} \right| \\ &= \left| \frac{b(n-m)}{nm} \right| \\ &\le \frac{1}{\min\{n, m\}}.\end{aligned}$$

Notice that $\rho(x_n, x_m) \to 0$ as $n, m \to \infty$. But clearly $x_n(t) \to x(t) = 1$, a constant function.

From the proof it is obvious that this counterexample does not work for the weaker requirement of nondecreasing functions.

The metric space in 3.3d. is not complete. The proof similar to 3.3c. and the same counterexample works in this case, with obvious modifications for the distance function.

The metric space in 3.3e. is not complete. The set of rational numbers is defined as

$$Q = \left\{ \frac{p}{r} : p, r \in Z, r \neq 0 \right\}$$

where Z is the set of integers. Let

$$x_n = 1 + \sum_{i=1}^{n} \frac{1}{i!}.$$

Clearly x_n is a rational number, however $x_n \to e \notin Q$.

The metric space in 3.4f. is not complete. Take the function

$$x_n(t) = \left(\frac{t-a}{b-a} \right)^n.$$

First, assume $a = 0,\ b = 1$, and $m > n$. Hence

$$\begin{aligned}\|x_n(t) - x_m(t)\| &= \int_0^1 (t^n - t^m)dt \\ &= \int_0^1 t^n(1 - t^{n-m})dt \\ &\leq \int_0^1 t^n dt \to 0\end{aligned}$$

But the sequence of functions $x_n(t) \to 0$ for $0 \leq t < 1$, and 1 for $t = 1$, a discontinuous function at 1.

In order to show that the space in 3.3c. is complete if "strictly increasing" is replaced by "nondecreasing," we can prove the existence of a limit sequence as we did before. It is left to prove that the limit sequence is nondecreasing. The proof is by contradiction. Take a Cauchy sequence f_n of nondecreasing functions converging to f, and contrary to the statement, suppose $f(t) - f(t') > \varepsilon$ for $t' > t$. Hence,

$$0 < \varepsilon < f(t) - f(t') = f(t) - f_n(t) + f_n(t) - f_n(t') + f_n(t') - f(t').$$

Using the fact that for every t, $\{f_n(t)\}$ converges to $f(t)$,

$$0 < \varepsilon < 2\,\|f_n - f\| + f_n(t) - f_n(t').$$

Choosing N_ε such that for all $n \geq N_\varepsilon$, $\|f_n - f\| \leq \varepsilon/2$, we get

$$0 < \varepsilon < f_n(t) - f_n(t'),$$

a contradiction.

b. Since $S' \subseteq S$ is closed, any convergent sequence in S' converges to a point in S'. Take the set of Cauchy sequences in S. They all converge to points in S since S is complete. Take the subset of those sequences that belong to S', then by the argument above they converge to a point in S', so S' is complete.

Exercise 3.7

a. First we have to prove that $C^1[a, b]$ is a normed vector space. By definition of absolute value, the nonnegativity property is clearly satisfied,

$$\|f\| = \sup_{x \in X} \{|f(x)| + |f'(x)|\} \geq 0.$$

To see that the second property is satisfied, note that

$$\begin{aligned}\|\alpha f\| &= \sup_{x\in X}\left\{|\alpha f(x)| + \left|\alpha f'(x)\right|\right\} \\ &= \sup_{x\in X}\left\{|\alpha|\left[|f(x)| + \left|f'(x)\right|\right]\right\} \\ &= |\alpha| \sup_{x\in X}\left\{|f(x)| + \left|f'(x)\right|\right\} \\ &= |\alpha|\, \|f\| .\end{aligned}$$

The triangle inequality is satisfied, since

$$\begin{aligned}\|f+g\| &= \sup_{x\in X}\left\{|f(x)+g(x)| + \left|f'(x)+g'(x)\right|\right\} \\ &\le \sup_{x\in X}\left\{|f(x)| + |g(x)| + \left|f'(x)\right| + \left|g'(x)\right|\right\} \\ &\le \sup_{x\in X}\left\{|f(x)| + \left|f'(x)\right|\right\} + \sup_{x\in X}\left\{|g(x)| + \left|g'(x)\right|\right\} \\ &= \|f\| + \|g\| .\end{aligned}$$

Hence, $C^1[a, b]$ is a normed vector space.

Let $\{f_n\}$ be a Cauchy sequence of functions in $C^1[a, b]$. Fix x, then

$$\left|f_n(x) - f_m(x)\right| + \left|f_n'(x) - f_m'(x)\right| \le \|f_n - f_m\| ,$$

and

$$\max\left\{\sup_{x\in X}\left|f_n(x) - f_m(x)\right| , \sup_{x\in X}\left|f_n'(x) - f_m'(x)\right|\right\} \le \|f_n - f_m\| ,$$

therefore the sequences of numbers $\{f_n(x)\}$ and $\{f_m'(x)\}$ converge and the limit values define the functions $f : X \to \mathbf{R}$ and $f' : X \to \mathbf{R}$. The proof is similar to the one outlined in Theorem 3.1, and repeatedly used in Exercise 3.6. It follows that f' is continuous. Our candidate for the limit is the function f defined by

$$f(a) = \lim_{n\to\infty} f_n(a),$$

and

$$f(x) = f(a) + \int_0^x f'(z)dz.$$

It is clear that f is continuously differentiable, so that $f \in C^1$.

To see that $\|f_n - f\| \to 0$ note that

$$\begin{aligned}
\|f_n - f\| &\le \sup_{x\in X} |f_n(x) - f(x)| + \sup_{x\in X} |f_n'(x) - f'(x)| \\
&\le \sup_{x\in X} \left| f_n(a) + \int_0^x f'(z)dz - f(a) - \int_0^x f'(z)dz \right| \\
&\quad + \sup_{x\in X} |f_n'(x) - f'(x)| \\
&\le |f_n(a) - f(a)| + \int_0^b |f_n'(z) - f'(z)|\, dz \\
&\quad + \sup_{x\in X} |f_n'(x) - f'(x)| \\
&\le |f_n(a) - f(a)| + (b+1) \sup_{x\in X} |f_n'(x) - f'(x)|.
\end{aligned}$$

Since $\{f_n(a)\} \to f(a)$, and $\{f_n'\} \to f'$ uniformly, both terms go to zero as $n \to \infty$.

b. See part c.

c. Consider $C^k[a, b]$, the space of k times continuously differentiable functions on $[a, b]$, with the norm given in the text. Clearly $\alpha_i \ge 0$ is needed for the norm to be well defined.

If $\alpha_i > 0$, all i, then the space is complete. The proof is a trivial adaptation of the one presented in a. However, if $\alpha_j = 0$, for any j, then the space is not complete. To see this, choose a function $h : [a, b] \to [a, b]$ that is continuous, satisfies $h(a) = a$ and $h(b) = b$, and is $(k - j)$ times continuously differentiable, with $h^i(a) = h^i(b) = 0$, $i = 1, 2, \ldots, k - j$.

Then consider the following sequence of functions

$$f_n^j(x) = \begin{cases} a & \text{if } x < \frac{a}{n} \\ h(nx) & \text{if } \frac{a}{n} \le x \le \frac{b}{n} \\ b & \text{if } x > \frac{b}{n} \end{cases}$$

and

$$f_n^{i-1}(x) = \int_0^x f_n^i(z)dz, \quad i = 1, \ldots, j$$

Each function f_n is k times continuously differentiable. However, the limiting function f has a discontinuous jth derivative.

So an example to be applied to part b. would be, for instance, $X = [-1, 1]$ and

$$f_n'(x) = \begin{cases} -1 & \text{if } x < -\frac{1}{n} \\ nx & \text{if } -\frac{1}{n} \leq x \leq \frac{1}{n} \\ 1 & \text{if } x > \frac{1}{n} \end{cases}.$$

Hence

$$f_n(x) = \begin{cases} -x & \text{if } x < -\frac{1}{n} \\ \frac{1}{2n} + \frac{n}{2}x^2 & \text{if } -\frac{1}{n} \leq x \leq \frac{1}{n} \\ x & \text{if } x > \frac{1}{n} \end{cases}.$$

This sequence is clearly not Cauchy in the norm of part a.

Exercise 3.8

The function $T : S \to S$ is uniformly continuous if for every $\varepsilon > 0$ there exists a $\delta > 0$ such that for all x and y in S with $|x - y| < \delta$ we have that $|Tx - Ty| < \varepsilon$.

If T is a contraction, then for some $\beta \in (0, 1)$

$$\frac{|Tx - Ty|}{|x - y|} \leq \beta < 1 \quad \text{all } x, y \in S \text{ with } x \neq y.$$

Hence to prove that T is uniformly continuous in S, let $\delta \equiv \varepsilon/\beta$, then for any arbitrary $\varepsilon > 0$, if $|x - y| < \delta$ then

$$|Tx - Ty| \leq \beta\, |x - y| < \beta\delta = \varepsilon.$$

Hence T is uniformly continuous.

Exercise 3.9

Observe that

$$\begin{aligned} \rho(T^n v_0, v) &\leq \rho(T^n v_0, T^{n+1} v_0) + \rho(T^{n+1} v_0, v) \\ &= \rho(T^n v_0, T^{n+1} v_0) + \rho(T^{n+1} v_0, Tv) \\ &\leq \rho(T^n v_0, T^{n+1} v_0) + \beta\rho(T^n v_0, v), \end{aligned}$$

where the first line uses the triangle inequality, the second the fact that v is the fixed point of T, and the third line follows from the Contraction Mapping Theorem. Rearranging terms, this implies that

$$\rho(T^n v_0, v) \leq \frac{1}{1-\beta}\rho(T^n v_0, T^{n+1}v_0).$$

Exercise 3.10

a. Since v is bounded, the continuous function f is bounded, say by M, on $[-\|v\|, +\|v\|]$. Hence

$$|(Tv)(s)| \leq |c| + sM,$$

so Tv is bounded on $[0, t]$. Since

$$\int_0^s f[v(z)]\,dz$$

is continuous for all f, Tv is continuous.

b. Let $w, v \in C(0, t)$ and let B be their common bound. Note that

$$\begin{aligned} |Tv(s) - Tw(s)| &\leq \int_0^s |f[v(z)] - f[w(z)]|\,dz \\ &\leq \int_0^s B\,|v(z) - w(z)|\,dz \\ &\leq Bs\,\|v - w\|. \end{aligned}$$

Choose $\tau = \beta/B$, where $0 < \beta < 1$, then $0 \leq s \leq \tau$ implies that $Bs\,\|v - w\| \leq \beta\,\|v - w\|$.

c. The fixed point is $x \in C[0, \tau]$, such that

$$x(s) = c + \int_0^s f[x(z)]\,dz.$$

Hence, for $0 \leq s, s' \leq \tau$,

$$\begin{aligned} x(s) - x(s') &= \int_{s'}^s f[x(z)]\,dz \\ &= f[x(\hat{z})](s - s'), \quad \text{for some } \hat{z} \in [s, s']. \end{aligned}$$

Therefore

$$\frac{x(s) - x(s')}{s - s'} = f\,[x(\hat{z})].$$

Let $s' \to s$, then $\hat{z} \to s$, and so $x'(s) = f\,[x(s)]$.

Exercise 3.11

a. We have to prove that Γ is lower hemi-continuous (l.h.c.) and then the result follows by the definition of a continuous correspondence. Toward a contradiction, assume Γ is not lower hemi-continuous. Then, for all $\varepsilon > 0$, and any N, $\exists\, n > N$ such that $|y_n - y| > \varepsilon$. Construct a subsequence $\{y_{n_k}\}$ from these and consider the corresponding subsequence $\{x_{n_k}\}$ where $y_{n_k} \in \Gamma(x_{n_k})$. As $x_n \to x$, $\{x_{n_k}\} \to x$. But as Γ is upper hemi-continuous (u.h.c.), there exist $y_{n_{k_j}} \to y$, a contradiction.

c. That Γ is compact comes from the fact that a finite union of compact sets is compact. To show that Γ is u.h.c., fix x and pick any arbitrary $x_n \to x$ and $\{y_n\}$ such that $y_n \in \Gamma(x_n)$. Hence $y_n \in \phi(x_n)$ or $y_n \in \psi(x_n)$, and therefore there is a subsequence of $\{y_n\}$ whose elements belong to $\phi(x_n)$ and/or a subsequence of $\{y_n\}$ whose elements belong to $\psi(x_n)$. Call them $\{y_{n_k}^{\phi}\}$ and $\{y_{n_k}^{\psi}\}$ respectively. By ϕ and ψ u.h.c., those sequences have a convergent subsequence that converges to $y \in \phi(x)$ or $\psi(x)$ respectively. By construction, those subsequences of $\{y_{n_k}^{\phi}\}$ and $\{y_{n_k}^{\psi}\}$ are convergent subsequences of $\{y_n\}$ that converge to $y \in \Gamma(x)$, which completes the proof.

e. For each x, the set of feasible y's is compact. Similarly, for each y, the set of feasible z's is compact. Hence, for each x, Γ is a finite union of compact sets, which is compact.

To see that Γ is u.h.c., pick any arbitrary $x_n \to x$ and $(\{z_n\}, \{y_n\})$ such that $z_n \in \psi(y_n)$ for $y_n \in \phi(x_n)$. By ϕ u.h.c. there is a convergent subsequence of $\{y_n\}$ whose limit point is in $\phi(x)$.

Take this convergent subsequence of $\{y_n\}$. Call it $\{y_{n_k}\}$. By ψ u.h.c. any sequence $\{z_{n_k}\}$ with $z_{n_k} \in \psi(y_{n_k})$ has a convergent subsequence that converges to $z \in \psi(y)$.

Hence, $\{z_{n_k}\}$ is a convergent subsequence of $\{z_n\}$ that converges to $z \in \Gamma(x)$.

Exercise 3.12

a. If Γ is l.h.c. and single valued, then Γ is nonempty and for every $y \in \Gamma(x)$ and every sequence $x_n \to x$, the sequence $\{y_n\}$ with $y_n = \Gamma(x_n)$ converges to y. Hence Γ is a continuous function.

c. Fix x. Clearly $\Gamma(x)$ is nonempty if ϕ or ψ are l.h.c. To show that Γ is l.h.c., pick any arbitrary $y \in \Gamma(x)$ and a sequence $x_n \to x$. By definition, either $y \in \phi(x)$, or $y \in \psi(x)$ or both. Hence, by ϕ and ψ l.h.c., there exist $N \geq 1$ and a sequence $\{y_n\}$ such that $y_n \in \phi(x_n)$ or $y_n \in \psi(x_n)$ for all $n \geq N$, so $\{y_n\}$ is a sequence such that $y_n \in \Gamma(x_n)$ and $y_n \to y$ for all $n \geq N$. Hence, $\Gamma(x)$ is l.h.c. at x. Because x was arbitrarily chosen, the proof is complete.

e. It is clear that Γ is nonempty if ϕ and ψ are nonempty. Pick any $z \in \Gamma(x)$ and a sequence $x_n \to x$. The objective is to find $N \geq 1$ and a sequence $\{z_n\}_{n=N}^{\infty} \to z$ such that $z_n \in \Gamma(x_n)$. To construct such a sequence, note that if $z \in \Gamma(x)$, then $z \in \psi(y)$ for some $y \in \phi(x)$. So pick any $y \in \phi(x)$ such that $z \in \psi(y)$.

By ϕ l.h.c. there exist $N_1 \geq 1$ and $\{y_n\}$ such that $y_n \to y$ and $y_n \in \phi(x_n)$ for all $n \geq N_1$. Call this sequence $\{y_n^{\phi}\}$.

By ψ l.h.c., for $\{y_n^{\phi}\} \to y$, there exist $N_2 \geq 1$ and $\{z_n\}$ such that $z_n \to z$ and $z_n \in \phi(y_n^{\phi})$ for all $n \geq N_2$. Take $N = \max\{N_1, N_2\}$. Hence, $\Gamma(x)$ is l.h.c. at x. Because x was arbitrarily chosen, the proof is complete.

Exercise 3.13

a. Same as part b. with $f(x) = x$.

b. Choose any x. Since $0 \in \Gamma(x)$, $\Gamma(x)$ is nonempty. Choose any $y \in \Gamma(x)$ and consider the sequence $x_n \to x$. Let $\gamma \equiv y/f(x) \leq 1$ and $y_n = \gamma f(x_n)$. Then $y_n \in \Gamma(x_n)$, all $n \geq 1$, and using the continuity of f

$$\lim y_n = \gamma \lim f(x_n) = \gamma f(x) = y.$$

Hence Γ is l.h.c. at x.

Given x, $[0, f(x)]$ is compact and hence $\Gamma(x)$ is compact valued. Take arbitrary sequences $x_n \to x$ and $y_n \in \Gamma(x_n)$. Define $\epsilon = \sup_{x_n} \|x_n - x\|$ and let $N(x, \epsilon)$ denote the closed ϵ neighborhood of x. Since the set

$$\{z : z \in [0, \bar{f}], \bar{f} = \max_{x' \in N(x,\epsilon)} f(x')\},$$

is compact, there exists a convergent subsequence of y_n, call it y_{n_k}, with $\lim y_{n_k} \equiv y$. Since $y_{n_k} \leq f(x_{n_k})$ all k, we know that $y \leq f(x)$ by the continuity of f and standard properties of the limit. Hence $y \in \Gamma(x)$ and Γ is u.h.c. at x.

Since x was chosen arbitrarily, Γ is a continuous correspondence.

c. Since the set

$$\left\{ \left(x^1, \ldots, x^l\right) : \sum_{i=1}^{l} x^i \leq x \right\},$$

is compact, fix $(x^1, \ldots, x^l)$ and proceed coordinate by coordinate using the proof in b. with $f(x) = f_i(x^i, z)$.

Exercise 3.14

a. Same as part b., with the following exceptions. Suppose $x \neq 0$; let 0 play the role of $\hat{y}$ (since $H(x, 0) > H(0, 0) = 0$), and use monotonicity rather than concavity to establish all the necessary inequalities. For $x = 0$, use monotonicity and the fact that the sequence $\{x_n\}$ must converge to $x = 0$ from above.

b. We prove first that Γ is l.h.c. Fix x. Choose $y \in \Gamma(x)$ and $\{x_n\} \to x$. We must find a sequence $\{y_n\} \to y$ such that $y_n \in \Gamma(x_n)$, all n.

Suppose that $H(x, y) > 0$. Since H is continuous, it follows that for some N, $H(x_n, y) > 0$, all $n \geq N$. Then the sequence $\{y_n\}_{n=N}^{\infty}$ with $y_n = y$, $n \geq N$, has the desired property.

Suppose that $H(x, y) = 0$. By hypothesis there exists some $\hat{y}$ such that $H(x, \hat{y}) > 0$. Since H is continuous, there exists some N such that $H(x_n, \hat{y}) > 0$, all $n \geq N$. Define $y^{\lambda} = (1 - \lambda)y + \lambda\hat{y}$, $\lambda \in [0, 1]$. Then for each $n \geq N$, define

$$\lambda_n = \min \left\{ \lambda \in [0, 1] : H(x_n, y^{\lambda}) \geq 0 \right\}.$$

Since $H(x_n, y^1) = H(x_n, \hat{y}) > 0$, the set on the right is nonempty; clearly it is compact. Hence the minimum is attained.

Next note that $\{\lambda_n\} \to 0$. To see this, notice that by the concavity of H,

$$H(x, y^{\zeta}) \geq (1 - \zeta)H(x, y) + \zeta H(x, \hat{y}) > 0, \quad \text{all } \zeta \in (0, 1].$$

Hence, for any ζ, there exist N_{ζ} such that $H(x, y^{\zeta}) \geq 0$, all $n \geq N_{\zeta}$. Therefore $\lambda_n \leq \zeta$, for all $n \geq N_{\zeta}$. Hence $\{\lambda_n\} \to 0$. Therefore, the sequence $y_n = y^{\lambda_n}$, $n \geq N$, has the desired properties. By construction, $H(x_n, y_n) \geq 0$, all n, so $y_n \in \Gamma(x_n)$, all n, and since $\{\lambda_n\} \to 0$, it follows that $\{y_n\} \to y$.

Next, we prove that Γ is u.h.c. Choose $\{x_n\} \to x$ and $\{y_n\}$ such that $y_n \in \Gamma(x_n)$, all n. We must show that there exists a convergent subsequence of $\{y_n\}$ whose limit point y is in $\Gamma(x)$. It suffices to show that the sequence $\{y_n\}$ is bounded. For if it is, then it has a convergent subsequence, call it $\{y_{n_k}\}$, with limit y. Then, since $H(x_{n_k}, y_{n_k}) \geq 0$, all k, $\{(x_{n_k}, y_{n_k})\} \to (x, y)$, and H is continuous, it follows that $H(x, y) \geq 0$.

Let $\|\cdot\|$ denote the Euclidean norm in $\mathbf{R}^m$. Choose $M < \infty$ such that $\|y\| < M$, all $y \in \Gamma(x)$. Since $\Gamma(x)$ is compact, this is possible. Suppose $\{y_n\}$ is not bounded. Then, there exists a subsequence $\{y_{n_k}\}$ such that $N < n_1 < n_2 \ldots$ and $\|y\| > M + k$, all k. Define $S = \{y \in \mathbf{R}^m : \|y\| = M + 1\}$, which is clearly a compact set. Since $\|\hat{y}\| < M$, and $\|y_{n_k}\| > M + k$, all k, for any element in the sequence $\{y_{n_k}\}$, there exists a unique value $\lambda \in (0, 1)$ such that

$$\|\tilde{y}_{n_k}\| = \|\lambda y_{n_k} + (1 - \lambda)\hat{y}\| + M + 1.$$

Moreover, since $H(x_{n_k}, \hat{y}) > 0$ and $H(x_{n_k}, y_{n_k}) \geq 0$, it follows from the concavity of H that $H(x_{n_k}, \tilde{y}_{n_k}) > 0$, all k. Since by construction the sequence $\{\tilde{y}_{n_k}\}$ lies in the compact set S, it has a convergent subsequence; call this subsequence $\{\tilde{y}_j\}$ and call its limit point $\tilde{y}$. Note that since $\tilde{y} \in S$, $\|\tilde{y}\| = M + 1$. Along the chosen subsequence, $H(x_j, \tilde{y}_j) > 0$, all j; and $\{(x_j, \tilde{y}_j)\} \to (x, \tilde{y})$. Since H is continuous, this implies that $H(x, \tilde{y}) \geq 0$. But then $\|\tilde{y}\| = M + 1$, a contradiction.

c. The correspondence can be written in this case as

$$\begin{aligned}\Gamma(x) &= \{y \in \mathbf{R} : H(x, y) \geq 0\} \\ &= \{y \in \mathbf{R} : 1 - \max\{|x|, |y|\} \geq 0\}.\end{aligned}$$

It can be checked that, at $x = 1$, $\Gamma(x)$ is not l.h.c. Notice that $\Gamma(1) = [-1, +1]$, which is compact and has a nonempty interior, but $\Gamma(1 + 1/n) = 0$, for all $n > 0$.

Exercise 3.15

Let $\{x_n, y_n\}$ be a sequence in A. We need to show that this sequence has a convergent subsequence. Because X is compact, the sequence $\{x_n\}$ has a convergent subsequence, say $\{x_{n_k}\}$ converging to $x \in X$. Because Γ is u.h.c., every sequence $x_n \to x \in X$ has an associated sequence $\{y_n\}$ such that $y_n \in \Gamma(x_n)$, all n, with a convergent subsequence, say $\{y_{n_k}\}$ whose limit point $y \in \Gamma(x)$. Then, $\{(x_n, y_n)\} \in A$ has a convergent subsequence with limit (x, y).

Exercise 3.16

a. The correspondence G is

$$\begin{aligned} G(x) &= \left\{ y \in [-1, 1] : xy^2 = \max_{\tilde{y} \in [-1,1]} x\tilde{y}^2 \right\} \\ &= \{ y \in [-1, 1] : y = 0 \text{ for } x < 0, \\ &\qquad y \in [-1, 1] \text{ for } x = 0, \;\; y = \pm 1 \text{ for } x > 0 \}. \end{aligned}$$

Thus, $G(x)$ can be drawn as shown in Figure 3.1.

Then, $G(x)$ is nonempty, and it is clearly compact valued. Furthermore, A, the graph of G, is closed in $\mathbf{R}^2$ since it is a finite union of closed sets. Hence, by Theorem 3.4, $G(x)$ is u.h.c.

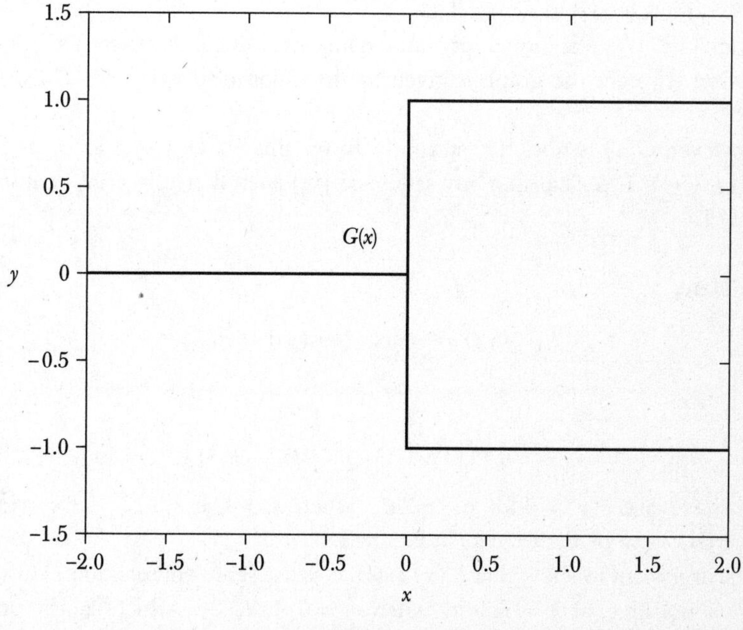

Figure 3.1

To see that $G(x)$ is not l.h.c. at $x = 0$, choose an increasing sequence $\{x_n\} \to x = 0$ and $y = 1/2 \in G(0)$. In this case, any $\{y_n\}$ such that $y_n \in G(x_n)$ implies that $y_n = 0$, so $\{y_n\} \to 0 \neq 1/2$.

b. Let $X = \mathbf{R}$.
Then,

$$\begin{aligned} h(x) &= \max_{y\in[0,4]} \left\{ \max\{2-(y-1)^2, x+1-(y-2)^2\}\right\} \\ &= \max\left\{ \max_{y\in[0,4]}[2-(y-1)^2], \max_{y\in[0,4]}[x+1-(y-2)^2]\right\} \\ &= \max\left\{2, x+1\right\} \end{aligned}$$

Hence,

$$h(x) = \begin{cases} 2 & \text{if } x \leq 1 \\ x+1 & \text{if } x > 1 \end{cases}$$

Then,

$$\begin{aligned} G(x) = \{ & y \in [0, 4] : y = 1 \text{ for } x < 1, \\ & y \in \{1, 2\} \text{ for } x = 1, \ y = 2 \text{ for } x > 1\}, \end{aligned}$$

which is represented in Figure 3.2.

Evidently, $G(x)$ is nonempty and compact valued. Further, its graph is closed in $\mathbf{R}^2$ since the graph is given by the union of closed sets. Thus, $G(x)$ is u.h.c.

However, $G(x)$ is not l.h.c. at $x = 1$. To see this, let $\{x_n\} \to 1$ for $x_n > 1$ and $y = 1 \in G(1)$. It is clear that any sequence $\{y_n\}$ such that $y_n \in G(x_n)$ converges to $2 \neq 1$.

c. Here,

$$h(x) = \max_{-x\leq y\leq x} \{\cos(y)\} = 1$$

and hence

$$G(x) = \left\{y \in [-x, x] : \cos(y) = 1\right\}.$$

Then, since $\cos(y) = 1$ for $y = \pm 2n\pi$, where $n = 0, 1, 2, \ldots$, the correspondence $G(x)$ can be depicted as in Figure 3.3.

The argument to show that $G(x)$ is u.h.c. is the same outlined in b. However, $G(x)$ is not l.h.c. at $x = \pm 2n\pi$, where $n = 0, 1, 2, \ldots$; which can be proved using the same kind of construction of sequences developed before.

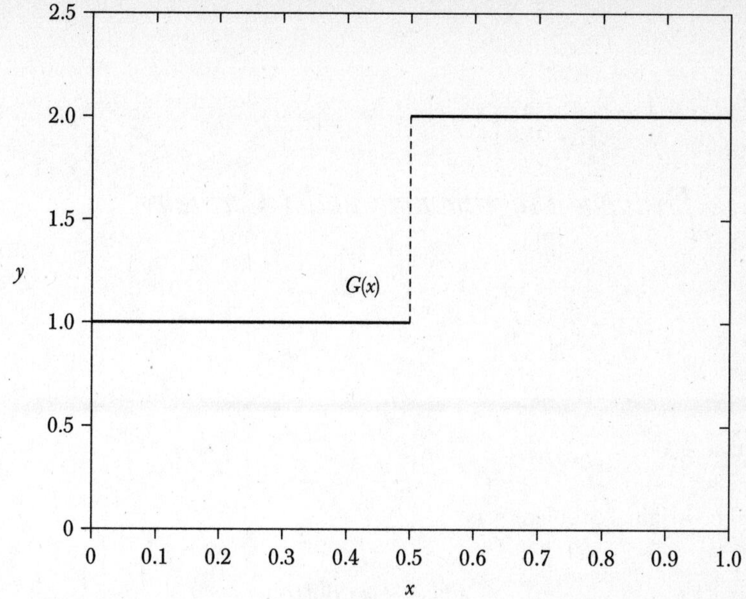

Figure 3.2

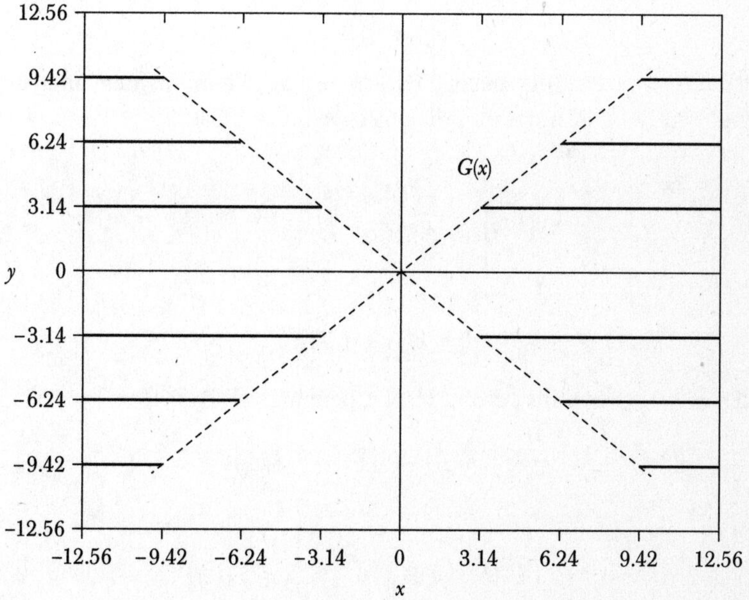

Figure 3.3

4 *Dynamic Programming under Certainty*

Exercise 4.1

a. The original problem was

$$\max_{\{c_t,k_{t+1}\}_{t+0}^{\infty}} \sum_{t=0}^{\infty} \beta^t u(c_t)$$

subject to

$$c_t + k_{t+1} \leq f(k_t),$$
$$c_t,\ k_{t+1} \geq 0,$$

for all $t = 0, 1, \ldots$ with k_0 given. This can be equivalently written, after substituting the budget constraint into the objective function, as

$$\max_{\{k_{t+1}\}_{t+0}^{\infty}} \sum_{t=0}^{\infty} \beta^t u[f(k_t) - k_{t+1}]$$

subject to

$$0 \leq k_{t+1} \leq f(k_t),$$

for all $t = 0, 1, \ldots$ with k_0 given. Hence, defining

$$F(k_t, k_{t+1}) = u[f(k_t) - k_{t+1}],$$

and

$$\Gamma(k_t) = \left\{k_{t+1} \in \mathbf{R}_+ : 0 \leq k_{t+1} \leq f(k_t)\right\},$$

we obtain the sequence problem (SP) formulation given in the text.

b. Note that in this case $c_t \in \mathbf{R}^l_+$ for all $t = 0, 1, \ldots$ and we cannot simply substitute for consumption in the objective function. Instead, define

$$\Gamma(k_t) := \{k_{t+1} \in \mathbf{R}^l_+ : (k_{t+1} + c_t,\ k_t) \in Y \subseteq \mathbf{R}^{2l}_+,\ c_t \in \mathbf{R}^l_+\},$$

and

$$\Phi(k_t, k_{t+1}) := \{c_t \in \mathbf{R}^l_+ : (k_{t+1} + c_t,\ k_t) \in Y \subseteq \mathbf{R}^{2l}_+\}.$$

Then, let

$$F(k_t, k_{t+1}) = \sup_{c_t \in \Phi(k_t, k_{t+1})} u(c_t),$$

and the problem is in the form of the (SP).

Exercise 4.2

a. Define x_{it} as the ith component of the l dimensional vector x_t. Hence,

$$\max_i x_{it} \leq \theta^t \left\| x_0 \right\| .$$

Let $e = (1, \ldots, 1, \ldots, 1)$ be an l dimensional vector of ones. Hence, the fact that F is increasing in its first l arguments and decreasing in its last l arguments implies that for all θ

$$F(x_1, x_2) \leq F(x_1, 0) \leq F(\theta \left\| x_0 \right\| e, 0)$$

Then, if $\theta \leq 1$, $F(\theta^t \left\| x_0 \right\| e, 0) \leq F(\left\| x_0 \right\| e, 0)$ and

$$\lim_{n\to\infty} \sum_{t=0}^{\infty} \beta^t F(x_t, x_{t+1}) \leq \lim_{n\to\infty} \sum_{t=0}^{\infty} \beta^t F(\left\| x_0 \right\| e, 0) = \frac{F(\left\| x_0 \right\| e, 0)}{(1-\beta)},$$

as $\beta < 1$. Otherwise, if $\theta > 1$, $F(\theta^t \left\| x_0 \right\| e, 0) \leq \theta^t F(\left\| x_0 \right\| e, 0)$ by the concavity of F and

$$\lim_{n\to\infty} \sum_{t=0}^{\infty} \beta^t F(x_t, x_{t+1}) \leq \lim_{n\to\infty} \sum_{t=0}^{\infty} (\theta\beta)^t F(\left\| x_0 \right\| e, 0) = \frac{F(\left\| x_0 \right\| e, 0)}{(1-\theta\beta)},$$

as $\beta\theta < 1$. Hence the limit exists.

b. By assumption, for all $x_0 \in X$, $F(x_1, 0) \leq \theta F(x_0, 0)$. Hence

$$F(x_t, x_{t+1}) \leq F(x_t, 0) \leq \theta F(x_{t-1}, 0) \leq \ldots \leq \theta^t F(x_0, 0).$$

Then,

$$\begin{aligned} \lim_{n\to\infty} \sum_{t=0}^{\infty} \beta^t F(x_t, x_{t+1}) &\leq \lim_{n\to\infty} \sum_{t=0}^{\infty} (\theta\beta)^t F(x_0, 0) \\ &= \frac{F(x_0, 0)}{1-\theta\beta}. \end{aligned}$$

Therefore, the limit exists.

Exercise 4.3

a. Let $\upsilon(x_0)$ be finite. Since υ satisfies the functional equation (FE), as shown in the proof of Theorem 4.3, for every $x_0 \in X$ and every $\varepsilon > 0$, there exists $\underset{\sim}{x} \in \Pi(x_0)$ such that

$$\upsilon(x_0) \leq u_n(\underset{\sim}{x}) + \beta^{n+1}\upsilon(x_{n+1}) + \frac{\varepsilon}{2}.$$

Taking the limit as $n \to \infty$ gives

$$\begin{aligned} \upsilon(x_0) &\leq u(\underset{\sim}{x}) + \limsup_{n\to\infty} \beta^{n+1}\upsilon(x_{n+1}) + \frac{\varepsilon}{2} \\ &\leq u(\underset{\sim}{x}) + \frac{\varepsilon}{2}. \end{aligned}$$

Since

$$u(\underset{\sim}{x}) \leq \upsilon^*(x_0),$$

for all $\underset{\sim}{x} \in \Pi(x_0)$, this gives

$$\upsilon(x_0) \leq \upsilon^*(x_0) + \frac{\varepsilon}{2},$$

for all $\varepsilon > 0$. Hence,

$$\upsilon(x_0) \leq \upsilon^*(x_0),$$

for all $x_0 \in X$.

If $\upsilon(x_0) = -\infty$, the result follows immediately. If $\upsilon(x_0) = +\infty$, the proof goes along the lines of the last part of Theorem 4.3. Hence $\upsilon(x_0) \leq \upsilon^*(x_0)$, all $x_0 \in X$.

b. Since υ satisfies FE, by the argument of Theorem 4.3, for all $x_0 \in X$ and $\underset{\sim}{x} \in \Pi(x_0)$

$$\upsilon(x_0) \geq u_n(\underset{\sim}{x}) + \beta^{n+1}\upsilon(x_{n+1}).$$

In particular, for $\underset{\sim}{x}$ and $\underset{\sim}{x}'$ as described,

$$\begin{aligned}\upsilon(x_0) &\geq \lim_{n\to\infty} u_n(\underset{\sim}{x}') + \lim_{n\to\infty} \beta^n \upsilon(x'_{n+1}) \\ &= u(\underset{\sim}{x}') \\ &\geq u(\underset{\sim}{x})\end{aligned}$$

all $\underset{\sim}{x} \in \Pi(x_0)$. Hence

$$\upsilon(x_0) \geq \upsilon^*(x_0) = \sup_{\underset{\sim}{x}\in\Pi(x_0)} u(\underset{\sim}{x}),$$

and in combination with the result proved in part a., the desired result follows.

Exercise 4.4

a. Let K be a bound on F and M be a bound on f. Then

$$(Tf)(x) \leq K + \beta M, \quad \text{for all } x \in X.$$

Hence $T : B(X) \to B(X)$.

In order to show that T has a unique fixed point $\upsilon \in B(X)$ we will use the Contraction Mapping Theorem. Note that $(B(X), \rho)$ is a complete metric space, where ρ is the metric induced by the sup norm.

We will use Blackwell's sufficient conditions to show that T is a contraction. To prove monotonicity, let $f, g \in B(X)$, with $f(x) \leq g(x)$ for all $x \in X$. Then

$$\begin{aligned}(Tf)(x) &= \max_{y\in\Gamma(x)} \{F(x, y) + \beta f(y)\} \\ &= F(x, y^*) + \beta f(y^*) \\ &\leq F(x, y^*) + \beta g(y^*) \\ &\leq \max_{y\in\Gamma(x)} \{F(x, y) + \beta g(y)\} = (Tg)(x),\end{aligned}$$

where

$$y^* = \arg\max_{y\in\Gamma(x)} \{F(x, y) + \beta f(y)\}.$$

For discounting, let $a \in \mathbf{R}$. Then

$$\begin{aligned} T(f+a)(x) &= \max_{y\in\Gamma(x)} \left\{F(x, y) + \beta\left[f(y) + a\right]\right\} \\ &= \max_{y\in\Gamma(x)} \{F(x, y) + \beta f(y)\} + \beta a \\ &= (Tf)(x) + \beta a. \end{aligned}$$

Hence by the Contraction Mapping Theorem, T has a unique fixed point $v \in B(X)$, and for any $v_0 \in B(X)$,

$$\left\|T^n v_0 - v\right\| \leq \beta^n \left\|v_0 - v\right\|.$$

That the optimal policy correspondence $G : X \to X$, where

$$G(x) = \{y \in \Gamma(x) : v(x) = F(x, y) + \beta v(y)\}$$

is nonempty is immediate from the fact that Γ is nonempty and finite valued for all x. Hence, the maximum is always attained.

b. Note that as F and f are bounded, $T_h f$ is bounded. Hence $T_h : B(X) \to B(X)$. That T_h satisfies Blackwell's sufficient conditions for a contraction can be proven following the same steps as in part a. with the corresponding adaptations. Hence, T_h is a contraction and by the Contraction Mapping Theorem it has a unique fixed point $w \in B(X)$.

c. First, note that

$$\begin{aligned} w_n(x) &= (T_{h_n} w_n)(x) \\ &= F\left[x, h_n(x)\right] + \beta w_n\left[h_n(x)\right] \\ &\leq \max_{y\in\Gamma(x)} \left\{F(x, y) + \beta w_n(y)\right\} \\ &= (Tw_n)(x) \\ &= (T_{h_{n+1}} w_n)(x). \end{aligned}$$

Hence for all $n = 0, 1, \ldots, w_n \leq Tw_n$. Applying the operator $T_{h_{n+1}}$ to both sides of this inequality and using monotonicity gives

$$Tw_n = T_{h_{n+1}} w_n \leq \left(T_{h_{n+1}}\right)(Tw_n) = T^2_{h_{n+1}} w_n.$$

Iterating on this operator gives

$$Tw_n \leq T^N_{h_{n+1}} w_n.$$

But $w_{n+1} = \lim_{N\to\infty} T^N_{h_{n+1}} w_n$, for $w_n \in B(X)$. Hence $Tw_n \leq w_{n+1}$ and

$$w_0 \leq Tw_0 \leq w_1 \leq Tw_1 \leq \ldots \leq Tw_{n-1} \leq Tw_n \leq v.$$

By the Contraction Mapping Theorem,

$$\left\| T^N w_n - v \right\| \leq \beta^N \left\| w_n - v \right\|.$$

Then,

$$\begin{aligned}\left\| w_n - v \right\| &\leq \left\| Tw_{n-1} - v \right\| \leq \beta \left\| w_{n-1} - v \right\| \\ &\leq \beta \left\| Tw_{n-2} - v \right\| \leq \beta^2 \left\| w_{n-2} - v \right\| \leq \ldots \\ &\leq \beta^n \left\| w_0 - v \right\|\end{aligned}$$

and hence $w_n \to v$ as $n \to \infty$.

Exercise 4.5

First, we prove that $g(x)$ is strictly increasing. Toward a contradiction, suppose that there exists $x, x' \in X$ with $x < x'$ such that $g(x) \geq g\left(x'\right)$. Then as f is increasing, using the first-order condition (5)

$$\begin{aligned}\beta v'[g(x')] &= U'[f(x') - g(x')] \\ &< U'[f(x) - g(x)] = \beta v'[g(x)]\end{aligned}$$

which contradicts v strictly concave.

We prove next that $0 < g(x') - g(x) < f(x') - f(x)$, if $x' > x$. Let $x' > x$. As $g(x)$ is strictly increasing, using the first-order condition we have

$$\begin{aligned}U'[f(x) - g(x)] &= \beta v'[g(x)] \\ &> \beta v'[g(x')] = U'[f(x') - g(x')].\end{aligned}$$

The result follows from U strictly concave.

Exercise 4.6

a. By Assumption 4.10 $\left\| x_t \right\|_E \leq \alpha \left\| x_{t-1} \right\|_E$ for all t. Hence

$$\alpha \left\| x_{t-1} \right\|_E \leq \alpha^2 \left\| x_{t-2} \right\|_E$$

and

$$\|x_t\|_E \leq \alpha^2 \|x_{t-2}\|_E$$

The desired result follows by induction.

b. By Assumption 4.10 $\Gamma : X \to X$ is nonempty.
Combining Assumptions 4.10 and 4.11,

$$\begin{aligned}|F(x_t, x_{t+1})| &\leq B\left(\|x_t\|_E + \|x_{t+1}\|_E\right)\\ &\leq B(1+\alpha)\|x_t\|_E\\ &\leq B(1+\alpha)\alpha^t \|x_0\|_E\end{aligned}$$

for $\alpha \in (0, \beta^{-1})$ and $0 < \beta < 1$. So by Exercise 4.2, Assumption 4.2 is satisfied.

c. By Assumption 4.11 F is homogeneous of degree one, so

$$F(\lambda x_t, \lambda x_{t+1}) = \lambda F(x_t, x_{t+1}).$$

Then

$$\begin{aligned}u(\lambda \underset{\sim}{x}) &= \lim_{n\to\infty} \sum_{t=0}^{n} \beta^t F(\lambda x_t, \lambda x_{t+1})\\ &= \lambda \lim_{n\to\infty} \sum_{t=0}^{n} \beta^t F(x_t, x_{t+1}) = \lambda u(\underset{\sim}{x}).\end{aligned}$$

By Assumption 4.10 the correspondence Γ displays constant returns to scale. Then clearly $\underset{\sim}{x} \in \Pi(x_0)$ if and only if $\lambda \underset{\sim}{x} \in \Pi(\lambda x_0)$. Hence

$$\begin{aligned}v^*(\lambda x_0) &= \sup_{\lambda \underset{\sim}{x} \in \Pi(\lambda x_0)} u(\lambda \underset{\sim}{x})\\ &= \lambda \sup_{\underset{\sim}{x} \in \Pi(x_0)} u(\underset{\sim}{x})\\ &= \lambda v^*(x_0).\end{aligned}$$

By Assumption 4.11,

$$\begin{aligned}|F(x_t, x_{t+1})| &\leq B\left(\|x_t\|_E + \|x_{t+1}\|_E\right)\\ &\leq B(1+\alpha)\|x_t\|_E \leq B(1+\alpha)\alpha^t \|x_0\|_E .\end{aligned}$$

Hence

$$\begin{aligned}
\left|v^*(x_0)\right| &= \left| \sup_{\underline{x}\in\Pi(x_0)} \sum_{t=0}^{\infty} \beta^t F(x_t, x_{t+1}) \right| \\
&\leq \sup_{\underline{x}\in\Pi(x_0)} \sum_{t=0}^{\infty} \beta^t \left|F(x_t, x_{t+1})\right| \\
&\leq \sum_{t=0}^{\infty} B(1+\alpha)(\alpha\beta)^t \left\|x_0\right\|_E \\
&= \frac{B(1+\alpha)}{1-\alpha\beta} \left\|x_0\right\|_E .
\end{aligned}$$

Therefore $v^*(x_0) \leq c \left\|x_0\right\|_E$, all $x_0 \in X$, where

$$c = \frac{B(1+\alpha)}{1-\alpha\beta}.$$

Exercise 4.7

a. Take f and g homogeneous of degree one, and $\alpha \in \mathbf{R}$, then $f + g$ and αf are homogeneous of degree one, and clearly $\|\cdot\|$ is a norm, so H is a normed vector space. We hence turn to the proof that H is complete. Let $\{f_n\}$ be a Cauchy sequence in H. Then $\{f_n\}$ converges pointwise to a limit function f. We need to show that $f_n \to f \in H$ where the convergence is in the norm of H. The proof of convergence, and that f is continuous, are analogous to the proof of Theorem 3.1. To see that f is homogeneous of degree one, note that for any $x \in X$ and any $\lambda \geq 0$

$$f(\lambda x) = \lim_{n\to\infty} f_n(\lambda x) = \lim_{n\to\infty} \lambda f_n(x) = \lambda f(x) .$$

b. Take $f \in H(X)$. Tf is continuous by the Theorem of the Maximum. To show that Tf is homogeneous of degree one, notice that

$$\begin{aligned}
(Tf)(\lambda x) &= \sup_{\lambda y\in\Gamma(\lambda x)} \{F(\lambda x, \lambda y) + \beta f(\lambda y)\} \\
&= \sup_{y\in\Gamma(x)} \lambda \{F(x, y) + \beta f(y)\} \\
&= \lambda (Tf)(x),
\end{aligned}$$

where the second line follows from Assumption 4.10.

Exercise 4.8

a. We prove the result under the additional restriction that f is nonnegative, and strictly positive on $X\setminus\{0\}$. To see that a further assumption is necessary, consider the following example. Let $X = \mathbf{R}^2_+$ and consider the function

$$f(x) = \begin{cases} x_1^{1/2} x_2^{1/2} & \text{if } x_2 \geq x_1 \\ 0 & \text{otherwise.} \end{cases}$$

This function is clearly not concave, but is homogeneous of degree one and quasi-concave. To see homogeneity, let $\lambda \in [0, \infty)$ and note that

$$f(\lambda x) = \begin{cases} \lambda x_1^{1/2} x_2^{1/2} & \text{if } x_2 \geq x_1 \\ 0 & \text{otherwise.} \end{cases}$$
$$= \lambda f(x).$$

To see quasi-concavity, let $x, x' \in X$ with $f(x) \geq f(x')$. If $f(x') = 0$ the result follows from f nonnegative. If $f(x') > 0$, then $x_2 \geq x_1$ and $x_2' \geq x_1'$, and as $f(x)$ is Cobb-Douglas in this range, it is quasi-concave.

Assume that f is nonnegative, and strictly positive on $X\setminus\{0\}$. Let $x, x' \in X$ with $f(x) \geq f(x')$. If $x' = 0$, the result follows from homogeneity. Letting $f(x') > 0$, then

$$f\left(\frac{x}{f(x)}\right) = f\left(\frac{x'}{f(x')}\right) = 1,$$

and for any $\theta \in (0, 1)$ define

$$\lambda = \frac{\theta f(x)}{\theta f(x) + (1-\theta) f(x')}.$$

Then

$$1 \leq f\left(\lambda \frac{x}{f(x)} + (1-\lambda)\frac{x'}{f(x')}\right)$$
$$= f\left(\frac{\theta x + (1-\theta) x'}{\theta f(x) + (1-\theta) f(x')}\right),$$

where the inequality is by quasi-concavity. But then using homogeneity of degree one,

$$f\left(\theta x + (1-\theta) x'\right) \geq \theta f(x) + (1-\theta) f\left(x'\right).$$

b. Let f be nonnegative and *strictly* quasiconcave, as well as homogeneous of degree one. But if so, f must be strictly positive except at the origin, for if $f(x) = 0$ for $x \neq 0$, then for $\lambda \in (0, 1)$

$$0 = \lambda f(x) = f(\lambda x + (1 - \lambda)\, 0) > 0,$$

a contradiction. With f nonnegative except at the origin, the proof is then identical to that for part a., with the weak inequality replaced by a strict inequality.

c. In order to prove that the fixed point v of the operator T defined in (2) is strictly quasi-concave, we need X, Γ, F and β to satisfy Assumptions 4.10 and 4.11. In addition, we need F to be strictly quasi-concave (see part b.). To show this, let $H'(X) \subset H(X)$ be the set of functions on X that are continuous, homogeneous of degree one, quasi-concave and bounded in the norm in (1), and let $H''(X)$ be the set of strictly quasi-concave functions. Since $H'(X)$ is a closed subset of the complete metric space $H(X)$, by Theorem 4.6 and Corollary 1 to the Contraction Mapping Theorem, it is sufficient to show that $T[H'(X)] \subseteq H''(X)$.

To verify that this is so, let $f \in H'(X)$ and let

$$x_0 \neq x_1, \quad \theta \in (0, 1), \quad \text{and } x_\theta = \theta x_0 + (1 - \theta) x_1.$$

Let $y_i \in \Gamma(x_i)$ attain $(Tf)(x_i)$, for $i = 0, 1$, and let $F(x_0, y_0) > F(x_1, y_1)$. Then by Assumption 4.10, $y_\theta = \theta y_0 + (1 - \theta) y_1 \in \Gamma(x_\theta)$. It follows that

$$\begin{aligned} (Tf)(x_\theta) &\geq F(x_\theta, y_\theta) + \beta f(y_\theta) \\ &> F(x_1, y_1) + \beta f(y_1) \\ &= (Tf)(x_1), \end{aligned}$$

where the first line uses (3) and the fact that $y_\theta \in \Gamma(x_\theta)$; the second uses the hypothesis that f is quasi-concave and the quasi-concavity restriction on F; and the last follows from the way y_0 and y_1 were selected. Since x_0 and x_1 were arbitrary, it follows that Tf is strictly quasi-concave, and since f was arbitrary, that $T[H'(X)] \subseteq H''(X)$. Hence the unique fixed point v is strictly quasi-concave.

d. We need X, Γ, F, and β to satisfy Assumptions 4.9, 4.10 and 4.11, and in addition F to be strictly quasi-concave. Considering $x, x' \in X$ with $x \neq \alpha x'$ for any $\alpha \in \mathbf{R}$, Theorem 4.10 applies.

Exercise 4.9

Construct the sequence $\{k_t^*\}_{t=0}^{\infty}$ using

$$k_{t+1} = g(k_t) = \alpha\beta k_t^{\alpha},$$

given some $k_0 \in X$. If $k_0 = 0$ we have that $k_t^* = 0$ for all $t = 0, 1, \ldots,$ which is the only feasible policy and is hence optimal. If $k_0 > 0$, then for all $t = 0, 1, \ldots$ we have that $k_{t+1}^* \in int\Gamma(k_t^*)$ as $\alpha\beta \in (0, 1)$.

Let

$$E(x_t, x_{t+1}) \equiv F_y(x_t, x_{t+1}) + \beta F_x(x_t, x_{t+1}).$$

Then for all $t = 0, 1, 2, \ldots$ we have that

$$\begin{aligned} E(k_t^*, k_{t+1}^*) &= \beta\frac{\alpha k_t^{*\alpha-1}}{k_t^{*\alpha} - k_{t+1}^*} - \frac{1}{k_{t-1}^{*\alpha} - k_t^*} \\ &= \beta\frac{\alpha k_t^{*\alpha-1}}{k_t^{*\alpha} - \alpha\beta k_t^{*\alpha}} - \frac{1}{k_{t-1}^{*\alpha} - \alpha\beta k_{t-1}^{*\alpha}} \\ &= \frac{\alpha\beta}{k_t^*(1-\alpha\beta)} - \frac{1}{k_{t-1}^{*\alpha}(1-\alpha\beta)} \\ &= \frac{1}{k_{t-1}^{*\alpha}(1-\alpha\beta)} - \frac{1}{k_{t-1}^{*\alpha}(1-\alpha\beta)} = 0, \end{aligned}$$

from repeated substitution of the policy function. Hence the Euler equation holds for all $t = 0, 1, \ldots$.

To see that the transversality condition holds, let

$$T(x_t, x_{t+1}) = \lim_{t\to\infty} \beta^t F_x(x_t, x_{t+1}) \cdot x_t.$$

Then,

$$\begin{aligned} T(k_t^*, k_{t+1}^*) &= \lim_{t\to\infty} \beta^t \frac{\alpha k_t^{*\alpha-1}}{k_t^{*\alpha} - k_{t+1}^*} k_t \\ &= \lim_{t\to\infty} \beta^t \frac{\alpha k_t^{*\alpha}}{k_t^{*\alpha} - \alpha\beta k_t^{*\alpha}} \\ &= \lim_{t\to\infty} \beta^t \frac{\alpha}{(1-\alpha\beta)} = 0, \end{aligned}$$

where the result comes from the fact that $0 < \beta < 1$.

5 *Applications of Dynamic Programming under Certainty*

Exercise 5.1

a.–c. The answers to parts a. through c. of this question require that Assumptions 4.1 through 4.8 be established. We verify each in turn.

A4.1: Here $\Gamma(x) = [0, f(x)]$, and since by T2 $f(0) = 0$, $0 \in \Gamma(x)$ for all x, and therefore Γ is nonempty for all x.

A4.2: Here $F(x_t, x_{t+1}) = U[f(x_t) - x_{t+1}]$. By U3 and the fact that $U : \mathbf{R}_+ \to \mathbf{R}$, U, and hence F, is bounded below and the result follows from U1.

A4.3: $X = [0, \overline{x}] \in \mathbf{R}_+$ which is a convex subset of $\mathbf{R}$. Refer to Exercise 3.13b. for Γ nonempty and compact valued. By T1 and Exercise 3.13, Γ is continuous.

A4.4: We showed above that F is bounded below. By T1–T3 $f(x_t) - x_{t+1}$ is bounded, and hence by assumption U2–U3 F is bounded above. By U2 and T1, F is continuous. And by U1, $0 < \beta < 1$.

A4.5: By U3 and T3, $F(\cdot, y)$ is a strictly increasing function.

A4.6: Let $x \leq x'$, then by T3, $f(x) \leq f(x')$, which implies that $[0, f(x)] \subseteq [0, f(x')]$.

A4.7: By T4 $f(x) - y$ is a concave function in (x, y). By U4 this implies that $F(x, y)$ is strictly concave in (x, y).

A4.8: Let $x, x' \in X$, $y \in \Gamma(x)$ and $y' \in \Gamma(x')$. Then $y \leq f(x)$ and $y' \leq f(x')$, which implies, by T4, that

$$\begin{aligned}\theta y + (1-\theta)y' &\leq \theta f(x) + (1-\theta) f(x') \\ &\leq f(\theta x + (1-\theta)x').\end{aligned}$$

d. $v(x)$ is differentiable at x: By Theorems 4.7 and 4.8 and parts b. and c., v is an increasing and strictly concave function. By U5, T5 and $g(x) \in (0, f(x))$, Assumption 4.9 is satisfied. Hence by Theorem 4.11 v is continuously differentiable and

$$v'(x) = F_x[f(x) - g(x)] = U'[f(x) - g(x)]f'(x).$$

$0 < g(x) < f(x)$: A sufficient condition for an interior solution is

$$\lim_{c\to 0} U'(c) = \infty.$$

To see that $g(x) = f(x)$ is never optimal under this condition, notice that v is differentiable for $x \in (0, \bar{x})$ when $g(x) \in (0, f(x))$. Hence, in this case we have that $g(x)$ satisfies

$$U'[f(x) - g(x)] = \beta v'[g(x)],$$

but

$$\lim_{g(x)\to f(x)} U'[f(x) - g(x)] = \infty,$$

while

$$\lim_{g(x)\to f(x)} \beta v'[g(x)] < \infty,$$

by the strict concavity of v.

To show that $g(x) = 0$ is not optimal, assume $g(\hat{x}) = 0$, for some $\hat{x} > 0$. Hence, it must be that $g(x) = 0$ for $x < \hat{x}$. But then, for $x < \hat{x}$

$$v(x) \equiv U[f(x)] + \beta \frac{U(0)}{1-\beta}.$$

Therefore v is differentiable and

$$v'(x) = U'[f(x)]\, f'(x).$$

Hence, when $x \to 0$, $v'(x) \to \infty$, and then $g(\hat{x}) = 0$ for $\hat{x}$ is not possible.

To see what happens when this condition fails, notice that at the steady state, we have that $g(x^*) < f(x^*)$, where x^* stands for the steady-state level of capital. By continuity of g, there is an interval $(x^* - \varepsilon, x^*)$, such that for any x belonging to that interval, $g(x) < f(x)$. Theorem 4.11 implies that v is differentiable in this range. For any other x, eventually this interval will be reached, or another point interval that implies $g(x) = 0$ or $g(x) < f(x)$. We established above that v is differentiable in those cases, so it must be that v is differentiable everywhere.

e. Let $\beta' > \beta$. Define T' as the operator T using β' as a discount factor instead of β, and v_k as the kth application of this operator.

Applying T' to $v(x; \beta)$ once (that is, using v as the inital condition of the iteration) we obtain $v_1(x; \beta')$ and $g_1(x; \beta')$, where using the first-order condition (assuming an interior solution for simplicity), $g_1(x; \beta')$ is defined as the solution y to

$$U'[f(x) - y] = \beta' v'(y, \beta).$$

It is clear that the savings function must increase since the right-hand side increases from β to β', that is $g_1(x; \beta') > g_1(x; \beta)$, which by Theorem 4.11 in turn implies

$$v_1'(x, \beta') > v'(x, \beta).$$

By a similar argument, if

$$v_k'(x; \beta') > v_{k-1}'(x; \beta'),$$

then

$$v_{k+1}'(x; \beta') > v_k'(x; \beta'),$$

and

$$g_{k+1}(x; \beta') > g_k(x; \beta').$$

Hence, $g_k(x; \beta')$ increases with k. The result then follows from applying Theorem 4.9 to the sequence $\{g_k(x; \beta')\}_{k=0}^{\infty}$ since $g_k(x; \beta') \to g(x; \beta')$.

Exercise 5.2

a. For $f(x) = x$, T1 and T3–T5 are easily proved as follows:

T1: To prove that the function f is continuous, we must show that for every $\varepsilon > 0$ and every $x \in \mathbf{R}_+$, there exist $\delta > 0$ such that

$$|f(x) - f(x')| < \varepsilon \text{ if } |x - x'| < \delta.$$

Choosing $\delta = \varepsilon$ the definition of continuity is trivially satisfied.

T3: Pick $x, x' \in \mathbf{R}_+$, with $x > x'$, then

$$f(x) = x > x' = f(x').$$

T4: Pick $x \neq x' \in \mathbf{R}_+$. Then, for any $\alpha \in (0, 1)$,

$$\alpha f(x) + (1-\alpha) f(x') = \alpha x + (1-\alpha)x' = f[\alpha x + (1-\alpha)x'],$$

so f is weakly concave.

T5: For every $x \in \mathbf{R}_+$,

$$\lim_{\varepsilon \to 0} \frac{f(x+\varepsilon) - f(x)}{\varepsilon} = 1,$$

so f is continuously differentiable.

Also, notice that given this technology, there is no growth in the economy. Hence the maximum level of capital is given by the initial condition $x_0 \geq 0$. Therefore, for the nontrivial case where the economy starts with a positive level of capital, we can always define $\bar{x} = x_0$ and restrict attention to the set $X = [0, x_0]$. Given the linear technology, it is always possible to maintain the preexisting capital stock; hence the desired result follows.

b. The problem can be stated as

$$\max_{\{x_{t+1}\}_{t=0}^{\infty}} \sum_{t=0}^{\infty} \beta^t \ln(x_t - x_{t+1}),$$

subject to

$$0 \leq x_{t+1} \leq x_t, \quad t = 0, 1, \ldots,$$

given $x_0 \geq 0$.

Since $\ln x_t \leq \ln x_0$ for all t,

$$\ln(x_t - x_{t+1}) \leq \ln(x_t) \leq \ln(x_0).$$

Then, for any feasible sequence,

$$\sum_{t=0}^{\infty} \beta^t \ln(x_t - x_{t+1}) \leq \frac{1}{1-\beta} \ln(x_0).$$

Hence,

$$v^*(x) \leq \frac{1}{1-\beta}\ln(x_0),$$

where v^* is the supremum function.

Define

$$\hat{v}(x) = \frac{1}{1-\beta}\ln(x).$$

It is clear that $\hat{v}$ satisfies conditions (1) to (3) of Theorem 4.14.

Define

$$Tf_n(x) = \max_{0 \leq y \leq x}\left\{\ln(x-y) + \beta f_n(y)\right\}.$$

Then

$$\begin{aligned} T\hat{v}(x) &= \max_{0 \leq y \leq x}\left\{\ln(x-y) + \frac{\beta}{1-\beta}\ln(y)\right\} \\ &= \frac{1}{1-\beta}\ln x + \ln(1-\beta) + \frac{\beta}{1-\beta}\ln\beta, \end{aligned}$$

where the second line uses the fact that the first-order condition of the right-hand side implies $y = \beta x$. Using the same procedure,

$$\begin{aligned} T^2\hat{v}(x) &= \max_{0 \leq y \leq x}\left\{\ln(x-y) + \frac{\beta}{1-\beta}\ln(y)\right. \\ &\quad \left. + \beta\left[\ln(1-\beta) + \frac{\beta}{1-\beta}\ln\beta\right]\right\} \\ &= \frac{1}{1-\beta}\ln x + (1+\beta)\left[\ln(1-\beta) + \frac{\beta}{1-\beta}\ln\beta\right] \end{aligned}$$

and more generally,

$$T^n\hat{v}(x) = \frac{1}{1-\beta}\ln x + \left[\ln(1-\beta) + \frac{\beta}{1-\beta}\ln\beta\right]\sum_{j=0}^{n}\beta^j.$$

Define $v = \lim_{n\to\infty} T^n\hat{v}$. Taking the limit of the expression above, we have

$$v(x) = \frac{1}{1-\beta}\ln x + \frac{1}{1-\beta}\left[\ln(1-\beta) + \frac{\beta}{1-\beta}\ln\beta\right]$$

which is clearly a fixed point of T. Hence, by Theorem 4.14, $v = v^*$.

Then, as

$$Tv(x) = \max_{0 \le y \le x} \left\{ \ln(x - y) + \beta v(y) \right\},$$

the first-order condition of the right-hand side implies that the policy function g is given by the expression $g(x) = \beta x$.

c. Notice that the only change between the current formulation and the one presented in Exercise 5.1 is the linearity of the technology. Restricting the state space to $X = [0, x_0]$ all the results obtained in Exercise 5.1 are still valid under this setup.

Exercise 5.6

a. Let $X = \mathbf{R}_+$. Define

$$\Gamma(Q) = \{y : y \ge Q,\ y \le Q + \bar{q}\} = [Q, Q + \bar{q}].$$

Since $\phi(\bar{q}) = \underline{c}$ and $\lim_{Q \to \infty} \gamma(Q) = \underline{c}$, it is never profitable to produce more than $\bar{q}$.

To show the existence of a unique bounded continuous function v satisfying the functional equation

$$v(Q) = \max_{y \ge Q} \left\{ (y - Q) \left[\phi(y - Q) - \gamma(Q) \right] + \beta v(y) \right\}$$

it is enough to show that the assumptions of Theorem 4.6 are satisfied. We establish each in turn.

A4.3: $X = \mathbf{R}_+$ is a convex subset of $\mathbf{R}^l$. Also, Γ is nonempty since $Q \in \Gamma(Q)$ for all Q, compact valued since it is a closed interval in $\mathbf{R}_+$, and clearly continuous since it has a continuous lower and upper bound.

A4.4: Let

$$F(Q, y) = (y - Q) \left[\phi(y - Q) - \gamma(Q) \right].$$

Then

$$0 \le F(Q, y) \le \bar{q} \left[\phi(0) - \gamma(Q) \right] < \bar{q} \left[\phi(0) - \underline{c} \right] < \infty.$$

Hence $F(Q, y)$ is bounded. Since ϕ and γ are continuous functions, $F(Q, y)$ is also continuous. Finally, $0 < \beta < 1$ since $r > 0$. Hence Theorem 4.6 applies.

To show that Assumption 4.6 does not hold, consider $Q < Q'$ with $Q' < Q + \bar{q}$. Then $\Gamma(Q) = [Q, Q + \bar{q}]$ and $\Gamma(Q') = [Q', Q' + \bar{q}]$. Hence,

$$\Gamma(Q) \cup \Gamma(Q') = [Q, Q' + \bar{q}] \neq [Q', Q' + \bar{q}],$$

which implies that $\Gamma(Q)$ is not a subset of $\Gamma(Q')$.

To show that Assumption 4.7 does not hold, an extra assumption about the curvatures of γ and ϕ is needed. Necessary and sufficient conditions for $F(x, y)$ to be jointly concave in (x, y) are F_{11}, $F_{22} < 0$, and $F_{11}F_{22} - F_{12}^2 > 0$. In this example

$$F(x, y) = (y - x)\,[\phi(y - x) - \gamma(x)],$$

so

$$F_1(x, y) = -\,[\phi(y - x) - \gamma(x)] - (y - x)\left[\phi'(y - x) + \gamma'(x)\right],$$
$$F_2(x, y) = [\phi(y - x) - \gamma(x)] + (y - x)\,\phi'(y - x),$$

and

$$F_{11} = 2\left[\phi' + \gamma'\right] + (y - x)\left[\phi'' - \gamma''\right],$$
$$F_{12} = -2\phi' - \gamma' - (y - x)\,\phi'',$$
$$F_{22} = 2\phi' + (y - x)\,\phi''.$$

Note that

$$F_{11} = F_{22} + 2\gamma' - (y - x)\,\gamma'',$$
$$F_{12} = -F_{22} - \gamma'.$$

The assumption that $\phi + q\phi'$ is decreasing implies $F_{22} < 0$, and the additional assumption that γ is decreasing and convex then implies $F_{11} < 0$. To ensure that $F_{11}F_{22} - F_{12}^2 > 0$, we need

$$0 < F_{22}\left[F_{22} + 2\gamma' - (y - x)\,\gamma''\right] - \left[F_{22} + \gamma'\right]^2$$
$$= -F_{22}\,(y - x)\,\gamma'' - (\gamma')^2.$$

The first term is positive, but a joint restriction on γ and ϕ is needed to ensure that it offsets the second term:

$$\frac{[\gamma'(x)]^2}{\gamma''(x)} < -[2q\phi'(q) + q^2\phi''(q)], \quad \text{all } q, x.$$

An alternative argument to show that v is strictly increasing can be constructed by examining the problem posed in terms of infinite sequences, then applying the Principle of Optimality. The principle holds because under Assumptions 4.3–4.4 we have that Assumptions 4.1–4.2 hold.

Consider two initial stocks of cumulative experience Q_0 and $Q_0' \in X$ with $Q_0 < Q_0'$. Let $\{Q_t^*\}$ be the optimal sequence from Q_0 and define $\{q_t^*\}$ as the optimal production levels from Q_0 by

$$q_t^* = Q_{t+1}^* - Q_t^*.$$

Then,

$$\begin{aligned} v(Q_0') &\geq \sum_{t=0}^{\infty} \beta^t q_t^* \left[\phi(q_t^*) - \gamma\left(Q_t^* + Q_0' - Q_0\right)\right] \\ &> \sum_{t=0}^{\infty} \beta^t q_t^* \left[\phi(q_t^*) - \gamma(Q_t^*)\right] = v(Q_0), \end{aligned}$$

where the strict inequality comes from the fact that γ is strictly decreasing. Hence, v is strictly increasing.

Next, we will show that $y^* \in G(Q)$ implies that

$$y^* > \arg\max_{y \geq Q}(y - Q)\left[\phi(y - Q) - \gamma(Q)\right] \equiv \tilde{y}.$$

Note that $\tilde{y}$ is implicitly determined by

$$\phi(\tilde{y} - Q) - \gamma(Q) + (\tilde{y} - Q)\phi'(\tilde{y} - Q) = 0,$$

or

$$\phi(\tilde{y} - Q) + (\tilde{y} - Q)\phi'(\tilde{y} - Q) = \gamma(Q),$$

where the left-hand side is strictly decreasing in y by the assumption of strictly decreasing marginal revenue.

On the other hand, y^* is determined by the first-order condition of the right-hand side of the Bellman equation, assuming v is differentiable (see Theorem 4.11), then

$$\phi(y^* - Q) + (y^* - Q)\phi'(y^* - Q) = \gamma(Q) - \beta v'(y^*).$$

Having shown that v is increasing, we can conclude that

$$\phi(y^* - Q) + (y^* - Q)\phi'(y^* - Q) < \gamma(Q),$$

which implies that $y^* > \tilde{y}$.

b. S is continuously differentiable since ϕ is continuously differentiable and integrals are linear operators. Using Leibniz's Rule, $S'(q) = \phi(q) > 0$, and $S''(q) = \phi'(q) < 0$.

To show that there is a unique bounded and continuous function w satisfying the functional equation

$$w(Q) = \max_{y \geq Q} \left\{ S(y - Q) - (y - Q)\gamma(Q) + \beta w(y) \right\},$$

let $\Gamma(Q) = [Q, Q + \bar{q}]$ by the same argument given in a. Hence Assumption 4.3 is satisfied.

Let

$$F(Q, y) = S(y - Q) - (y - Q)\gamma(Q),$$

then $F(Q, y) \leq S(\bar{q}) < \infty$, so F is bounded.

Since S and γ are continuous functions, F is a continuous function, so Assumption 4.4 is also satisfied and the desired result follows from Theorem 4.6.

To show that $w \leq S(\bar{q})/(1 - \beta)$, define the operator T by

$$(Tw)(Q) = \max_{y \in \Gamma(Q)} \left\{ S(y - Q) - (y - Q)\gamma(Q) + \beta w(y) \right\}.$$

That T is monotone follows from the fact that if $w(Q) > w'(Q)$ for all Q, then

$$\begin{aligned} (Tw)(Q) &= \max_{y \in \Gamma(Q)} \left\{ S(y - Q) - (y - Q)\gamma(Q) + \beta w(y) \right\} \\ &> \max_{y \in \Gamma(Q)} \left\{ S(y - Q) - (y - Q)\gamma(Q) + \beta w'(y) \right\} \\ &= (Tw')(Q). \end{aligned}$$

We have shown already that

$$\lim_{n \to \infty} (T^n w_0)(Q) = w(Q),$$

where $w(Q)$ satisfies the Bellman equation. Start with $w_0(Q) = 0$. Then

$$\begin{aligned} w_1(Q) &= \max_{y \in \Gamma(Q)} \left\{ S(y - Q) - (y - Q)\gamma(Q) \right\} \\ &\leq S(\bar{q}), \end{aligned}$$

and applying T to both sides of this inequality we get

$$\begin{aligned} (Tw_1)(Q) &\leq (TS)(\bar{q}) \\ &= \max_{y \in \Gamma(Q)} \left\{ S(y - Q) - (y - Q)\gamma(Q) + \beta S(\bar{q}) \right\} \\ &\leq (1 + \beta)S(\bar{q}). \end{aligned}$$

Therefore,

$$\lim_{n\to\infty}(Tw_1)(Q) \le \lim_{n\to\infty}(TS)(\bar{q}) \le (1+\beta+\beta^2+\ldots)S(\bar{q}),$$

and hence

$$w(Q) \le \frac{S(\bar{q})}{(1-\beta)},$$

for all $Q \in X$.

As before, Assumption 4.6 is not satisfied, so in order to show that w is strictly increasing, pick two arbitrary initial stocks Q_0, $Q_0' \in X$, with $Q_0 < Q_0'$. Consider an increasing function w' and let y^* be the optimal choice of next-period cumulative experience when Q_0 is the current stock and w' is the continuation value function. Then

$$(Tw')(Q_0) = S(y^* - Q_0) - (y^* - Q_0)\gamma(Q_0) + \beta w'(y^*),$$

and

$$\begin{aligned}(Tw')(Q_0') &\ge S(y^* - Q_0) - (y^* - Q_0)\gamma(Q_0') + \beta w'\left[y^* - Q_0 + Q_0'\right] \\ &> S\left(y^* - Q_0\right) - \left(y^* - Q_0\right)\gamma\left(Q_0\right) + \beta w'\left(y^*\right) \\ &= (Tw')(Q_0),\end{aligned}$$

since w' is strictly increasing, and γ is strictly decreasing. Then T maps increasing into strictly increasing functions and by Corollary 1 to the Contraction Mapping Theorem, $w(Q)$ is a strictly increasing function.

The proof that any output level that is optimal exceeds the level that maximizes current surplus is a straightforward adaptation of the proof outlined in a.

c. Competitive firms take prices and aggregate production as given. Normalize the total number of firms to one. The sequential problem for an individual firm can be stated as

$$\max_{\{q_t\}_{t=0}^{\infty}} \sum_{t=0}^{\infty} \beta^t q_t \left[p_t - \gamma(Q_t)\right].$$

The equilibrium conditions are

$$p_t = \phi\left(q_t\right)$$

$$\sum_i q_t^i = Q_{t+1} - Q_t.$$

where we have exploited the fact that under our normalization, aggregate production in the industry is q_t. The first-order condition of the firm's problem implies zero production at time t if

$$p_t < \gamma(Q_t),$$

infinite production at t if

$$p_t > \gamma(Q_t),$$

and indeterminate production at t if

$$p_t = \gamma(Q_t).$$

After substituting the equilibrium conditions we obtain

$$p_t = \phi\left(Q_{t+1} - Q_t\right) = \gamma(Q_t).$$

Since ϕ and γ are strictly decreasing functions, production is an increasing function of Q.

As a result, production will rise through time, but since γ is a convex function the growth rate has to be declining, with $\lim_{t\to\infty} q_t = \bar{q}$. Concurrently, the price will be declining through time at a decreasing rate with an asymptote at $\underline{c}$ since $\phi(Q_{t+1} - Q_t)$ declines with Q_t.

The equation describing the efficient path of production implies

$$\phi(y^E - Q) < \gamma(Q).$$

In the competitive equilibrium,

$$\phi(y^C - Q) = \gamma(Q).$$

Therefore $y^E > y^C$ as ϕ is strictly decreasing. Hence the competitive output level is lower.

d. Instead of building a stock of cumulative experience, we have an initial stock of a nonrenewable resource that will be depleted over time. The recursive formulation of the problem can be stated as

$$w(Q) = \max_{y \le Q} \left\{S(Q - y) - (Q - y)\gamma(Q) + \beta w(y)\right\}.$$

Assuming that the cost of extraction γ is strictly increasing and strictly convex and defining $\Gamma(Q) = [0, Q]$ which satisfies Assumption 4.3, the problem is well defined. All of the proof presented above applies with slight modifications. Posed in terms of infinite sequences, the monopolist's problem can be stated as

$$\max_{\{Q_{t+1}\}_{t=0}^{\infty}} \sum_{t=0}^{\infty} \beta^t (Q_t - Q_{t+1}) \left[\phi(Q_t - Q_{t+1}) - \gamma(Q_t)\right],$$

subject to

$$Q_t \geq Q_{t+1} \quad t = 0, 1, \ldots,$$

with Q_0 given.

Exercise 5.7

a. Define

$$\Gamma(k) = \left\{y : (1-\delta)k \leq y \leq (1+\lambda)k\right\},$$

and set $v_0(k) = 0$ for all k. Then for $n = 1$,

$$\begin{aligned} v_1(k) &= (T v_0)(k) \\ &= \max_{y \in \Gamma(k)} \left\{k\phi(y/k) + \beta v_0(y)\right\} = a_1 k \end{aligned}$$

where

$$a_1 = \max_{y \in \Gamma(k)} \phi(y/k) = \phi(1-\delta) = 1.$$

Now assume that $v_n(k) = (T^n v_0)(k) = a_n k$. To see that the result holds for $n+1$, note that

$$\begin{aligned} v_{n+1}(k) &= (T^{n+1} v_0)(k) \\ &= \max_{y \in \Gamma(k)} \left\{k\phi(y/k) + \beta v_n(y)\right\} \\ &= \max_{y \in \Gamma(k)} \left\{k\phi(y/k) + \beta a_n y\right\}. \end{aligned}$$

There are three cases to consider, depending upon whether the optimal choice of y is interior or at a corner. First, consider the case of an interior solution. The first-order condition of the problem is

$$\phi'(y/k) + \beta a_n = 0,$$

and hence

$$y = k\phi'^{-1}(-\beta a_n).$$

Plugging this expression into the Bellman equation, we have that

$$v_{n+1}(k) = k\phi[\phi'^{-1}(-\beta a_n)] + \beta k \phi'^{-1}(-\beta a_n)a_n = a_{n+1}k,$$

where

$$a_{n+1} = \phi[\phi'^{-1}(-\beta a_n)] + \beta \phi'^{-1}(-\beta a_n)a_n.$$

Second, consider the case of a corner solution with $y = (1-\delta)k$, which occurs when

$$\phi'(1-\delta) + \beta a_n \leq 0.$$

Plugging $y = (1-\delta)k$ into the Bellman equation gives

$$v_{n+1}(k) = k\phi(1-\delta) + \beta(1-\delta)ka_n = a_{n+1}k,$$

where

$$a_{n+1} = 1 + \beta(1-\delta)a_n.$$

Finally, consider the case of a corner solution with $y = (1+\lambda)k$, which occurs when

$$\phi'(1+\lambda) + \beta a_n \geq 0.$$

Although we have shown that it is never optimal to choose $y = (1+\lambda)k$ when there is just one period left in which to work, we cannot rule out corner solutions in other periods without making further assumptions about ϕ and some of the parameters of the problem. Plugging $y = (1+\lambda)k$ into the Bellman equation we get

$$v_{n+1}(k) = k\phi(1+\lambda) + \beta(1+\lambda)ka_n = a_{n+1}k,$$

where

$$a_{n+1} = \beta(1+\lambda)a_n.$$

Hence the result is true for $n+1$ and the result follows by induction.

The proof that $a_{n+1} > a_n$ for all n is by induction. Note that we have shown above that $a_1 = 1$. Next, assume $a_n > a_{n-1}$. Let y^n denote the optimal choice of next period capital when the worker has n periods left to work, that is

$$v_n(k) = k\phi(y^n/k) + \beta v_{n-1}(y^n).$$

Hence,

$$\begin{aligned} a_{n+1}k = v_{n+1}(k) &= \max_{y\in\Gamma(k)} \{k\phi(y/k) + \beta v_n(y)\} \\ &\geq k\phi(y^n/k) + \beta v_n(y^n) \\ &= k\phi(y^n/k) + \beta a_n y^n \\ &> k\phi(y^n/k) + \beta a_{n-1} y^n = v_n(k) = a_n k, \end{aligned}$$

and the result follows.

Next, we establish conditions under which the sequence $\{a_n\}_{n=0}^{\infty}$ is bounded. Notice that either

$$\begin{aligned} a_{n+1} &= 1 + \beta(1-\delta)a_n, \\ a_{n+1} &= f(a_n), \text{ or} \\ a_{n+1} &= \beta(1+\lambda)a_n, \end{aligned}$$

and $\phi'^{-1}: R_- \to [(1-\delta), (1+\lambda)]$. Therefore

$$\beta(1-\delta) \leq \frac{\partial f(a_n)}{\partial a_n} = \beta\phi'^{-1}(-\beta a_n) \leq \beta(1+\lambda),$$

and hence the required condition is $\lambda < r$.

b. We can show, using the fact that $a_{n+1} > a_n$ for all n, that if in the nth period it is optimal to invest at the minimum feasible level (complete depletion), then it is optimal to continue investing at the minimum level in future periods $(n-1, n-2, \ldots)$, hence $y = (1-\delta)k$ from then on.

From the first-order conditions of the problem, if minimum feasible accumulation is optimal,

$$-\phi'(1-\delta) > \beta a_n.$$

But $a_n > a_{n-1} > a_{n-2} \cdots$ implies that $-\phi'(1-\delta) > \beta a_n > \beta a_{n-1} \cdots$.

We can also show that if in the nth period it is optimal to invest at the maximum feasible level $y = (1+\lambda)k$, then it is optimal to invest at that level for earlier periods also, namely $n+1, n+2, \ldots$

In this case, from the first-order conditions of the problem

$$-\phi'(1+\lambda) < \beta a_n.$$

But $a_{n+1} > a_n > \ldots$ implies that $-\phi'(1+\lambda) < \beta a_n < \beta a_{n+1} \cdots$.

A plausible path for capital (remember we cannot rule out some weird path without making some further assumptions) would be increasing at early stages of the individual's life, reaching a peak, and decreasing after that point.

Notice that we can have an interior solution and $k_{t+1} < k_t$, so capital may start decreasing before decreasing at the maximum allowed rate. We cannot ensure from the first-order conditions that $k_{t+1} = g(k_t)$ is strictly increasing for an interior solution.

In order to characterize the path of k_t corresponding to the region of interior solutions, from the first-order conditions we have

$$-\phi'(y/k) = \beta a_n,$$

hence

$$k_{t+1} = \phi'^{-1}(-\beta a_n)k_t.$$

Since $\{a_n\}_{n=0}^{\infty}$ is an increasing sequence, higher a's imply higher values for ϕ'^{-1}, and because ϕ'^{-1} goes from ranges of $\phi'^{-1} > 1$ (for high values of a) to ranges of $\phi'^{-1} < 1$ (for low values of a), when $a_n \to a_1$ capital may increase at the beginning ($\phi'^{-1} > 1$) and then gradually decrease ($\phi'^{-1} < 1$).

The age-earnings profile will also be hump-shaped, with a flat segment at the level of zero earnings for the periods in which it is optimal to accumulate capital at the rate λ.

Exercise 5.9

a. In order to find exact solutions for $v(k)$ and $g(k)$ we can use standard calculus, but this requires that v satisfy certain properties.

First, notice that $f(k)$ is unbounded, so we cannot apply the standard theorems for bounded returns. One way to get around this problem is by judiciously restricting the state space. Define k^m as

$$k^m = \frac{p}{q} f(k^m) + (1-\delta)k^m.$$

That is, if $k > k^m$, the output in terms of capital that can be obtained is less than k^m. Hence it is never optimal to set k_{t+1} higher than k^m. Set $\bar{k} = \max\{k^m, k_0\}$. Then, let $k \in K = [0, \bar{k}]$ where K is the restricted state space and let $y \in \Gamma(k) = K$ be the restricted feasible correspondence.

Next, we need to check that v is differentiable, for which it suffices to check that the assumptions of Theorem 4.11 are satisfied.

A4.3: Since $K = [0, \bar{k}] \subseteq R_+$, K is a convex subset of R. Since $\Gamma(k) = K$, Γ is nonempty, compact valued and continuous by Exercise 3.13. Define

$$A = \{(k, y) \in K \times K : y \in \Gamma(k)\},$$

and $F : A \to \mathbf{R}$ as

$$F(k, y) = pf(k) - q[y - (1-\delta)k].$$

A4.4: Since we have restricted the state space, F is bounded, and clearly continuous. Finally $0 < \beta < 1$ by $r > 0$.

A4.7: Take two arbitrary pairs (k, y) and (k', y') and let $\theta \in (0, 1)$. Define $k^\theta = \theta k + (1-\theta)k'$ and $y^\theta = \theta y + (1-\theta)y'$. Then

$$\begin{aligned} F(k^\theta, y^\theta) &= pf(k^\theta) - q[y^\theta - (1-\delta)k^\theta] \\ &= pf(\theta k + (1-\theta)k') \\ &\quad - q\{\theta y + (1-\theta)y' - (1-\delta)[\theta k + (1-\theta)k']\} \\ &> \theta\{pf(k) - q[y - (1-\delta)k]\} \\ &\quad + (1-\theta)\{pf(k') - q[y' - (1-\delta)k']\} \\ &= \theta F(k, y) + (1-\theta)F(k', y'), \end{aligned}$$

where the strict inequality is the result of the strict concavity of f.

A4.8: Since $\Gamma(k) = \{y : 0 \leq y \leq \bar{k}\}$ for all k it follows trivially that if $y \in \Gamma(k)$ and $y' \in \Gamma(k')$ then

$$y^\theta \in \Gamma(k^\theta) = \Gamma(k) = \Gamma(k') = K.$$

A4.9: By assumption, f is continuously differentiable. Hence, by Theorem 4.11, v is differentiable. The Bellman equation for this problem is

$$v(k) = \max_{y \in \Gamma(k)} \{pf(k) - q[y - (1-\delta)k] + \beta v(y)\}$$

so the Euler equation (Inada conditions rule out corner solutions) is

$$q = \beta[pf'(y^*) + (1-\delta)q] \tag{5.1}$$

where y^* is the value of y that satisfies this equation. Notice that y^* does not depend on the current level of capital, so independently of it, it is optimal to adjust to y^* and stay at that level of capital forever.

The interpretation of (5.1) is as follows. The left-hand side of the Euler equation measures the marginal cost of increasing the stock of capital by one more unit.

The right-hand side measures the marginal benefit of an additional unit of capital when the capital stock is already at the y^* level. Since it takes one period for the capital to be effective, the current marginal benefit must be discounted. It is composed of a first term which measures the value of its marginal product and a second term which is its scrap value if it is sold next period. Hence,

$$v(y^*) = pf(y^*) - q[y^* - (1-\delta)y^*] + \beta v(y^*),$$

which implies that

$$v(y^*) = \frac{1}{1-\beta}[pf(y^*) - q\delta y^*].$$

So for any arbitrary $k \in K$,

$$v(k) = pf(k) - q[y^* - (1-\delta)k] + \frac{\beta}{1-\beta}[pf(y^*) - q\delta y^*].$$

Within one period, then, all firms end up with the same capital stock irrespective of their initial capital endowment. The intuition behind this result is that the marginal cost of adjusting capital is constant, so there is no reason to adjust capital in a gradual fashion. Hence $y = g(k) = y^*$, a constant function.

The economic interpretation of the absence of a nonnegativity constraint in gross investment is the existence of perfect capital markets, so investment is reversible.

If we have some upper and lower bounds on investment, the feasible correspondence is now

$$\Gamma(k) = \{y : (1-\delta)k \le y \le (1-\delta)k + a\}$$

To ensure differentiability of the value function, we need to check Assumptions 4.3 and 4.8.

A4.3: We still maintain the assumption that $K = [0, \bar{k}]$. It is clear that $\Gamma(k)$ is nonempty ($y = (1-\delta)k \in \Gamma(k)$), compact valued and continuous.

A4.8: Take two arbitrary pairs (k, y) and (k', y') where $y \in \Gamma(k)$ and $y' \in \Gamma(k')$, and $\theta \in (0, 1)$, and define k^θ and y^θ as before. We need to show that $y^\theta \in \Gamma(k^\theta)$.

By definition

$$\Gamma(k^\theta) = \{y : (1-\delta)k^\theta \leq y \leq (1-\delta)k^\theta + a\}.$$

Note that $y \in \Gamma(k)$ implies that $(1-\delta)k \leq y$, which implies in turn that $(1-\delta)\theta k \leq \theta y$, and $\theta y < (1-\delta)\theta k + a$. Hence $\theta y \in \Gamma(\theta k)$. Proceeding in the same fashion it can be shown that $(1-\theta)y' \in \Gamma[(1-\theta)k']$. Therefore, since $(1-\delta)k^\theta \leq y^\theta$ and $y^\theta \leq (1-\delta)k^\theta + a$, Γ is convex.

At this point it would be convenient to show that indeed v is increasing and strictly concave. Unfortunately $\Gamma(k)$ is not monotone, so we cannot apply Theorem 4.7. To show that v is strictly increasing we will use Corollary 1 of the Contraction Mapping Theorem. Let $v \in C'(k)$ where $C'(k)$ is the space of continuous and (weakly) increasing functions. Then,

$$\begin{aligned}(Tv)(k) &= \max_{y \in \Gamma(k)} \{pf(k) - q[y - (1-\delta)k] + \beta v(y)\} \\ &= \{pf(k) - q[\hat{y} - (1-\delta)k] + \beta v(\hat{y})\},\end{aligned}$$

where $\hat{y} \in \arg\max_{y\in\Gamma(k)} \{pf(k) - q[y - (1-\delta)k] + \beta v(y)\}$.

Take $\tilde{k} > k$. Then,

$$\begin{aligned}(Tv)(k) &< pf(\tilde{k}) + (1-\delta)\tilde{k}q - q[\hat{y} + (1-\delta)(\tilde{k} - k)] \\ &\quad + \beta v[\hat{y} + (1-\delta)(\tilde{k} - k)] \\ &= pf(\tilde{k}) - q[\tilde{y} - (1-\delta)\tilde{k}] + \beta v(\tilde{y}) \\ &\leq \max_{y \in \Gamma(\tilde{k})} \left\{pf(\tilde{k}) - q[y - (1-\delta)\tilde{k}] + \beta v(y)\right\} \\ &= (Tv)(\tilde{k}).\end{aligned}$$

Note that $\tilde{y} \in \Gamma(\tilde{k})$ since $\tilde{y} = \hat{y} + (1-\delta)(\tilde{k} - k)$ implies that $\tilde{y} + (1-\delta)k = \hat{y} + (1-\delta)\tilde{k}$ and $\hat{y} \in \Gamma(k)$. Hence $T : C'(k) \to C''(k)$ where $C''(k)$ is the space of continuous and strictly increasing functions. Therefore $v \in C''(k)$ where v is the fixed point of T.

That v is strictly concave follows immediately from f being strictly concave and Γ convex, so Theorem 4.8 applies.

Let λ and μ be the Lagrange multiplier for the lower and the upper bounds respectively. Then the first-order condition of the problem is

$$q = \beta v'(y) + \lambda - \mu.$$

Hence, $\lambda > 0$ implies $v'(y) < q/\beta$ and $y = (1-\delta)k$; $\mu > 0$ implies $v'(y) > q/\beta$ and $y = (1-\delta)k + a$; and finally $\lambda = \mu = 0$ implies $v'(y) = q/\beta$.

Let k_λ and k_μ be defined as

$$v'\left[(1-\delta)k_\lambda\right] = q/\beta,$$

and

$$v'\left[(1-\delta)k_\mu + a\right] = q/\beta,$$

so if the level of capital is higher than k_λ the firm has too much of it, and the only way of depleting it is by letting it depreciate. If the current level of capital is lower than k_μ then the firm wants to accumulate as much capital as possible, but there is a bound on how much capital can be accumulated in a single period.

The policy function is then,

$$g(k) = \begin{cases} (1-\delta)k + a & \text{if } k \le k_\mu \\ y^* & \text{if } k_\mu \le k \le k_\lambda \\ (1-\delta)k & \text{if } k \ge k_\lambda. \end{cases}$$

b. Under this new setup the functional equation is

$$v(k) = \max_{y \in \Gamma(k)} \left\{ pf(k) - c[y - (1-\delta)k] + \beta v(y) \right\}$$

The proofs that v is differentiable, strictly increasing and strictly concave are similar to the ones presented in part a. The optimal level of next period's capital is implicitly determined by the first-order condition

$$c'[y - (1-\delta)k] = \beta v'(y).$$

Since c is strictly convex and v is strictly concave there is a unique y^* that solves the above equation.

The policy function $g(k)$ is a single-valued correspondence (see Theorem 4.8) and it is nondecreasing. Pick any arbitrary k, k' with $k' > k$. The proof is by contradiction. Suppose $g(k') < g(k)$. Then, by v strictly concave,

$$\begin{aligned} c'[g(k) - (1-\delta)k] &= \beta v'[g(k)] \\ &< \beta v'[g(k')] = c'[g(k') - (1-\delta)k'], \end{aligned}$$

which implies, by c strictly convex, that

$$0 < (1-\delta)(k'-k) < g(k') - g(k),$$

a contradiction.

Also note that

$$c'[g(k) - (1-\delta)k] > c'[g(k') - (1-\delta)k']$$

implies that

$$(1-\delta) > \frac{g(k') - g(k)}{(k' - k)},$$

hence the policy function has a slope that is strictly less than one.

The envelope condition is

$$v'(k) = pf'(k) + (1-\delta)c'[y - (1-\delta)k].$$

Combining it with the first-order condition we get the Euler equation

$$c'[y - (1-\delta)k] = \beta \left\{ pf'(y) + (1-\delta)c'[y' - (1-\delta)y] \right\}.$$

Notice that, in contrast with the Euler equation obtained in a., now the marginal cost of investing is no longer constant. Hence the steady state capital level k^* satisfies

$$c'(\delta k^*) = \frac{\beta}{1 - \beta(1-\delta)} pf'(k^*).$$

Notice that in this case, capital will adjust slowly to this level.

c. Let

$$\phi(k) = \arg\max_{l \geq 0} \{pF(k, l) - wl\}.$$

For Π and ϕ to be well-defined functions, we need the maximum to exist and ϕ to be single valued. If $F(k, l)$ is a continuous function for all pairs $(k, l) \in K \times L$, then Π and ϕ will be continuous functions. If, in addition, $F(k, l)$ is strictly concave in l, then ϕ will be single valued.

We consider each property of Π in turn. For $\Pi(0)$ we need $F(0, l) = 0$ for all l. For then

$$\Pi(0) = \max_{l \in L(k)} -wl = 0,$$

and the optimal choice of l is zero. To show that $\lim_{k\to 0} \Pi'(k) = \infty$ and $\lim_{k\to\infty} \Pi'(k) = 0$, we need Inada conditions for k on $F(k, l)$. By the envelope condition $\Pi'(k) = pF_k(k, l)$ so it is enough that $\lim_{k\to 0} F_k(k, l) = \infty$ and $\lim_{k\to\infty} F_k(k, l) = 0$. To show that Π is strictly concave we need $F(k, l)$ to be strictly concave.

Exercise 5.10

a. Define

$$\Pi(k_0) = \{\{k_{t+1}\}_{t=0}^{\infty} : (1-\delta)k_t \leq k_{t+1} \leq (1+\alpha)k_t, \quad t = 0, 1, \ldots\}.$$

Let

$$\{k_t^*\}_{t=0}^{\infty} \in \underset{\{k_t\}_{t=0}^{\infty} \in \Pi(k_0)}{\operatorname{argmax}} \sum_{t=0}^{\infty} \beta^t \{pF(k_t, k_{t+1}) - q\,[k_{t+1} - (1-\delta)k_t]\},$$

and $\lambda > 0$. Then,

$$\begin{aligned} v^*(\lambda k_0) &\geq \sum_{t=0}^{\infty} \beta^t \{pF(\lambda k_t^*, \lambda k_{t+1}^*) - q\,[\lambda k_{t+1}^* - (1-\delta)\lambda k_t^*]\} \\ &= \lambda v^*(k_0). \end{aligned}$$

Now let $\{k_t^{\lambda *}\}_{t=0}^{\infty}$ be optimal from λk_0. Then, clearly, $\{\lambda^{-1} k_t^{\lambda *}\}_{t=0}^{\infty}$ is feasible from k_0, and

$$\begin{aligned} v^*(k_0) &\geq \sum_{t=0}^{\infty} \beta^t \left\{pF(\frac{1}{\lambda}k_t^*, \frac{1}{\lambda}k_{t+1}^*) - q\left[\frac{1}{\lambda}k_{t+1}^* - (1-\delta)\frac{1}{\lambda}k_t^*\right]\right\} \\ &= \frac{1}{\lambda} v^*(\lambda k_0), \end{aligned}$$

which completes the proof.

b. We will prove that there is a function v satisfiying the functional equation that is homogeneous of degree one. For that, we have to check that Assumptions 4.10 and 4.11 are satisfied.

Let

$$\Gamma(k) = \{y \in \mathbf{R}_+ : (1-\delta)k \leq y \leq (1+\alpha)k\}.$$

Clearly, the graph of Γ is a cone.

Also,

$$\frac{y}{k} - 1 \leq \alpha.$$

Hence, Assumption 4.10 is satisfied.

To see that Asumption 4.11 is also satisfied, notice that

$$pF(k, y) - q\,[y - (1-\delta)k] \le pF(k, (1-\delta)k) = pF(1, (1-\delta))k.$$

By Theorem 4.13 the desired result follows.

c. Since the return function and the correspondence describing the feasible set are constant returns to scale, Assumption 4.4 no longer holds. Here, imposing a bound on the state space is not a good idea. Instead, the strategy will be to prove that the structure of the model satisfies Assumptions 4.10–4.11 and then to make use of Theorem 4.13.

Define

$$H(k, y) = pF(k, y) - q[y - (1-\delta)k].$$

A 4.10: K is a convex cone since $K = \mathbf{R}_+ \subseteq \mathbf{R}^l$.
If $y \in \Gamma(k)$ then $\lambda y \in \Gamma(\lambda k)$ since

$$\Gamma(k) = \left\{y : (1-\delta)k \le y \le (1+\alpha)k\right\}.$$

Also, $y \le \gamma k$ for all $k \in K$ for some $\gamma \in \left(0, \beta^{-1}\right)$. Since

$$y \le (1+\alpha)k,$$

and

$$(1+\alpha)k \le \gamma k \le \beta^{-1}k,$$

is needed, we need to assume that $(1+\alpha)\beta \le 1$. Notice that the assumption about the marginal adjustment cost, as the rate of growth of capital approaches $\alpha > 0$, allows the use of the weak inequality.

A 4.11: $\beta \in (0, 1)$.
$H : \mathbf{R}_+ \times \mathbf{R}_+ \to \mathbf{R}_+$ is continuous and homogeneous of degree one. It follows directly from the assumptions about F.

Since F is nonnegative, decreasing in y and homogeneous of degree one,

$$\begin{aligned} pF(k, y) &\le pF[k, (1-\delta)k] \\ &= pkF[1, (1-\delta)]. \end{aligned}$$

This implies that

$$|H(k, y)| \le pkF[1, (1-\delta)] + q(1-\delta)k + qy.$$

Let

$$B = \max \left\{ pF[1, (1-\delta)] + q(1-\delta), q \right\},$$

then $|H(k, y)| \leq B(|k| + |y|)$.

Hence, we can define the operator

$$(Tv)(k) = \max_{y \in \Gamma(k)} \{H(k, y) + \beta v(y)\},$$

and by Theorem 4.13, v, the unique fixed point of the operator T, is homogeneous of degree one and the optimal policy correspondence

$$G = \left\{ y \in \Gamma(k) : v^*(k) = pF(k, y) - q[y - (1-\delta)k] + \beta v^*(y) \right\},$$

is compact valued, u.h.c. and homogeneous of degree one. The quasi-concavity of F implies that G is single valued.

Since G is homogeneous of degree one, it must be the case that $y \in G(k)$ implies that $y = \theta k$ for some $\theta \in [(1-\delta), (1+\alpha)]$. Also, v homogeneous of degree one implies that $v(k) = Ak$, therefore

$$Ak = \max_{\theta} \left\{ pF(1, \theta) - q[\theta - (1-\delta)] + \beta A\theta \right\} k,$$

so $\theta^* = \text{argmax}_\theta \left\{ pF(1, \theta) - q[\theta - (1-\delta)] + \beta A\theta \right\}$ is defined by

$$pF_\theta(1, \theta^*) - q + \beta A = 0,$$

and

$$A = \frac{pF(1, \theta^* - q[\theta^* - (1-\delta)]}{1 - \beta\theta^*}.$$

Now

$$v^*(k_0) = \sum_{t=0}^{\infty} \beta^t H(k_t^*, k_{t+1}^*) \leq H[1, (1-\delta)]k_0 \sum_{t=0}^{\infty} [\beta(1+\alpha)]^t$$

so imposing $\beta(1+\alpha) < 1$ the hypothesis of Theorems 4.2 and 4.3 are satisfied and the connection between the functional equation and the sequential problem can then be established.

Also, the strict quasi-concavity of F allows us to conclude that v is strictly quasi-concave (see Exercise 4.8) since the operator T preserves quasi-concavity.

Assumptions 4.9–4.11 are satisfied and F is strictly quasi-concave, so by Exercise 4.8d., v is differentiable.

Exercise 5.11

a. To prove boundedness, let $B \in \mathbf{R}$ and take any $c \in L$. Then, $U(c_t) \leq B$ for all t implies that

$$\begin{aligned} u(c) &= \sum_{t=0}^{\infty} \beta^t U(c_t) \\ &\leq \sum_{t=0}^{\infty} \beta^t B = \frac{B}{1-\beta}. \end{aligned}$$

To prove continuity, let $c \in L$. We need to show that for every $c' \in L$ and $\varepsilon > 0$ there is a $\delta' > 0$ with $|u(c') - u(c)| < \varepsilon$ whenever $\|c' - c\|_L < \delta'$.

Equivalently, we need to show that for some sequence $\{c^n\}_{n=1}^{\infty}$, where $c^n \in L$ for all n, and $c^n \to c$ in $\|\cdot\|_L$ norm, $|u(c^n) - u(c)| \to 0$.

Clearly,

$$\begin{aligned} |u(c^n) - u(c)| &= \left| \sum_{t=0}^{\infty} \beta^t U(c_t^n) - \sum_{t=0}^{\infty} \beta^t U(c_t) \right| \\ &\leq \sum_{t=0}^{\infty} \beta^t \left| U(c_t^n) - U(c_t) \right| \\ &= \sum_{t=0}^{N} \beta^t \left| U(c_t^n) - U(c_t) \right| + \sum_{t=N+1}^{\infty} \beta^t \left| U(c_t^n) - U(c_t) \right|. \end{aligned}$$

for any N.

Fix ε. Because $U(\cdot) \leq B$,

$$\left| U(c_t^n) - U(c_t) \right| \leq 2B.$$

Choose $\overline{N}$ such that for all $N \geq \overline{N}$,

$$\sum_{t=N+1}^{\infty} \beta^t \left| U(c_t') - U(c_t) \right| \leq \beta^{N+1} \frac{2B}{1-\beta} < \frac{\varepsilon}{2}.$$

For the first part of the sequence, we know that $c_t' \to c_t$. Hence, choose $\overline{n}$ such that for all $n \geq \overline{n}$

$$\left| U(c_t^n) - U(c_t) \right| \leq \frac{(1-\beta)}{(1-\beta^{N+1})} \frac{\varepsilon}{2},$$

as $\|\cdot\|_L$ convergence implies pointwise convergence.

Then, if $n > \bar{n}$ and $N > \overline{N}$,

$$\left|u(c^n) - u(c)\right| < \sum_{t=0}^{N} \beta^t \frac{(1-\beta)}{(1-\beta^{N+1})} \frac{\varepsilon}{2} + \frac{\varepsilon}{2} = \varepsilon.$$

Since ε was arbitrarily chosen, this completes the proof.

b. S is complete. Straightforward adaptation of the proof outlined in Exercise 3.6.

To see that it is not true that $\lim_{n\to\infty} |u\ (c) - u\ (c^n)| = 0$ for all $u \in S$, consider

$$u\ (c) = \inf_t c_t.$$

Let $c \in L$ be a sequence with elements $c_t = 1$ for all t. But then $|u\ (c) - u\ (c^n)| = 1$ for all n, and hence $\lim_{n\to\infty} |u\ (c) - u\ (c^n)| \neq 0$.

c. We first check that T satisfies the Blackwell's sufficient conditions for a contraction. To show that T satisfies monotonicity, let $u,\ v \in S$ with $u(c) > v(c)$ for all c. Then

$$\begin{aligned}(Tu)(c) &= U(c_0) + \beta u({}_1c) \\ &> U(c_0) + \beta v({}_1c) = (Tv)(c).\end{aligned}$$

To show discounting, note that

$$\begin{aligned}[T(u+a)](c) &= U(c_0) + \beta[u({}_1c) + a] \\ &= U(c_0) + \beta u({}_1c) + \beta a \\ &= (Tu)(c) + \beta a.\end{aligned}$$

Hence the operator $T : S \to S$ is a contraction and therefore $\hat{u}(c) = U(c_0) + \beta\hat{u}({}_1c)$ where $\hat{u}$ is the unique fixed point of T. Notice that $\hat{u}({}_1c) = U(c_1) + \beta\hat{u}({}_2c)$. Hence

$$\hat{u}(c) = U(c_0) + \beta U(c_1) + \beta^2\hat{u}({}_2c).$$

Continuing the recursion in this fashion, $\hat{u}(c) = \sum_{t=0}^{\infty} \beta^t U(c_t)$.

d. For any $u,\ v \in S$, the fact that $\left\|T_W u - T_W v\right\| \leq \beta\ \|u - v\|$ follows immediately from the definition of T_W and W3. Hence, T_W is a contraction and the existence of a unique fixed point u_W is implied by the Contraction

Mapping Theorem. It is also a consequence of the Contraction Mapping Theorem that

$$\left\| T_W^n u_0 - u \right\| \leq \beta^n \frac{B}{1-\beta}, \tag{5.2}$$

where B is an upper bound for W.

To prove that $\left| u_W(c) - u_W(c^n) \right| \leq \beta^n \left\| u_W \right\|$, define $u_W^n(c) = u_W(c^n)$. Then, for any $c \in L$,

$$\begin{aligned} u_W^n(c) &= u(c_0, c_1, \ldots, c_{n-1}, 0, 0, \ldots) \\ &= W(c_0, u_W(c_1, \ldots, c_{n-1}, 0, 0, \ldots)) \\ &= W(c_0, u_W^{n-1}({}_1c)), \end{aligned}$$

while $u_W(c) = W[c_0, u_W({}_1c)]$, hence, by the contraction property, W3,

$$\begin{aligned} \left\| u_W - u_W^n \right\| &< \beta \left\| u_W - u_W^{n-1} \right\| \\ &\leq \beta^2 \left\| u_W - u_W^{n-2} \right\| \\ &\vdots \\ &\leq \beta^n \left\| u_W - u_W^0 \right\|. \end{aligned}$$

To complete the proof, we need $u^0(c) = u(0, 0, \ldots) = 0$, which is true by W1 and the definition of T_W.

By W4 observe that T_W takes increasing functions into increasing functions. Applying (5.2) to an increasing initial guess u_0 the argument is complete.

To prove the concavity of u_w we prove first that if $u \in S$ is concave, so is $T_w u$. Take $c, c' \in L$, $\theta \in (0, 1)$ and define $c^\theta = \theta c + (1-\theta)c'$. Then,

$$\begin{aligned} &\theta(T_W u)(c) + (1-\theta)(T_W u)(c') \\ &= \theta W[c_0, u({}_1c)] + (1-\theta) W[c_0', u({}_1c')] \\ &\leq W[\theta c_0 + (1-\theta)c_0', \theta u({}_1c) + (1-\theta)u({}_1c')] \\ &\leq W[c_0^\theta, u({}_1c^\theta)] \\ &= (T_W u)(c^\theta) \end{aligned}$$

where the first inequality follows from the concavity of W and the second from the assumed concavity of u and the assumption that W is increasing in all arguments. To complete the proof, use Corollary 1 of the Contraction Mapping Theorem for an initial u_0 concave and apply (5.2).

e. The utility function can be written as

$$u_W(c) = W(c_0, u_W({}_1c)).$$

Hence the marginal rate of substitution between $c_{i,t}$ and $c_{j,t+k}$ is given by

$$\frac{W_2[c_t, u_w({}_{t+1}c)]W_{1j}[c_{t+k}, u_w({}_{t+k+1}c)]}{W_{1i}[c_t, u_w({}_{t+1}c)]},$$

where $W_{1i}[c_t, u_w({}_{t+1}c)]$ is the partial derivative of W_1 with respect to the ith good in period t, and W_2 is the partial derivative of W with respect to the second argument.

6 *Deterministic Dynamics*

Exercise 6.1

a. Pick any $k \in (0, \bar{k}]$. To see that $g(k) \in (0, \bar{k})$, suppose $g(k) = 0$. Then,

$$U'[f(k)] \geq \beta v'(0) = \beta U'[f(0) - g(0)]f'(0)$$

but the left-hand side is finite while the right-hand side is not. Therefore, it cannot be optimal to set $g(k) = 0$.

Similarly, suppose $g(k) = \bar{k}$. Because $k \in (0, \bar{k}]$, and consumption is nonnegative, it must be that $k = \bar{k}$. Hence,

$$U'[f(\bar{k}) - \bar{k}] \leq \beta v'(\bar{k}) = \beta U'[f(\bar{k}) - g(\bar{k})]f'(\bar{k}),$$

but the left-hand side of the inequality stated above is not finite. On the other hand, feasibility requires that $g(\bar{k}) \leq \bar{k}$. If $g(\bar{k}) = \bar{k}$, this implies zero consumption ever after, which is suboptimal. Hence $g(\bar{k}) < \bar{k}$. But

$$\infty = U'(0) = U'[f(\bar{k}) - \bar{k}] \leq \beta U'[f(\bar{k}) - g(\bar{k})]f'(\bar{k}),$$

and the right-hand side is finite, a contradiction.

Since $g(k) \in (0, \bar{k})$, we can use Theorem 4.11 to prove that v is differentiable and derive (2) and (3) .

b. Pick $k, k' \in (0, \bar{k}]$ with $k < k'$. The proof is by contradiction. Suppose $g(k) \geq g(k')$. Then, v strictly concave implies

$$U'[f(k) - g(k)] = \beta v'[g(k)] \leq \beta v'[g(k')] = U'[f(k') - g(k')].$$

Hence, by U strictly concave,

$$f(k) - g(k) \geq f(k') - g(k').$$

Then, f strictly increasing implies

$$g(k') - g(k) \geq f(k') - f(k) > 0$$

and so $g(k') > g(k)$, a contradiction.

Exercise 6.2

a. Toward a contradiction, pick $k, k' \in [0, 1]$ with $k < k'$. Suppose $g(k') \geq g(k)$. For this specific case, (7) is given by

$$\alpha \left[(1 - g(k)) \left(\frac{k}{1 - g(k)} \right)^{\theta} \right]^{\alpha - 1} \times \left[\left(\frac{k}{1 - g(k)} \right)^{\theta} - \frac{\theta k}{1 - g(k)} \left(\frac{k}{1 - g(k)} \right)^{\theta - 1} \right] = \beta v'[g(k)].$$

As v is strictly concave, we have

$$\alpha \left[1 - g(k')) \left(\frac{k'}{1 - g(k')} \right)^{\theta} \right]^{\alpha - 1} \times \left[\left(\frac{k'}{1 - g(k')} \right)^{\theta} - \frac{\theta k'}{1 - g(k')} \left(\frac{k'}{1 - g(k')} \right)^{\theta - 1} \right]$$
$$\leq \alpha \left[(1 - g(k)) \left(\frac{k}{1 - g(k)} \right)^{\theta} \right]^{\alpha - 1} \times \left[\left(\frac{k}{1 - g(k)} \right)^{\theta} - \frac{\theta k}{1 - g(k)} \left(\frac{k}{1 - g(k)} \right)^{\theta - 1} \right],$$

and after some straightforward algebra,

$$1 < \frac{k'}{k} < \left[\frac{1 - g(k')}{1 - g(k)} \right]^{\gamma},$$

where

$$\gamma = -\left[\frac{(1 - \theta)(\alpha - 1) - \theta}{\theta \alpha} \right] > 0.$$

Hence,

$$\frac{1-g(k')}{1-g(k)} > 1,$$

and so $g(k') < g(k)$, a contradiction.

Exercise 6.3

a. To see that g maps [0, 1] into itself, note that $g(0) = g(1) = 0$ and that $g(x_t)$ is a quadratic equation with a maximum at $x_{t+1} = 1$ when $x_t = 1/2$. Figure 6.1 presents x_{t+1} as a function of x_t on the interval [0, 1]. The stationary points are the values of x that solve $x = 4x - 4x^2$, which are $x = 0$ and $x = 3/4$.

b. The function $g^2(x_t)$ is obtained by simply plugging $x_{t+1} = g(x_t) = 4x_t - 4x_t^2$ into $g(x_{t+1}) = 4x_{t+1} - 4x_{t+1}^2$.

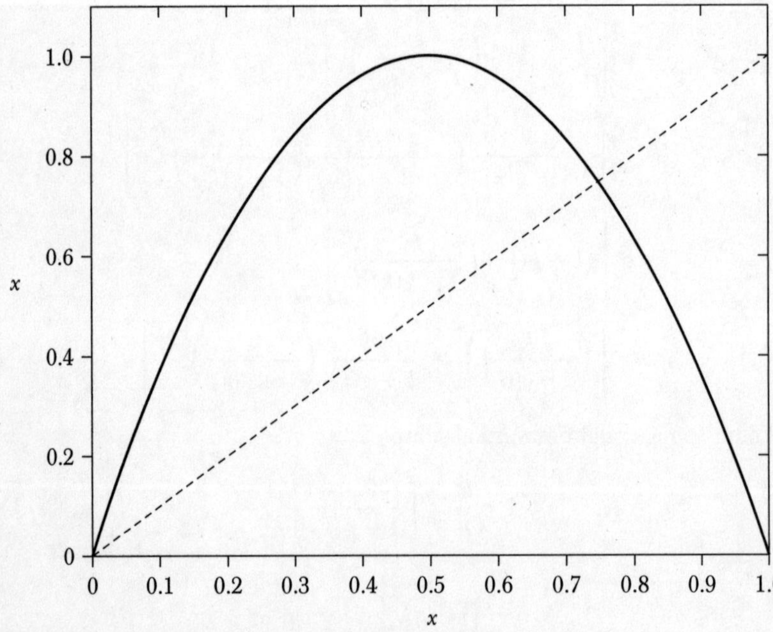

Figure 6.1

Hence,

$$x_{t+2} = g^2(x_t) = 4[4x_t - 4x_t^2] - 4[4x_t - 4x_t^2]^2$$
$$= 16x_t - 80x_t^2 + 128x_t^3 - 64x_t^4,$$

and so $g^2(0) = 0$, $g^2(1/4) = 3/4$, $g^2(1/2) = 0$, $g^2(3/4) = 3/4$, $g^2(1) = 0$. Figure 6.2 shows the presence of two-cycles. The four stationary points are $\{0, 0.3455, 0.75, 0.9045\}$.

When $x_t = 0$ or $x_t = 3/4$ we know from part a. that $x_{t+1} = 0$ or $x_{t+1} = 3/4$, respectively. Hence, those points cannot represent a two-cycle. Similarly, when $x_t = 0.3455$ or $x_t = 0.9045$ we know from part a. that $x_{t+1} \neq 0.3455$ or $x_{t+1} \neq 0.9045$ respectively, but we also know from above that $x_{t+2} = 0.3455$ or $x_{t+2} = 0.9045$; therefore those stationary points are our candidates for a two-cycle.

Starting the system at $x = 0.3455$ or $x = 0.9045$ we can see that the system oscillates between those two numbers, showing the presence of a two-cycle.

The function $g^3(x)$ can be obtained in a similar fashion.

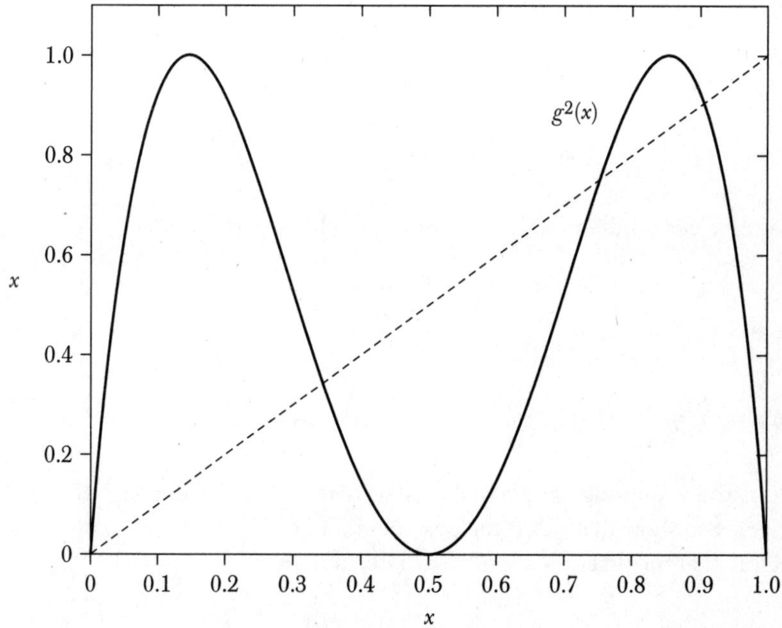

Figure 6.2

Exercise 6.4

The sufficient condition for (8) to hold is

$$bd - \frac{(1+\beta)^2 c^2}{4\beta} \geq 0.$$

In this setup, we can write the right-hand side of (8) as

$$\beta(x-\bar{x})[b(x-\bar{x}) + c(y-\bar{x})] + (y-\bar{x})\,[c(x-\bar{x}) + d(y-\bar{x})]$$

or

$$b\beta(x-\bar{x})^2 + (1+\beta)c(x-\bar{x})(y-\bar{x}) + d(y-\bar{x})^2.$$

Adding and subtracting

$$\left[\frac{(1+\beta)^2 c^2}{4b\beta}\right](y-\bar{x})^2$$

to the above expression to "complete the square" we obtain

$$b\beta[(x-\bar{x})^2 + \frac{(1+\beta)c}{b\beta}\,(x-\bar{x})\,(y-\bar{x}) + \frac{(1+\beta)^2 c^2}{4b\beta}\,(y-\bar{x})^2]$$

$$+ [d - \frac{(1+\beta)^2 c^2}{4b\beta}]\,(y-\bar{x})^2$$

$$= b\beta\left[(x-\bar{x}) + \frac{(1+\beta)c}{2b\beta}\,(y-\bar{x})\right]^2 + \frac{1}{b}[bd - \frac{(1+\beta)^2 c^2}{4\beta}]\,(y-\bar{x})^2,$$

so a sufficient condition for this expression to be negative is that

$$bd - \frac{(1+\beta)^2 c^2}{4\beta} \geq 0.$$

Exercise 6.5

A matrix is nonsingular if and only if its determinant is not equal to zero. We are going to show that this is the case for A and $(I-A)$.

Recall that the determinant of a partitioned matrix

$$C = \begin{bmatrix} C_{11} & C_{12} \\ C_{21} & C_{22} \end{bmatrix}$$

can be written (if C_{11} and C_{22} are invertible) as

$$\det(C) = |C_{22}| \cdot \left|C_{11} - C_{12}C_{22}^{-1}C_{21}\right|$$
$$= |C_{11}| \cdot \left|C_{22} - C_{21}C_{11}^{-1}C_{12}\right|.$$

For the case of A, we can write its determinant as

$$\begin{aligned}\det(A) &= |J| \cdot \left|-J^{-1}K\right| \\ &= c \det(K) \\ &= c\left|-\beta^{-1}F_{xy}^{-1}F'_{xy}\right| \\ &= cb \\ &= \beta^{-l},\end{aligned}$$

where $c = (-1)^l$, $b = (-\beta)^{-l}$.

Similarly, we can write the determinant of $(I - A)$ as

$$\begin{aligned}\det(I - A) &= |I - J - K| \\ &= \left|I - (-\beta^{-1}F_{xy}^{-1}(F_{yy} + \beta F_{xx})) - (-\beta^{-1}F_{xy}^{-1}F'_{xy})\right| \\ &= \left|\beta^{-1}F_{xy}^{-1}(\beta F_{xy} + F_{yy} + \beta F_{xx} + F'_{xy})\right| \\ &= \left|\beta^{-1}F_{xy}^{-1}\right| \cdot \left|\beta F_{xy} + F_{yy} + \beta F_{xx} + F'_{xy}\right|.\end{aligned}$$

Therefore, F_{xy}^{-1} and $(\beta F_{xy} + F_{yy} + \beta F_{xx} + F'_{xy})$ nonsingular implies that $(I - A)$ is nonsingular.

Exercise 6.6

a. The characteristic polynomial for A is

$$\lambda^2 + \lambda\beta^{-1}F_{xy}^{-1}(F_{yy} + \beta F_{xx}) + \beta^{-1} = 0.$$

Hence,

$$\lambda_1, \lambda_2 = \frac{-\beta^{-1}F_{xy}^{-1}(F_{yy} + \beta F_{xx}) \pm \sqrt{\beta^{-2}F_{xy}^{-2}(F_{yy} + \beta F_{xx})^2 - 4\beta^{-1}}}{2},$$

and for (λ_1, λ_2) to both be real it must be that

$$(F_{yy} + \beta F_{xx})^2 \geq 4\beta F_{xy}^2.$$

Also, F strictly concave implies that $F_{xx} < 0$ and $F_{yy}F_{xx} > F_{xy}^2$. Hence it is enough to show that

$$(F_{yy} + \beta F_{xx})^2 \geq 4\beta F_{yy}F_{xx}.$$

But

$$\begin{aligned} &F_{yy}^2 - 2\beta F_{xx}F_{yy} + F_{xx}^2 \\ &= (F_{yy} - \beta F_{xx})^2 \\ &= (\beta F_{xx} - F_{yy})^2 \geq 0. \end{aligned}$$

b. The result comes from simple inspection of the equation determining (λ_1, λ_2). It is obvious from the result obtained in a. that

$$\lambda_1 = \frac{-\beta^{-1}F_{xy}^{-1}(F_{yy} + \beta F_{xx}) + \sqrt{\beta^{-2}F_{xy}^{-2}(F_{yy} + \beta F_{xx})^2 - 4\beta^{-1}}}{2} > 0$$

To see that $\lambda_2 > 0$, it is straightforward that if $\lambda_2 < 0$ then

$$-\beta^{-1}F_{xy}^{-1}(F_{yy} + \beta F_{xx}) < \sqrt{\beta^{-2}F_{xy}^{-2}(F_{yy} + \beta F_{xx})^2 - 4\beta^{-1}},$$

which implies

$$\beta^{-2}F_{xy}^{-2}(F_{yy} + \beta F_{xx})^2 < \beta^{-2}F_{xy}^{-2}(F_{yy} + \beta F_{xx})^2 - 4\beta^{-1},$$

a contradiction with $\beta > 0$.

c. The proof parallels the argument in b.

Exercise 6.7

a. Actually, Assumption 4.9 is not needed for uniqueness of the optimal capital sequence.

A4.3: $K = [0, 1] \subseteq R^l$ and the correspondence

$$\Gamma(k) = \{y : y \in K\}$$

is clearly compact valued and continuous.

A4.4: $F(k, y) = (1-y)^{(1-\theta)\alpha} k^{\theta\alpha}$ is clearly bounded in K, and it is also continuous. Also, $0 \leq \beta \leq 1$.

A4.7: Clearly, F is continuously differentiable, so

$$F_k = \theta\alpha(1-y)^{(1-\theta)\alpha} k^{\theta\alpha-1}$$

$$F_y = -(1-\theta)\alpha(1-y)^{(1-\theta)\alpha-1} k^{\theta\alpha}$$

$$F_{kk} = \theta\alpha(1-y)\ (\theta\alpha-1)^{(1-\theta)\alpha}\ k^{\theta\alpha-2} < 0$$

$$F_{yy} = (1-\theta)\alpha[(1-\theta)\ \alpha - 1](1-y)^{(1-\theta)\alpha-2} k^{\theta\alpha} < 0$$

$$F_{xy} = -\theta\alpha\ (1-\theta)\ \alpha(1-y)^{(1-\theta)\alpha-1} k^{\theta\alpha-1} < 0,$$

and $F_{kk}F_{yy} - F_{xy}^2 > 0$, hence F is strictly concave.

A4.8: Take two arbitrary pairs (k, y) and (k', y') and $0 < \pi < 1$. Define $k^\pi = \pi k + (1-\pi)k'$, $y^\pi = \pi y + (1-\pi)y'$. Then, since $\Gamma(k) = \{y : 0 \leq y \leq 1\}$ for all k it follows trivially that if $y \in \Gamma(k)$ and $y' \in \Gamma(k')$ then $y^\pi \in \Gamma(k^\pi) = \Gamma(k) = \Gamma(k') = K$.

A4.9: Define $A = K \times K$ as the graph of Γ. Hence F is continuously differentiable because U and f are continuously differentiable. The Euler equation is

$$\alpha(1-\theta)(1-k_{t+1})^{(1-\theta)\alpha-1} k_t^{\theta\alpha} = \beta\alpha\theta \left(1-k_{t+2}\right)^{(1-\theta)\alpha} k_{t+1}^{\theta\alpha-1}.$$

b. Evaluating the Euler equation at $k_{t+1} = k_t = k^*$, we get

$$(1-\theta)k^* = \beta\theta\left(1-k^*\right),$$

or

$$k^* = \frac{\beta\theta}{1-\theta+\beta\theta}.$$

c. From the Euler equation, define

$$\begin{aligned} &W(k_t, k_{t+1}, k_{t+2}) \\ &\equiv \alpha(1-\theta)(1-k_{t+1})^{(1-\theta)\alpha-1}k_t^{\theta\alpha} \\ &- \beta\alpha\theta(1-k_{t+2})^{(1-\theta)\alpha}k_{t+1}^{\theta\alpha-1} \\ &= 0. \end{aligned}$$

Hence, expanding W around the steady state

$$\begin{aligned} W(k_t, k_{t+1}, k_{t+2}) = W(k^*, k^*, k^*) &+ W_1(k^*)(k_t - k^*) \\ &+ W_2(k^*)(k_{t+1} - k^*) + W_3(k^*)(k_{t+2} - k^*), \end{aligned}$$

where

$$\begin{aligned} W_1(k^*) &= \alpha^2(1-\theta)\theta(1-k^*)^{(1-\theta)\alpha-1}(k^*)^{\theta\alpha-1}, \\ W_2(k^*) &= -\alpha(1-\theta)\left[(1-\theta)\,\alpha - 1\right](1-k^*)^{(1-\theta)\alpha-2}\,(k^*)^{\theta\alpha} \\ &\quad - \beta\theta\alpha(\theta\alpha - 1)(1-k^*)^{(1-\theta)\alpha}(k^*)^{\theta\alpha-2}, \\ W_3(k^*) &= \beta\theta\alpha^2(1-\theta)(1-k^*)^{(1-\theta)\alpha-1}(k^*)^{\theta\alpha-1}. \end{aligned}$$

Normalizing by $W_3(k^*)$ and using the expression obtained for the steady-state capital we finally get

$$\beta^{-1}\left(k_t - k^*\right) + B\left(k_{t+1} - k^*\right) + \left(k_{t+2} - k^*\right) = 0,$$

where

$$B = \frac{1-\alpha(1-\theta)}{\alpha(1-\theta)} + \frac{1-\alpha\theta}{\alpha\theta\beta}.$$

That both of the characteristic roots are real comes from the fact that the return function satisfies Assumptions 4.3–4.4 and 4.7–4.9 and it is twice differentiable, so the results obtained in Exercise 6.6 apply.

To see that $\lambda_1 = (\beta\lambda_2)^{-1}$ is straightforward from the fact that

$$\begin{aligned} \lambda_1\lambda_2 &= \left(\frac{(-B) + \sqrt{B^2 - 4\beta^{-1}}}{2}\right)\left(\frac{(-B) - \sqrt{B^2 - 4\beta^{-1}}}{2}\right) \\ &= \frac{(-B)^2 - (B^2 - 4\beta^{-1})}{4} \\ &= \beta^{-1}. \end{aligned}$$

To see that $\lambda_1 + \lambda_2 = -B$, just notice that

$$\lambda_1 + \lambda_2 = \frac{(-B) + \sqrt{B^2 - 4\beta^{-1}}}{2} + \frac{(-B) - \sqrt{B^2 - 4\beta^{-1}}}{2} = -B.$$

Then, $\lambda_1\lambda_2 > 0$ and $\lambda_1 + \lambda_2 < 0$ implies that both roots are negative.

In order to have a locally stable steady-state k^* we need one of the characteristic roots to be less than one in absolute value. Given that both roots are negative, this implies that we need $\lambda_1 > -1$, or

$$-B + \sqrt{B^2 - 4\beta^{-1}} > -2,$$

which after some straightforward manipulation implies

$$B > \frac{1+\beta}{\beta}.$$

Substituting for B we get

$$\frac{1-\theta+\theta\beta}{2\theta(1+\beta)(1-\theta)} > \alpha,$$

or equivalently

$$\beta > \frac{(2\theta\alpha - 1)(1-\theta)}{[1 - 2\alpha(1-\theta)]\theta}.$$

d. To find that $k^* = 0.23$, evaluate the equation for k^* obtained in b. at the given parameter values. To see that k^* is unstable, evaluate λ_1 at the given parameter values. Notice also that those parameter values do not satisfy the conditions derived in c.

e. Note that since F is bounded, the two-cycle sequence satisfies the transversality conditions

$$\lim_{t\to\infty} \beta^t F_1(x, y) \cdot x = 0$$

and

$$\lim_{t\to\infty} \beta^t F_1(x, y) \cdot y = 0,$$

for any two numbers $x, y \in [0, 1]$, $x \neq y$. Hence, by Theorem 4.15, if the two-cycle (x, y) satisfies

$$F_y(x, y) + \beta F_x(y, x) = 0$$

and

$$F_y(y, x) + \beta F_x(x, y) = 0,$$

it is an optimal path.

Conversely, if (x, y) is optimal and the solution is interior, then it satisfies

$$F_y(x, y) + \beta v'(y) = 0 \text{ and } v'(y) = F_x(y, x),$$

and

$$F_y(y, x) + \beta v'(x) = 0 \text{ and } v'(x) = F_x(x, y),$$

and hence it satisfies the Euler equations stated in the text.

Notice that the pair (x, y) defining the two-cycle should be restricted to the open interval $(0, 1)$.

f. We have that

$$\begin{aligned} F_y(x, y) + \beta F_x(y, x) = {} & \beta\alpha\theta y^{\alpha\theta-1}(1-x)^{\alpha(1-\theta)} \\ & - \alpha(1-\theta)x^{\alpha\theta}(1-y)^{\alpha(1-\theta)-1}, \end{aligned}$$

and

$$\begin{aligned} F_y(y, x) + \beta F_x(x, y) = {} & \beta\alpha\theta x^{\alpha\theta-1}(1-y)^{\alpha(1-\theta)} \\ & - \alpha(1-\theta)y^{\alpha\theta}(1-x)^{\alpha(1-\theta)-1} \end{aligned}$$

The pair (0.29, 0.18) makes the above set of equations equal to zero, and from the result proved in part e. we already know this is a necessary and sufficient condition for the pair to be a two-cycle.

g. Define

$$\begin{aligned} E^1(k_t, k_{t+1}, k_{t+2}, k_{t+3}) & \equiv -\alpha(1-\theta)k_{t+1}{}^{\alpha\theta}(1-k_{t+2})^{\alpha(1-\theta)-1} \\ & \quad + \beta\alpha\theta k_{t+2}^{\alpha\theta-1}(1-k_{t+3})^{\alpha(1-\theta)} \\ & = -\alpha(1-\theta)x^{\alpha\theta}(1-y)^{\alpha(1-\theta)-1} \\ & \quad + \beta\alpha\theta y^{\alpha\theta-1}(1-x)^{\alpha(1-\theta)} \\ & = 0 \\ E^2(k_t, k_{t+1}, k_{t+2}, k_{t+3}) & \equiv -\alpha(1-\theta)k_t{}^{\alpha\theta}(1-k_{t+1})^{\alpha(1-\theta)-1} \\ & \quad + \beta\alpha\theta k_{t+1}^{\alpha\theta-1}(1-k_{t+2})^{\alpha(1-\theta)} \\ & = -\alpha(1-\theta)y^{\alpha\theta}(1-x)^{\alpha(1-\theta)-1} \\ & \quad + \beta\alpha\theta x^{\alpha\theta-1}(1-y)^{\alpha(1-\theta)} \\ & = 0. \end{aligned}$$

Let E_i^j be the derivative of E^j with respect to the ith argument. Then, the derivatives are

$$
\begin{aligned}
E_1^1 &= 0, \\
E_2^1 &= -\alpha^2\theta(1-\theta)x^{\alpha\theta-1}(1-y)^{\alpha(1-\theta)-1}, \\
E_3^1 &= -\alpha(1-\theta)x^{\alpha\theta}[\alpha(1-\theta)-1](1-y)^{\alpha(1-\theta)-2} \\
&\quad + \beta\alpha\theta(\alpha\theta-1)y^{\alpha\theta-2}(1-x)^{\alpha(1-\theta)}, \\
E_4^1 &= \beta\alpha\theta y^{\alpha\theta-1}(1-x)^{\alpha(1-\theta)-1}, \\
E_1^2 &= -\alpha^2\theta(1-\theta)y^{\alpha\theta-1}(1-x)^{\alpha(1-\theta)-1}, \\
E_2^2 &= -\alpha(1-\theta)y^{\alpha\theta}[\alpha(1-\theta)-1](1-x)^{\alpha(1-\theta)-2} \\
&\quad + \beta\alpha\theta(\alpha\theta-1)x^{\alpha\theta-2}(1-y)^{\alpha(1-\theta)}, \\
E_3^2 &= \beta\alpha\theta x^{\alpha\theta-1}(1-y)^{\alpha(1-\theta)-1}, \\
E_4^2 &= 0.
\end{aligned}
$$

Using the fact that $k_{t+2} = k_t$ in E_1, expand this system around (0.29, 0.18). Denoting by $\hat{K}$ deviations around the stationary point $\bar{K}$, we can express the linearized system as

$$\hat{K}_{t/2+1} = \begin{bmatrix} \hat{k}_{t+3} \\ \hat{k}_{t+2} \end{bmatrix} = \hat{H} \begin{bmatrix} \hat{k}_{t+1} \\ \hat{k}_t \end{bmatrix} = \hat{H}\hat{K}_{t/2}$$

where

$$\hat{H} = \begin{bmatrix} E_4^1 & 0 \\ 0 & E_3^2 \end{bmatrix}^{-1} \begin{bmatrix} E_2^1 & E_1^1 \\ E_2^2 & E_1^2 \end{bmatrix}.$$

By evaluating $\hat{H}$ for the given parameters, it can be verified that the system is unstable around the stationary point $\bar{K} = (0.29, 0.18)$.

Exercise 6.9

a. To show that the functional equation

$$v(x) = \max_{y\in[0,\alpha x]} \left\{ S\left[x\phi\left(\frac{y}{x}\right)\right] - \theta\,[y-(1-\delta)x] + \beta v(y) \right\}$$

has a unique continuous bounded solution, it is sufficient to check that the assumptions of Theorem 4.6 are satisfied.

A4.3: $X = \mathbf{R}_+ \subseteq \mathbf{R}^l$. Define the correspondence

$$\Gamma(x) = \{y \in X : 0 \leq y \leq \alpha x\}.$$

Hence Γ is nonempty because $y = 0 \in \Gamma$ for all $x \in X$. It is also clearly compact valued and continuous (see Exercise 3.13a.).

A4.4: Define

$$F(x, y) = S\left[x\phi\left(\frac{y}{x}\right)\right] - \theta\left[y - (1-\delta)x\right].$$

Hence F is a bounded and continuous function by S bounded and continuous and $x \in \mathbf{R}_+$. Also, $\beta \in (0, 1)$. Notice that S is homothetic, but not necessarily homogeneous in (x, y). Hence Theorem 4.6 applies.

Next, we prove that v, the unique solution to the functional equation above, is strictly increasing and strictly concave.

A4.5: $F(x, y)$ strictly increasing in x follows from S being strictly increasing in q and q strictly increasing in x (the last fact implied by ϕ being nonnegative and strictly decreasing).

A4.6: Γ is monotone. Pick two arbitrary $x, x' \in X$ with $x \leq x'$. Then, if $0 \leq y \leq \alpha x$, we have $0 \leq y \leq \alpha x'$ and hence $\Gamma(x) \subseteq \Gamma(x')$.
Therefore, by Theorem 4.7, v is strictly increasing.

A4.7: By assumption S and ϕ are strictly concave functions. As F is a composition of weakly concave and strictly concave functions, F is strictly concave.

A4.8: Pick two arbitrary pairs (x, y) and (x', y') where $y \in \Gamma(x)$ and $y' \in \Gamma(x')$, for $0 < \pi < 1$. Define x^π and y^π as before. We need to show that $y^\pi \in \Gamma(x^\pi)$. By definition $\Gamma(x^\pi) = \{y^\pi : 0 \leq y^\pi \leq \alpha x^\pi\}$. Note that also by definition, if $y \in \Gamma(x)$ then $y \geq 0$ and $y \leq \alpha x$, and therefore $\pi y \geq 0$ and $\pi y < \pi \alpha x$. Hence $\pi y \in \Gamma(\pi x)$. Proceeding in the same fashion it can be shown that $(1-\pi)y' \in \Gamma((1-\pi)x')$. Therefore, $0 \leq y^\pi \leq \alpha x^\pi$. Hence Γ is convex.

So, by Theorem 4.8, v is strictly concave and the optimal policy function g is single valued and continuous. Define

$$A = \{(x, y) \in X \times X : y \in \Gamma(x)\}$$

as the graph of Γ.

A4.9: The return function F is continuously differentiable in the interior of A, by S and ϕ continuously differentiable.

Hence, by Theorem 4.11 υ is differentiable, with

$$\begin{aligned}\upsilon'(x) &= F_x(x, y)\\ &= S'\left[x\phi\left(\frac{g(x)}{x}\right)\right]\left\{\phi\left(\frac{g(x)}{x}\right) - \frac{g(x)}{x}\phi'\left(\frac{g(x)}{x}\right)\right\}\\ &\quad + \theta(1-\delta).\end{aligned}$$

b. The proof is by contradiction. Take $x, x' \in X$. with $x < x'$. Suppose $g(x) > g(x')$. Then, using the first-order condition,

$$\begin{aligned}&\theta - S'\left[x\phi\left(\frac{g(x)}{x}\right)\right]\phi'\left(\frac{g(x)}{x}\right)\\ &= \beta\upsilon'[g(x)]\\ &< \beta\upsilon'[g(x')]\\ &= \theta - S'\left[x'\phi\left(\frac{g(x')}{x'}\right)\right]\phi'\left(\frac{g(x')}{x'}\right),\end{aligned}$$

where the inequality comes from the strict concavity of υ. Hence,

$$-S'\left[x\phi\left(\frac{g(x)}{x}\right)\right]\phi'\left(\frac{g(x)}{x}\right) < -S'\left[x'\phi\left(\frac{g(x')}{x'}\right)\right]\phi'\left(\frac{g(x')}{x'}\right),$$

but

$$-\phi'\left(\frac{g(x)}{x}\right) > -\phi'\left(\frac{g(x')}{x'}\right),$$

and therefore

$$S'\left[x\phi\left(\frac{g(x)}{x}\right)\right] < S'\left[x'\phi\left(\frac{g(x')}{x'}\right)\right],$$

and $S' < 0$ implies that

$$x\phi\left(\frac{g(x)}{x}\right) > x'\phi\left(\frac{g(x')}{x'}\right),$$

or

$$\phi\left(\frac{g\ (x)}{x}\right) > \phi\left(\frac{g(x')}{x'}\right).$$

Hence,

$$g(x) < g(x'),$$

a contradiction.

c. Combining the first-order condition

$$\theta - S'\left[x\phi\left(\frac{g\ (x)}{x}\right)\right]\phi'\left(\frac{g\ (x)}{x}\right) = \beta\upsilon'[g(x)],$$

and the envelope condition, the Euler equation is given by the expression

$$\theta - S'\left[x_t\phi\left(\frac{x_{t+1}}{x_t}\right)\right]\phi'\left(\frac{x_{t+1}}{x_t}\right)$$

$$= \beta\left\{S'\left[x_{t+1}\phi\left(\frac{x_{t+2}}{x_{t+1}}\right)\right]\right.$$

$$\times\left[\phi\left(\frac{x_{t+2}}{x_{t+1}}\right) - \frac{x_{t+2}}{x_{t+1}}\phi'\left(\frac{x_{t+2}}{x_{t+1}}\right)\right] + \theta(1-\delta)\right\}.$$

At a stationary point, $x_{t+1} = x_t = \bar{x}$. Hence, a necessary condition for a stationary point is

$$S'[\bar{x}\phi(1)] = \frac{\theta\ [1 - \beta(1 - \delta)]}{[\beta\phi(1) + \phi'(1)(1 - \beta)]}.$$

Therefore, by the strict concavity of S there is a unique $\bar{x} > 0$ satisfying the condition above.

Notice that

$$\frac{\beta}{(1 - \beta)} > -\frac{\phi'(1)}{\phi(1)}.$$

If this condition is not satisfied, the steady state does not exist.

To decide if our candidate is indeed a stationary point, we can use the fact that υ is strictly concave, then

$$\{\upsilon'(x) - \upsilon'[g(x)]\}\ [x - g(x)] \leq 0, \quad \text{all } x \in X$$

with equality if and only if $g(x) = x$. Substituting for $v'(x)$ from the envelope condition and for $v'[g(x)]$ from the first-order condition,

$$\left\{S'\left[x\phi\left(\frac{g(x)}{x}\right)\right]\left\{\phi\left(\frac{g(x)}{x}\right)+\phi'\left(\frac{g(x)}{x}\right)\left[\frac{1}{\beta}-\frac{g(x)}{x}\right]\right\}\right.$$
$$\left. +\theta(1-\delta)-\frac{\theta}{\beta}\right\}[x-g(x)] \leq 0,$$

all $x \in X$, $S'[\bar{x}\phi(1)]\phi''(1)$ with equality if and only if $g(x) = x$. Since the left-hand side of the above inequality is zero when evaluated at $\bar{x}$, it follows that $g(\bar{x}) = \bar{x}$, so $\bar{x}$ is a stationary point.

d. Expanding the Euler equation at the stationary point we obtain that

$$\left\{\frac{S'[\bar{x}\phi(1)]\phi''(1)}{\bar{x}} - S''[\bar{x}\phi(1)]\phi'(1)[\phi(1)-\phi'(1)]\right\}(x_t - \bar{x})$$
$$-\left\{\frac{S'[\bar{x}\phi(1)]\phi''(1)}{\bar{x}} + S''[\bar{x}\phi(1)]\phi'^2(1)\right\}(x_{t+1} - \bar{x})$$

equals

$$\beta\left\{\frac{S'[\bar{x}\phi(1)]\phi''(1)}{\bar{x}} + S''[\bar{x}\phi(1)][\phi(1)-\phi'(1)]^2\right\}(x_{t+1} - \bar{x})$$
$$-\beta\left\{\frac{S'[\bar{x}\phi(1)]\phi''(1)}{\bar{x}} - S''[\bar{x}\phi(1)]\phi'(1)[\phi(1)-\phi'(1)]\right\}(x_{t+2} - \bar{x}).$$

Rearranging terms we obtain

$$Ax_{t+2} = Bx_{t+1} + Cx_t,$$

where

$$A = \beta\left\{S''[\bar{x}\phi(1)]\phi'(1)[\phi(1)-\phi'(1)] - \frac{S'[\bar{x}\phi(1)]\phi''(1)}{\bar{x}}\right\},$$

$$B = S''[\bar{x}\phi(1)]\phi'^2(1) - \frac{S'[\bar{x}\phi(1)]\phi''(1)}{\bar{x}(1+\beta)}$$
$$-\beta S''[\bar{x}\phi(1)][\phi(1)-\phi'(1)]^2,$$

and

$$C = \frac{S'[\bar{x}\phi(1)]\phi''(1)}{\bar{x}} - S''[\bar{x}\phi(1)]\phi'(1)[\phi(1)-\phi'(1)].$$

By inspection $A > 0$, $B > 0$ and $C < 0$. We can define $X_t' = (x_{t+1}, x_t)$ to write the second-order difference equation as

$$\begin{bmatrix} x_{t+2} \\ x_{t+1} \end{bmatrix} = X_{t+1} = DX_t = \begin{bmatrix} B/A & C/A \\ 1 & 0 \end{bmatrix} \begin{bmatrix} x_{t+1} \\ x_t \end{bmatrix}$$

Note that

$$F_{xy} = \left\{ S'\left[x\phi\left(\frac{y}{x}\right)\right]\left[\phi\left(\frac{y}{x}\right) - \phi'\left(\frac{y}{x}\right)\frac{y}{x}\right]\phi\left(\frac{y}{x}\right) \right.$$
$$\left. -S'\left[x\phi\left(\frac{y}{x}\right)\right]\phi''\left(\frac{y}{x}\right)\frac{y}{x^2}\right\} > 0,$$

so both roots are positive.

The characteristic function $H(\lambda)$ is

$$H(\lambda) = \lambda^2 - B/A\lambda - C/A,$$

so $H(0) = -C/A > 0$, and $H'(\lambda) = 2\lambda - B/A$. In order to prove local stability, we need to prove that one of the roots is less than one. If there is a root that is less than one, it must be the case that $H(1) = 1 - B/A - C/A < 0$, or equivalently that $B > A - C$. The proof is by contradiction. Suppose $B < A - C$, then

$$S''[\bar{x}\phi(1)]\phi'^2(1) - \frac{S''[\bar{x}\phi(1)]\phi''(1)}{\bar{x}(1+\beta)}$$
$$- \beta S''[\bar{x}\phi(1)][\phi(1) - \phi'(1)]^2$$
$$> \beta\left\{S''[\bar{x}\phi(1)]\phi'(1)[\phi(1) - \phi'(1)] - \frac{S''[\bar{x}\phi(1)]\phi''(1)}{\bar{x}}\right\}$$
$$- \frac{S''\bar{x}\phi(1)]\phi''(1)}{\bar{x}} + S''[\bar{x}\phi(1)]\phi'(1)[\phi(1) - \phi'(1)],$$

which after some manipulation can be written as

$$\beta[\phi(1) - \phi'(1)] + \phi'(1) < 0.$$

But, as we mentioned before, a necessary condition for the steady state to exist is $\beta[\phi(1) - \phi'(1)] + \phi'(1) > 0$, a contradiction.

e. The local stability of the Euler equation and the fact that $F_{xy} > 0$ implies, by Theorem 6.9 and Exercise 6.6, that in a neighborhood U of the steady state $\bar{x}$,

$$0 < \frac{g(x') - g(\bar{x})}{x' - \bar{x}} < 1, \quad \text{for } x' \in U.$$

Hence, for any $x' \in U$, $g(x')$ is greater than, equal to, or less than x' as x' is greater than, equal to, or less than $\bar{x}$. Next, pick any $x' \in \partial U$ with $x' < \bar{x}$, and $x'' = x' - \varepsilon$, for any arbitrary $\varepsilon > 0$. Therefore, $g(x'') > x''$, otherwise $g(x' - \varepsilon) < x' - \varepsilon$ and $g(x') > x'$ which implies, by the continuity of g, that there exist $\hat{x} \in (x' - \varepsilon, x')$ such that $g(\hat{x}) = \hat{x}$, a contradiction to the uniqueness of the stationary point $\bar{x} > 0$. A similar argument can be made for any $x' \in \partial U$ with $x' > \bar{x}$.

Hence $g(x)$ is greater than, equal to, or less than x' as x' is greater than, equal to, or less than $\bar{x}$ for any $x > 0$, which coupled with g being continuous and strictly increasing implies that for all $x_0 > 0$, the solution to $x_{t+1} = g(x_t)$ will converge monotonically to $\bar{x}$. An argument constructing a Liapunov function $L : X \to X$ defined by $L = (x - \bar{x})[v'(x) - v'(\bar{x})]$ for any compact set $X \subseteq \mathbf{R}_{++}$ including $\bar{x}$ completes the proof.

7 Measure Theory and Integration

Exercise 7.1

Let

$$\sigma\langle\mathcal{A}\rangle = \cap_{\{\sigma\text{-algebras } \mathcal{F}:\ \mathcal{A}\subset\mathcal{F}\}}\mathcal{F}$$

be the smallest σ-algebra containing $\mathcal{A}$. We will refer to this as the σ-algebra generated by $\mathcal{A}$. This is nonempty because the power set of S (that is, the set of all subsets of S) is a σ-algebra containing $\mathcal{A}$.

$\mathcal{A} \in \sigma\langle\mathcal{A}\rangle$: Let $A \in \mathcal{A}$. Then $A \in \mathcal{F}$ for all σ-algebras $\mathcal{F}$ containing $\mathcal{A}$. Hence $A \in \sigma\langle\mathcal{A}\rangle$.

$S, \emptyset \in \sigma\langle\mathcal{A}\rangle$: $S, \emptyset$ are elements of all σ-algebras of subsets of S.

$A \in \sigma\langle\mathcal{A}\rangle$ implies $A^c \in \sigma\langle\mathcal{A}\rangle$: If $A \in \sigma\langle\mathcal{A}\rangle$ then A is an element of all σ-algebras $\mathcal{F}$ containing $\mathcal{A}$. Hence A^c is an element of every $\mathcal{F}$ and $A^c \in \sigma\langle\mathcal{A}\rangle$.

$A_n \in \sigma\langle\mathcal{A}\rangle$, $n \geq 1$ implies $\cup_{n=1}^{\infty} A_n \in \sigma\langle\mathcal{A}\rangle$: If $A_n \in \sigma\langle\mathcal{A}\rangle$, $n \geq 1$, then A_n is an element of all σ-algebras $\mathcal{F}$ containing $\mathcal{A}$. Hence $\cup_{n=1}^{\infty} A_n$ is an element of every $\mathcal{F}$ and $\cup_{n=1}^{\infty} A_n \in \sigma\langle\mathcal{A}\rangle$.

Exercise 7.2

There are multiple ways to define the Borel σ-algebra for a Euclidean space. On page 169, the text (*RMED*) defines $\mathcal{B}^1$, the Borel algebra for $\mathbf{R}^1$, as the σ-algebra generated by the open sets. However, on page 170, the text defines the Borel algebra for higher-dimension Euclidean spaces as the σ-algebra generated by the open balls, or equivalently, the open rectangles, which in $\mathbf{R}^1$ are the open intervals. We will start by showing that these two definitions are equivalent, before turning to Exercise 7.2 itself.

Following the text denote by $\mathcal{A}$ the collection of open intervals in $\mathbf{R}$, and denote by $\mathcal{A}_1$ the collection of open sets in $\mathbf{R}$. We will show that $\sigma\langle\mathcal{A}\rangle = \sigma\langle\mathcal{A}_1\rangle$. Note that as $\mathcal{A} \subset \mathcal{A}_1$, $\sigma\langle\mathcal{A}_1\rangle$ is a σ-algebra containing $\mathcal{A}$ and hence $\sigma\langle\mathcal{A}\rangle \subset \sigma\langle\mathcal{A}_1\rangle$. To show the reverse, we will establish that $\mathcal{A}_1 \subset \sigma\langle\mathcal{A}\rangle$, which follows from the result that every open set can be written as a countable union of open intervals. To see this, let C be an arbitrary open set, and let $D = C \cap \mathbf{Q}$ where $\mathbf{Q}$ is the set of rational numbers. As C is open, for all $x \in D$ there exists an $\epsilon > 0$ such that

$$E_x \equiv (x - \epsilon, x + \epsilon) \subset C.$$

As D is countable,

$$\cup_{x \in D} E_x \in \sigma\langle\mathcal{A}\rangle.$$

Clearly $\cup_{x\in D} E_x \subset C$. That $\cup_{x\in D} E_x \supset C$ follows from the fact that C is open and the fact that the rationals are dense in $\mathbf{Q}$.

Let $\mathcal{A}_2$ be the collection of closed intervals in $\mathbf{R}$. That is, the collection of sets of the form $(-\infty, b]$, $[a, b]$, $[a, +\infty)$, $(-\infty, +\infty)$ for $a, b \in \mathbf{R}$, $a \le b$. Let $\sigma\langle\mathcal{A}_2\rangle$ be the σ-algebra generated by $\mathcal{A}_2$. For any $a, b \in \mathbf{R}$, we can write the open intervals as countable unions of closed sets according to

$$(-\infty, b) = \cup_{n=1}^{\infty} \left(-\infty, b - \frac{1}{n}\right],$$

$$(a, b) = \cup_{n=1}^{\infty} \left[a + \frac{1}{n}, b - \frac{1}{n}\right],$$

$$(a, +\infty) = \cup_{n=1}^{\infty} \left[a + \frac{1}{n}, +\infty\right).$$

Hence, the collection of open intervals $\mathcal{A} \subset \sigma\langle\mathcal{A}_2\rangle$ and as $\sigma\langle\mathcal{A}_2\rangle$ is a σ-algebra containing $\mathcal{A}$, $\mathcal{B}^1 \subset \sigma\langle\mathcal{A}_2\rangle$. Similarly,

$$(-\infty, b] = \cap_{n=1}^{\infty} \left(-\infty, b + \frac{1}{n}\right),$$

$$[a, b] = \cap_{n=1}^{\infty} \left(a - \frac{1}{n}, b + \frac{1}{n}\right),$$

$$[a, +\infty) = \cup_{n=1}^{\infty} \left(a - \frac{1}{n}, +\infty\right),$$

and hence $\sigma\langle\mathcal{A}_2\rangle \subset \mathcal{B}^1$.

Let $\mathcal{A}_3$ be the collection of intervals in $\mathbf{R}$ open from the left and closed from the right (that is, of the form $(a, b]$ for $a, b \in \mathbf{R}$, $a \leq b$), and let $\sigma\langle\mathcal{A}_3\rangle$ be the σ-algebra generated by $\mathcal{A}_3$. The proof that $\sigma\langle\mathcal{A}_3\rangle = \mathcal{B}^1$ proceeds analogously to that for $\mathcal{A}_2$.

Let $\mathcal{A}_4$ be the collection of half rays in $\mathbf{R}$ of the form $(a, +\infty)$ for some $a \in \mathbf{R}$, and let $\sigma\langle\mathcal{A}_4\rangle$ be the σ-algebra generated by $\mathcal{A}_4$. We will show that $\sigma\langle\mathcal{A}_4\rangle = \sigma\langle\mathcal{A}_3\rangle$. Clearly, $\mathcal{A}_4 \subset \sigma\langle\mathcal{A}_3\rangle$ and hence $\sigma\langle\mathcal{A}_4\rangle \subset \sigma\langle\mathcal{A}_3\rangle$. To see that $\sigma\langle\mathcal{A}_3\rangle \subset \sigma\langle\mathcal{A}_4\rangle$, note that $\mathcal{A}_3 \subset \sigma\langle\mathcal{A}_4\rangle$ from the fact that

$$\begin{aligned}(a, b] &= (a, +\infty) \cap (-\infty, b] \\ &= (a, +\infty) \cap (b, +\infty)^c .\end{aligned}$$

Exercise 7.3

Let $S \in \mathcal{B}^l$. Clearly, $\emptyset$ and S are in $\mathcal{B}_S$.

Let $A \in \mathcal{B}_S$. Then the complement of A relative to S, or

$$S \backslash A = S \cap A^c \in \mathcal{B}_S ,$$

as $\mathcal{B}^l$ is closed under complementation and finite intersections.

Let $A_n \in \mathcal{B}_S$ for $n = 1, 2, \ldots$. Then $\cup_{n=1}^{\infty} A_n$ is an element of $\mathcal{B}^l$ and a subset of S. Hence,

$$\cup_{n=1}^{\infty} A_n \in \mathcal{B}_S .$$

Exercise 7.4

We need to establish that the λ in a. and b. are extended real-valued functions satisfying the properties of measures. Typically, these properties are obvious with the possible exception of countable additivity.

a. Let $\{A_n\}_{n=1}^{\infty}$ be a countable sequence of disjoint subsets in $\mathcal{S}$. Then

$$\begin{aligned}\lambda\left(\cup_{n=1}^{\infty} A_n\right) &= \mu_1\left(\cup_{n=1}^{\infty} A_n\right) + \mu_2\left(\cup_{n=1}^{\infty} A_n\right) \\ &= \sum_{n=1}^{\infty} \mu_1(A_n) + \sum_{n=1}^{\infty} \mu_2(A_n) \\ &= \sum_{n=1}^{\infty} \lambda(A_n) .\end{aligned}$$

b. Let $\{A_n\}_{n=1}^{\infty}$ be a countable sequence of disjoint subsets in $\mathcal{S}$. Then

$$\begin{aligned}\lambda\left(\cup_{n=1}^{\infty}A_n\right) &= \mu_1\left(\left(\cup_{n=1}^{\infty}A_n\right)\cap B\right)\\ &= \mu_1\left(\cup_{n=1}^{\infty}\left(A_n\cap B\right)\right)\\ &= \sum_{n=1}^{\infty}\mu_1\left(A_n\cap B\right)\\ &= \sum_{n=1}^{\infty}\lambda\left(A_n\right),\end{aligned}$$

where the second inequality comes from the fact that the intersection distributes, and the third equality comes from the fact that the sets $\{A_n \cap B\}$, $n = 1, 2, \ldots,$ are disjoint.

Exercise 7.5

As $A \subseteq B$ there exists a $C = B\backslash A = B \cap A^c \in \mathcal{S}$ such that $A \cup C = B$ and $A \cap C = \emptyset$. Hence,

$$\mu(A) + \mu(C) = \mu(B).$$

As $\mu(C) \geq 0$ we have $\mu(A) \leq \mu(B)$. Further, if $\mu(A)$ is finite, $\mu(B) - \mu(A)$ is well defined and

$$\mu(C) = \mu(B\backslash A) = \mu(B) - \mu(A).$$

Exercise 7.6

a. Let $\mathcal{A}$ be the family of all complements and finite unions of intervals of the form $(a, b]$, $(-\infty, b]$, $(a, +\infty)$, and $(-\infty, +\infty)$ for $a, b \in \mathbf{R}$, $a \leq b$. Let $\mathcal{C}$ be the collection of sets that can be written as a finite disjoint union of such intervals. We follow the Hint and show that $\mathcal{A} \subset \mathcal{C}$.

Let $A \in \mathcal{A}$. Then by the definition of $\mathcal{A}$, there are three possibilities. If A is an interval of this form, then $A \in \mathcal{C}$. If A is a finite union of such intervals, A can always be written as a disjoint finite union of such intervals, and hence $A \in \mathcal{C}$. Finally, if A is a complement of such an interval, note that

$$\begin{aligned}(-\infty, b]^c &= (b, +\infty) \in \mathcal{C},\\ (a, b]^c &= (-\infty, a] \cup (b, +\infty) \in \mathcal{C}.\end{aligned}$$

Hence $\mathcal{A} \subset \mathcal{C}$.

To show that $\mathcal{A}$ is an algebra, note that it obviously contains $\emptyset$ and $\mathbf{R}$, and is closed under finite unions. Closure under complementation follows from the fact that, for $a, b, c, d \in \mathbf{R}$, $a \leq b \leq c \leq d$,

$$\begin{aligned}((a, b] \cup (c, d])^c &= (-\infty, a] \cup (b, c] \cup (d, +\infty) \in \mathcal{A}, \\ ((-\infty, b] \cup (c, d])^c &= (b, c] \cup (d, +\infty) \in \mathcal{A}, \\ ((a, b] \cup (c, +\infty))^c &= (-\infty, a] \cup (b, c] \in \mathcal{A}.\end{aligned}$$

b. We showed in Exercise 7.2 that $\mathcal{B}^1$ is the smallest σ-algebra containing the intervals in $\mathbf{R}$ open from the left and closed from the right. Hence, $\mathcal{B}^1 \subset \sigma \langle \mathcal{A} \rangle$. To show that $\sigma \langle \mathcal{A} \rangle \subset \mathcal{B}^1$, we need to show that $\mathcal{A} \subset \mathcal{B}^1$. But $\mathcal{B}^1$ contains the half-open intervals and is closed under complementation and finite unions.

Exercise 7.7

a. To show that μ is a measure on an algebra $\mathcal{A}$, it is necessary to show that μ is an *extended* real-valued function satisfying the properties of a measure. Obviously, μ is extended real valued (although not necessarily real valued) and $\mu(\emptyset) = 0$. Let $A \in \mathcal{A}$. Then by Exercise 7.6a. there exists a finite number of disjoint half-open intervals A_n for $n = 1, \ldots, N$ such that $\cup_{n=1}^N A_n = A$. By Property 4,

$$\mu(A) = \mu\left(\cup_{n=1}^N A_n\right) = \sum_{n=1}^N \mu(A_n),$$

which is nonnegative as for all $n = 1, \ldots, N$ the $\mu(A_n)$ are nonnegative from Properties 2 and 3.

To show countable additivity, let $\{A_i\}_{i=1}^\infty$ be a countably infinite sequence of disjoint sets in $\mathcal{A}$ with $\cup_{i=1}^\infty A_i \equiv A \in \mathcal{A}$. Since A is a finite disjoint union of intervals of the form

$$(a, b], (-\infty, b], (a, +\infty), (-\infty, +\infty),$$

the sequence $\{A_i\}$ can be partitioned into finitely many subsequences such that the union of the intervals in each subsequence is a single interval of this form.

By using such subsequences separately, and using the finite additivity of μ we can equivalently write A in this form. Then

$$\begin{aligned}\mu(A) &= \mu\left(\cup_{i=1}^{n} A_i\right) + \mu\left(A \setminus \cup_{i=1}^{n} A_i\right) \\ &\geq \mu\left(\cup_{i=1}^{n} A_i\right) = \sum_{i=1}^{n} \mu(A_i),\end{aligned}$$

where the equalities comes from finite additivity and the inequality by non-negativity. Letting $n \to \infty$ we get

$$\mu(A) \geq \sum_{i=1}^{\infty} \mu(A_i).$$

To see the converse, first assume that $A = (a, b]$ for $a, b \in \mathbf{R}$. Let $\varepsilon > 0$ and $\{\varepsilon_n\}_{n=1}^{\infty}$ be a sequence of real numbers such that $\sum_{n=1}^{\infty} \varepsilon_n < \varepsilon$. Renumber the collection of intervals A_i such that

$$a = a_1 < b_1 \leq a_2 < \ldots < b_{n-1} \leq a_n < b_n \leq a_{n+1} < \ldots,$$

and construct the collection of open intervals B_n such that

$$B_1 = (a_1 - \varepsilon_1, b_1 + \varepsilon_1),$$

and for $n \geq 2$

$$B_n = (a_n, b_n + \varepsilon_n).$$

Clearly, these intervals form an open covering of the set $[a, b]$. But this set is compact, and hence there exists a finite open subcover, say $\{B_{n_k}\}_{k=1}^{K}$. We may renumber these intervals such that

$$a = a_{n_1} \leq a_{n_2} < b_1 + \varepsilon_1 < \ldots < a_{n_k} < b_{n_{k-1}} + \varepsilon_{n_{k-1}} \leq b < b_{n_k} + \varepsilon_{n_k}.$$

Hence

$$\mu((a, b]) = b - a \leq (b_{n_K} + \varepsilon_{n_K} - a_{n_1})$$
$$\leq \sum_{k=1}^{K} [b_{n_k} + \varepsilon_{n_k} - a_{n_k}]$$
$$< \sum_{k=1}^{K} [b_{n_k} - a_{n_k}] + \varepsilon$$
$$\leq \sum_{n=1}^{\infty} [b_n - a_n] + \varepsilon.$$

But as ε is arbitrary

$$\mu((a, b]) = b - a \leq \sum_{n=1}^{\infty} \mu((a_n, b_n]).$$

To see the result for A of the form $(-\infty, b]$, note that the intervals B_n cover $[-M, b]$ for some M finite, and hence using the above argument

$$b + M \leq \sum_{n=1}^{\infty} \mu((a_n, b_n]).$$

Similarly, for $(a, +\infty)$ these intervals cover $[a, M]$ and we get

$$M - a \leq \sum_{n=1}^{\infty} \mu((a_n, b_n]).$$

The desired result follows in each case by letting $M \to \infty$.

b. As $\emptyset = (a, a]$, we have

$$\mu(\emptyset) = \int_a^a \pi(s)\, ds = 0.$$

Further, as $\pi(s)$ is nonnegative on S, $\mu(A)$ is nonnegative for all $A \in \mathcal{A}$, while, by definition of π

$$\mu(S) = \int_a^b \pi(s)\, ds = 1.$$

To see countable additivity, let $\{A_i\}_{i=1}^{\infty}$ be a countably infinite sequence of disjoint sets in $\mathcal{A}$ with $\cup_{i=1}^{\infty} A_i \equiv A \in \mathcal{A}$. Since A is a finite union of disjoint intervals of the form $(c, d]$ for $a \le c < d \le b$, by the same argument as for part a., we can assume A is of the form $(c, d]$. Note that

$$\mu\left((c, d]\right) = \int_c^d \pi(s)\, ds \le \int_a^b \pi(s)\, ds = 1,$$

and hence $\mu\left((c, d]\right)$ is bounded above.

Note first that

$$\begin{aligned}\int_c^d \pi(s)\, ds &= \mu\left((c, d]\right) = \mu\left(\cup_{i=1}^{\infty} A_i\right) \\ &= \mu\left(\cup_{i=1}^{\infty}(a_i, b_i]\right) \\ &= \mu\left(\cup_{i=1}^{n}(a_i, b_i]\right) + \mu\left((c, d] \setminus \cup_{i=1}^{n}(a_i, b_i]\right) \\ &\ge \mu\left(\cup_{i=1}^{n}(a_i, b_i]\right) = \sum_{i=1}^{n} \int_{a_i}^{b_i} \pi(s)\, ds.\end{aligned}$$

Letting $n \to \infty$, and noting that the limit exists in $\mathbf{R}$ as this is a monotone increasing sequence bounded above, we get

$$\mu\left((c, d]\right) = \int_c^d \pi(s)\, ds \ge \sum_{i=1}^{\infty} \int_{a_i}^{b_i} \pi(s)\, ds.$$

To see the converse, let $\varepsilon > 0$ and $\left\{\varepsilon_n\right\}_{n=1}^{\infty}$ be a sequence of real numbers such that

$$\sum_{n=1}^{\infty} \int_{b_{n_k}}^{b_{n_k}+\varepsilon_{n_k}} \pi(s)\, ds < \varepsilon.$$

Renumber the collection of intervals $A_i = (a_i, b_i]$ such that

$$c = a_1 < b_1 \le a_2 < \ldots < b_{n-1} \le a_n < b_n \le a_{n+1} < \ldots \le d,$$

and construct the collection of open intervals B_n such that

$$B_1 = (a_1 - \varepsilon_1, b_1 + \varepsilon_1),$$

and for $n \ge 2$

$$B_n = \left(a_n, b_n + \varepsilon_n\right).$$

Clearly, these intervals form an open covering of the set $[c, d]$. But this set is compact, and hence there exists a finite open subcover, say $\{B_{n_k}\}_{k=1}^{K}$. We may renumber these intervals such that

$$a = a_{n_1} \leq a_{n_2} < b_1 + \varepsilon_1 < \ldots < a_{n_k} < b_{n_{k-1}} + \varepsilon_{n_{k-1}} \leq b < b_{n_k} + \varepsilon_{n_k}.$$

Hence

$$\begin{aligned}
\mu\left((c, d]\right) &= \int_c^d \pi(s)\, ds \\
&\leq \int_{a_{n_1}}^{b_{n_K} + \varepsilon_{n_K}} \pi(s)\, ds \\
&\leq \sum_{k=1}^{K} \int_{a_{n_k}}^{b_{n_k} + \varepsilon_{n_k}} \pi(s)\, ds \\
&= \sum_{k=1}^{K} \int_{a_{n_k}}^{b_{n_k}} \pi(s)\, ds + \sum_{k=1}^{K} \int_{b_{n_k}}^{b_{n_k} + \varepsilon_{n_k}} \pi(s)\, ds \\
&< \sum_{k=1}^{K} \int_{a_{n_k}}^{b_{n_k}} \pi(s)\, ds + \varepsilon \\
&\leq \sum_{n=1}^{\infty} \int_{a_n}^{b_n} \pi(s)\, ds + \varepsilon.
\end{aligned}$$

But as ε is arbitrary

$$\mu\left((c, d]\right) = \int_c^d \pi(s)\, ds \leq \sum_{n=1}^{\infty} \int_{a_n}^{b_n} \pi(s)\, ds = \sum_{n=1}^{\infty} \mu\left((a_n, b_n]\right).$$

Exercise 7.8

Clearly, $\mathcal{S}'$ contains $\emptyset$ and S. To see closure under complementation, let $A' \in \mathcal{S}'$. Then there exists $A \in \mathcal{S}$, $C_1, C_2 \in \mathcal{C}$ such that

$$A' = \left(A \cup C_1\right) \backslash C_2.$$

Hence

$$A'^c = (A^c \cap C_1^c) \cup C_2$$
$$= (A^c \cup C_2) \setminus (C_1 \setminus C_2),$$

which is in $\mathcal{S}'$.

To see closure under countable unions, for all $n = 1, 2, \ldots$ let $A'_n \in \mathcal{S}'$. Then for each n there exists an $A_n \in \mathcal{S}$ and $C_{1n}, C_{2n} \in \mathcal{C}$ such that

$$A'_n = (A_n \cup C_{1n}) \setminus C_{2n}.$$

Define $A' = \cup_{n=1}^{\infty} A'_n$, $A = \cup_{n=1}^{\infty} A_n$, $C_1 = \cup_{n=1}^{\infty} C_{1n}$, and $C_2 = \cup_{n=1}^{\infty} C_{2n}$. Then

$$(A \cup C_1) \setminus C_2 \subseteq A' = A \cup C_1,$$

and

$$\mu\left((A \cup C_1) \setminus C_2\right) = \mu\left(A \cup C_1\right).$$

Hence, there exists a $C'_2 \in \mathcal{C}$ such that $A' = (A \cup C_1) \setminus C'_2$. Hence, $A' \in \mathcal{S}'$.

Exercise 7.9

a. The definitions differ as to whether the "$\leq$" in

(7.1) $$\{s \in S : f(s) \leq a\} \in \mathcal{S}, \text{ all } a \in \mathbf{R}$$

is replaced with $\geq$, $<$ or $>$. Proof of equivalence requires establishing that (7.1) is equivalent to the equivalent statement sets defined by $\geq$, $<$ or $>$.

$\leq$ if and only if $>$: Follows from the fact that, for all $a \in \mathbf{R}$

$$\{s \in S : f(s) \leq a\} \in \mathcal{S}, \text{ if and only if}$$
$$\{s \in S : f(s) \leq a\}^c \in \mathcal{S}, \text{ if and only if}$$
$$\{s \in S : f(s) > a\} \in \mathcal{S},$$

as $\mathcal{S}$ is closed under complementation.

$\geq$ if and only if $<$: Follows analogously.

$\leq$ implies $<$: for any $a \in \mathbf{R}$, for $n \geq 1$ consider the sequence of sets $A_n = \left\{s \in S : f(s) \leq a - \frac{1}{n}\right\}$ which are in $\mathcal{S}$ by (7.1). Then

$$A \equiv \{s \in S : f(s) < a\} = \cup_{n=1}^{\infty} A_n$$

is in $\mathcal{S}$ by closure under countable unions.

$\leq$ is implied by $<$: for any $a \in \mathbf{R}$, for $n \geq 1$ consider the sequence of sets $A_n = \left\{s \in S : f(s) < a + \frac{1}{n}\right\}$ in $\mathcal{S}$. Then

$$A \equiv \{s \in S : f(s) \leq a\} = \cap_{n=1}^{\infty} A_n$$

is in $\mathcal{S}$ by closure under countable intersections.

b. Assume that $\{s \in S : f(s) \leq a\} \in \mathcal{S}$ for all $a \in \mathbf{R}$. Then by the result of part a., for all $a \in \mathbf{R}$ $\{s \in S : f(s) \geq a\} \in \mathcal{S}$. Hence

$$\{s \in S : f(s) = a\} = \{s \in S : f(s) \geq a\} \cap \{s \in S : f(s) \leq a\} \in \mathcal{S}$$

for all $a \in \mathbf{R}$ by closure under finite intersections.

To show that the converse is false, as a counterexample let $S = (0, 1]$ and let $\mathcal{S}$ be the set of all countable and co-countable subsets of S (where a co-countable set is a set with a countable complement). It is easily verified that $\mathcal{S}$ is a σ-algebra. Consider the function $f(s) = s$. Then the set

$$\{s \in S : f(s) = a\} = \begin{cases} \emptyset & a \notin (0, 1] \\ a & a \in (0, 1] \end{cases}.$$

The empty set is finite and hence countable. Hence these sets are in $\mathcal{S}$. However, the set $\{s \in S : f(s) \leq a\}$ for any $a \in (0, 1)$ is equal to $(0, a]$, which is neither countable nor co-countable.

c. The sets

$$A \equiv \{s \in S : f(s) = -\infty\} = \cap_{n=1}^{\infty} \{s \in S : f(s) < -n\},$$
$$B \equiv \{s \in S : f(s) = +\infty\} = \cap_{n=1}^{\infty} \{s \in S : f(s) > n\}$$

are in $\mathcal{S}$ because $\mathcal{S}$ is closed under countable intersections.

Exercise 7.10

a. Let f be monotone increasing. Then for some $a \in \mathbf{R}$ the set

$$\{s \in \mathbf{R} : f(s) \leq a\}$$

is either of the form $\{s \in \mathbf{R} : s \leq a\}$ or $\{s \in \mathbf{R} : s < a\}$. Both are in $\mathcal{B}$ by Exercise 7.6. The proof for monotone decreasing f is analogous.

Let f be continuous. By Exercise 7.9 a. it is sufficient to show that for all $a \in \mathbf{R}$ the set $\{s \in \mathbf{R} : f(s) < a\}$ is in $\mathcal{B}$. But as f is continuous, this set is open and hence in $\mathcal{B}$.

b. For any $f : S \rightarrow \mathbf{R}$ the set $\{s \in S : f(s) \leq a\}$ is a subset of S and is hence in $\mathcal{S}$. Hence, all functions are measurable.

Exercise 7.11

Let $A_i \in \mathcal{S}$, $i = 1, \ldots, n$ and without loss of generality, reorder $i = 1, \ldots, n$ such that $a_1 < a_2 < \ldots < a_n$, which is possible as the a_i are distinct. Then for all $a \in \mathbf{R}$, the set

$$\{s \in S : \phi(s) \geq a\}$$

is either $\emptyset \in \mathcal{S}$ if $a > a_n$, $S \in \mathcal{S}$ if $a \leq a_1$, or, for $j = 2, \ldots, n$, $B_j = \cup_{k=j}^n A_k$ if $a_{j-1} < a \leq a_j$. As S is closed under finite unions, $B_j \in \mathcal{S}$ for $j = 2, \ldots, n$ and hence ϕ is measurable.

Let ϕ be measurable. Without loss of generality, reorder $i = 1, \ldots, n$ such that $a_1 < a_2 < \ldots < a_n$. Then for all $a \in \mathbf{R}$

$$\{s \in S : \phi(s) \geq a\} \in \mathcal{S}$$

and hence $\{s \in S : \phi(s) < a\} \in \mathcal{S}$ as $\mathcal{S}$ is closed under complementation. For all i there exist $b_i, c_i \in \mathbf{R}$ such that $a_{i-1} < b_i < a_i < c_i < a_{i+1}$. Then

$$A_i = \{s \in S : \phi(s) \geq b_i\} \cap \{s \in S : \phi(s) < c_i\} \in \mathcal{S}$$

as $\mathcal{S}$ is closed under finite intersections.

Exercise 7.12

a. Let f and g be measurable functions and $c \in \mathbf{R}$. By Theorem 7.5 there exists sequences of measurable simple functions $\{f_n\}$ and $\{g_n\}$ such that $f_n \to f$ and $g_n \to g$ pointwise. In each case we will exhibit a sequence of measurable simple functions that converges pointwise to the desired function. The result will then follow by Theorem 7.4.

$f + g$: Let $h_n \equiv f_n + g_n$, which converges pointwise to $h \equiv f + g$, because for any sequences of real numbers $\{x_n\}$ and $\{y_n\}$ we know $x_n + y_n \to x + y$. To see that each h_n is a measurable simple function, note that it can take on at most a finite number of values on a finite number of sets, all of which are measurable by the fact that $\mathcal{S}$ is closed under finite intersections and set differences.

fg : Let $h_n \equiv f_n g_n$, which converges pointwise to $h \equiv fg$, because for any sequences of real numbers $\{x_n\}$ and $\{y_n\}$ we know $x_n y_n \to xy$. That the h_n's are measurable simple functions follows from the fact that each h_n is nonzero only if both f_n and g_n are nonzero. This can happen on only a finite number of sets, all of which are measurable as $\mathcal{S}$ is closed under finite intersections.

$|f|$: Let $h_n \equiv |f_n| = f_n^+ - f_n^-$, which converges pointwise to $h \equiv |f|$, because for any sequence of real numbers $\{x_n\}$ we know $-x_n \to -x$. The h_n are measurable simple functions, for if

$$\sum_{i=1}^{N_n} a_i \chi_{A_n}(s)$$

is the standard representation of f_n, then

$$\sum_{i=1}^{N_n} |a_i| \chi_{A_n}(s)$$

is the standard representation of h_n.

cf : Let $h_n \equiv cf_n$, which obviously converges pointwise to $h \equiv cf$. The h_n are measurable simple functions with standard representation $\sum_{i=1}^{N_n} ca_i \chi_{A_n}(s)$.

b. To show that $\sup_n f_n$ is measurable, we need to show that for all $a \in R$

$$\left\{s \in S : \sup_n f_n \leq a\right\} \in \mathcal{S}.$$

As for all $n = 1, 2, \ldots$ the f_n are measurable, $\{s \in S : f_n \leq a\} \in \mathcal{S}$ for all n. But

$$\left\{s \in S : \sup_n f_n \leq a\right\} = \cap_{n=1}^{\infty} \{s \in S : f_n \leq a\},$$

which is measurable because $\mathcal{S}$ is closed under countable intersections.

That $\inf_n f_n$ is measurable comes from

$$\inf_n f_n = -\sup_n(-f_n),$$

which is measurable by part a. and the fact that $\sup_n f_n$ is measurable. Similarly, noting that

$$\liminf f_n = \sup_{m \geq 1}\left(\inf_{n \geq m} f_n\right)$$

and

$$\limsup f_n = \inf_{m \geq 1}\left(\sup_{n \geq m} f_n\right),$$

we can iterate on the above results to get that $\liminf f_n$ and $\limsup f_n$ are measurable.

Exercise 7.13

a. By the result of Exercise 7.9a., a continuous function f on $\mathbf{R}^l$ will be $\mathcal{B}^l$-measurable if, for all $a \in \mathbf{R}$

$$\{x \in \mathbf{R}^l : f(x) < a\} \in \mathcal{B}^l.$$

But the set $(-\infty, a)$ is open in R, and as f is continuous

$$\{x \in \mathbf{R}^l : f(x) < a\}$$

is open and is hence an element of $\mathcal{B}^l$.

b. In answering part b., we will follow Billingsley (*Probability and Measure,* 3d ed., 1995, pp. 183–186) in defining the Baire functions to be real-valued functions (as opposed to extended real valued). Let $\mathcal{X}$ be the smallest class of real-valued functions on $\mathbf{R}^l$ containing the continuous functions and closed under pointwise passages to the limit that do not give rise to $\pm\infty$. That is, if $\{f_n\}$ is a sequence of real-valued functions in $\mathcal{X}$ converging pointwise to f, and if f is real valued, then $f \in \mathcal{X}$. Let $\mathcal{Y}$ denote the Borel measurable real-valued functions on $\mathbf{R}^l$.

$\mathcal{X} \subset \mathcal{Y}$: Note that the argument of Exercise 7.10a. extends to continuous real-valued functions on $\mathbf{R}^l$. Hence, all continuous real valued functions are in $\mathcal{Y}$. Further, by Exercise 7.12b., $\mathcal{Y}$ is closed under pointwise passages to the limit that do not give rise to $\pm\infty$. As $\mathcal{X}$ is the smallest such class of functions, $\mathcal{X} \subset \mathcal{Y}$.

$\mathcal{Y} \subset \mathcal{X}$: The argument proceeds in the following four steps. First, note that if $f, g \in \mathcal{X}$ and $a, b \in \mathbf{R}$, by the result of Exercise 7.12 (which applies because $\mathcal{X} \subset \mathcal{Y}$), $\max\{f, g\} \in \mathcal{X}$ (where the maximum is pointwise) and $af + bg \in \mathcal{X}$.

Second, let $\mathcal{A} = \{A \subset \mathbf{R}^l : \chi_A \in \mathcal{X}\}$. We will use the first result to show that this is a σ-algebra. Note that as $\chi_{\mathbf{R}^l}$ is continuous, $\mathbf{R}^l \subset \mathcal{A}$. To show closure under complementation, let $A \in \mathcal{A}$. Then

$$\chi_{A^c} = \chi_{\mathbf{R}^l} - \chi_A,$$

which is in $\mathcal{X}$ by the first result. To show closure under countable unions, for $n \geq 1$, let $A_n \in \mathcal{A}$. To show that $\cup_{n=1} A_n \in \mathcal{A}$, let

$$f_1 = \chi_{A_1}$$

and
$$f_n = \max\left\{f_n, \chi_{A_{n-1}}\right\},$$

where the first is in $\mathcal{X}$ by assumption, and the second by the first result. Therefore,

$$\chi_A = \lim_{n\to\infty} f_n,$$

which is in $\mathcal{X}$. Third, for $x \in \mathbf{R}^l$ note that

$$C = \{s \in \mathbf{R}^l : s_n \leq x_n,\ n = 1, \ldots, l\} \in \mathcal{A}.$$

To see this, define for $i = 1, \ldots, l$

$$C_i = \{s \in \mathbf{R}^l : s_i \leq x_i\}$$

and

$$g_i(s) = \begin{cases} 1 & \text{if } s \in C_i \\ x_i + 1 - s_i & \text{if } s_i \in [x_i, x_i + 1] \\ 0 & \text{if } s_i > x_i + 1 \end{cases}$$

As the g_i are continuous, and as

$$\chi_C = -\max\left\{-g_1, -g_2, \ldots, -g_l\right\},$$

by the first result above, $C \in \mathcal{A}$. Hence, as $\mathcal{A}$ is a σ-algebra containing the sets of the form C, which generate $\mathcal{B}^l$, we have $\mathcal{B}^l \subset \mathcal{A}$.

Finally, by Theorem 7.5 all Borel functions can be written as the pointwise limit of a sequence of Borel simple functions that do not give rise to $\pm\infty$. But as $\mathcal{B}^l \subset \mathcal{A}$, the indicator functions of Borel sets are in $\mathcal{X}$. Further, by the first result, finite combinations of indicator functions are in $\mathcal{X}$, and hence $\mathcal{X}$ includes all Borel simple functions. Hence as $\mathcal{X}$ is closed under pointwise passages to the limit that do not give rise to $\pm\infty$, $\mathcal{Y} \subset \mathcal{X}$.

Exercise 7.14

Denote $f^{-1}(A) = \{x \in S : f(x) \in A\}$ and let

$$\mathcal{G} = \{A \subset R : f^{-1}(A) \in \mathcal{S}\}.$$

We will show that $\mathcal{G}$ is a σ-algebra containing the open intervals in $\mathbf{R}$, and hence that $\mathcal{B} \subset \mathcal{G}$.

$\mathcal{G}$ is a σ-algebra, from the fact that $f^{-1}(\mathbf{R}) = S$, the fact that

$$\begin{aligned}\left(f^{-1}(A)\right)^c &= \{x \in S : f(x) \in A\}^c \\ &= \{x \in S : f(x) \in A^c\} \\ &= f^{-1}\left(A^c\right),\end{aligned}$$

and that

$$\begin{aligned}f^{-1}\left(\cup_{n=1}^{\infty} A_n\right) &= \left\{x \in S : f(x) \in \cup_{n=1}^{\infty} A_n\right\} \\ &= \cup_{n=1}^{\infty}\{x \in S : f(x) \in A_n\} \\ &= \cup_{n=1}^{\infty} f^{-1}(A_n).\end{aligned}$$

By definition of f measurable and Exercise 7.9, $\mathcal{G}$ contains the open intervals.

Exercise 7.15

Suppose f_i for $i = 1, \ldots, m$ is $\mathcal{B}^l$-measurable. Then for all $i = 1, \ldots, m$, for all $a_i, b_i \in \mathbf{R}$, $a_i \leq b_i$,

$$A_i \equiv \{s \in R^l : f_i(s) \in (a_i, b_i)\} \in \mathcal{B}^l.$$

Let $B = \{s \in R^m : s_i \in (a_i, b_i), i = 1, \ldots, m\}$. Then

$$\{s \in R^l : f(s) \in B\} = \cap_{i=1}^m A_i \in \mathcal{B}^l.$$

Now suppose that f is measurable, and for all $i = 1, \ldots, m$, for all $a_i, b_i \in \mathbf{R}$, $a_i \leq b_i$ let

$$B_i(a_i, b_i) = \{s \in R^m : s_i \in (a_i, b_i), i = 1, \ldots, m\}.$$

Then

$$\{s \in R^l : f(s) \in B_i(a_i, b_i)\} = \{s \in R^l : f_i(s) \in (a_i, b_i)\} \in \mathcal{B}^l$$

and f_i is $\mathcal{B}^l$-measurable.

Exercise 7.16

Consider any finite partition of [0, 1] into intervals of the form $[a_{i-1}, a_i]$ for $i = 1, \ldots, n$. As each interval contains both rational and irrational numbers, if we choose the $y_i \leq f(x)$, all $x \in [a_{i-1}, a_i]$, the sum $\sum_{i=1}^n y_i(a_i - a_{i-1}) \leq 0$. Moreover, we can always choose the y_i so that this sum is equal to zero. Hence, the supremum over all such partitions, which is the lower Reimann integral, is zero. Similarly, if we choose $y_i \geq f(x)$, all $x \in [a_{i-1}, a_i]$ the sum $\sum_{i=1}^n y_i(a_i - a_{i-1}) \geq 1$, and the y_i can be chosen so that this sum equals one. Hence, the infimum over all such partitions, which is the upper Riemann integral, is one. As they are not equal, the function is not Riemann integrable.

Exercise 7.17

Let ϕ and ψ have standard representations

$$\phi(s) = \sum_{i=1}^{n_1} a_i \chi_{A_i}(s),$$

and

$$\psi(s) = \sum_{j=1}^{n_2} b_j \chi_{B_j}(s).$$

Then $\phi + \psi$ has a representation

$$(\phi + \psi)(s) = \sum_{i=1}^{n_1} \sum_{j=1}^{n_2} (a_i + b_j) \chi_{A_i \cap B_j}(s),$$

where the sets $A_i \cap B_j$ are disjoint from the fact that the A_i and B_j are separately disjoint. However, this need not be the standard representation of $\phi + \psi$, as the $a_i + b_j$ need not be distinct. Let $k = 1, \ldots, K$ index the distinct numbers c_k in the set

$$\{a_i + b_j : i = 1, \ldots, n_1, \ j = 1, \ldots, n_2\}$$

and denote by $\{k\}$ the collection of indices (i, j) that deliver this number,

$$\{k\} = \{(i, j), i = 1, \ldots, n_1, \ j = 1, \ldots, n_2 : a_i + b_j = c_k\}.$$

Define C_k as the union over all sets $A_i \cap B_j$ such that $a_i + b_j = c_k$, so that

$$\mu(C_k) = \sum_{\{k\}} \mu(A_i \cap B_j).$$

Then the standard representation of $\phi + \psi$ is given by

$$(\phi + \psi)(s) = \sum_{k=1}^{K} c_k \chi_{C_k}.$$

Then

$$
\begin{aligned}
\int (\phi + \psi) d\mu &= \sum_{k=1}^{K} c_k \mu(C_k) \\
&= \sum_{k=1}^{K} \sum_{\{k\}} c_k \mu(A_i \cap B_j) \\
&= \sum_{k=1}^{K} \sum_{\{k\}} (a_i + b_j) \mu(A_i \cap B_j) \\
&= \sum_{i=1}^{n_1} \sum_{j=1}^{n_2} (a_i + b_j) \mu(A_i \cap B_j) \\
&= \sum_{i=1}^{n_1} \sum_{j=1}^{n_2} a_i \mu(A_i \cap B_j) + \sum_{i=1}^{n_1} \sum_{j=1}^{n_2} b_j \mu(A_i \cap B_j) \\
&= \sum_{i=1}^{n_1} a_i \mu(A_i) + \sum_{j=1}^{n_2} b_j \mu(B_j) \\
&= \int \phi d\mu + \int \psi d\mu,
\end{aligned}
$$

where the second-last equality follows from the fact that

$$\mu(A_i) = \sum_{j=1}^{n_2} \mu(A_i \cap B_j)$$

and
$$\mu(B_j) = \sum_{i=1}^{n_1} \mu(A_i \cap B_j).$$

If $c = 0$, then $c\phi$ vanishes identically and the equality holds. If $c > 0$, then $c\phi$ has standard representation

$$\sum_{i=1}^{n_1} c a_i \chi_{A_i}.$$

Therefore,

$$\int c\phi d\mu = \sum_{i=1}^{n_1} c a_i \mu(A_i) = c \sum_{i=1}^{n_1} a_i \mu(A_i) = c \int \phi d\mu.$$

Exercise 7.18

a. By definition

$$\int f d\mu = \sup \int \phi d\mu,$$

where the sup is over all simple functions ϕ in $M^+(S, \mathcal{S})$ with $0 \le \phi \le f$. As $f \le g$, the subset of simple functions ϕ in $M^+(S, \mathcal{S})$ satisfying $0 \le \phi \le g$ is at least as large as that for f. Hence,

$$\int f d\mu \le \int g d\mu.$$

b. Note that

$$\int_A f d\mu = \int f \chi_A d\mu,$$

and

$$\int_B f d\mu = \int f \chi_B d\mu.$$

As $A \subseteq B$ we have that $f\chi_A \le f\chi_B$ and hence by the result of part a.

$$\int_A f d\mu \le \int_B f d\mu.$$

Exercise 7.19

Consider the constant function $f : S \to \mathbf{R}_+$ defined by $f(s) = a \ge 1$ for all $s \in S$, and for all $n = 1, 2, \ldots$, let $f_n(s) = a - 1/n$. Then the f_n form a monotone increasing sequence of functions in $M^+(S, \mathcal{S})$. Let $\alpha = 1$ and consider the simple function $\varphi(s) = f(s)$ which satisfies $0 \le \varphi \le f$. Then

$$\begin{aligned} A_n &= \{s \in S : f_n(s) \ge \alpha\varphi(s)\} \\ &= \{s \in S : f_n(s) \ge f(s)\} = \emptyset \end{aligned}$$

for all n. Hence, $\cup_{n=1}^{\infty} A_n = \emptyset \ne S$.

Exercise 7.20

a. Let $f, g \in M^+(S, \mathcal{S})$. By Theorem 7.5 there exist sequences of nonnegative simple functions f_n and g_n such that

$$0 \le f_1 \le \ldots \le f_n \le \ldots \le f \text{ for all } n,$$

and

$$0 \le g_1 \le \ldots \le g_n \le \ldots \le g \text{ for all } n.$$

Then for all $n = 1, 2, \ldots$, the function $s_n \equiv f_n + g_n$ is a nonnegative simple function satisfying

$$0 \le s_1 \le \ldots \le s_n \le \ldots \le s \equiv f + g \quad \text{for all } n.$$

Hence,

$$\begin{aligned} \int s d\mu &= \lim_{n\to\infty} \int s_n d\mu \\ &= \lim_{n\to\infty} \int f_n d\mu + \lim_{n\to\infty} \int g_n d\mu \\ &= \int f d\mu + \int g d\mu, \end{aligned}$$

where the first and third equalities come from the Monotone Convergence Theorem (Theorem 7.8) and the second comes from the additivity of the integrals of simple functions (Exercise 7.17).

Now let $c \ge 0$, and define for all $n = 1, 2, \ldots$ $s_n = cf_n$, which is a pointwise monotone increasing sequence of nonnegative simple functions bounded above by $s = cf$. Hence

$$\int s d\mu = \lim_{n\to\infty} \int s_n d\mu = c \lim_{n\to\infty} \int f_n d\mu = c \int f d\mu,$$

by Exercise 7.17 and the Monotone Convergence Theorem.

b. Following the text, for $n = 1, 2, \ldots$, let

$$A_{kn} = \{s \in S : (k-1)2^{-n} \le f(s) < k2^{-n}\},$$

$$C_n = \{s \in S : f(s) \ge n\},$$

and

$$\phi_n(s) = \sum_{k=1}^{n2^n} (k-1)2^{-n} \chi_{A_{kn}}(s) + n\chi_{C_n}(s).$$

Then the ϕ_n form a monotone increasing sequence of simple functions converging pointwise to f. Hence, the sequence of functions $\phi_n \chi_A$ is a monotone increasing sequence of simple functions converging pointwise to $f\chi_A$, and

$$\int \phi_n \chi_A d\mu = \int \left(\sum_{k=1}^{n2^n} (k-1)2^{-n} \chi_{A_{kn} \cap A} + n\chi_{C_n \cap A} \right) d\mu$$

$$= \sum_{k=1}^{n2^n} (k-1)2^{-n} \mu(A_{kn} \cap A) + n\mu(C_n \cap A) = 0,$$

for all n. Then

$$\int_A f d\mu = \int f\chi_A d\mu$$

$$= \lim_{n\to\infty} \int \phi_n \chi_A d\mu = 0,$$

where the second equality comes from the Monotone Convergence Theorem.

c. Note that $f \geq f^* \equiv \infty\chi_A$. Hence, by Exercise 7.18a.,

$$\infty > \int f d\mu \geq \int f^* d\mu = \infty\mu(A),$$

which implies $\mu(A) = 0$.

Exercise 7.21

Defined this way, λ is clearly nonnegative and satisfies $\lambda(\emptyset) = 0$. To see countable additivity, let $\{A_i\}$ $i \geq 1$ be a sequence of disjoint sets in S with $A = \cup_{i=1}^{\infty} A_i$. For $n \geq 1$, let $f_n = \sum_{i=1}^{n} f\chi_{A_i}$. Then by Exercise 7.20a. we have

$$\int f_n d\mu = \sum_{i=1}^{n} \int f\chi_{A_i} d\mu = \sum_{i=1}^{n} \lambda(A_i).$$

As $\{f_n\}$ is a monotone increasing sequence of nonnegative functions converging pointwise to $f\chi_{A_i}$, the above result and the Monotone Convergence Theorem (Theorem 7.8) imply that

$$\lambda(A) = \int f\chi_{A.} d\mu = \lim_{n\to\infty} \int f_n d\mu$$

$$= \sum_{i=1}^{\infty} \lambda(A_i).$$

Exercise 7.22

As the g_i are nonnegative, the sequence $\{f_n\}$ defined by $f_n = \sum_{i=1}^{n} g_i$, $n = 1, 2, \ldots$, is nondecreasing and converges pointwise to $f = \sum_{i=1}^{\infty} g_i$. By Exercise 7.20, we have

$$\int f_n d\mu = \int \sum_{i=1}^{n} g_i d\mu = \sum_{i=1}^{n} \int g_i d\mu,$$

and taking limits gives

$$\lim_{n\to\infty} \int \sum_{i=1}^{n} g_i d\mu = \lim_{n\to\infty} \sum_{i=1}^{n} \int g_i d\mu.$$

But, by the Monotone Convergence Theorem (Theorem 7.8)

$$\lim_{n\to\infty} \int \sum_{i=1}^{n} g_i d\mu = \lim_{n\to\infty} \int f_n d\mu = \int f d\mu = \int \sum_{i=1}^{\infty} g_i d\mu,$$

and the result follows.

Exercise 7.23

Let $S = (0, 1]$, $\mathcal{S} = \mathcal{B}_{(0,1]}$, and μ the Lebesgue measure, and consider the sequence of functions for $n = 1, 2, \ldots$

$$f_n = n\chi_{(0,1/n]}.$$

As $\inf_n f_n \geq 0$ Fatou's Lemma applies. Noting that $\liminf_n f_n = 0$ and $\int f_n d\mu = 1$ for all n we have

$$0 = \int \liminf_n f_n d\mu < \liminf_n \int f_n d\mu = 1.$$

Exercise 7.24

a. For $f \in M^+$ the sequence of sets $B_n \equiv \left\{s \in S : f(s) \geq \frac{1}{n}\right\}$ and the sequences of functions $f_n \equiv f\chi_{B_n}$ satisfy

$$B_1 \subseteq B_2 \subseteq \ldots \subseteq B_n \subseteq \ldots \subseteq B \equiv \{s \in S : f(s) > 0\},$$

and

$$f_1 \leq f_2 \leq \ldots \leq f_n \leq \ldots \leq f = f\chi_B.$$

Then

$$\int f d\mu = 0 \text{ implies } \int f_n d\mu = 0,$$

for all $n = 1, 2, \ldots$ as $\int f_n d\mu$ converges to $\int f d\mu = 0$ from below by the Monotone Convergence Theorem (Theorem 7.8). This implies that $\mu(B_n) = 0$ from the fact that

$$0 \leq \frac{1}{n}\chi_{B_n} \leq f_n,$$

and so

$$0 \leq \frac{1}{n}\mu(B_n) \leq \int f_n d\mu.$$

But this implies that $\mu(B) = 0$ by Theorem 7.1a.

Now suppose that $\mu\ (B) = 0$. Then for all $n = 1, 2, \ldots$ we must have $\mu(B_n) = 0$. Noting that

$$f_n \leq \infty\chi_{B_n}.$$

Exercise 7.18a. gives

$$0 \leq \int f_n d\mu \leq \infty\mu(B_n),$$

from which we get that $\int f_n d\mu = 0$. The result follows from the Monotone Convergence Theorem.

b. Let $\{f_n\}$ be a monotone increasing sequence of functions in M^+ that converges to f μ-almost everywhere and let f^* be the pointwise limit of this sequence. By Theorem 7.4 f^* is measurable, and by the Monotone Convergence Theorem (Theorem 7.8) we have

$$\lim_{n\to\infty} \int f_n d\mu = \int f^* d\mu.$$

We know that $\mu\ (\{s \in S : f\ (s) \neq f^*\ (s)\}) = 0$. Therefore, by part a.,

$$\int (f - f^*) d\mu = 0,$$

and hence by Exercise 7.20a., we get

$$\int f d\mu = \int f^* d\mu.$$

Exercise 7.25

If f is bounded, there exists a $B \in \mathbf{R}$ such that for all $s \in S$ we have $|f|(s) \leq B$. Hence

$$\int f^+ d\mu \leq B\mu(S) < \infty,$$

and

$$\int f^- d\mu \leq B\mu(S) < \infty.$$

Exercise 7.26

a. Note that $|f| = f^+ + f^-$ and hence that $|f|^+ = f^+ + f^-$ while $|f|^- = 0$. If f is μ-integrable, then f^+ and f^- have finite integrals with respect to μ and hence so does $|f|^+$. Therefore, $|f|$ is integrable. If $|f|$ is integrable, $|f|^+$ has a finite integral with respect to μ and hence so must f^+ and f^-. Finally,

$$\begin{aligned} \left| \int f d\mu \right| &= \left| \int f^+ d\mu - \int f^- d\mu \right| \\ &\leq \int f^+ d\mu + \int f^- d\mu = \int |f| \, d\mu. \end{aligned}$$

b. Note that

$$f^+ + f^- = |f| \leq |g| = g^+ + g^-.$$

Hence by Exercise 7.18a.,

$$\int f^+ d\mu \leq \int |g| \, d\mu < \infty$$

and

$$\int f^- d\mu \leq \int |g|\, d\mu < \infty,$$

which implies that $|f|$ is μ-integrable, and moreover

$$\int |f|\, d\mu \leq \int |g|\, d\mu < \infty.$$

c. Let $\alpha \in [0, +\infty)$. Then $(\alpha f)^+ = \alpha f^+$ and $(\alpha f)^- = \alpha f^-$. Hence, $\int \alpha f^+ d\mu = \alpha \int f^+ d\mu < \infty$ and $\int \alpha f^- d\mu = \alpha \int f^- d\mu < \infty$ by Exercise 7.20. Hence, αf is integrable and

$$\int \alpha f d\mu = \int \alpha f^+ d\mu - \int \alpha f^- d\mu = \alpha \int f d\mu.$$

Now let $\alpha \in (-\infty, 0]$. Then $(\alpha f)^+ = -\alpha f^-$ and $(\alpha f)^- = -\alpha f^+$. Integrability follows as above, and hence

$$\int \alpha f d\mu = \int -\alpha f^- d\mu - \int -\alpha f^+ d\mu$$
$$= \alpha \int \left(f^+ - f^-\right) d\mu = \alpha \int f d\mu.$$

Note that $(f+g)^+ \leq f^+ + g^+$ and $(f+g)^- \leq f^- + g^-$. Then as f and g are integrable, by Exercise 7.20 $f+g$ is integrable. Then as

$$(f+g)^+ - (f+g)^- = f + g = \left(f^+ - f^-\right) + \left(g^+ - g^-\right),$$

we get

$$(f+g)^+ + f^- + g^- = (f+g)^- + f^+ + g^+.$$

By Exercise 7.20

$$\int (f+g)^+ d\mu + \int f^- d\mu + \int g^- d\mu$$
$$= \int (f+g)^- d\mu + \int f^+ d\mu + \int g^+ d\mu.$$

Subtracting the finite numbers $\int f^- d\mu$, $\int g^- d\mu$, and $\int (f+g)^- d\mu$ from both sides gives

$$\begin{aligned}\int (f+g)\, d\mu &= \int (f+g)^+\, d\mu - \int (f+g)^-\, d\mu \\ &= \int f^+ d\mu - \int f^- d\mu + \int g^+ d\mu - \int g^- d\mu \\ &= \int f d\mu + \int g d\mu.\end{aligned}$$

Exercise 7.27

Let $\mathcal{F}$ be the set of all finite unions of disjoint measurable rectangles, and let $\mathcal{G}$ be the algebra generated by the measurable rectangles. We will show that $\mathcal{E} = \mathcal{F} = \mathcal{G}$.

Obviously, $\mathcal{F} \subset \mathcal{E} \subset \mathcal{G}$. The proof will be complete if we can establish that $\mathcal{G} \subset \mathcal{F}$. But $\mathcal{F}$ contains the measurable rectangles, and so we only need to show that it is an algebra.

$\emptyset$, $X \times Y \in \mathcal{F} : \emptyset$ and $X \times Y$ are measurable rectangles.

To establish closure under complementation, we will first establish that $\mathcal{F}$ is closed under finite intersections. First, let B and $C \in \mathcal{F}$. Therefore there exist $\{B_n\}_{n=1}^N$ and $\{C_m\}_{m=1}^M$ sequences of disjoint measurable rectangles such that $\cup_{n=1}^N B_n = B$ and $\cup_{m=1}^M C_m = C$. Then

$$\begin{aligned}B \cap C &= \left(\cup_{n=1}^N B_n\right) \cap \left(\cup_{m=1}^M C_m\right) \\ &= \left(\cup_{n=1}^N B_{1n} \times B_{2n}\right) \cap \left(\cup_{m=1}^M C_{1m} \times C_{2m}\right) \\ &= \cup_{n=1}^N \cup_{m=1}^M (B_{1n} \times B_{2n}) \cap (C_{1m} \times C_{2m}) \\ &= \cup_{n=1}^N \cup_{m=1}^M (B_{1n} \cap C_{1m}) \times (B_{2n} \cap C_{2m}),\end{aligned}$$

which is a finite union of disjoint measurable rectangles. Iterating on this gives us the result for arbitrary finite unions.

$A \in \mathcal{F}$ implies $A^c \in \mathcal{F}$: Let $A \in \mathcal{F}$. Then there exists $\{A_n\}_{n=1}^N$ disjoint measurable rectangles such that $\cup_{n=1}^N A_n = A$ and $A^c = \cap_{n=1}^N A_n^c$. For any measurable rectangle $A_n = X_A \times Y_A$, A_n^c can be written as the union of three measurable rectangles $(X_A^c \times Y_A)$, $(X_A \times Y_A^c)$, and $(X_A^c \times Y_A^c)$. To see this, note that if $(x, y) \in A_n^c$, then either $x \notin X_A$, or $y \notin Y_A$, or both. Hence, (x, y) is an element of one of these rectangles. The reverse is obvious.

But these rectangles are also disjoint. Hence, the result follows by closure under finite intersections.

To establish closure under finite unions, we first establish closure under finite differences. If $A, B \in \mathcal{F}$ they can be written as $A = \cup_{n=1}^N A_n$ and $B = \cup_{m=1}^M B_m$ for finite disjoint collections of $\mathcal{C}$ sets $\{A_n\}$ and $\{B_m\}$. Then

$$\begin{aligned} A \backslash B &= \left(\cup_{n=1}^N A_n\right) \cap \left(\cup_{m=1}^M B_m\right)^c \\ &= \left(\cup_{n=1}^N A_n\right) \cap \left(\cap_{m=1}^M B_m^c\right) \\ &= \cup_{n=1}^N \left(\cap_{m=1}^M \left(A_n \backslash B_m\right)\right). \end{aligned}$$

Writing $A_n = X_n \times Y_n$ and $B_m = U_m \times V_m$, we have that for all n, m, $A_n \backslash B_m$ is the union of the disjoint measurable rectangles $(X_n \backslash U_m) \times Y_n$ and $(X_n \cap U_m) \times (Y_n \backslash V_m)$. But we saw above that $\mathcal{F}$ is closed under finite intersections, and hence $A \backslash B$ is a finite union of disjoint measurable rectangles.

$A_n \in \mathcal{F}$, $n = 1, \ldots, N$ implies $\cup_{n=1}^N A_n \in \mathcal{F}$: We demonstrate the result for $N = 2$. Iterating on the argument gives the result for arbitrary finite N. Note that

$$A_1 \cup A_2 = (A_1 \backslash A_2) \cup (A_2 \backslash A_1) \cup (A_1 \cap A_2)$$

is a finite union of disjoint measurable rectangles using the facts proven above that $\mathcal{F}$ is closed under finite set differences and finite intersections.

Exercise 7.28

It is sufficient to show that each σ-algebra contains the generators of the other.

$\mathcal{B}^{k+l} \subset \mathcal{B}^k \times \mathcal{B}^l$: $\mathcal{B}^{k+l}$ is generated by $\mathcal{A}$, the collection of sets of the form

$$A = \{x \in R^{k+l} : x_i \in (a_i, b_i),\ i = 1, \ldots, k+l\}.$$

We will refer to these sets as the *measurable pavings* in R^{k+l}. But such pavings are measurable rectangles and are in $\mathcal{E}$. Hence $\mathcal{B}^k \times \mathcal{B}^l$ is a σ-algebra containing $\mathcal{A}$ and $\mathcal{B}^{k+l} \subset \mathcal{B}^k \times \mathcal{B}^l$.

$\mathcal{B}^{k+l} \supset \mathcal{B}^k \times \mathcal{B}^l$: The text defines $\mathcal{B}^k \times \mathcal{B}^l$ as the σ-algebra generated by $\mathcal{E}$; it is easily seen that it is also the σ-algebra generated by $\mathcal{C}$. It is sufficient to show that $\mathcal{C} \subset \mathcal{B}^{k+l}$. That is, if $B \in \mathcal{B}^k$ and $C \in \mathcal{B}^l$, $B \times C \in \mathcal{B}^{k+l}$.

Let B be a measurable paving in $\mathbf{R}^k$ and consider the class

$$\mathcal{M} = \{C \subset R^l : B \times C \in \mathcal{B}^{k+l}\}.$$

It is easily verified that $\mathcal{M}$ is a σ-algebra, and as $\mathcal{B}^{k+l}$ contains the measurable pavings in $\mathbf{R}^{k+l}$, $\mathcal{M}$ must contain the measurable pavings in $\mathbf{R}^l$. Hence $\mathcal{B}^l \subset \mathcal{M}$.

Now fix $C \in \mathcal{B}^l$ and consider the class of sets

$$\mathcal{N} = \{B \subset R^k : B \times C \in \mathcal{B}^{k+l}\}.$$

This is a σ-algebra, and by the result immediately above contains the measurable pavings in $\mathbf{R}^k$. Hence $\mathcal{B}^k \subset \mathcal{N}$.

From this, if $B \in \mathcal{B}^k$ and $C \in \mathcal{B}^l$, $B \times C \in \mathcal{B}^{k+l}$ and $\mathcal{B}^{k+l} \supset \mathcal{B}^k \times \mathcal{B}^l$.

Exercise 7.29

Let $E \in \mathcal{E}$. If we can show that E can be written as a finite union of disjoint measurable rectangles (that is, if we can adapt Exercise 7.27 to this setup), we can use the argument in the proof of Theorem 7.13 to show that we can extend μ to $\mathcal{E}$. The extension to $\mathcal{Z}$ will then follow from the Hahn and Caratheodory Extension Theorems.

Let $\mathcal{F}$ be the set of all finite unions of disjoint measurable rectangles. Once again we only need to show that it is an algebra. That it contains $\emptyset$ and Z is immediate. To show closure under complementation and finite unions, we first establish that $\mathcal{F}$ is closed under finite intersections and finite differences.

To establish closure under finite intersections, first let B and $C \in \mathcal{F}$. Therefore there exist $\{B_k\}_{k=1}^{K}$ and $\{C_m\}_{m=1}^{M}$ sequences of disjoint measurable rectangles such that $\cup_{k=1}^{K} B_k = B$ and $\cup_{m=1}^{M} C_m = C$. Then $B \cap C$ equals

$$
\begin{aligned}
&\left(\cup_{k=1}^{K} B_k\right) \cap \left(\cup_{m=1}^{M} C_m\right) \\
&= \left(\cup_{k=1}^{K} B_{1k} \times B_{2k} \times \ldots \times B_{nk}\right) \cap \left(\cup_{m=1}^{M} C_{1m} \times C_{2m} \times \ldots \times C_{nm}\right) \\
&= \cup_{k=1}^{K} \cup_{m=1}^{M} \left(B_{1k} \cap C_{1m}\right) \times \left(B_{2k} \cap C_{2m}\right) \times \ldots \times \left(B_{nk} \cap C_{nm}\right),
\end{aligned}
$$

which is a finite union of disjoint measurable rectangles.

To establish closure under finite differences, let A, $B \in \mathcal{F}$. Hence they can be written as $A = \cup_{k=1}^{K} A_n$ and $B = \cup_{m=1}^{M} B_m$ for finite disjoint collections of $\mathcal{C}$ sets $\{A_n\}$ and $\{B_m\}$. Then

$$
\begin{aligned}
A \backslash B &= \left(\cup_{k=1}^{K} A_k\right) \cap \left(\cup_{m=1}^{M} B_m\right)^c \\
&= \left(\cup_{k=1}^{K} A_k\right) \cap \left(\cap_{m=1}^{M} B_m^c\right) \\
&= \cup_{k=1}^{K} \left(\cap_{m=1}^{M} \left(A_k \backslash B_m\right)\right).
\end{aligned}
$$

But we saw above that $\mathcal{F}$ is closed under finite intersections. Hence $A \backslash B$ will be a finite union of disjoint measurable rectangles if we can prove that for all k, m, $A_k \backslash B_m$ is a finite union of disjoint measurable rectangles. The proof of this is constructive. Writing $A_k = X_{1A_k} \times X_{2A_k} \times \ldots \times X_{nA_k}$ and $B_m = X_{1B_m} \times X_{2B_m} \times \ldots \times X_{nA_m}$, we have that

$$
\begin{aligned}
A_k &= X_{1A_k} \times X_{2A_k} \times \ldots \times X_{nA_k} \\
&= \left(\left(X_{1A_k} \backslash X_{1B_m}\right) \cup \left(X_{1A_k} \cap X_{1B_m}\right)\right) \times X_{2A_k} \times \ldots \times X_{nA_k} \\
&= \left[\left(X_{1A_k} \backslash X_{1B_m}\right) \times X_{2A_k} \times \ldots \times X_{nA_k}\right] \\
&\quad \cup \left[\left(X_{1A_k} \cap X_{1B_m}\right) \times X_{2A_k} \times \ldots \times X_{nA_k}\right] \\
&= \left[\left(X_{1A_k} \backslash X_{1B_m}\right) \times X_{2A_k} \times \ldots \times X_{nA_k}\right] \\
&\quad \cup \left[\left(X_{1A_k} \cap X_{1B_m}\right) \times \left(X_{2A_k} \backslash X_{2B_m}\right) \times \ldots \times X_{nA_k}\right] \\
&\quad \cup \left[\left(X_{1A_k} \cap X_{1B_m}\right) \times \left(X_{2A_k} \cap X_{2B_m}\right) \times \ldots \times X_{nA_k}\right].
\end{aligned}
$$

Iterating on this process gives the result.

We can now prove closure under complementation and finite unions.

$A \in \mathcal{F} \Rightarrow A^c \in \mathcal{F}$: Let $A \in \mathcal{F}$. Then there exist $\{A_k\}_{k=1}^K$ disjoint measurable rectangles such that $\cup_{k=1}^K A_k = A$ and $A^c = \cap_{k=1}^K A_k^c$. For any measurable rectangle $A_k = X_{1A_k} \times X_{2A_k} \times \ldots \times X_{nA_k}$, A_k^c can be written as the union of disjoint measurable rectangles constructed the following way. For $j = 0, \ldots, n-1$, let $\mathcal{A}^j$ represent the collection of measurable rectangles constructed from products of the X_{mA_k}'s with exactly j of the $X_{mA_k}^c$'s. Thus, $\mathcal{A}^0 = \{X_{1A_k}^c \times X_{2A_k}^c \times \ldots \times X_{nA_k}^c\}$. Then taking the union of all the elements of these collections for $j = 0, \ldots, n-1$ gives us $A_k^c \in \mathcal{F}$. Hence, the result follows by closure under finite intersections.

$A_n \in \mathcal{F},\ n = 1, \ldots, N \Rightarrow \cup_{n=1}^N A_n \in \mathcal{F}$: We demonstrate the result for $N = 2$. Iterating on the argument gives the result for arbitrary finite N. Note that

$$A_1 \cup A_2 = (A_1 \backslash A_2) \cup (A_2 \backslash A_1) \cup (A_1 \cap A_2)$$

is a finite union of disjoint measurable rectangles using the facts proven above that $\mathcal{F}$ is closed under finite set differences and finite intersections.

Exercise 7.30

Let E be a subset of $\mathbf{R}$ that is not Lebesgue measurable, and let $F \in \mathcal{L}^1$ be such that $\lambda(F) = 0$. Then the set $E \times F$ is a subset of $\mathbf{R} \times F$ and has Lebesgue measure zero. Hence, $E \times F \in \mathcal{L}^2$.

Exercise 7.31

We need to show that for all $A \in \mathcal{S}$,

$$\phi^{-1}(A) \equiv \{(w, x) \in W \times X : \phi(w, x) \in A\},$$

is an element of $\mathcal{W} \times \mathcal{X}$. Define the function $b : W \times X \to Y \times Z$ by $b(w, x) = (f(x), g(y))$. Then we can write $\phi = h \circ b$. The proof will be complete if we can show that b is measurable between $\mathcal{W} \times \mathcal{X}$ and $\mathcal{Y} \times \mathcal{Z}$, and that compositions of measurable functions are measurable. To see that compositions of measurable functions are measurable in general, let $(\Omega, \mathcal{F})$, $(\Omega', \mathcal{F}')$

and $(\Omega'', \mathcal{F}'')$ be measurable spaces, and let $T : \Omega \to \Omega'$ be measurable between $\mathcal{F}$ and $\mathcal{F}'$, and $T' : \Omega' \to \Omega''$ be measurable between $\mathcal{F}'$ and $\mathcal{F}''$. Then $T' \circ T : \Omega \to \Omega''$ is measurable between $\mathcal{F}$ and $\mathcal{F}''$ because, if $A'' \in \mathcal{F}''$, then

$$(T' \circ T)^{-1}(A'') = T^{-1}((T')^{-1}(A'')) \in \mathcal{F},$$

because $(T')^{-1}(A'') \in \mathcal{F}'$ as T' is measurable, and T is measurable.

To see that b is measurable between $\mathcal{W} \times \mathcal{X}$ and $\mathcal{Y} \times \mathcal{Z}$, we first establish that if E is a measurable rectangle in $\mathcal{Y} \times \mathcal{Z}$, then $b^{-1}(E)$ is a measurable rectangle in $\mathcal{W} \times \mathcal{X}$. We then show that the set of all subsets in $Y \times Z$ with inverse images in $\mathcal{W} \times \mathcal{X}$, call it $\mathcal{G}$, is a σ-algebra. Then by construction, we will have $\mathcal{Y} \times \mathcal{Z} \subset \mathcal{G}$ and the result will be proven.

Let E be a measurable rectangle in $\mathcal{Y} \times \mathcal{Z}$. Then $b^{-1}(E)$ is a measurable rectangle in $\mathcal{W} \times \mathcal{X}$ because f and g are measurable. Now define

$$\mathcal{G} = \{B \subset Y \times Z : b^{-1}(B) \in \mathcal{W} \times \mathcal{X}\}.$$

But $\mathcal{G}$ contains the measurable rectangles in $\mathcal{W} \times \mathcal{X}$, and is a σ-algebra. To see the latter, note first that

$$b^{-1}(Y \times Z) = W \times X.$$

Also, if $B \in \mathcal{G}$, then as

$$b^{-1}(B^c) = (b^{-1}(B))^c,$$

we must have $B^c \in \mathcal{G}$. Finally, if $\{B_n\}_{n=1}^{\infty}$ is in $\mathcal{G}$, then $\cup_{n=1}^{\infty} B_n \in \mathcal{G}$ as

$$\begin{aligned} b^{-1}(\cup_{n=1}^{\infty} B_n) &= \{(w, x) \in W \times X : b(w, x) \in \cup_{n=1}^{\infty} B_n\} \\ &= \cup_{n=1}^{\infty}\{(w, x) \in W \times X : b(w, x) \in B_n\} \\ &= \cup_{n=1}^{\infty} b^{-1}(B_n). \end{aligned}$$

Then as $\mathcal{G}$ is a σ-algebra on $Y \times Z$ containing the measurable rectangles, we must have $\mathcal{Y} \times \mathcal{Z} \subset \mathcal{G}$. But then b is measurable between $\mathcal{W} \times \mathcal{X}$ and $\mathcal{Y} \times \mathcal{Z}$.

Exercise 7.32

a. There are two things to note. First, all functions in the equivalence class are $\mathcal{A}$-measurable and are hence constant on sets A_i in the countable partition $\{A_i\}_{i=1}^{\infty}$. Second, all of these functions have the same integral over any $\mathcal{A}$ set.

Hence, the equivalence class is the class of discrete random variables on the $\{A_i\}_{i=1}^{\infty}$ that differ only on A_i such that $i \in J^c$. That is, we can write

$$E(f|\mathcal{A})(\widehat{\omega}) = \sum_{n=1}^{\infty} E(f|A_n)\chi_{A_n}(\widehat{\omega}),$$

where $E(f|A_n)$ is the number defined in (1).

b. The equivalence class is given by the class of step functions on the $\{A_i\}_{i=1}^{\infty}$. For all $i \in J$, if $\omega \in A_i$ we have

$$E(\chi_B|\mathcal{A})(\omega) = \frac{\mu(B \cap A_i)}{\mu(A_i)}.$$

Members of this class differ only on A_i such that $i \in J^c$.

Exercise 7.33

a. Defined in this way, all sets $A \in \mathcal{A}$ display no variation in y, in the sense that for all y and A, the y-sections of A, call them A_y, are identical. Consequently, each version of the conditional expectation $E(f|\mathcal{A})$ cannot display any variation in y, in the sense that its y-sections are identical. That is, for all $A \in \mathcal{A}$, and for all y and y' we have

$$E(f|\mathcal{A})_y = E(f|\mathcal{A})_{y'}.$$

Therefore, each function in this equivalence class is defined by its y-section for $y = 0$. As members of this equivalence class have the same integral over any $\mathcal{A}$ set, they can vary only on sets of μ measure zero.

b. Given $B \in \mathcal{F}$, the conditional probability $E(\chi_B|\mathcal{A})$ is any member of the equivalence class of functions that are $\mathcal{A}$-measurable, and satisfy

$$\int_A E(\chi_B|\mathcal{A})(\omega)p(\omega)d\lambda = \int_A \chi_B p(\omega)d\lambda = \mu(B \cap A),$$

for all $A \in \mathcal{A}$. As for part a., there is a sense in which $\mathcal{A}$ contains no information about the dimension y. Consequently, if $y, y' \in B_x$ for some x, we have

$$E(\chi_B|\mathcal{A})_x(y) = E(\chi_B|\mathcal{A})_x(y').$$

8 Markov Processes

Exercise 8.1

As f and $g \in B(Z, \mathcal{Z})$, and $\alpha, \beta \in \mathbf{R}$, then $\alpha f + \beta g \in B(Z, \mathcal{Z})$ (see Exercise 7.12a.). Hence, $T(\alpha f + \beta g)$ is well defined and

$$[T(\alpha f + \beta g)](z) = \int [\alpha f + \beta g](z')Q(z, dz'),$$

all $z \in Z$. As $f, g \in B(Z, \mathcal{Z})$, they are integrable, so we can use the fact that integrals are linear operators (see Exercise 7.26c.) to get

$$\begin{aligned}[T(\alpha f + \beta g)](z) &= \int \alpha f(z')Q(z, dz') + \int \beta g(z')Q(z, dz') \\ &= \alpha \int f(z')Q(z, dz') + \beta \int g(z')Q(z, dz') \\ &= \alpha(Tf)(z) + \beta(Tg)(z).\end{aligned}$$

Exercise 8.2

Define $\gamma(A) = \alpha\lambda(A) + (1 - \alpha)\mu(A)$, which is a well-defined measure by Exercise 7.4. Let ϕ_n be a sequence of simple functions converging to Q. Because Q is a probability measure, by Theorem 7.5 such a sequence exists. Let the sequence of sets $\{Z_i\}$ form a partition of Z. Then $T^*\gamma$ is well defined, and

$$
\begin{aligned}
(T^*\gamma)(A) &= \int Q(z, A)\gamma(dz) \quad \text{all } A \in \mathcal{Z} \\
&= \lim_{n\to\infty} \int \phi_n(z, A)\gamma(dz) \quad \text{all } A \in \mathcal{Z} \\
&= \lim_{n\to\infty} \sum_i \phi_n(Z_i, A)\gamma(Z_i) \\
&= \lim_{n\to\infty} \sum_i \phi_n(Z_i, A)[\alpha\lambda(Z_i) + (1-\alpha)\mu(Z_i)] \\
&= \lim_{n\to\infty} \left[\alpha \sum_i \phi_n(Z_i, A)\lambda(Z_i)\right] \\
&\quad + \lim_{n\to\infty} \left[(1-\alpha) \sum_i \phi_n(Z_i, A)\mu(Z_i)\right] \\
&= \alpha \lim_{n\to\infty} \int \phi_n(z, A)\lambda(dz) \\
&\quad + (1-\alpha) \lim_{n\to\infty} \int \phi_n(z, A)\mu(dz) \\
&= \alpha \int Q(z, A)\lambda(dz) + (1-\alpha) \int Q(z, A)\mu(dz) \\
&= \alpha(T^*\lambda)(A) + (1-\alpha)(T^*\mu)(A),
\end{aligned}
$$

where the second line uses Theorem 7.5 and the rest of the proof relies on repeated applications of the definition of Lebesgue integration.

Exercise 8.3

a. Note that

$$
\begin{aligned}
\langle af + bg, \lambda \rangle &= \int (af + bg)(z)\lambda(dz) \\
&= a \int f(z)\lambda(dz) + b \int g(z)\lambda(dz) \\
&= a \langle f, \lambda \rangle + b \langle g, \lambda \rangle,
\end{aligned}
$$

where the second line uses Exercise 7.26c.

b. Note that

$$\begin{aligned}\langle f, \alpha\lambda + (1-\alpha)\mu\rangle &= \int f(z)[\alpha\lambda + (1-\alpha)\mu](dz) \\ &= \alpha \int f(z)\lambda(dz) + (1-\alpha) \int f(z)\mu(dz) \\ &= \alpha \langle f, \lambda\rangle + (1-\alpha)\langle f, \mu\rangle,\end{aligned}$$

where the second line comes from applying an argument similar to the one used in Exercise 8.2.

Exercise 8.4

a. The proof is by induction. By assumption, $Q(z, A) = Q^1(z, A)$ is a transition function. Hence, by Theorem 8.2,

$$\begin{aligned}Q^2(z, A) &= (T^* Q_z)(A) \\ &= \int Q^1(z', A) Q(z, dz'),\end{aligned}$$

all $(z, A) \in (Z, \mathcal{Z})$, is a probability measure on $(Z, \mathcal{Z})$ for each $z \in Z$.

To prove that for each $A \in \mathcal{Z}$, $Q^2(\cdot, A)$ is a measurable function, notice that $Q^2(\cdot, A) \in M^+(Z, \mathcal{Z})$ and Theorem 8.1 applies.

Next, assume $Q^{n-1}(z, A)$ is a transition function, hence

$$\begin{aligned}Q^n(z, A) &= (T^* Q_z^{n-1})(A) \\ &= \int Q^{n-1}(z', A) Q(z, dz'),\end{aligned}$$

all $(z, A) \in (Z, \mathcal{Z})$, is a probability measure on $(Z, \mathcal{Z})$ for each $z \in Z$ by the same argument as before. That $Q^n(\cdot, A)$, all $z \in Z$, is a measurable function, follows again from a direct application of Theorem 8.1.

b. Using the properties of the transition functions established in part a.,

$$
\begin{aligned}
Q^{(n+m)}(z_0, A) &= \int Q^{(n+m-1)}(z_1, A)Q(z_0, dz_1) \\
&= \int\int Q^{(n+m-2)}(z_2, A)Q(z_1, dz_2)Q(z_0, dz_1) \\
&= \int Q^{(n+m-2)}(z_2, A)\int Q(z_1, dz_2)Q(z_0, dz_1) \\
&= \int Q^{(n+m-2)}(z_2, A)Q^2(z_0, dz_2),
\end{aligned}
$$

where z_i is the state i periods ahead. Continuing the recursion in this fashion we can write

$$
Q^{(n+m)}(z_0, A) = \int Q^m(z_n, A)Q^n(z_0, dz_n).
$$

To show that $T^{(n+m)}f = (T^n)(T^m f)$, notice that

$$
\begin{aligned}
[T^{(n+m)}f](z_0) &= \int f(z_{n+m})Q^{n+m}(z_0, dz_{n+m}) \\
&= \int f(z_{n+m})Q^m(z_n, z_{n+m})Q^n(z_0, dz_n) \\
&= \int\left[\int f(z_{n+m})Q^m(z_n, z_{n+m})\right]Q^n(z_0, dz_n) \\
&= \int (T^m f)(z_n)Q^n(z_0, dz_n) \\
&= (T^n)(T^m f)(z_0).
\end{aligned}
$$

To show that $T^{*(n+m)}\lambda = (T^{*n})(T^{*m}\lambda)$, all $\lambda \in \Lambda(Z, \mathcal{Z})$, note that by definition,

$$
\begin{aligned}
T^{*(n+m)}\lambda(A) &= \int Q^{n+m}(z_0, A)\lambda(dz_0) \\
&= \int\int Q^n(z_m, A)Q^m(z_0, dz_m)\lambda(dz_0) \\
&= \int Q^n(z_m, A)\int Q^m(z_0, dz_m)\lambda(dz_0) \\
&= \int Q^n(z_m, A)(T^{*m}\lambda)(dz_m) \\
&= (T^{*n})(T^{*m}\lambda)(A),
\end{aligned}
$$

where both results rely on a repeated application of Theorem 8.3 and the results obtained in part a.

Exercise 8.5

Clearly $\mu^t(z_0, \emptyset) = 0$, so that condition a. of Exercise 7.29 is satisfied. In addition, $\mu^t(z_0, B) \geq 0$, as Q is a transition function.

The proof that $\mu^t(z_0, \cdot)$ satisfies condition b. of Exercise 7.29 is by induction. Take any arbitrary sequence

$$\{C_i^t\}_{i=1}^{\infty} = \{(A_{1i} \times A_{2i} \times \ldots \times A_{ti})\}_{i=1}^{\infty},$$

of disjoint sets in $\mathcal{C}$, such that

$$C^t = \cup_{i=1}^{\infty} C_i^t \in \mathcal{C}.$$

For $t = 1$ is trivial. For $t = 2$,

$$\{C_i^2\}_{i=1}^{\infty} = \{(A_{1i} \times A_{2i})\}_{i=1}^{\infty}$$
$$C^2 = A_1 \times A_2 = \cup_{i=1}^{\infty}(A_{1i} \times A_{2i}).$$

Fix a point $z_1 \in A_1$. Then for each $z_2 \in A_2$ the point (z_1, z_2) belongs to exactly one rectangle $(A_{1i} \times A_{2i})$. Thus A_2 is the disjoint union of those A_{2i} such that z_1 is in the corresponding A_{1i}. Hence

$$\sum_{i+1}^{\infty} Q(z_1, A_{2i})\chi_{A_{1i}}(z_1) = Q(z_1, A_2)\chi_{A_1}(z_1),$$

since Q is countably additive. Therefore, by the corollary of the Monotone Convergence Theorem (see Exercise 7.22), we have that

$$\sum_{i=1}^{\infty} \int_Z Q(z_1, A_{2i})\chi_{A_{1i}}(z_1) Q(z_0, dz_1) = \int_Z Q(z_1, A_2)\chi_{A_1}(z_1) Q(z_0, dz_1),$$

which implies that

$$\sum_{i=1}^{\infty} \int_{A_{1i}} Q(z_1, A_{2i}) Q(z_0, dz_1) = \int_A Q(z_1, A_2) Q(z_0, dz_1).$$

Hence,

$$\sum_{i=1}^{\infty} \int_{A_{1i}} \int_{A_{2i}} Q(z_1, dz_2) Q(z_0, dz_1) = \int_{A_1} \int_{A_2} Q(z_1, dz_2) Q(z_0, dz_1),$$

and so

$$\sum_{i=1}^{\infty} \mu^2(z_0, C_i) = \mu^2(z_0, C).$$

Next, suppose $\mu^{t-1}[z_0, (A_1 \times \ldots \times A_{t-1})]$ satisfies condition b. We will show that $\mu^t[z_0, (A_1 \times \ldots \times A_{t-1} \times A_t)]$ satisfies the stated hypothesis also. Fix a point

$$z^{t-1} = (z_1, \ldots, z_{t-1}) \in (A_1 \times \ldots \times A_{t-1}).$$

Then, for each $z_t \in A_t$, the point (z^{t-1}, z_t) belongs to exactly one rectangle $(A_{1i} \times \ldots \times A_{ti})$. Thus A_t is the disjoint union of those A_{ti} such that z^{t-1} is in the corresponding $(A_{1i} \times \ldots \times A_{t-1i})$. Hence,

$$\sum_{i=1}^{\infty} Q(z_{t-1}, A_{ti})\chi_{A_{1i}\times\ldots\times A_{t-1i}}(z^{t-1}) = Q(z_{t-1}, A_t)\chi_{A_1\times\ldots\times A_t}(z^{t-1}),$$

since Q is countably additive. Then, as before, by the corollary of the Monotone Convergence Theorem,

$$\sum_{i=1}^{\infty} \int_{Z^{t-1}} Q(z_{t-1}, A_{ti})\chi_{A_{1i}\times\ldots\times A_{t-1i}}(z^{t-1})\mu^{t-1}(z_0, dz^{t-1})$$
$$= \int_{Z^{t-1}} Q(z_1, A_2)\chi_{A_1}(z_1)\mu^{t-1}(z_0, dz^{t-1}),$$

so

$$\sum_{i=1}^{\infty} \int_{A_{1i}} \cdots \int_{A_{ti}} Q(z_{t-1}, dz_t) \ldots Q(z_0, dz_1)$$
$$= \int_{A_1} \cdots \int_{A_t} Q(z_{t-1}, dz_t) \ldots Q(z_0, dz_1),$$

which implies

$$\sum_{i=1}^{\infty} \mu^t(z_0, C_i) = \mu^t(z_0, C),$$

where the second line makes use of the definition of μ. Hence condition b. of Exercise 7.29 also holds.

To show that $\mu^t(z_0, Z^t) = 1$, note that

$$\mu^t(z_0, Z^t) = \int_Z \cdots \int_Z Q(z_{t-1}, dz_t) \ldots Q(z_0, dz_1).$$

But

$$\int_Z Q(z_{i-1}, dz_i) = 1$$

as Q is a probability measure. Applying this recursively to $\mu^t(z_0, Z^t)$ we obtain the result.

Exercise 8.6

a. For $B \in \mathcal{Z}^t$, $C \in \mathcal{Z}$, define $\widehat{C} \equiv Z \times \ldots \times Z \times C \times Z \times \ldots$, $\widehat{B} \equiv Z \times \ldots \times Z \times B \times Z \times \ldots \in \mathcal{Z}^\infty$, and for $t = 1, 2, \ldots$, the conditional probability $P_{t+1}(C \mid [z_0(\omega), \ldots, z_t(\omega)] \in B)$ can be written (generalizations to $P_{t+1,\ldots,t+n}(C \,|[z_0(\omega), \ldots, z_t(\omega)] \in B)$ are straightforward) as

$$\begin{aligned}
&P_{t+1}(C \,|[z_0(\omega), \ldots, z_t(\omega)] \in B) \\
&= \mu^\infty(z_0, \widehat{B} \cup \widehat{C}) \\
&= \int_Z \cdots \int_Z \chi_C(z_{t+1}, \ldots, z_{t+n}) \chi_B(z_0, \ldots, z_t) Q(z_t, dz_{t+1}) \ldots Q(z_0, dz_1) \\
&= \int_Z \cdots \int_Z Q(z_t, C) \chi_B(z_0, \ldots, z_t) Q(z_{t-1}, dz_t) \ldots Q(z_0, dz_1).
\end{aligned}$$

Hence

$$P_{t+1}(C \,|[z_0(\omega) = a_0, \ldots, z_t(\omega) = a_t]) = Q(a_t, C) \text{ (a.s.)}.$$

Similarly, we can verify that

$$P_{t+1}(C \,|z_t(\omega) = a_t) = Q(a_t, C) \text{ (a.s.)}.$$

Hence the desired result follows.

b. Follows from the proof outlined in part a.

c. For $C \in \mathcal{Z}^n$, define $\widehat{C} = Z \times Z \times \ldots \times C \times Z \times \ldots \in \mathcal{Z}^\infty$. Then

$$\begin{aligned}
&P_{t+1,\ldots,t+n}(C) \\
&= P(\{\omega \in \Omega : [z_{t+1}(\omega), \ldots, z_{t+n}(\omega)] \in C = C^1 \times \ldots \times C^n\}) \\
&= P(\{\omega \in \Omega : z_{t+1}(\omega) \in C^1, \ldots, z_{t+n}(\omega) \in C^n\}),
\end{aligned}$$

$t = 1, 2, \ldots$; all $C \in \mathcal{Z}^n$, as

$$\begin{aligned} P_{t+1,\ldots,t+n}(C) &= \mu^\infty(z_0, \widehat{C}) \\ &= \int_{C^1} \cdots \int_{C^n} Q(z_{t+n-1}, dz_{t+n}) \ldots Q(z_t, dz_{t+1}) \\ &= \prod_{j=1}^{n} \lambda(C^j). \end{aligned}$$

Because t, n and $C \in \mathcal{Z}^n$ were arbitrarily chosen, the proof is complete.

Exercise 8.7

a. Define the canonical process through the sequence of functions $z_t(\omega) = \omega_t$, $\omega_t \in \{H, T\}$, $t = 1, 2, \ldots$, and

$$\mathcal{A}^t = \left\{B \in \Omega : B = \left\{\omega : \omega_\tau = a_\tau \in \{H, T\}, \tau \leq t\right\}\right\}.$$

Then we can define the sequence of sigma algebras as

$$\begin{aligned} \mathcal{F}_0 &= \{\emptyset, \Omega\} \\ \mathcal{F}_t &= \sigma\{\mathcal{A}^1, \ldots, \mathcal{A}^t\}, \ t = 1, 2, \ldots, \end{aligned}$$

where $\sigma\{\cdot\}$ is the smallest sigma algebra containing the sets $\mathcal{A}^1, \ldots, \mathcal{A}^t$. So the sigma field generated by $\omega_1, \ldots, \omega_t$ corresponds to the knowledge of the outcomes of the first t trials. Clearly, $\mathcal{F}_t$ is an increasing sequence of sigma algebras, and each function $z_t(\omega)$ is $\mathcal{F}_t$-measurable by construction.

b. We just need to show that the sequence of functions $\sigma_t : \Omega \to \{0, 1\}$, $t = 1, 2, \ldots$, are $\mathcal{F}_t$-measurable. We can redefine σ_t as

$$\begin{aligned} \sigma_t(\omega) &= \chi[z_t(\omega)] \\ &= \chi(\omega_t) = \begin{cases} 1 & \text{if } \omega_t = H \\ 0 & \text{otherwise.} \end{cases} \end{aligned}$$

We need to show that if z_t is $\mathcal{F}_t$-measurable, then σ_t is also $\mathcal{F}_t$-measurable.

To see this, fix $B \in \mathcal{Z}$, and $C \in \{0, 1\}$, then

$$\begin{aligned} \left\{\omega : z_t(\omega) \in B\right\} &= \left\{\omega : \chi[z_t(\omega)] \in C\right\} \\ &= \left\{\omega : z_t(\omega) \in \chi^{-1}(C)\right\} \in \mathcal{F}_t, \end{aligned}$$

$t = 1, 2, \ldots$, and therefore, since χ is $\mathcal{F}_t$-measurable, so is σ_t.

c. Same argument as in part b., but here σ_t being $\mathcal{F}_t$- measurable implies that g_t is $\mathcal{F}_t$-measurable too. This comes from $\mathcal{F}_t \subset \mathcal{F}_{t+1}$ and Exercise 7.12.

Exercise 8.8

a. To show that for $t = 1, 2, \ldots, \mu^t(\cdot, \cdot)$ is a stochastic kernel on $\{Z, \mathcal{Z}^t\}$ we have to show that for each $z_0 \in Z$, $\mu^t(z_0, \cdot)$ is a probability measure on $\{Z^t, \mathcal{Z}^t\}$. By Exercise 8.5, Caratheodory and Hahn Extension Theorems (Theorems 7.2 and 7.3), $\mu^t(z_0, \cdot)$ has a unique extension to a probability measure on $\mathcal{Z}^t$.

In addition, it has to be shown that for each $B \in \mathcal{Z}^t$, $\mu^t(\cdot, B)$ is a $\mathcal{Z}$-measurable function. The proof is by induction.

Let Q be a transition function on $(Z, \mathcal{Z})$. Clearly Q is a stochastic kernel on $(Z, \mathcal{Z})$. For $t = 1$

$$\mu(z_0, A_1) = \int_{A_1} Q(z_0, dz_1)$$

is a measurable function. The result comes from a direct application of Theorem 8.4, with $F(z_0, z_1) = \chi_{A_1}(z_1)$.

Suppose $\mu^{t-1}(\cdot, B)$ is a measurable function. Then, by construction (see part b. of this exercise)

$$\begin{aligned}\mu^t(z_0, B) &= \int_{A_1}\int_{A_2} \cdots \int_{A_t} Q(z_{t-1}, dz_t)Q(z_{t-2}. dz_{t-1}) \ldots Q(z_0. dz_1) \\ &= \int_{A_1} \mu^{t-1}[z_1, (A_2 \times \ldots \times A_t)]Q(z_0, dz_1)\end{aligned}$$

and therefore, by Theorem 8.4, $\mu^t(z_0, B)$ is a measurable function. Because z_0 and B are arbitrary, the proof is complete.

b. This is a consistency property. By definition, for any measurable set $B = (A_1 \times \ldots \times A_{t-1}) \in \mathcal{Z}^{t-1}$

$$\mu^{t-1}(z_0, B) = \int_{A_1} \cdots \int_{A_{t-1}} Q(z_{t-2}, dz_{t-1}) \ldots Q(z_0, dz_1)$$

and

$$Q(z_{t-1}, A_t) = \int_{A_t} Q(z_{t-1}, dz_t).$$

In part a. we proved that $\mu^t(\cdot, \cdot)$ is a stochastic kernel. Hence, by Theorem 8.5 and the definition of $\mu^t(\cdot, \cdot)$,

$$Q \times \mu^{t-1} = \int_{A_1} \dots \int_{A_{t-1}} Q(z_{t-1}, A_t)\mu^{t-1}(z_0, dz^{t-1})$$

$$= \int_{A_1} \dots \int_{A_{t-1}} \int_{A_t} Q(z_{t-1}, dz_t)Q(z_{t-2}, dz_{t-1}) \dots Q(z_0, dz_1)$$

$$= \mu^t(z_0, B \times A_t).$$

Equivalently, for any measurable set $\hat{B} = (A_2 \times \dots \times A_t) \in \mathcal{Z}^{t-1}$

$$\mu^{t-1}(z_1, \hat{B}) = \int_{A_2} \dots \int_{A_t} Q(z_{t-1}, dz_t) \dots Q(z_1, dz_2).$$

Hence by Theorem 8.5,

$$\mu^{t-1} \times Q = \int_{A_1} \mu^{t-1}(z_1, \hat{B})Q(z_0, dz_1)$$

$$= \int_{A_1} \dots \int_{A_{t-1}} \int_{A_t} Q(z_{t-1}, dz_t)Q(z_{t-2}, dz_{t-1}) \dots Q(z_0, dz_1)$$

$$= \mu^t(z_0, A_1 \times \hat{B})$$

and the desired result holds for $B \times A_t = A_1 \times \hat{B}$.

c. This should be read as a Corollary of Theorems 8.6 to 8.8. For $t = 2$ the results come from a direct application of Theorems 8.6 to 8.8. For $t > 2$ results follow from the application of the aforementioned theorems plus the properties of μ^t shown in part b.

Exercise 8.9

a. Let E_x be the x section of $E \subseteq Z = X \times Y$. By Theorem 7.14, if E in Z is $\mathcal{Z}$-measurable, then every section of E is measurable, and $\nu(E_x)$ is a well-defined function of x.

Next, we must show that $\lambda(A \times B) = \mu(A)\nu(B)$ is a measure on $\mathcal{Z}$. Clearly λ is nonnegative, and $\lambda(\emptyset) = 0$. It remains to show countable additivity. Let $\{E^j \in \mathcal{Z}, j \in \mathbf{N}\}$ be a disjoint collection, such that there exist sets $A^j \in \mathcal{X}$ and $B^j \in \mathcal{Y}$ with $E^j = A^j \times B^j$; and suppose $E = \cup_j E^j \in \mathcal{Z}$, such that there exist sets A and B with $E = A \times B$. Any point $(x, y) \in A \times B$ belongs to one and only one of the sets $A^j \times B^j$, so that for any $x \in A$, the sets of the subcollection $\{B^j\}$ for which $x \in A^j$ must constitute a partition of B. Hence,

$$\nu(E_x) = \nu\left[\left(\cup_j E^j\right)_x\right] = \nu\left[\cup_j \left(E^j\right)_x\right] = \sum_j \chi_{A^j}(x)\nu(B^j),$$

where we used the fact that B^j are disjoint sets, so we can use the additivity of ν. Since we can write

$$\nu(E_x) = \nu(B)\chi_A(x),$$

we get

$$\begin{aligned}\lambda(E) &= \mu(A)\nu(B)\\ &= \int \nu(E_x)\mu(dx)\\ &= \int \left(\sum_j \chi_{A^j}(x)\nu(B^j)\right)\mu(dx)\\ &= \sum_j \mu(A^j)\nu(B^j) = \sum_j \lambda(E^j),\end{aligned}$$

as required.

Finally, the products $A^j \times B^k$ for $\{A^j\}$ and $\{B^k\}$ as above decompose $X \times Y$ into measurable rectangles of finite measure. Hence, by Theorem 7.13, Theorem 7.2 (Caratheodory Extension Theorem) and Theorem 7.3 (Hahn Extension Theorem), there exists a unique probability measure λ on $(X \times Y, \mathcal{X} \times \mathcal{Y})$ such that $\lambda(A \times B) = \mu(A)\nu(B)$, all $A \in \mathcal{X}$, $B \in \mathcal{Y}$.

b. Let $E = (A \times B) \in (\mathcal{X} \times \mathcal{Y})$. By Theorem 7.14, $F_x(y) = F(x, y)$ is $\mathcal{Y}$-measurable with respect to y for each $x \in X$, and $F_y(x) = F(x, y)$ is $\mathcal{X}$-measurable with respect to x for each $y \in Y$.

Let $F(x, y) \geq 0$. Then, since the function $F(x, y)$ is $\mathcal{Y}$-measurable for each x, the integral

$$\int_Y F(x, y)\nu(dy)$$

is well defined. Next, we will show that this integral is an $\mathcal{X}$-measurable function and

$$\int_X \left[\int_Y F(x, y)\nu(dy)\right]\mu(dx) = \int_{X\times Y} F(x, y)\lambda(dx \times dy).$$

Consider first $F(x, y) = \chi_{A\times B}(x, y)$, $A \in \mathcal{X}$, $B \in \mathcal{Y}$. Then, since $\chi_{A\times B}(x, y) = \chi_A(x)\chi_B(y)$, we have

$$\int_Y \chi_{A\times B}(x, y)\nu(dy) = \chi_A(x) \int_Y \chi_B(y)\nu(dy)$$

and consequently the integral on the left is an $\mathcal{X}$-measurable function. Clearly the same result holds if F is an indicator function for a finite union of disjoint measurable rectangles.

Let

$$\mathcal{E} = \left\{E \in \mathcal{X} \times \mathcal{Y} : \int_Y \chi_E(x, y)\nu(dy) \text{ is } \mathcal{X}\text{-measurable}\right\},$$

we need to show that $\mathcal{E}$ is a monotone class. Then, it will follow from the Monotone Class Lemma that $\mathcal{E} = \mathcal{X} \times \mathcal{Y}$.

Let $\{E_n\}$ be an increasing sequence of sets in $\mathcal{E}$, with $E = \cup_{n=1}^{\infty} E_n$. Then

$$\left\{\int_Y \chi_{E_n}(x, y)\nu(dy)\right\}_{n=1}^{\infty}$$

is an increasing sequence of $\mathcal{X}$-measurable functions, converging pointwise to

$$\int_Y \chi_E(x, y)\nu(dy).$$

Hence

$$\int_Y \chi_E(x, y)\nu(dy)$$

is also $\mathcal{X}$-measurable. A similar argument holds if $\{E_n\}$ is a decreasing sequence. Hence $\mathcal{E}$ is a monotone class.

If $F(x, y)$ is an arbitrary nonnegative $\mathcal{X}$-measurable function, the $\mathcal{X}$-measurability of the integral

$$\int_Y F(x, y)\nu(dy)$$

follows from the Monotone Convergence Theorem. A similar argument is valid for

$$\int_X F(x, y)\mu(dx).$$

In part a. we showed that there is a unique probability measure λ on $(X \times Y, \mathcal{X} \times \mathcal{Y})$ such that

$$\lambda(A \times B) = \mu(A)\nu(B), \text{ all } A \in \mathcal{X},\ B \in \mathcal{Y}.$$

If $F(x, y) = \chi_{A\times B}(x, y)$, $A \in \mathcal{X}$, $B \in \mathcal{Y}$, then

$$\int_{X\times Y} \chi_{A\times B}(x, y)\lambda(dx \times dy) = \lambda(A \times B),$$

and since $\chi_{A\times B}(x, y) = \chi_A(x)\chi_B(y)$, we have

$$\begin{aligned}&\int_X \left[\int_Y \chi_{A\times B}(x, y)\nu(dy)\right]\mu(dx)\\ &= \int_X \left[\chi_A(x)\int_Y \chi_B(y)\nu(dy)\right]\mu(dx)\\ &= \mu(A)\nu(B).\end{aligned}$$

Hence, by definition of λ, it follows that the statement we need to prove holds for $F(x, y) = \chi_{A\times B}(x, y)$.

Next, let $F(x, y) = \chi_E(x, y)$, $E \in \mathcal{X} \times \mathcal{Y}$. Let

$$\begin{aligned}\mathcal{F} = \Bigg\{E \in \mathcal{X} \times \mathcal{Y} : &\int_{X\times Y} \chi_E(x, y)\lambda(dx \times dy)\\ &= \int_X \left[\int_Y \chi_E(x, y)\nu(dy)\right]\mu(dx)\\ &= \int_Y \left[\int_X \chi_E(x, y)\mu(dy)\right]\nu(dx)\Bigg\}.\end{aligned}$$

We have shown that $\mathcal{F}$ contains the algebra generated by the measurable rectangles, so it suffices to show that $\mathcal{F}$ is a monotone class, and it will follow from the Monotone Class Lemma that $\mathcal{F} = \mathcal{X} \times \mathcal{Y}$. Let $\{E_n\}$ be an increasing sequence of sets in $\mathcal{F}$, with $E = \cup_{n=1}^{\infty} E_n$. Then $\{\chi_{E_n}\}$ is an increasing sequence of $(\mathcal{X} \times \mathcal{Y})$-measurable functions converging pointwise to χ_E. Then by Theorem 7.4, χ_E is also measurable. Define the functions

$$g_n(x) = \int_Y \chi_{E_n}(x, y)\nu(dy), \quad n = 1, 2, \ldots,$$

and

$$g(x) = \int_Y \chi_E(x, y)\nu(dy).$$

We have shown that those functions are measurable, and so by the Monotone Convergence Theorem, $g_n \to g$ pointwise. Hence,

$$\int_{X\times Y} \chi_{E_n}(x, y)\lambda(dx \times dy) = \int_X \left[\int_Y \chi_{E_n}(x, y)\nu(dy)\right]\mu(dx),$$

$n = 1, 2, \ldots.$

Taking the limit as $n \to \infty$ and applying the Monotone Convergence Theorem to both sides, we find that

$$\begin{aligned}
\int_{X \times Y} \chi_E(x, y)\lambda(dx \times dy) &= \lim_{n\to\infty} \int_{X \times Y} \chi_{E_n}(x, y)\lambda(dx \times dy) \\
&= \lim_{n\to\infty} \int_X \left[\int_Y \chi_{E_n}(x, y)\nu(dy)\right] \mu(dx) \\
&= \lim_{n\to\infty} \int_X g_n(x)\mu(dx) \\
&= \int_X g(x)\mu(dx) \\
&= \int_X \left[\int_Y \chi_E(x, y)\nu(dy)\right] \mu(dx),
\end{aligned}$$

hence $E \in \mathcal{F}$. If $\{E_n\}$ is a decreasing sequence in $\mathcal{F}$, apply the argument above to the increasing sequence $\{E_n^c\}$, and use the fact that $E^c \in \mathcal{F}$. Hence $\mathcal{F}$ is a monotone class. An argument similar to the one used in Theorem 8.3 can be used to extend the result to all measurable simple functions, and then by Theorem 7.5 and the Monotone Convergence Theorem the result is established for all measurable (λ-integrable) functions.

For the case of nonnegative measurable functions F, the only point in the proof above where the integrability of F was used was to infer the existence of an increasing sequence of simple functions converging to F. But if μ and v are σ-finite, then so is λ, and any nonnegative measurable function on $X \times Y$ can be approximated in this way.

Exercise 8.10

First, we will prove that the stated condition holds for all indicator functions of measurable sets, all measurable simple functions, and all measurable functions.

Let $A \in \mathcal{Z}$ a measurable set, and let $f(z) = \chi_A(z)$ then

$$\begin{aligned}
\int_Z \chi_A(z')\, Q(z, dz') &= Q(z, A) \\
&= \mu\left([\Gamma(A)]_z\right) \\
&= \int_W \chi_{\{w \in W : g(z,w) \in A\}}(w)\, \mu(dw),
\end{aligned}$$

so the condition holds for indicator functions of a measurable set. By the linearity of the integral (see Exercise 7.26c.) the result can be extended to all measurable simple functions and finally by Theorem 7.5 and the Monotone Convergence Theorem to all nonnegative $\mathcal{Z}$-measurable functions. The general case is covered by representing f as $f^+ - f^-$ if f is integrable.

Q has the Feller property, if for $z_n \to z$ and a continuous function h, $(Th)(z_n) \to (Th)(z)$.

Fix $w \in W$. If f, g are continuous functions then $h = f \circ g$ is a continuous function too. Hence, if $z_n \to z$, $f[g(z_n, w)] \to f[g(z, w)]$. Define $h_n = f[g(z_n, w)]$, then $h \in C(Z)$. Then, by the Lebesgue Dominated Convergence Theorem,

$$\lim_{n\to\infty} Th_n = \lim_{n\to\infty} \int_W h_n \mu(dw) = \int_W h\mu(dw) = Th.$$

Hence Q has the Feller property.

Exercise 8.11

First, we must show that Q is well defined on $(Z, \mathcal{Z})$, that is, $Q : Z \times \mathcal{Z} \to [0, 1]$. Clearly, Q takes values on $[0, 1]$, and for any $((w, w'), A \times B)$ it is well defined because P is well defined.

Next, we need to show that for each $(w, w') \in W \times W$, $Q[(w, w'), \cdot]$ is a probability measure on $(Z \times \mathcal{Z})$, and that for each $(A \times B) \in \mathcal{Z}$, $Q[\cdot, (A \times B)]$ is a $\mathcal{Z}$-measurable function.

Let $\mathcal{C}$ be the class of all measurable rectangles, and let $\mathcal{E}$ be the algebra consisting of all finite unions of sets in $\mathcal{C}$. Fix (w, w'); then $Q[(w, w'), \cdot]$ defined on $\mathcal{C}$ clearly satisfies the hypothesis of Theorem 7.13 and $Q[(w, w'), W \times W] = 1$. Hence it can be extended to a measure on all of $\mathcal{E}$. Since $\mathcal{Z}$ is the σ-algebra generated by $\mathcal{E}$, it then follows immediately from the Caratheodory and Hahn Extension Theorems that $Q[(w, w'), \cdot]$ has a unique extension to all of $\mathcal{Z}$.

Finally, we must show that for each $C \in \mathcal{Z}$, the function $Q(\cdot, C) : Z \to [0, 1]$ is measurable. Let $\mathcal{S} \subseteq \mathcal{Z}$ be the family of sets for which $Q(\cdot, C)$ is a measurable function. By the Monotone Class Lemma, it suffices to show that $\mathcal{S}$ contains $\mathcal{C}$ and that $\mathcal{S}$ is a monotone class.

Fix $C = (A \times B) \in \mathcal{Z}$. Then we can write Q as

$$Q[(w, w'), A \times B] = P(w, w', B)\chi_A(w'),$$

where χ_A is the indicator function for A. Since $P(\cdot, \cdot, B)$ and χ_A are measurable functions, and since the products of measurable functions are measurable, it follows that $Q[\cdot, A \times B]$ is measurable.

Hence $\mathcal{S}$ contains the measurable rectangles in $\mathcal{Z}$. Using the fact that every set in $\mathcal{C}$ can be written as the finite union of disjoint measurable rectangles, we can conclude that $\mathcal{C} \subseteq \mathcal{Z}$.

In order to show that $\mathcal{S}$ is a monotone class, let $C_1 \subseteq C_2 \subseteq \ldots$ be an increasing sequence of sets in $\mathcal{S}$, with $C = \cup_{i=1}^{\infty} C_i$. Thus, by Theorem 7.1, for each $(w, w') \in Z$,

$$Q[(w, w'), C] = \lim_{n \to \infty} Q[(w, w'), C_n].$$

Hence $Q[(w, w'), C]$ is the pointwise limit of a sequence of measurable functions, and therefore by Theorem 7.4 is measurable. Therefore $C \in \mathcal{S}$. A similar argument applies for decreasing sequences. Therefore $\mathcal{S}$ is a monotone class.

9 Stochastic Dynamic Programming

Exercise 9.1

By definition,

$$
\begin{aligned}
& u\left[C(\pi, z_1), (\pi_0, z_1)\right] \\
&= \lim_{n\to\infty} u_n\left[C(\pi, z_1), (\pi_0, z_1)\right] \\
&= \lim_{n\to\infty} \{F\left[\pi_0, C_0(\pi, z_1), z_1\right] \\
&+ \int_{Z^1} F\left[C_0(\pi, z_1), C_1(z_2; \pi, z_1), z_2\right]\mu^1(z_1, dz_2) \\
&+ \sum_{t=3}^{n} \int_{Z^{t-1}} \beta^{t-1} F\left[C_{t-2}(z_2^{t-1}; \pi, z_1), C_{t-1}(z_2^t; \pi, z_1), z_1\right] \\
&\times \mu^{t-1}(z_1, dz_2^t)\}.
\end{aligned}
$$

By Assumption 9.2, F is measurable. By Theorem 7.14, $C_0(\pi, \cdot)$ and $C_t(z_2^{t-1}; \pi, \cdot)$ are measurable functions of z_1, and then F is a measurable function of z_1 by Exercise 7.31. Therefore, u is a measurable function of z_1. That u is measurable follows from Exercise 7.12.

Exercise 9.2

a. First, notice that by assumption F is bounded and $\mathcal{A}$-measurable, and so it is $\mathcal{Z}$-measurable (see Exercise 7.31). Therefore, $F\left[\pi_{t-1}(z^{t-1}), \pi_t(z^t), z_t\right]$ is $\mu^t(z_0, \cdot)$-integrable, $t = 1, 2, \ldots$

If F is uniformly bounded above,

$$F\left[\pi_{t-1}(z^{t-1}), \pi_t(z^t), z_t\right] \le C, \quad \text{all } z^t \in Z^t, \; t = 1, 2, \ldots,$$

where C is the upper bound. Hence F^+ is bounded and coupled with $0 < \beta < 1$,

$$F^+\left[x_0, \pi_0, z_0\right]$$
$$+ \lim_{n\to\infty} \textstyle\sum_{t=1}^{n} \int_{Z^t} \beta^t F^+ \left[\pi_{t-1}(z^{t-1}), \pi_t(z^t), z_t\right] \mu^t(z_0, dz^t)$$
$$\leq \frac{C}{1-\beta} < \infty,$$

and hence the limit exists (although it may be minus infinity).

An analogous proof applies if F is uniformly bounded below. Hence, $u(\pi, s_0) = \lim_{n\to\infty} u_n(\pi, s_0)$ is well defined.

If in addition, Assumption 9.1 holds, then by Lemma 9.1, $\Pi(s_0)$ is non-empty for all s_0, and therefore $\sup_{\pi\in\Pi(s)} u(\pi, s)$ exists, so v^* is well defined.

b. The proof of Theorem 9.2 remains the same, but now the part a. of this exercise (instead of Assumption 9.2) provides the justification needed to take the limit of $u_n(\pi, s_0)$ in the first part of the proof.

In order to show that Lemma 9.3 still holds, let $(x_0, z_0) = s_0 \in S$ and $\pi \in \Pi(s_0)$ be given and suppose F is uniformly bounded above. Then $u(\pi, s_0)$ is well defined, and we can write (10) in the text as

$$u(\pi, s_0) = F(x_0, \pi_0, z_0)$$
$$+ \lim_{n\to\infty} \sum_{t=1}^{n} \int_{Z^t} \beta^t F \left[\pi_{t-1}(z^{t-1}), \pi_t(z^t), z_t\right] \mu^t(z_0, dz^t).$$

We wish to make use of the Monotone Convergence Theorem to justify exchanging the order of limit and integration. Toward this, we split F into its positive and negative parts. The second term on the right can then be re-expressed as

$$\lim_{n\to\infty} \int_Z \beta F^+ \left[\pi_0, \pi_1(z_1), z_1\right] Q(z_0, dz_1)$$
$$+ \lim_{n\to\infty} \int_Z \left\{\sum_{t=2}^{n} \int_{Z^{t-1}} \beta^t F^+[\pi_{t-1}(z^{t-1}), \pi_t(z^t), z_t] \mu^{t-1}(z_1, dz_2^t)\right\}$$
$$\times Q(z_0, dz_1) - \lim_{n\to\infty} \int_Z \beta F^- \left[\pi_0, \pi_1(z_1), z_1\right] Q(z_0, dz_1)$$
$$- \lim_{n\to\infty} \int_Z \left\{\sum_{t=2}^{n} \int_{Z^{t-1}} \beta^t F^-[\pi_{t-1}(z^{t-1}), \pi_t(z^t), z_t] \mu^{t-1}(z_1, dz_2^t)\right\}$$
$$\times Q(z_0, dz_1).$$

We then use the upper bound on F and the fact that $0 < \beta < 1$ to make sure the limits exist and u is well defined. By the Monotone Convergence Theorem, the above expression then equals

$$\int_Z \lim_{n\to\infty} \beta F^+ \left[\pi_0, \pi_1(z_1), z_1\right] Q(z_0, dz_1)$$

$$+ \int_Z \lim_{n\to\infty} \left\{ \sum_{t=2}^{n} \int_{Z^{t-1}} \beta^t F^+[\pi_{t-1}(z^{t-1}), \pi_t(z^t), z_t] \mu^{t-1}(z_1, dz_2^t) \right\}$$

$$\times Q(z_0, dz_1) - \int_Z \lim_{n\to\infty} \beta F^- \left[\pi_0, \pi_1(z_1), z_1\right] Q(z_0, dz_1)$$

$$- \int_Z \lim_{n\to\infty} \left\{ \sum_{t=2}^{n} \int_{Z^{t-1}} \beta^t F^-[\pi_{t-1}(z^{t-1}), \pi_t(z^t), z_t] \mu^{t-1}(z_1, dz_2^t) \right\}$$

$$\times Q(z_0, dz_1),$$

which equals

$$\beta \int_Z u\left[C(\pi, z_1), (\pi_0, z_1)\right] Q(z_0, dz_1).$$

by the definition of u. A similar argument applies if F is uniformly bounded below. Substituting into (10) above gives the desired result.

Finally, Theorem 9.4 remains intact, because the assumptions made about F and β enter into the proof only through Theorem 9.2 and Lemma 9.3.

Exercise 9.3

Choose a measurable selection h from Γ. Fix $s_0 = (x_0, z_0) \in S$, and define π by

$$\pi_0 = h(s_0)$$

$$\pi_t(z^t) = h[x_t^\pi(z^t), z_t]$$

$$= h[\phi(x_{t-1}^\pi(z^{t-1}), \pi_{t-1}(z^{t-1}), z_t), z_t],$$

for all $z^t \in Z^t$; $t = 1, 2, \ldots$.

Clearly π satisfies (1a′) and (1b′) and π_0 is measurable. That each π_t is measurable for all t then follows by induction from the fact that ϕ is measurable and compositions of measurable functions are measurable (see Exercise 7.31). Since s_0 was arbitrarily chosen, the proof is complete.

Exercise 9.4

Notice that under Assumptions 9.1′ and 9.2′, v^* is well defined. Hence, in order to show that $v = v^*$ we have to show that

$$v(s) \geq u(\pi, s), \quad \text{all } \pi \in \Pi(s) \text{ and}$$
$$v(s) = \lim_{k\to\infty} u(\pi^k, s), \quad \text{for some sequence } \{\pi^k\}_{k=1}^{\infty} \text{ in } \Pi(s).$$

Choose any $s_0 = (x_0, z_0) \in S$. Then for any $\pi \in \Pi(s_0)$,

$$\begin{aligned} v(s_0) &= \sup_{y\in\Gamma(s_0)} \left\{F(x_0, y, z_0) + \beta \int_Z v[\phi(x_0, y, z_1), z_1]Q(z_0, dz_1)\right\} \\ &\geq F(x_0, \pi_0, z_0) + \beta \int_Z v[\phi(x_0, \pi_0, z_1), z_1]Q(z_0, dz_1) \\ &= u_0(\pi, s_0) + \beta \int_Z v[\phi(x_0, \pi_0, z_1), z_1]\mu^1(z_0, dz^1), \end{aligned}$$

where the second line used the fact that π is feasible from s_0, and the third uses the definitions of u_0 and μ^1. Iterating on this process, gives

$$\begin{aligned} &u_0(\pi, s_0) + \beta \int_Z v[\phi(x_0, \pi_0, z_1), z_1]\mu^1(z_0, dz^1) \\ &= u_0(\pi, s_0) + \beta \int_Z \sup_{y\in\Gamma[x_1^\pi(z^1), z_1]} F[x_1^\pi(z^1), y, z_1]\mu^1(z_0, dz^1) \\ &\quad + \beta \int_Z v[\phi(x_1^\pi(z^1), y, z_2), z_2]Q(z_1, dz_2)\mu^1(z_0, dz^1) \\ &\geq u_0(\pi, s_0) + \beta \int_Z F[x_1^\pi(z^1), \pi_1(z^1), z_1]\mu^1(z_0, dz^1) \\ &\quad + \beta \int_Z v[\phi(x_1^\pi(z^1), \pi_1(z^1), z_2), z_2]Q(z_1, dz_2)\mu^1(z_0, dz^1) \\ &= u_1(\pi, s_0) + \beta^2 \int_{Z^2} v[\phi(x_1^\pi(z^1), \pi_1(z^1), z_2), z_2]\mu^2(z_0, dz^2), \end{aligned}$$

where the last line uses the definition of u_1 and that the two integrals can be combined into one (see Exercise 8.8). Therefore, it follows by induction that

$$v(s_0) \geq u_n(\pi, s_0) + \beta^{n+1} \int_{Z^{n+1}} v[\phi(x_n^\pi(z^n), \pi_n(z^n), z_{n+1}), z_{n+1}]$$
$$\times \mu^{n+1}(z_0, dz^{n+1}),$$

$n = 1, 2, 3, \ldots.$

Taking the limit as $n \to \infty$ and using (7′) we obtain that

$$v(s_0) \geq u(\pi, s_0),$$

and since $\pi \in \Pi(s_0)$ was arbitrary, $v(s) \geq u(\pi, s)$, for all $\pi \in \Pi(s)$.

To show that the second condition is also satisfied, let π^* be any plan generated by G from s_0. If G is nonempty and permits at least one measurable selection, there is at least one such plan. Then repeating the argument above with equality at every step, we can show that $v(s) = \lim_{k\to\infty} u(\pi^k, s)$ for the sequence $\pi^k = \pi^*$, $k = 1, 2, \ldots.$

Since $s_0 \in S$ was arbitrary, this establishes that $v = v^*$.

Exercise 9.5

a. Let $(x_0, z_0) = s_0 \in S$ and $\pi \in \Pi(s_0)$ be given and suppose that $F \geq 0$. Under Assumption 9.2′, $u(\pi, s_0)$ is well defined, and

$$u(\pi, s_0)$$
$$= F(x_0, \pi_0, z_0) + \lim_{n\to\infty} \sum_{t=1}^{n} \int_{Z^t} \beta^t F\left[x_t^\pi(z^t), \pi_t(z^t), z_t\right] \mu^t(z_0, dz^t).$$

For the second term on the right we have

$$\lim_{n\to\infty} \sum_{t=1}^{n} \int_{Z^t} \beta^t F[x_t^\pi(z^t), \pi_t(z^t), z_t]\mu^t(z_0, dz^t)$$
$$= \int_Z \lim_{n\to\infty} \beta F[x_1^\pi(z^1), \pi_1(z_1), z_1] Q(z_0, dz_1)$$
$$+ \int_Z \lim_{n\to\infty} \left\{ \sum_{t=2}^{n} \int_{Z^{t-1}} \beta^t F[x_t^\pi(z^t), \pi_t(z^t), z_t]\mu^{t-1}(z_1, dz_2^t) \right\}$$
$$\times Q(z_0, dz_1)$$

$$= \int_Z \beta \lim_{n\to\infty} F[x_1^\pi(z^1), C_0(\pi, z_1), z_1]Q(z_0, dz_1)$$

$$+ \int_{Z^1} \beta \lim_{n\to\infty} F[\phi[x_1^\pi(z^1), C_0(\pi, z_1), z_1], C_1(z_2; \pi, z_1), z_2]$$

$$\times \mu^1(z_1, dz_2)Q(z_0, dz_1)$$

$$+ \sum_{t=3}^{n} \int_{Z^{t-1}} \beta^t F[\phi[x_{t-1}^\pi(z^{t-1}), C_{t-2}(z_2^{t-1}; \pi, z_1), z_t],$$

$$C_{t-1}(z_2^t; \pi, z_1), z_t]\mu^{t-1}(z_1, dz_2^t)Q(z_0, dz_1)$$

$$= \beta \int_Z u[C(\pi, z_1), (x_1^\pi(z_1), z_1)]Q(z_0, dz_1),$$

where the steps are justified as in Lemma 9.3 in the text. Hence, substituting into the original equation the desired result follows.

If $F \le 0$, a similar argument can be applied to the function $-F$.

If F takes on both signs, then we can make use of Assumption 9.3′, and define the sequence of functions $\hat{H}_n(z_1) : Z \to \mathbf{R}$ by

$$\hat{H}_n(z_1) = \beta F\left[x_1^\pi(z^1), \pi_1(z_1), z_1\right]$$

$$+ \sum_{t=2}^{n} \int_{Z^{t-1}} \beta^t F\left[x_t^\pi(z^t), \pi_t(z^t), z_t\right] \mu^t(z_1, dz_2^t),$$

$n = 2, 3, \ldots,$ and Assumption 9.3′ implies that there exists a constant $\bar{L} = \sum_{t=0}^{\infty} \beta^t L_t(s_0)$ such that $\left|\hat{H}_n(z_1)\right| \le \bar{L}$, all $z_1 \in Z$, all n. Hence, as in Lemma 9.3, we can use the Lebesgue Dominated Convergence Theorem to justify the change in the order of limit and integration.

b. Let π^* be a plan that attains the supremum in (2). Since G is defined by (6′), it is sufficient to show that

$$v^*(s_0) = F(x_0, \pi_0^*, z_0) + \beta \int_Z v^*[x_1^{\pi^*}(z_1), z_1]Q(z_0, dz_1)$$

and

$$v^*(x_t^{\pi^*}, z_t) = F[x_t^{\pi^*}(z^t), \pi_t^*(z^t), z_t]$$

$$+ \beta \int_Z v^*[x_{t+1}^{\pi^*}(z^{t+1}), z_{t+1}]Q(z_t, dz_{t+1}),$$

$$\mu^t(z_0, \cdot)\text{-a.e., } t = 1, 2, \ldots.$$

To show that the first equation holds, notice that by hypothesis π^* satisfies

$$v^*(s_0) = u(\pi^*, s_0) \geq u(\pi, s_0), \quad \text{all } \pi \in \Pi(s_0).$$

Therefore, using the result shown in part a., we can write the above expression as

$$F(x_0, \pi_0^*, z_0) + \beta \int_Z u[C(\pi^*, z_1), (x_1^{\pi^*}(z_1), z_1)]Q(z_0, dz_1)$$

$$\geq F(x_0, \pi_0, z_0) + \beta \int_Z u[C(\pi, z_1), (x_1^{\pi}(z_1), z_1)]Q(z_0, dz_1),$$

for all $\pi \in \Pi(s_0)$. In particular, the above inequality holds for any plan $\pi \in \Pi(s_0)$, with $\pi_0 = \pi_0^*$. Next, choose a measurable selection g from G, and define the plan $\pi^g \in \Pi(s_0)$ as follows:

$$\pi_0^g = \pi_0^*,$$

$$\pi_t^g(z^t) = g[x_t^{\pi^g}(z^t), z_t], \quad \text{all } z^t \in Z^t,\ t = 1, 2, \ldots.$$

For each $z_1 \in Z$, the continuation $C(\pi^g, z_1)$ is a plan generated by G from $(\phi(x_0, \pi_0^*, z_1), z_1)$. Hence, $C(\pi^g, z_1)$ attains the supremum in (2) for $s = (\phi(x_0, \pi_0^*, z_1), z_1)$ (see Exercise 9.4). That is,

$$v^*[x_1^{\pi^*}(z_1), z_1] = u[C(\pi^g, z_1), (x_1^{\pi^*}(z_1), z_1)] \geq u[\pi, (x_1^{\pi^*}(z_1), z_1)],$$

all $\pi \in \Pi(x_1^{\pi^*}(z_1), z_1)$, all $z_1 \in Z$. In particular, since $C(\pi^*, z_1) \in \Pi(x_1^{\pi^*}(z_1), z_1)$, all $z_1 \in Z$, the equation above implies that

$$u[C(\pi^g, z_1), (x_1^{\pi^*}(z_1), z_1)] \geq u[C(\pi^*, z_1), (x_1^{\pi^*}(z_1), z_1)], \quad \text{all } z_1 \in Z;$$

and since $\pi^g \in \Pi(s_0)$ and $\pi_0^g = \pi_0^*$,

$$\int_Z u[C(\pi^*, z_1), (x_1^{\pi^*}(z_1), z_1)]Q(z_0, dz_1)$$

$$\geq \int_Z u[C(\pi^g, z_1), (x_1^{\pi^*}(z_1), z_1)]Q(z_0, dz_1).$$

By Exercise 7.24, these two inequalities together imply that

$$u[C(\pi^g, z_1), (x_1^{\pi^*}(z_1), z_1)] = u[C(\pi^*, z_1), (x_1^{\pi^*}(z_1), z_1)], \quad Q(z_0, \cdot)\text{-a.e.}$$

It then follows that

$$v^*[x_1^{\pi^*}(z_1), z_1] = u[C(\pi^*, z_1), (x_1^{\pi^*}(z_1), z_1)], \quad Q(z_0, \cdot)\text{-a.e.}$$

Hence,

$$\begin{aligned} v^*(s_0) &= u(\pi^*, s_0) \\ &= F(x_0, \pi_0^*, z_0) + \beta \int_Z u[C(\pi^*, z_1), (x_1^{\pi^*}(z_1), z_1)]Q(z_0, dz_1) \\ &= F(x_0, \pi_0^*, z_0) + \beta \int_Z v^*[x_1^{\pi^*}(z_1), z_1]Q(z_0, dz_1), \end{aligned}$$

where the second line uses the result obtained in part a. and the last uses Exercise 7.24.

Using an analogous argument, with

$$v^*[x_1^{\pi^*}(z_1), z_1] = u[C(\pi^*, z_1), (x_1^{\pi^*}(z_1), z_1)], \quad Q(z_0, \cdot)\text{ -a.e.}$$

as the starting point, we can show the second equation at the beginning holds for $t = 1$, and continue by induction.

Exercise 9.6

To see that Assumption 9.1 is satisfied, notice that by Assumption 9.6, Γ is nonempty valued. Assumptions 9.4, 9.5 and 9.6 imply that the graph of Γ is $(\mathcal{X} \times \mathcal{X} \times \mathcal{Z})$-measurable. To see this, recall that, A, the graph of Γ, is defined by

$$A = \{(x, y, z) \in X \times X \times Z : y \in \Gamma(x, z)\}.$$

We need to show that $A \in \mathcal{X} \times \mathcal{X} \times \mathcal{Z}$.

Let Z be countable. Then $A = A_1 \cup A_2 \cup A_3 \cup \ldots$, where

$$A_i = \hat{A}_i \times \{z_i\}, \quad i = 1, 2, \ldots,$$

and $\hat{A}_i = \{(x, y) \in X \times X : y \in \Gamma(x, z_i)\}$.

By Assumption 9.6, for z fixed, Γ is continuous. But if $\hat{A}_i \in \mathcal{X} \times \mathcal{X}$ for $i = 1, 2, \ldots$, then $A_i \in \mathcal{X} \times \mathcal{X} \times \mathcal{Z}$, and so is its countable union. The extension of this result for the case when Z is a compact (Borel) set in $\mathbf{R}^k$ is similar to the second part of the proof of Theorem 8.9.

As Γ is continuous by Assumption 9.6, it is upper hemi-continuous. As it is compact valued, Theorem 7.6 applies and it has a measurable selection.

To see that Assumption 9.2 holds, note that, because F is continuous, it is measurable with respect to the Borel sets, and so it is $\mathcal{A}$-measurable (see

Exercise 7.10). Assumption 9.7 assures that $F[\pi_{t-1}(z^{t-1}), \pi_t(z^t), z_t]$ is $\mu^t(z_0, \cdot)$-integrable for $t = 1, 2, \ldots$, and that the limit

$$F[x_0, \pi_0, z_0] + \lim_{n\to\infty} \sum_{t=1}^{n} \int_{Z^t} \beta^t F[\pi_{t-1}(z^{t-1}), \pi_t(z^t), z_t]\mu^t(z_0, dz^t)$$

exists (see Exercise 9.2). Therefore Assumption 9.2 holds.

Finally, Assumption 9.7 says that $\left|F[\pi_{t-1}(z^{t-1}), \pi_t(z^t), z_t]\right| \le B < \infty$ for all t. Hence defining $L_t(s_0) = B$ for all t, and using the fact that $0 < \beta < 1$, Assumption 9.3 is satisfied.

Exercise 9.7

a. The proof that Assumption 9.1′ holds parallels the one presented in Exercise 9.6, but in addition it must be proved that the function $\phi : D \times Z \to X$ is measurable. With Assumptions 9.16 and 9.17 at hand the result obtained in Exercise 7.10 applies, which completes the proof that Assumption 9.1′ is satisfied.

The proofs needed to show that Assumptions 9.2′ and 9.3′ hold are a straightforward adaptation of the ones developed in Exercise 9.6.

b. Let $u = (x, y)$ and define $\psi(u, z') = f[\phi(u, z'), z']$ as in the proof of Lemma 9.5′. Since $f \in C(S)$ and ϕ is continuous, then $\psi \in C(S)$. The rest of the proof is similar to the proof of Theorem 9.6, with ψ playing the role of f.

c. Under the stated assumptions, an argument analogous to the one used in Theorem 9.7 in the text applies. To see this, fix $z \in Z$. Let $f(\cdot, z) \in C'(S)$ and take $x_1, x_2 \in X$, with $x_1 > x_2$. Also, let $y_i \in \Gamma(x_i, z)$ attain the supremum in

$$(Tf)(x_i, z) = \sup_{y\in\Gamma(x_i,z)} \left\{F(x_i, y, z) + \beta \int f[\phi(x_i, y, z'), z']Q(z, dz')\right\}.$$

Then

$$\begin{aligned}(Tf)(x_1, z) &= F(x_1, y_1, z) + \beta \int f[\phi(x_1, y_1, z'), z']Q(z, dz') \\ &\ge F(x_1, y_2, z) + \beta \int f[\phi(x_1, y_2, z'), z']Q(z, dz') \\ &> F(x_2, y_2, z) + \beta \int f[\phi(x_2, y_2, z'), z']Q(z, dz') \\ &= (Tf)(x_2, z),\end{aligned}$$

where the second line uses Assumption 9.9 and the fact that y_1 maximizes the right-hand side, and the third line uses Assumptions 9.8 and 9.9 and ϕ nondecreasing. Hence $(Tf)(\cdot, z)$ is strictly increasing.

d. The first part of the proof is similar to the proof of Theorem 9.8 in the text. The only difference is the proof that $T[C'(S)] \subseteq C''(S)$, where $C'(S)$ and $C''(S)$ are defined as in the proof of Theorem 9.8. In order to show this, let $f \in C'(S)$ and let $x_0 \neq x_1$, $\theta \in (0, 1)$, and $x_\theta = \theta x_0 + (1-\theta)x_1$. Let $y_i \in \Gamma(x_i, z)$ attain $(Tf)(x_i, z)$ for $i = 0, 1$. Then by Assumption 9.10, $y_\theta = \theta y_0 + (1-\theta)y_1 \in \Gamma(x_\theta, z)$. It follows that

$$
\begin{aligned}
&(Tf)(x_\theta, z) \\
&\geq F(x_\theta, y_\theta, z) + \beta \int_Z f[\phi(x_\theta, y_\theta, z'), z']Q(z, dz') \\
&> \theta\left[F(x_0, y_0, z) + \beta \int_Z f[\phi(x_0, y_0, z'), z']Q(z, dz')\right] \\
&\quad + (1-\theta)\left[F(x_1, y_1, z) + \beta \int_Z f[\phi(x_1, y_1, z'), z']Q(z, dz')\right] \\
&= \theta(Tf)(x_0, z) + (1-\theta)(Tf)(x_1, z),
\end{aligned}
$$

where the first line uses (7) and the fact that $y_\theta \in \Gamma(x_\theta, z)$; the second line the hypothesis that f is concave, and the concavity restriction on F in Assumption 9.10 and the assumption that $\phi(\cdot, \cdot, z')$ is concave. Since x_0 and x_1 were arbitrary, it follows that Tf is strictly concave, and since f was arbitrary, that $T[C'(S)] \subseteq C''(S)$. Hence, the unique fixed point v is strictly concave. Since F is strictly concave (Assumption 9.10) and, for each $s \in S$, $\Gamma(s)$ is convex (Assumption 9.11), it follows that the maximum in (7) is attained at a unique y value. Hence G is a single-valued function. The continuity of G then follows from the fact that it is u.h.c. by the Theorem of the Maximum (Theorem 3.6).

e. Let $C''(S) \subseteq C'(S)$ be as defined in the proof of Theorem 9.8. As shown in part d., $T[C'(S)] \subseteq C''(S)$ and $v \in C''(S)$. Let $v_0 \in C'(S)$, and define the functions $\{f_n\}$ and f by

$$f_n(x, y, z) = F(x, y, z) + \beta \int_Z v_n[\phi(x, y, z'), z']Q(z, dz'),$$

$n = 1, 2, \ldots,$ and

$$f(x, y, z) = F(x, y, z) + \beta \int_Z v[\phi(x, y, z'), z']Q(z, dz').$$

Since $v_0 \in C'(S)$, each function v_n, $n = 1, 2, \ldots$, is in $C''(S)$, as is v. Hence for any $s \in S = X \times Z$, the functions $\{f_n(s, \cdot)\}$ and $f(s, \cdot)$ are all strictly concave in y, and so Theorem 3.8 applies.

f. Fix z_0. Let $(x_0, z_0) \in \text{int } X \times Z$ and $g(x_0, z_0) \in \text{int } \Gamma(x_0, z_0)$. Then, there is some open neighborhood D of x_0 such that $g(x_0, z_0) \in \text{int } \Gamma(x, z_0)$, all $x \in D$. Hence we can define $W : D \to R$ by

$$W(x) = F[x, g(x_0, z_0), z_0] + \beta \int v[\phi(g(x_0, z_0), z'), z']Q(z_0, dz').$$

As F, v and ϕ are concave, W is concave, continuously differentiable on D and

$$W(x) \leq v(x, z_0), \quad \text{all } x \in D,$$

with equality at x_0. Hence Theorem 4.10 applies and the desired result follows.

g. In order to show that $v(x, z)$ is strictly increasing in z, we need to make the additional assumption that ϕ is nondecreasing in z.

Paralleling Theorem 9.11, it is enough to show that $T[C'(S)] \subseteq C''(S)$, where $C'(S)$ and $C''(S)$ are defined as in Theorem 9.11. Fix $x \in X$. Assume $f \in C'(S)$, and choose $z_1 < z_2$. As before, let $y_i \in \Gamma(x, z_i)$ attain the supremum in

$$(Tf)(x, z_i) = \sup_{y \in \Gamma(x, z_i)} \left\{ F(x, y, z_i) + \beta \int f[\phi(x, y, z'), z']Q(z_i, dz') \right\}.$$

Hence,

$$\begin{aligned}
(Tf)(x, z_1) &= F(x, y_1, z_1) + \beta \int f[\phi(x, y_1, z'), z']Q(z_1, dz') \\
&< F(x, y_1, z_2) + \beta \int f[\phi(x, y_1, z'), z']Q(z_2, dz') \\
&\leq F(x, y_2, z_2) + \beta \int f[\phi(x, y_2, z'), z']Q(z_2, dz') \\
&= (Tf)(x, z_2),
\end{aligned}$$

where the second line uses Assumptions 9.13, 9.15 and the added assumption about ϕ, and the third line uses Assumption 9.14. Hence, $(Tf)(x, \cdot)$ is strictly increasing.

Exercise 9.8

To see that Assumption 9.1 holds, note that Assumption 9.19 implies that Γ is nonempty, while Assumptions 9.5 and 9.18 imply that A is $(\mathcal{X} \times \mathcal{X} \times \mathcal{Z})$ measurable. In addition, Assumptions 9.5, 9.18 and 9.19 imply that the assumptions of Theorem 7.6 (Measurable Selection Theorem) are satisfied. Hence, Γ has a measurable selection.

To show that Assumption 9.2 holds, notice that under assumption 9.1 $\mathcal{A} = \{C \in \mathcal{X} \times \mathcal{X} \times \mathcal{Z} : C \subseteq A\}$ is a σ-algebra, and by Assumption 9.20 $F : A \to R$ is $\mathcal{A}$-measurable (see Exercise 7.10).

We showed already that $\|x_t\|_l \leq \alpha^t \|x_0\|_l$, $t = 1, 2, \ldots$ (see Exercise 4.6). Hence for any $\pi \in \Pi(s_0)$, all $s_0 \in S$, by Assumption 9.19 and 9.20 is it straightforward that

$$\left|F[\pi_{t-1}(z^{t-1}), \pi_t(z^t), z_t]\right| \leq \alpha^t B(1+\alpha) \|x_0\|_l,$$

all $z^t \in Z^t$, $t = 1, 2, \ldots$.

Therefore, for all $t = 1, 2, \ldots$, the positive and negative parts of F are bounded and then $F[\pi_{t-1}(z^{t-1}), \pi_t(z^t), z_t]$ is $\mu^t(z_0, \cdot)$-integrable (see Exercises 7.25 and 7.26). Finally, by the bound imposed on F for each t, and the fact that $\alpha \in (0, \beta^{-1})$,

$$\begin{aligned} & F[x_0, \pi_0, z_0] + \lim_{n\to\infty} \sum_{t=1}^{n} \int_{Z^t} \beta^t F[\pi_{t-1}(z^{t-1}), \pi_t(z^t), z_t]\mu^t(z_0, dz^t) \\ & \leq F[x_0, \pi_0, z_0] + \lim_{n\to\infty} \sum_{t=1}^{n} (\beta\alpha)^t B(1+\alpha) \|x_0\|_l \leq \infty. \end{aligned}$$

Hence, the limit exists. Therefore Assumption 9.2 is satisfied. Moreover, the limit is finite.

Define $L_t(s_0) = \alpha^t B(1+\alpha) \|x_0\|_l$. Then, using the results above, Assumption 9.3 is clearly satisfied.

Exercise 9.9

To show that $M : H(S) \to H(S)$, first note that if f is homogeneous of degree one,

$$\begin{aligned}(Mf)(\lambda y, z) &= \int f(\lambda y, z')Q(z, dz') \\ &= \int \lambda f(y, z')Q(z, dz') \\ &= \lambda \int f(y, z')Q(z, dz') \\ &= \lambda(Mf)(y, z),\end{aligned}$$

hence Mf is homogeneous of degree one.

To prove that Mf is a continuous function, notice that the proof of Lemma 9.5 applies with the obvious change of norm for $H(S)$.

To show that the operator M preserves quasi-concavity, choose $y_1, y_2 \in X$, with $y_1 \neq y_2$ and $f(y_1, z) > f(y_2, z)$. If f is quasi-concave, then for $\theta \in (0, 1)$, $f[\theta y_1 + (1-\theta)y_2, z] \geq f(y_2, z)$. Then,

$$\begin{aligned}(Mf)[\theta y_1 + (1-\theta)y_2, z] &= \int f[\theta y_1 + (1-\theta)y_2, z']Q(z, dz') \\ &\geq \int f(y_2, z')Q(z, dz') \\ &= (Mf)(y_2, z),\end{aligned}$$

all $z \in Z$, all $\theta \in (0, 1)$. If f is strictly quasi-concave, then the inequality above is also strict.

Exercise 9.10

a. The proofs that $H(S)$ is a complete metric space and $T : H(S) \to H(S)$ parallel that of Exercise 4.7. Define T as

$$Tf(x, z) = \sup_{y \in \Gamma(x,z)} \left\{ F(x, y, z) + \beta \int_Z f(y, z')Q(z, dz') \right\}.$$

Choose $f, g \in H(S)$ and $f \leq g$. Clearly $Tf \leq Tg$, so T satisfies the monotonicity property. Similarly, choose $f \in H(S)$ and $a > 0$. Then

$$\begin{aligned}
&T(f + a)(x, z) \\
&= \sup_{y \in \Gamma(x,z)} \left\{ F(x, y, z) + \beta \int_Z [f(y, z') + a] Q(z, dz') \right\} \\
&= \sup_{y \in \Gamma(x,z)} \left\{ F(x, y, z) + \beta \int_Z f(y, z') Q(z, dz') + \beta a \|y\| \right\} \\
&\leq \sup_{y \in \Gamma(x,z)} \left\{ F(x, y, z) + \beta \int_Z f(y, z') Q(z, dz') \right\} + \beta a \alpha \|x\| \\
&= (Tf)(x, z) + \beta a \alpha \|x\|,
\end{aligned}$$

where the third line uses Assumption 9.19. Since $s \in S$ was arbitrary, it follows that $T(f + a) \leq Tf + \alpha\beta a$. Hence T satisfies the discounting condition, and by Theorem 4.12, T is a contraction of modulus $\alpha\beta < 1$. It then follows from the Contraction Mapping Theorem that T has a unique fixed point $v \in H(S)$.

That G is nonempty, compact valued and u.h.c. then follows from the Theorem of the Maximum (Theorem 3.6). Finally, suppose that $y \in G(x, z)$. Then $y \in \Gamma(x, z)$ and

$$v(x, z) = F(x, y, z) + \beta \int_Z v(y, z') Q(z, dz').$$

It then follows from Assumption 9.19 that $\lambda y \in \Gamma(\lambda x, z)$ and from the homogeneity of F and v that for each $z \in Z$,

$$v(\lambda x, z) = F(\lambda x, \lambda y, z) + \beta \int_Z v(\lambda y, z') Q(z, dz').$$

Hence $\lambda y \in G(\lambda x)$.

b. For v to be strictly quasi-concave, $(X, \mathcal{X})$, $(Z, \mathcal{Z})$, Q, Γ, F, and β have to satisfy Assumptions 9.5, 9.18–9.20 and in addition for each $z \in Z$, $F(\cdot, \cdot, z)$ must be strictly quasi-concave. The proof parallels the ones in Theorem 9.8 and Exercise 4.8c.

c. Adding Assumptions 9.8 and 9.9 we obtain monotonicity of v. The proof is similar to Theorem 9.7, with $H(X)$, $H'(X)$ and $H''(X)$ as defined in Exercise 4.8c., instead of $C(X)$, $C'(X)$ and $C''(X)$.

For differentiability of v, we need the same assumptions as in part b., plus Assumption 9.12. Then, for each $z \in Z$, $x, x' \in X$ with $x \neq \alpha x'$, for any $\alpha \in \mathbf{R}$, Theorem 4.10 applies.

Exercise 9.11

For this particular example,

$$\begin{aligned}
&v[\pi_{t-1}(z^{t-1}), z_t] \\
&= A_0 + \frac{\alpha}{1-\alpha\beta} \ln \pi_{t-1}(z^{t-1}) + \frac{1}{1-\alpha\beta} \ln z_t \\
&= \frac{\alpha}{1-\alpha\beta} \left\{ \sum_{n=0}^{t-1} \alpha^{t-1-n}[\ln(\alpha\beta) + \ln(z_n)] + \alpha^t \ln x_0 \right\} \\
&\quad + A_0 + \frac{1}{1-\alpha\beta} \ln z_t.
\end{aligned}$$

Using the fact that $0 < \beta < 1$, $0 < \alpha\beta < 1$ and $E(\ln z) = m < \infty$, it is straightforward to show that

$$\lim_{t\to\infty} \beta^t \int_{Z^t} v[\pi_{t-1}(z^{t-1}), z_t]\mu^t(z_0, dz^t) = 0,$$

and hence that condition a. of Theorem 9.12 is satisfied.

Exercise 9.12

Denote by λ the probability measure on u. Then,

$$\begin{aligned}
&\int_{Z^t} |z_t|\, \mu^t(z_0, dz^t) \\
&= \int_{Z^{t-1}} \left[\int_Z |\rho z_{t-1} + u_t|\, Q(z_{t-1}, dz_t) \right] \mu^{t-1}(z_0, dz^{t-1}) \\
&\leq \int_{Z^{t-1}} (|\rho z_{t-1}| + |u_t|)\, \mu^t(z_0, dz^t) \\
&= \int_Z |u_t|\, \lambda(du_t) + \int_{Z^{t-1}} |\rho z_{t-1}|\, \mu^{t-1}(z_0, dz^{t-1}).
\end{aligned}$$

Hence, since $0 \leq \rho \leq 1$, $z_0 \in \mathbf{R}$, and $|u|$ has finite mean since $Z = \mathbf{R}$, there exist an $A > 0$, such that

$$\int_{Z^t} |z_t| \, \mu^t(z_0, dz^t) = \sum_{i=1}^{t} \rho^{t-i} \int |u_i| \, \lambda(du_i) + \rho^t \, |z_0| \leq A, \quad \text{all } t.$$

The second part is proved by induction. For $t = 1$, since u has finite mean and variance, there exists a $B > 0$ such that

$$\begin{aligned} \int z_1^2 \mu(z_0, dz^1) &= \int \left(\rho^2 z_0^2 + 2\rho z_0 u_1 + u_1^2\right) Q(z_0, dz^1) \\ &= \rho^2 z_0^2 + 2\rho z_0 \int u_1 \lambda(du_1) + \int u_1^2 \lambda(du_1) < B. \end{aligned}$$

Next, assume $\int_{Z^{t-1}} z_{t-1}^2 \mu^{t-1}(z_0, dz^{t-1}) < B$, then

$$\begin{aligned} \int_{Z^t} z_t^2 \mu^t(z_0, dz^t) &= \int_{Z^{t-1}} \left[\rho^2 z_{t-1}^2 + 2\rho z_{t-1} \int u_t \lambda(du_t) + \int u_t^2 \lambda(du_t)\right] \\ &\quad \times \mu^{t-1}(z_0, dz^{t-1}) \\ &= \rho^2 \int_{Z^{t-1}} z_{t-1}^2 \mu^{t-1}(z_0, dz^{t-1}) \\ &\quad + \int u_t \lambda(du_t) \left[2\rho \int_{Z^{t-1}} z_{t-1} \mu^{t-1}(z_0, dz^{t-1})\right] \\ &\quad + \int u_t^2 \lambda(du_t) \\ &< B, \end{aligned}$$

where the inequality comes from the result obtained in the first part of the exercise.

Exercise 9.13

a. The most general solution to (1) would be

$$v(x, z) = v_0 + v_1 z + v_2 x + v_3 z x - v_4 x^2 + v_5 z^2.$$

That is, it may be the case that $v_5 \neq 0$. In fact, the proposed solution (with $v_5 = 0$) does not satisfy (1) .

To show that the equation above constitutes a solution to (1), substitute this guess in (1) to get

$$v_0 + v_1 z + v_2 x + v_3 zx - v_4 x^2 + v_5 z^2$$
$$= \sup_y \left\{ zx - \frac{1}{2} b x^2 - \frac{1}{2} c\,(y - x)^2 \right.$$
$$\left. + \beta \int_Z \left(v_0 + v_1 z' + v_2 y + v_3 z y - v_4 y^2 + v_5 z'^2 \right) Q\left(z, dz'\right) \right\}.$$

The first-order condition of the maximization problem of the right-hand side is

$$-c\,(y - x) + v_3 \beta \int_Z z' Q\left(z, dz'\right) - 2\beta v_4 y + \beta v_2 = 0.$$

Let $\bar{u}$ and σ^2 denote the mean and variance of u. Then,

$$y = \frac{1}{\left(c + 2v_4 \beta\right)} \left[cx + \beta \left(v_2 + v_3 \left(\rho z + \bar{u} \right) \right) \right].$$

We can plug this into the functional equation above, group terms, and solve for the coefficients. The values of the coefficients that satisfy (1) are implicitly given by

$$v_0 = \frac{\beta^2 (v_2 + v_3 \bar{u})^2}{(1 - \beta)\, 2(c + 2\beta v_4)} + \frac{\beta}{1 - \beta} \left[v_1 \bar{u} + v_5 (\bar{u}^2 + \sigma^2) \right],$$

$$v_1 = \beta \rho v_1 + \frac{\beta^2 \rho v_3 \left(v_2 + \bar{u} \right)}{(c + 2\beta v_4)},$$

$$v_2 = \frac{c\beta}{(c + 2\beta v_4)} \left(v_2 + v_3 \bar{u} \right),$$

$$v_3 = 1 + \frac{c \beta \rho v_3}{(c + 2\beta v_4)},$$

$$v_4 = \frac{b}{2} + \frac{c \beta v_4}{(c + 2\beta v_4)},$$

$$v_5 = \frac{(\beta \rho v_3)^2}{(c + 2\beta v_4)}.$$

To verify that one of the solutions to v_4 is strictly positive, notice that

$$2\beta v_4^2 + [(1-\beta)c - \beta b] v_4 - \frac{cb}{2} = 0,$$

and therefore

$$v_4 = \frac{[(1-\beta)c - \beta b] \pm \sqrt{[(1-\beta)c - \beta b]^2 + 4\beta cb}}{4\beta},$$

which clearly implies the result.

b. From part a. we know that the first-order condition for the problem above implies that

$$y = g(x, z) = \frac{1}{(c + 2v_4\beta)} \left[cx + \beta\left(v_2 + v_3\left(\rho z + \bar{u}\right)\right)\right],$$

which can be written as

$$y = g(x, z) = g_0 + g_1 x + g_2 z,$$

where

$$g_0 = \frac{\beta\left(v_2 + v_3\bar{u}\right)}{(c + 2v_4\beta)},$$

$$g_1 = \frac{c}{(c + 2v_4\beta)},$$

$$g_2 = \frac{\beta v_3 \rho}{(c + 2v_4\beta)},$$

and clearly $0 < g_1 < 1$ since in part a. we showed that $v_4 > 0$.

Exercise 9.14

Using (10) we can write the measurable functions that conform to the plan $\pi^*(\cdot\,;s_0)$ generated by g as

$$\pi_t^*(z^t, s_0) = g_0 \sum_{i=0}^{t} g_1^i + g_1^{t+1} x_0 + g_2 \sum_{i=0}^{t} g_1^{t-i} z_i.$$

Hence, (11) becomes

$$\lim_{t\to\infty} \beta^t \int_{Z^t} v_0 + v_1 z_t + v_2 \left(g_0 \sum_{i=0}^{t-1} g_1^i + g_1^t x_0 + g_2 \sum_{i=0}^{t-1} g_1^{t-1-i} z_i \right)$$
$$+ v_3 z_t \left(g_0 \sum_{i=0}^{t-1} g_1^i + g_1^t x_0 + g_2 \sum_{i=0}^{t-1} g_1^{t-1-i} z_i \right)$$
$$- v_4 \left(g_0 \sum_{i=0}^{t-1} g_1^i + g_1^t x_0 + g_2 \sum_{i=0}^{t-1} g_1^{t-1-i} z_i \right)^2 \mu^t(z_0, dz^t),$$

or

$$\lim_{t\to\infty} M_t + \lim_{t\to\infty} N_t,$$

where

$$M_t = \beta^t \left\{ v_0 + v_2 \left(g_0 \sum_{i=0}^{t-1} g_1^i + g_1^t x_0 \right) \right\},$$

and

$$N_t = \beta^t \int_{Z^t} \left[v_1 z_t + v_2 \left(g_2 \sum_{i=0}^{t-1} g_1^{t-1-i} z_i \right) \right.$$
$$+ v_3 z_t \left(g_0 \sum_{i=0}^{t-1} g_1^i + g_1^t x_0 + g_2 \sum_{i=0}^{t-1} g_1^{t-1-i} z_i \right)$$
$$\left. - v_4 \left(g_0 \sum_{i=0}^{t-1} g_1^i + g_1^t x_0 + g_2 \sum_{i=0}^{t-1} g_1^{t-1-i} z_i \right)^2 \right] \mu^t(z_0, dz^t)$$
$$< \beta^t A \left(v_1 + v_2 g_2 \sum_{i=0}^{t-1} g_1^{t-1-i} + v_3 g_0 \sum_{i=0}^{t-1} g_1^i + g_1^t x_0 \right)$$
$$+ \beta^t B \left(v_3 g_2 \sum_{i=0}^{t-1} g_1^{t-1-i} \right),$$

where A and B are the same constants used in Exercise 9.12, and the last inequality comes from the fact that $v_4 > 0$.

That $\lim_{t\to\infty} M_t = 0$ comes from the fact that $0 < g_1 < 1$, which makes the sum converge.

That $\lim_{t\to\infty} N_t = 0$ comes from $\beta < 1$, $0 < g_1 < 1$, and A, B, υ_1, υ_2, and υ_3 are finite.

Exercise 9.15

a. We will prove that the stated condition holds for all indicator functions of measurable sets, then all nonnegative measurable simple functions, and then all nonnegative measurable functions.

Let $C = A \times B \in \mathcal{S}$, and let $f(x, z) = \chi_{A\times B}(x, z)$. Then

$$\begin{aligned}
&\int_{X\times Z} \chi_{A\times B}(x', z')P[(x, z), dx' \times dz'] \\
&= P[(x, z), A \times B] \\
&= Q(z, B)\chi_A[g(x, z)] \\
&= \int_Z \chi_A[g(x, z)]\chi_B(z')Q(z, dz') \\
&= \int_Z \chi_{A\times B}[g(x, z), z']Q(z, dz'),
\end{aligned}$$

hence the statement is true for indicator functions of measurable sets. Clearly, the argument also holds if f is an indicator function for a finite union of measurable rectangles. Let

$$\begin{aligned}
\mathcal{C} = \Big\{C \in \mathcal{S} : &\int_{X\times Z} f(x', z')P[(x, z), dx' \times dz'] \\
&= \int_Z f[g(x, z), z']Q(z, dz') \text{ for } f = \chi_C\Big\}.
\end{aligned}$$

We need to show that $\mathcal{C}$ is a monotone class; it will follow from the Monotone Class Lemma that $\mathcal{C} = \mathcal{S}$.

Let $\{C_n\}_{n=1}^{\infty}$ be an increasing sequence in $\mathcal{C}$, with $C = \cup_{n=1}^{\infty} C_n$. Then χ_{C_n} is an increasing sequence of $\mathcal{S}$-measurable functions converging pointwise to χ_C; hence by Theorem 7.4, χ_C is also $\mathcal{S}$-measurable. By hypothesis,

$$\int_{X\times Z} \chi_{C_n}(x', z')P[(x, z), dx' \times dz'] = \int_Z \chi_{C_n}[g(x, z), z']Q(z, dz'),$$

for $n = 1, 2, \ldots$.

Hence, taking the limit as $n \to \infty$ and applying the Monotone Convergence Theorem to both sides, we find that

$$\begin{aligned}
&\int_{X\times Z} \chi_C(x', z') P[(x, z), dx' \times dz'] \\
&= \lim_{n\to\infty} \int_{X\times Z} \chi_{C_n}(x', z') P[(x, z), dx' \times dz'] \\
&= \lim_{n\to\infty} \int_Z \chi_{C_n}[g(x, z), z'] Q(z, dz') \\
&= \int_Z \chi[g(x, z), z'] Q(z, dz'),
\end{aligned}$$

so $C \in \mathcal{C}$. Similar argument applies if $\{C_n\}_{n=1}^{\infty}$ is a decreasing sequence.

We can use the linearity of the integral to extend the result to all measurable simple functions, and Theorem 7.5 and the Monotone Convergence Theorem to establish the result for all measurable functions.

b. The proof that a. holds also for f being $P(s, \cdot)$-integrable comes from the fact that this requirement is sufficient for the integral above to be well defined. Hence proceeding as in part a. for the positive and negative parts of f we can complete the proof.

Exercise 9.16

Define $\Pr(z_t = i)$, $i = 0, 1$ as the unconditional probability of $z_t = i$. Conditioning on x_t only, we don't have any information about past realizations of the z_t process, so

$$P(x_{t+1} \in A \mid x_t) = \sum_{i=0}^{1} \chi_A[g(x_t, i)] \Pr(z_t = i).$$

Conditioning on x_t and x_{t+1}, due to the specific functional form of $g(x, z)$, we can infer the value of z_{t-1}, and hence we can use that information to calculate the conditional probability, therefore

$$P(x_{t+1} \in A \mid x_t, x_{t-1}) = \sum_{i=0}^{1} \chi_A[g(x_t, i)] Q(z_{t-1}, i).$$

Hence, as long as $\Pr\left(z_t = i\right) \neq Q\left(z_{t-1}, i\right)$, we will have that

$$P\left(x_{t+1} \in A \mid x_t\right) \neq P\left(x_{t+1} \in A \mid x_t, x_{t-1}\right).$$

As an example, let $\theta = 1/2$ and $A = [1/2, 1]$. Also, assume $x_t = 1/2$, $x_{t-1} = 1$. Therefore, $z_{t-1} = 0$, and

$$\begin{aligned}\Pr\left[x_{t+1} \in A \mid x_t = 1/2\right] &= \Pr\left[z_t \geq 1/2\right] \\ &= \Pr\left[z_t = 1\right].\end{aligned}$$

On the other hand,

$$\begin{aligned}\Pr\left[x_{t+1} \in A \mid x_t = 1/2, x_{t-1} = 1\right] &= \Pr\left[z_t \geq 1/2 \mid z_{t-1} = 0\right] \\ &= Q(0, 1) \\ &= 0.1.\end{aligned}$$

Exercise 9.17

a. Define

$$\hat{H}(A) = \left\{(x, z, z') \in X \times Z \times Z : \phi[x, g(x, z), z'] \in A\right\}.$$

Then, $H(x, z, A)$ is the (x, z)-section of $\hat{H}(A)$, and $B \cap H(x, z, A)$ is the (x, z)-section of $B \cap \hat{H}(A)$.

First, we need to show that P is well defined. To do this, it suffices to show that $B \cap H(x, z, A) \in \mathcal{Z}$, all $(x, z) \in X \times Z$, all $B \in \mathcal{Z}$, and all $A \in \mathcal{X}$. Since by hypothesis ϕ and g are measurable, $B \cap \hat{H}(A) \in \mathcal{X} \times \mathcal{Z} \times \mathcal{Z}$. As shown in Theorem 7.14, any section of a measurable set is measurable, so the desired result follows.

Next, we must show that for each $(x, z) = s \in S = X \times Z$, $P(s, \cdot)$ is a probability measure on $\mathcal{S} = \mathcal{X} \times \mathcal{Z}$. Fix s. Clearly $P(s, \emptyset) = Q[z, \emptyset \cap H(x, z, \emptyset)] = 0$, and $P(s, S) = Q[z, Z \cap H(x, z, X)] = 1$. Also, for any disjoint sequence $\left\{(B \times A)_i\right\}$ in $\mathcal{S}$, the sets $C_i = B_i \cap \hat{H}\left(A_i\right)$, $i = 1, 2, \ldots$ in $\mathcal{X} \times \mathcal{Z} \times \mathcal{Z}$ are disjoint, and therefore their (x, z)-sections are also disjoint. Then

$$
\begin{aligned}
P[(x, z), \cup_{i=1}^{\infty}(B \times A)_i] &= Q[z, (\cup_{i=1}^{\infty} C_i)_{(x,z)}] \\
&= Q[z, \cup_{i=1}^{\infty}(C_i)_{(x,z)}] \\
&= \sum_{i=1}^{\infty} Q[z, B_i \cap H(x, z, A_i)] \\
&= \sum_{i=1}^{\infty} P[(x, z), (B \times A)_i].
\end{aligned}
$$

Therefore $P(s, \cdot)$ is countably additive.

Finally, it must be shown that for each $(B \times A) \in \mathcal{S}$, $P[\cdot, (B \times A)]$ is a $\mathcal{S}$-measurable function. Since for each $(B \times A) \in \mathcal{S}$, the set $C = B \cap \hat{H}(A)$ is in $\mathcal{X} \times \mathcal{Z} \times \mathcal{Z}$, it suffices to show that the function $Q\left[z, C_{(x,z)}\right]$, as a function of s, is $\mathcal{S}$-measurable for all C in $\mathcal{X} \times \mathcal{Z} \times \mathcal{Z}$. Let

$$
\mathcal{B} = \left\{C \in \mathcal{X} \times \mathcal{Z} \times \mathcal{Z} : Q[z, C_{(x,z)}] \text{ is } (\mathcal{X} \times \mathcal{Z})\text{-measurable}\right\}.
$$

By the Monotone Class Lemma (Lemma 7.15), it suffices to show that $\mathcal{B}$ contains all finite unions of measurable rectangles and that $\mathcal{B}$ is a monotone class.

First, let $C = A \times B \times D$. Then

$$
Q[z, C_{(x,z)}] = \begin{cases} Q(z, D) & \text{if } (x, z) \in (A \times B) \\ 0 & \text{if } (x, z) \notin (A \times B). \end{cases}
$$

Since $(A \times B)$ is a measurable set, $Q\left[z, C_{(x,z)}\right]$ is a measurable (simple) function of (x, z). Hence $\mathcal{B}$ contains all measurable rectangles. The rest of the proof is a straightforward adaptation of the proof of Theorem 8.9 to show that if $E_1, \ldots, E_n$ are measurable rectangles, then $\cup_{i=1}^{n} E_i \in \mathcal{B}$, and that $\mathcal{B}$ is a monotone class.

b. First, we need to show that

$$
\int_{X \times Z} f(x', z') P[(x, z), dx' \times dz'] = \int_Z f[\phi(x, g(x, z), z')] Q(z, dz').
$$

We will prove that the stated condition holds for all indicator functions of measurable sets, then all measurable simple functions, and then all measurable functions.

Let $C = A \times B \in \mathcal{S}$, and let $f(x, z) = \chi_{A\times B}(x, z)$. Then

$$\begin{aligned}
&\int_{X\times Z} \chi_{A\times B}(x', z')P[(x, z), dx' \times dz'] \\
&= P[(x, z), A \times B] \\
&= Q[z, B \cap H(x, z, A)] \\
&= \int_Z \chi_{H(x,z,A)}(z')\chi_B(z')Q(z, dz') \\
&= \int_Z \chi_A[\phi(x, g(x, z), z')]\chi_B(z')Q(z, dz') \\
&= \int_Z \chi_{A\times B}[\phi(x, g(x, z), z'), z']Q(z, dz'),
\end{aligned}$$

so the stated condition holds for indicator functions of $\mathcal{S}$-measurable sets. Clearly, it also holds if f is an indicator function for a finite union of measurable rectangles. The proof parallels the one presented in Exercise 9.15. Similarly, the linearity of the integral allows us to extend the result to all measurable simple functions. Theorem 7.5 and the Monotone Convergence Theorem then establish the result for all measurable functions.

Let M_Q and M_P be the Markov operators associated with Q and P, respectively; and let $f : S \to \mathbf{R}$ be any bounded continuous functions. Then for any $(x, z) = s \in S$, it follows from the argument above that

$$\begin{aligned}
(M_P f)(s) &= \int_{X\times Z} f(s')P(s, ds') \\
&= \int_Z f[\phi(x, g(s), z'), z']Q(z, dz') \\
&= (M_Q f)[\phi(x, g(s)), z].
\end{aligned}$$

Hence, the desired result follows immediately from Lemma 9.5′ (which requires Assumptions 9.4, 9.5, 9.16 and 9.17) and the fact that g and ϕ are continuous.

10 Applications of Stochastic Dynamic Programming

Exercise 10.1

a. Define

$$\mu^t(z^t) = \Pi_{i=1}^t \lambda(z_i).$$

Then, equation (1) can be rewritten as

$$\sup \sum_{t=0}^{\infty} \int_{Z^t} \beta^t U\left[z_t f(x_t) - x_{t+1}\right] \mu(dz^t),$$

subject to

$$0 \le x_{t+1} \le z_t f(x_t), \;\; t = 0, 1, \ldots,$$
$$x_0 \ge 0 \text{ and } z_0 \ge 0 \text{ given.}$$

The set of feasible plans is a sequence $\{x_t\}_{t=0}^{\infty}$ of measurable functions $x_t : Z^{t-1} \to X$ such that $0 \le x_{t+1} \le z_t f(x_t)$.

b. Assumption 9.4 is trivially satisfied since $0 \le x_{t+1} \le z_t f(x_t)$ defines a convex Borel set in $\mathbf{R}$ given $x_t \in [0, \bar{x}]$ and $z_t \in Z$. Assumptions Z1 and Z2 guarantee that Assumption 9.5 is satisfied since $Q(z, dz') = \lambda(dz')$, which does not depend on z. Define the correspondence

$$\Gamma(x, z) = \{y : 0 \le y \le zf(x), \; y \in X, \; z \in Z\},$$

then since $f(x) \in \Gamma(x, z)$, $\Gamma(x, z)$ is nonempty. Since

$$0 \le f(0) \le zf(x) \le \bar{z} f(\bar{x}) < \infty,$$

for $x \in X$ and $z \in Z$, $\Gamma(x, z)$ is compact valued and since $zf(x)$ is continuous in x and z, $\Gamma(x, z)$ is continuous. Hence Assumption 9.6 is satisfied. Define

$$F(x, y, z) \equiv U[zf(x) - y],$$

then since f and U are continuous and X and Z are compact, $F(x, y, z)$ is bounded and continuous. This, together with U1, implies that Assumption 9.7 is satisfied. Hence we can use Theorem 9.6 to show the first set of results.

Theorem 9.2 establishes then that the optimum for the FE is the optimum for the SP and that the plans generated by the FE attain the supremum in the SP. Theorem 9.4 establishes that a solution of the SP is also a solution for the FE. Notice that Exercise 9.6 establishes that Assumptions 9.4–9.7 imply Assumptions 9.1–9.3.

c. By U3 and T3, $F(\cdot, y, z)$ is strictly increasing and $\Gamma(x, z)$ is increasing in x. Hence Assumptions 9.8 and 9.9 are satisfied and we can use Theorem 9.7 to show that $v(\cdot, z)$ is strictly increasing.

By U4 and T4 Assumptions 9.10 and 9.11 are satisfied (see Exercise 5.1) and so we can use Theorem 9.8 to prove the rest of the results.

d. The FE for this problem can be written as

$$\begin{aligned}\hat{v}(s) &= v(x, z) \\ &= \max_{0 \le y \le zf(x)} \left\{ U[zf(x) - y] + \beta \int_Z v(y, z')\lambda(dz') \right\} \\ &= \max_{0 \le y \le s} \left\{ U[s - y] + \beta \int_Z \hat{v}[z' f(y)]\,\lambda(dz') \right\},\end{aligned}$$

where $s = zf(y)$ and $s' = z'f(y)$.

Hence the policy function $g(x, z)$ only depends on the new state variable s, and so $g(x, z) = h(s)$. Since $g(x, z)$ is a continuous single-valued function, so is h. To show that h is strictly increasing, suppose not. Then for $x > x'$, $s > s'$ and $h(s) < h(s')$ and so by U4

$$U'[s - h(s)] < U'[s' - h(s')],$$

which implies using the first-order condition that

$$\beta \int_Z v'(h(s), z')\lambda(dz') < \beta \int_Z v'(h(s'), z')\lambda(dz'),$$

a contradiction with v concave in x. Hence $h(s)$ is increasing in s and by T4, $g(x, z)$ is increasing in both arguments.

Since $v(x, z)$ is strictly concave in x, for $x > x'$, $v'(x, z) < v'(x', z)$, $s > s'$ and $h(s) > h(s')$, hence

$$\beta \int_Z v'(h(s), z')\lambda(dz') < \beta \int_Z v'(h(s'), z')\lambda(dz'),$$

which implies that

$$U'[s - h(s)] < U'\left[s' - h(s')\right],$$

which implies by U4, that $s - h(s) > s' - h(s')$, so $c(x, z)$ is increasing in s and so in x and z by T4.

e. Assumption 9.12 is satisfied by T5 and U5. Hence we can use Theorem 9.10 to show that v is differentiable at s with the given derivatives since $s_x = zf'(x)$ and $s_z = f(x)$. Notice that we are using Theorem 9.10 to prove differentiability with respect to s, and since s is differentiable with respect to x and z, $v(x, z)$ is differentiable with respect to both variables. Hence differentiability with respect to z comes from the possibility of reducing the problem to one state variable.

f. If we replace Z2 with Z3, Assumption 9.5 is still satisfied so 10.1a.–c. hold. The FE for this problem can be written as

$$v(x, z) = \max_{0 \le y \le zf(x)} \left\{ U[zf(x) - y] + \beta \int_Z v(y, z')Q(z, dz') \right\}$$

with $x, z \ge 0$ given.

Notice that now the problem depends on z through the transition function so that we cannot reduce the state variables to s only. Hence g depends on both arguments independently. It is no longer guaranteed that $g(x, z)$ is increasing in z since we are not assuming that for $z > z' \in Z$, $Q(z, A) > Q(z', A)$ for all $A \in \mathcal{Z}$. If Q does satisfy this condition, we can prove that $g(x, z)$ is increasing in z. Toward a contradiction suppose that for $z > \hat{z}$, $g(x, z) < g(x, \hat{z})$. Then, by U4,

$$U'[zf(x) - g(x, z)] < U'\left[\hat{z}f(x) - g(x, \hat{z})\right],$$

which implies that

$$\int_Z v'(g(x, z), z')Q(z, dz') < \int_Z v'(g(x, \hat{z}), z')Q(\hat{z}, dz').$$

A contradiction with v concave. Hence $g(x, z)$ is increasing in z.

Because of the new dependence of the FE on z in the transition function we can only apply Theorem 9.10 to the differentiability with respect to x.

Exercise 10.3

a. We need to prove that Γ is well defined and that it is nonempty, compact valued and continuous.

Define Γ as,

$$\Gamma(x, z) = \{y \in X : (c, y) \in \Phi(x, z) \text{ for some } c \in \mathbf{R}_+^M\}.$$

The correspondence is well defined since for every pair $(x, z) \in X \times Z$, it assigns feasible consumption vectors and capital values. Since by Assumption a. Φ is nonempty, compact valued and continuous, Γ is nonempty, compact valued and continuous. Hence Assumption 9.6 is satisfied.

The definition of A (the graph of Γ) is standard. In the definition of F we are using the fact that the choice of the consumption basket is a static problem. That is, we can maximize which basket of goods to consume first and then attack the intertemporal problem. We know $\beta \in (0, 1)$ by assumption. Since U is a bounded and continuous function and $\Phi(x, z)$ is compact valued and continuous we can use the Theorem of the Maximum (Theorem 3.6) to obtain that Assumption 9.7 is satisfied. To show that F is increasing in the first argument notice that by Assumption b., for $x \leq x'$ and $z \in Z$, $\Phi(x, z) \subseteq \Phi(x', z)$. Hence since the possible choices are more restricted in the first case and U is strictly increasing, for $y \in X$,

$$F(x, y, z) \leq F(x', y, z),$$

hence Assumption 9.8 is satisfied.

Assumption 9.9 is also satisfied because of Assumption b. Since $\Phi(x, z) \subseteq \Phi(x', z)$ for $x \leq x'$, and so for $c \in \mathbf{R}_+^M$, $\Gamma(x, z) \subseteq \Gamma(x', z)$. U strictly concave and Assumption c. imply Assumption 9.10, since for $x, x' \in X$ and $y, y' \in X$, we have that

$$F(\theta x + (1-\theta)x', \theta y + (1-\theta)y', z),$$

is defined by

$$\max_{c \in \mathbf{R}_+^M} U(c),$$

subject to

$$(c, \theta y + (1-\theta)y') \in \Phi(\theta x + (1-\theta)x', z).$$

But by Assumption c., the value of this problem is at least as large as the value of maximizing the same function subject to the constraint that c satisfy

$$(c, y) \in \Phi(x, z) \text{ and } (c, y') \in \Phi(x', z).$$

But then by U strictly concave, this is strictly greater than

$$\theta F(x, y, z) + (1-\theta)F(x', y', z).$$

Assumption 9.11 is guaranteed by Assumption c.

b. First notice that in this case we have shown that $\Gamma(x, z)$ is nonempty, compact valued and u.h.c. and this guarantees that it has a measurable selection. Hence Assumption 9.1 is satisfied. Notice also that F is bounded, and so Assumption 9.2 is also satisfied. Hence we can use the Theorem 9.2 to show the result. The sketch of the proof is as in the proof of this theorem.

Let

$$v^*(x_0, z_0) = \max_{\{c_t, x_{t+1}\}_{t=0}^{\infty}} \sum_{t=0}^{\infty} \beta^t \int_{Z^t} U(c_t)\, \mu^t(z_0, dz^t),$$

subject to $(c_t, x_{t+1}) \in \Phi(x_t, z_t)$ for all t, given x_0, z_0. But this is equivalent to the problem

$$\max_{\{x_t\}_{t=1}^{\infty}} \sum_{t=0}^{\infty} \beta^t \int_{Z^t} F(x_t, x_{t+1}, z_t) \mu^t(z_0, dz^t),$$

subject to $x_{t+1} \in \Gamma(x_t, z_t)$ for all t, given x_0, z_0.

Then for an arbitrary plan π and the consumption plan γ^* such that $[\gamma_t^*(z_t), \pi_t(z^t)] \in \Phi[\pi_{t-1}(z^{t-1}), z_t]$ and given x_0 and z_0,

$$\begin{aligned} v(x_0, z_0) &\geq F(x_0, \pi_0, z_0) + \beta \int_Z v(\pi_0, z_1) Q(z_0, dz_1) \\ &= F(x_0, \pi_0, z_0) + \beta \int_Z F\left[x_1, \pi_1(z^1), z_1\right] Q(z_0, dz_1) \\ &\quad + \beta^2 \int_Z \int_Z v\left[\pi_1(z^1), z_2\right] Q(z_0, dz_1) Q(z_1, dz_2), \end{aligned}$$

and by Exercise 8.8 and using induction

$$\begin{aligned} v(x_0, z_0) &\geq \sum_{t=0}^{\infty} \beta^t \int_{Z^t} F(x_t, \pi_t(z^t), z_t) \mu^t(z_0, dz^t) \\ &\quad + \lim_{t\to\infty} \beta^t \int_{Z^t} F(x_t, \pi_t(z^t), z_t) \mu^t(z_0, dz^t). \end{aligned}$$

Notice that the last term exists since Assumption 9.2 is satisfied and it is positive. Hence $v(x_0, z_0) \geq v^*(x_0, z_0)$ which yields the result.

Exercise 10.4

a. Let $\mu^t(z_0, \cdot)$, $z_0 \in Z$, $t = 1, 2 \ldots$, be as defined in section 8.2. Then a precise statement of (1) is given by

$$\sup_{\{x_t\}_{t=1}^{\infty}} \sum_{t=0}^{\infty} (1+r)^{-t} \int_{Z^t} \left[U(x_t, z_t) - x_t c(x_{t+1}/x_t)\right] \mu^t(z_0, dz^t),$$

subject to $x_t > 0$ for all $t = 1, 2, \ldots$, given (x_0, z_0).

We need to show that Assumptions 9.1 to 9.3 hold. $\Gamma(x) = \mathbf{R}_{++}$ is trivially nonempty, has a measurable graph, and letting $h(x) = B \in \mathbf{R}_{++}$, then $h(x)$ is a measurable selection. Let

$$F(x, y, z) = U(x, z) - xc(\frac{y}{x}).$$

Since $U(\cdot, z)$ is bounded and $xc(y/x)$ is bounded from below, $F(x, y, z)$ is bounded from above. Hence Assumptions 9.2 and 9.3 are satisfied. This guarantees by Theorem 9.2 that the optimum for the FE is an optimum for the SP, and that the value generated by the policy function attains the supremum in the SP. By Theorem 9.4, we have that a solution for (1) is also a solution for (2).

b. $X = \mathbf{R}_{++}$ satisfies Assumption 9.4 trivially. Assumption 9.6 is guaranteed since Q is assumed to have the Feller property. Assumption 9.7 is guaranteed by the definition of Γ. Γ is nonempty since $(1-\delta)x \in \Gamma(x)$ all x, compact-valued since it is defined by closed intervals and continuous since the functions that define the boundaries of the intervals are continuous in x. Since U and c are continuous functions, F is continuous, and by the reasoning above it is bounded. Hence Assumption 9.6 is also satisfied and so existence of a unique bounded and continuous function v is guaranteed by Theorem 9.6.

To show that the function v satisfying (2′) also satisfies (2) we need to show that for any $x \in X$, the solution, y, to the maximization problem in (2) is such that $y \in \Gamma(x)$. Let M be such that for all $y \geq M$,

$$A - Mc\left(\frac{y}{M}\right) + \frac{A}{r} < 0$$

and for all $x \leq M$,

$$A - xc\left(\frac{M}{x}\right) + \frac{A}{r} < 0.$$

Let $x > M$, then $y \leq x$, since otherwise the first part of the definition of M implies that the value of the problem in (1) is negative given $x_0 \geq M$ which is clearly not the case. To see that the value in problem (1) is not negative, choose for example a policy $y = (1-\delta)x$ and notice that this yields a positive value for the problem. Since by part a. the optimal plans implied by the sequential and recursive problems are the same, so $y \leq x$. Let $x \leq M$, then $y < M$ by the same argument but using the second part of the definition of M. Hence, if the capital stock today is larger than M tomorrow's capital stock will be smaller than today's capital stock, and if today's capital stock is smaller than M tomorrow's capital stock will be smaller that M as well.

Since $c(a) = 0$ for all $a \leq (1-\delta)$, clearly $y > (1-\delta)x$. Hence $y \in \Gamma(x)$, which implies that the restriction added in (2′) is not binding.

c. v strictly increasing in x. We need to show that Assumptions 9.8–9.9 hold. F strictly increasing in x comes from $U_x(x, z) = D(x, z)$ strictly increasing in x, and that

$$\frac{\partial xc(\frac{y}{x})}{\partial x} = c\left(\frac{y}{x}\right) - \frac{y}{x}c'\left(\frac{y}{x}\right) < 0,$$

by the strict convexity of c for $y/x > 1-\delta$ and $c(y/x) = 0$ for $y/x \leq 1-\delta$. Hence Assumption 9.8 is satisfied.

Since $\Gamma(x)$ is defined by intervals with increasing functions of x as boundaries, it is increasing in x in the sense of Assumption 9.9. Hence we can use Theorem 9.7.

To show that v is strictly increasing in z we need to check that Assumptions 9.13–9.15 hold. U is strictly increasing in z since D is, and so F is strictly increasing in z. And the transition function Q is monotone by assumption. Hence we can use Theorem 9.11 to prove the result.

To show that v is strictly concave in x we need to show that Assumptions 9.10 and 9.11 hold. The strict concavity of U, together with the strict convexity of c, implies that

$$F_{xx} = U_{xx} - \frac{y^2}{x^3}c''(\frac{y}{x}) < 0,$$

$$F_{yy} = -\frac{1}{x}c''(\frac{y}{x}) < 0,$$

$$F_{yx} = \frac{y}{x^2}c''(\frac{y}{x}) > 0,$$

and so

$$F_{xx}F_{yy} - F_{xy}^2 = -\frac{1}{x}c''(\frac{y}{x})U_{xx} > 0,$$

(notice that for simplicity we are assuming that c is twice continuously differentiable). Hence the characteristic roots are all negative and so the Hessian is negative definite, which yields Assumption 9.10.

Assumption 9.11 is satisfied since Γ is defined by intervals with boundaries that are linear functions of x. Hence we can use Theorem 9.8 to show that v is strictly concave and also that the optimal policy correspondence is single valued, call it $g(x, z)$. Since $c(1-\delta) = 0$ and c is continuously differentiable,

$$\lim_{h \to (1-\delta)} c'(h) = 0.$$

And since $v(x, z)$ is increasing in x this implies that it is never optimal to choose $g(x, z) < (1-\delta)x$. In part b. we showed that if $x \in (0, M]$, $g(x, y) < M$, and if $x \in (M, \infty]$, $g(x, y) < x$.

To show that $v(\cdot, z)$ is continuously differentiable we need to show that Assumption 9.12 holds and use Theorem 9.10. The differentiability of c and U yield this result.

d. The first-order condition with respect to y is

$$-c'(\frac{y}{x}) + (1+r)^{-1} \int v'(y, z')Q(z, dz') = 0.$$

By contradiction, suppose $g(x, z)$ is nonincreasing in x. Since v is strictly concave in x, for $x < x'$,

$$c'\left[\frac{g(x, z)}{x}\right] < c'\left[\frac{g(x', z)}{x'}\right],$$

and $g(x, z) \geq g(x', z)$, a contradiction since c is convex.

We will prove that for $x' > x$, $g(x', z)/x' < g(x, z)/x$ (notice that g increasing and with slope less than one does not imply this). By contradiction. Suppose that for $x' > x$, $g(x', z)/x' \geq g(x, z)/x$. Then convexity of c implies that

$$c'\left[\frac{g(x, z)}{x}\right] \leq c'\left[\frac{g(x', z)}{x'}\right],$$

but then

$$\int v'\left[g(x, z), z'\right] Q(z, dz') \leq \int v'\left[g(x', z), z'\right] Q(z, dz').$$

Since g is increasing this contradicts that v is concave in x.

e. The envelope condition of the problem is given by

$$v_x(x, z) = D(x, z) - c(\frac{y}{x}) + \frac{y}{x}c'(\frac{y}{x}),$$

since D is increasing in z this implies that $v_x(x, z)$ is increasing in z and so by the monotonicity assumption $\int v'(y, z')Q(z, dz')$ is nondecreasing in z. By contradiction. Assume $g(x, z)$ is nonincreasing in z. Then by the first-order condition, for $z \leq \bar{z}$,

$$\begin{aligned} c'\left[\frac{g(x, z)}{x}\right] &= (1+r)^{-1} \int v'\left[g(x, z), z'\right] Q(z, dz') \\ &\leq (1+r)^{-1} \int v'\left[g(x, \bar{z}), z'\right] Q(\bar{z}, dz') \\ &= c'\left[\frac{g(x, \bar{z})}{x}\right], \end{aligned}$$

a contradiction since c is convex. For $y/x > 1 - \delta$, c is strictly convex and so the proof holds with strict inequality.

f. In this case $Q(z, \cdot) = \mu(\cdot)$, so the Bellman equation becomes

$$v(x, z) = \max_{y \in \Gamma(x)} \left[U(x, z) - xc(\frac{y}{x}) + (1+r)^{-1} \int v(y, z')\mu(dz') \right].$$

Since only the result in part e. was obtained using properties of the transition function of z, everything holds except that the policy function is a nondecreasing function of z. In this case, the first-order condition of the Bellman equation above becomes

$$c' \left[\frac{g(x, z)}{x} \right] = (1+r)^{-1} \int v_x \left[g(x, z), z' \right] \mu(dz').$$

And since neither side depends on z, $\bar{g}(x) \equiv g(x, z)$ for all $z \in Z$.

In part d. we showed that for $x < x'$,

$$\frac{\bar{g}(x')}{x'} < \frac{\bar{g}(x)}{x}.$$

Let x_0 be such that $\bar{g}(x_0) \le x_0$, then $\{x_t\}_{t=0}^{\infty}$ is a monotone decreasing sequence since $\bar{g}(x)$ is strictly increasing. Hence by the result of part d., $\{x_{t+1}/x_t\}_{t=0}^{\infty}$ is a monotone increasing sequence with an upper bound,

$$1 \ge \frac{\bar{g}(x_t)}{x_t}.$$

So it converges. Conversely, if $\bar{g}(x_0) > x_0$, then $\{x_t\}_{t=0}^{\infty}$ is a monotone increasing sequence and so $\{x_{t+1}/x_t\}_{t=0}^{\infty}$ is a monotone decreasing sequence with a lower bound,

$$\frac{\bar{g}(x_t)}{x_t} > 1 - \delta.$$

Hence it converges. Notice that at both limits, say $\hat{x}$,

$$\frac{\bar{g}\left[\bar{g}(\hat{x})\right]}{\bar{g}(\hat{x})} = \frac{\bar{g}(\hat{x})}{\hat{x}},$$

and since $\bar{g}(x)/x$ is a strictly decreasing function of x, this implies that $\bar{g}(\hat{x}) = \hat{x}$. So both sequences converge to one and $\{x_t\}_{t=0}^{\infty}$ converges to a point $\hat{x}$ independent of x_0.

Combining the envelope and first-order conditions for this problem,

$$v_x(x, z) = D(x, z) - c\left[\frac{g(x)}{x}\right] + \frac{g(x)}{x}c'\left[\frac{g(x)}{x}\right],$$

$$c'\left[\frac{g(x)}{x}\right] = (1+r)^{-1}\int v_x\left[g(x), z'\right]\mu(dz'),$$

we obtain

$$(1+r)c'\left[\frac{x}{g^{-1}(x)}\right]$$

$$= \int\left[D(x, z') - c\left[\frac{g(x)}{x}\right] + \frac{g(x)}{x}c'\left[\frac{g(x)}{x}\right]\right]\mu(dz').$$

Now suppose $x_t \to 0$, we know by the proof above that $g(x_t)/x_t \to 1$, and so since 0 is the lower bound for x,

$$c(1) + rc'(1) \geq \int D(0, z')\mu(dz').$$

Hence a sufficient condition to rule out $\bar{x} = 0$ is

$$c(1) + rc'(1) < \int D(0, z')\mu(dz').$$

Exercise 10.7

a. By choice of y_t the agent can, given a wage offer w_t, decide to work for that wage or search. If he searches he will get an offer of z_{t+1}. If the agent works he either gets the current wage or loses his job (depending on the value of d_{t+1}). Hence the law of motion of the wage, $w_{t+1} = \phi(w_t, y_t, d_{t+1}, z_{t+1})$, is given by

$$w_{t+1} = d_{t+1}y_t w_t + (1 - y_t)z_{t+1}.$$

b. The worker decision problem is

$$v^*(w_0) = \sup_{\{y_t\}_{t=0}^{\infty}}\Bigg\{y_0 U(w_0) + \sum_{t=1}^{\infty}\beta^t\int_{Z^t} y_t U(w_t)\,\mu^t(dz^t \times dd^t)\Bigg\}$$

s.t. $w_{t+1} = d_{t+1}y_t w_t + (1 - y_t)z_{t+1},$ given w_0, where

$$\mu^t(dz^t \times dd^t) = \Pi_{t=1}^t f(z_t)\left[\chi_{1\in dd_t}(1-\theta) + \chi_{0\in dd_t}\theta\right].$$

Notice that this problem depends only on w_0. This is so because once the agent has an offer at the beginning of the period, the pair of shocks that generated that offer is not important for the decision making. That is, the wage offer at the beginning of the period is the only relevant state variable.

c. Define the operator T by

$$Tv(w) = \max\Big\{U(w) + \beta[(1-\theta)v(w) + \theta v(0)],$$
$$\beta\int_0^{\bar{w}} v(w')f(w')dw'\Big\}.$$

First notice that since $w \in [0, \bar{w}]$, both parts of the right-hand side are bounded if v is bounded so the operator maps the space of bounded functions into itself. Since both parts are continuous, if v is continuous and since the maximum of continuous functions is continuous, the operator maps continuous functions into continuous functions.

We will use the Blackwell conditions to show first that $v(w)$ is a contraction. For monotonicity just notice that for $\psi(w) > v(w)$, $T\psi(w) > Tv(w)$, since both choices increase. For discounting,

$$T[v(w)+a] = \max\Big\{U(w) + \beta[(1-\theta)(v(w)+a) + \theta(v(0)+a)],$$
$$\beta\int_0^{\bar{w}} (v(w')+a)f(w')dw'\Big\}$$
$$= Tv(w) + \beta a.$$

Hence by the Contraction Mapping Theorem and Corollary 2, there exists a unique, continuous and bounded function v that satisfies $Tv(w) = v(w)$.

We can rewrite the problem in part b. by noting that

$$
\begin{aligned}
& v^*(w_0) \\
&= \sup_{\{y_t\}_{t=0}^{\infty}} \left\{ y_0 U(w_0) \right. \\
&\quad \left. + \sum_{t=1}^{\infty} \beta^t \int_{Z^t} y_t U(w_t)\, \mu^t(dz^t \times dd^t) \right\} \\
&= \max \left\{ U(w_0) + \sup_{\{y_t\}_{t=1}^{\infty}} [\beta y_1 [(1-\theta)U(w_0) + \theta U(0)] \right. \\
&\quad + \beta(1-\theta) \sum_{t=2}^{\infty} \beta^{t-1} \int_{Z^t} y_t U\left(w_t|_{w_1=w_0}\right) \mu^t(dz^t \times dd^t) \\
&\quad + \beta\theta \sum_{t=2}^{\infty} \beta^{t-1} \int_{Z^t} y_t U\left(w_t|_{w_1=0}\right) \mu^t(dz^t \times dd^t)], \\
&\quad \sup_{\{y_t\}_{t=1}^{\infty}} [\beta \int_Z y_1 U(z_1)\, f(dz_1) \\
&\quad \left. + \beta \int_Z \sum_{t=2}^{\infty} \beta^{t-1} \int_{Z^t} y_t U\left(w_t|_{w_1=z_1}\right) \mu^t(dz^t \times dd^t) f(dz_1)] \right\},
\end{aligned}
$$

which can be rearranged to get

$$
\max \left\{ U(w_0) + \beta(1-\theta)v^*(w_0) + \theta v^*(0), \right.
\qquad \left. \beta \int_Z v^*(z_1) f(z_1) dz_1 \right\}.
$$

Hence $v(w) = v^*(w)$ for all $w \in [0, \bar{w}]$. Alternatively, we could prove that Assumptions 9.1–9.2 hold and use Theorem 9.2.

Let w be such that

$$
v(w) = U(w) + \beta\left[(1-\theta)v(w) + \theta v(0)\right],
$$

then since $U(w)$ is increasing in w,

$$
v(w) = \frac{U(w) + \beta\theta v(0)}{1 - \beta(1-\theta)}
$$

is also increasing in w. If

$$v(w) = \beta \int_Z v(w')f(w')dw',$$

$v(w)$ is constant and hence $v(w)$ is weakly increasing.

d. First we will show that $v(0) = A$.

$$v(0) = \max\{\beta v(0), A\},$$

if $v(0) = \beta v(0)$, then $v(0) = 0$. If $v(0) = A$, then $v(0) > 0$. Hence $v(0) = A$.

Since $U(w)$ is strictly increasing and $v(w)$ is weakly increasing by part c., $U(w) + \beta(1-\theta)v(w) + \theta v(0)$ is strictly increasing in w. Notice also that since $v(0) = A$,

$$\beta v(0) < A,$$

and that

$$U(\bar{w}) + \beta\left[(1-\theta)\, v(\bar{w}) + \theta v(0)\right] > \beta \int_0^{\bar{w}} v(w')f(w')dw' = A,$$

since if not, $v(\bar{w}) = A$, a contradiction with $\beta < 1$. These conditions, together with U and v continuous, guarantee that there exists a unique w^* that satisfies

$$U(w^*) + \beta\left[(1-\theta)\, v(w^*) + \theta A\right] = A.$$

e. If $w < w^*$,

$$U(w) + \beta\left[(1-\theta)\, v(w) + \theta A\right] < A,$$

since the left-hand side is increasing in w and so $v(w) = A$.

If $w \geq w^*$,

$$U(w) + \beta\left[(1-\theta)\, v(w) + \theta A\right] \geq A,$$

and so $v(w) = U(w) + \beta\left[(1-\theta)\, v(w) + \theta A\right]$, hence the result.

f. From (2)

$$A = \beta \int_0^{\bar{w}} v(w')f(w')dw',$$

and substituting (4),

$$A = \beta AF(w^*) + \beta \int_{w^*}^{\bar{w}} \frac{U(w') + \beta\theta A}{1 - \beta(1-\theta)} f(w')dw'$$

$$= \beta AF(w^*) + \frac{\beta^2\theta A(1 - F(w^*))}{1 - \beta(1-\theta)}$$

$$+ \beta \int_{w^*}^{\bar{w}} \frac{U(w')}{1 - \beta(1-\theta)} f(w')dw',$$

and rearranging terms, we arrive at equation (5).

g. First notice that

$$0 = U(0)[1 + \beta\theta] < \beta \int_0^{\bar{w}} U(w')f(w')dw'.$$

Also notice that

$$U(\bar{w})[1 + \beta\theta - \beta] > \beta \int_{\bar{w}}^{\bar{w}} U(w')f(w')dw' = 0.$$

Rewrite equation (6) as

$$U(w^*)[1 + \beta\theta] = \beta \int_{w^*}^{\bar{w}} U(w')f(w')dw' + \beta U(w^*) \int_0^{w^*} f(w')dw'$$

$$= \beta \int_{w^*}^{\bar{w}} (U(w') - U(w^*))f(w')dw' + \beta U(w^*),$$

which implies that

$$U(w^*)[1 + \beta\theta - \beta] = \beta \int_{w^*}^{\bar{w}} (U(w') - U(w^*))f(w')dw'.$$

The left-hand side is strictly increasing in w since U is strictly increasing in w, and the right-hand side is decreasing in w, since

$$\frac{\partial}{\partial w}\beta \int_w^{\bar{w}} (U(w') - U(w))f(w')dw' = -\beta \int_w^{\bar{w}} U'(w)f(w')dw' < 0.$$

h. Equation (5) can be rewritten as

$$U(w^*)[1 + \beta\theta - \beta] = \beta \int_{w^*}^{\bar{w}} (U(w') - U(w^*))f(w')dw',$$

as shown in part g., so

$$U(w^*)\left[\frac{1}{\beta}+\theta-1\right]=\int_{w^*}^{\bar{w}}(U(w')-U(w^*))f(w')dw'.$$

The left-hand side of the equation above decreases with β and the right-hand side does not depend on β. Hence w^* is increasing in β. The intuition for this result is that if the agent is more patient, he is more ready to wait for a good wage offer. With an increase in θ, the left-hand side increases, so w^* is decreasing in θ. Again the intuition is that if one is more likely to lose one's job, then the future expected utility derived from a good offer decreases.

i. If the change in the variance is given by a mean preserving spread in the wage distribution, the weight of the tail of the distribution increases. Hence

$$\int_{w^*}^{\bar{w}}(U(w')-U(w^*))f(w')dw'$$

increases, and since this term is decreasing in w^*, w^* increases when the variance increases. The result for expected utility is ambiguous. Figure 10.4 shows that the function v is neither globally convex nor concave, hence the term

$$\beta\int_{0}^{\bar{w}}v(w')f(w')dw'$$

may increase or decrease with a mean preserving spread in the wage distribution.

Exercise 10.8

a. To show that the difference equation is stable, use equation (2) to obtain

$$\begin{aligned}\left|\lambda_{t+1}(A^c)-\lambda_t(A^c)\right| &= \left|\theta+\lambda_t(A^c)\left[\mu(A^c)-\theta\right]-\lambda_t(A^c)\right|\\ &= \left|\mu(A^c)-\theta\right|\left|\lambda_t(A^c)-\lambda_{t-1}(A^c)\right|.\end{aligned}$$

And since $|\mu(A^c)-\theta|<1$, the difference equation is stable.

To find the limit, find the fixed point of (2). Denote the fixed point $\bar{\lambda}(A^c)=\lim_{t\to\infty}\lambda_t(A^c)$. Then,

$$\bar{\lambda}(A^c)=\theta+\bar{\lambda}(A^c)\left[1-\mu(A)-\theta\right],$$

which implies that

$$\bar{\lambda}(A^c)=\frac{\theta}{\theta+\mu(A)}.$$

b. If $0 \in C$ then $P(w, C) = \theta$ for all $w \in A$. Hence

$$\begin{aligned}\lambda_{t+1}(C) &= \int_W P(w, C)\lambda_t(dw) \\ &= \lambda_t(A^c)\mu(C) + \lambda_t(A)\theta \\ &= \theta + \lambda_t(A^c)\,[\mu(C) - \theta].\end{aligned}$$

Taking the limit of the equation above we obtain

$$\begin{aligned}\bar{\lambda}(C) &= \theta + \bar{\lambda}(A^c)\,[\mu(C) - \theta] \\ &= \theta + \frac{\theta\,[\mu(C) - \theta]}{\theta + \mu(A)},\end{aligned}$$

which yields equation (4) after rearranging terms.
If $0 \notin C$ then $P(w, C) = 0$ for all $w \in A$, hence

$$\begin{aligned}\lambda_{t+1}(C) &= \lambda_t(A^c)\mu(C) + \lambda_t(A)0 \\ &= \lambda_t(A^c)\mu(C).\end{aligned}$$

Again

$$\bar{\lambda}(C) = \bar{\lambda}(A^c)\mu(C),$$

which implies that

$$\bar{\lambda}(C) = \frac{\theta\mu(C)}{\theta + \mu(A)}.$$

c. Take limits of

$$\lambda_{t+1}(C) = \lambda_t(A^c)\mu(C) + \lambda_t(C)(1 - \theta)$$

to obtain

$$\bar{\lambda}(C) = \bar{\lambda}(A^c)\mu(C) + \bar{\lambda}(C)(1 - \theta),$$

so

$$\bar{\lambda}(C) = \frac{\mu(C)}{\theta + \mu(A)}.$$

d. The result in (3) gives the probability of obtaining an offer that is not accepted. Equation (4) gives the equilibrium probability of staying unemployed, searching or getting fired. Equation (5) gives the probability of staying unemployed searching and equation (6) the probability of staying employed. The average wage in this economy is then

$$w_a = \int_A w \frac{\mu(dw)}{\theta + \mu(A)}.$$

Let $h(n)$ be the probability of staying on average n periods unemployed, then

$$h(n) = \int_{A^c} n \left[\frac{\theta\mu(dw)}{\theta + \mu(A)} + \frac{\theta\mu(A)}{\theta + \mu(A)} \right]^n .$$

Exercise 10.10

a. Because of the specification of μ, we just need to check that

$$\frac{\Gamma(n+2)}{\Gamma(k+1)\Gamma(n+1-k)} = \frac{1}{\int_0^1 u^k(1-u)^{n-k}du}.$$

First notice that

$$\begin{aligned}\Gamma(n) &= \int_0^\infty t^{n-1}e^{-t}dt \\ &= \frac{t^n}{n}e^{-t}|_0^\infty + \int_0^\infty \frac{t^n}{n}e^{-t}dt \\ &= \frac{\Gamma(n+1)}{n}.\end{aligned}$$

Hence, applying the result above repeatedly,

$$\frac{\Gamma(n+2)}{\Gamma(k+1)\Gamma(n+1-k)} = \frac{(n+1)!}{(k)!(n-k)!}.$$

Using integration by parts repeatedly

$$\begin{aligned}\int_0^1 u^k(1-u)^{n-k}du &= u^k\frac{(1-u)^{n-k+1}}{n+1-k}|_0^1 \\ &\quad + \int_0^1 ku^{k-1}\frac{(1-u)^{n-k+1}}{n+1-k}du \\ &= \frac{k!(n-k)!}{(n+1)!}.\end{aligned}$$

So

$$\frac{\Gamma(n+2)}{\Gamma(k+1)\Gamma(n+1-k)} = \frac{1}{\int_0^1 u^k(1-u)^{n-k}du}.$$

b. We need to show that

$$\frac{\Gamma(\alpha+\beta+n)}{\Gamma(\alpha+k)\Gamma(\beta+n-k)} = \frac{1}{\int_0^1 u^{\alpha+k-1}(1-u)^{\beta+n-k-1}du}.$$

Following the proof in a.,

$$\frac{\Gamma(\alpha+\beta+n)}{\Gamma(\alpha+k)\Gamma(\beta+n-k)} = \frac{(\alpha+\beta+n-1)!}{(\alpha+k-1)!(\beta+n-k-1)!}.$$

Also as in part a.,

$$\int_0^1 u^{\alpha+k-1}(1-u)^{\beta+n-k-1}du = \frac{(\alpha+k-1)!(\beta+n-k-1)!}{(\alpha+\beta+n-1)!},$$

using integration by parts.

11 *Strong Convergence of Markov Processes*

Exercise 11.1

To show that the matrix Q takes the given form, we will use the fact that Q satisfies

$$Q = \Pi Q = Q\Pi.$$

First notice that following the same block matrix notation as in the text,

$$\Pi Q = \begin{pmatrix} 0 & \begin{matrix} R_{00}w_1Q_1 \\ +R_{01}Q_1 \end{matrix} & \begin{matrix} R_{00}w_2Q_2 \\ +R_{02}Q_2 \end{matrix} & \cdots & \begin{matrix} R_{00}w_MQ_M \\ +R_{0M}Q_M \end{matrix} \\ 0 & R_{11}Q_1 & 0 & \cdots & 0 \\ 0 & 0 & R_{22}Q_2 & \cdots & 0 \\ \vdots & \vdots & \vdots & \ddots & \vdots \\ 0 & 0 & 0 & \cdots & R_{MM}Q_M \end{pmatrix},$$

and

$$Q\Pi = \begin{pmatrix} 0 & w_1Q_1R_{11} & w_2Q_2R_{22} & \cdots & w_MQ_MR_{MM} \\ 0 & Q_1R_{11} & 0 & \cdots & 0 \\ 0 & 0 & Q_2R_{22} & \cdots & 0 \\ \vdots & \vdots & \vdots & \ddots & \vdots \\ 0 & 0 & 0 & \cdots & Q_MR_{MM} \end{pmatrix}.$$

Since E_i is an ergodic set, Theorem 11.1 implies that there is only one invariant distribution and hence all the rows of Q_i are equal. Also, because each matrix

R_{ii} is a stochastic matrix and by the definition of Q_i, $i = 1, \ldots, M$, we know that $Q_i = Q_i R_{ii}$. Hence $Q\Pi = Q$ and

$$\Pi Q = \begin{pmatrix} 0 & \begin{matrix} R_{00}w_1Q_1 \\ +R_{01}Q_1 \end{matrix} & \begin{matrix} R_{00}w_2Q_2 \\ +R_{02}Q_2 \end{matrix} & \cdots & \begin{matrix} R_{00}w_MQ_M \\ +R_{0M}Q_M \end{matrix} \\ 0 & Q_1 & 0 & \cdots & 0 \\ 0 & 0 & Q_2 & \cdots & 0 \\ \vdots & \vdots & \vdots & \ddots & \vdots \\ 0 & 0 & 0 & \cdots & Q_M \end{pmatrix}.$$

We still need to show that there exists a set of matrices $\{w_i\}_{i=1}^{M}$ such that

$$R_{00}w_iQ_i + R_{0i}Q_i = w_iQ_i, \quad i = 1, \ldots, M.$$

Notice that w_i is a vector only if the transient set is a singleton. We will use a guess and verify strategy to prove the existence of the set of matrices $\{w_i\}_{i=1}^{M}$. So guess that

$$w_i = \left(\sum_{n=0}^{\infty} R_{00}^n\right) R_{0i}, \quad i = 1, \ldots, M.$$

Substitute the guess in the equation above to get

$$\left(\sum_{n=1}^{\infty} R_{00}^n\right) R_{0i}Q_i = \left(\sum_{n=0}^{\infty} R_{00}^n - I_{\dim(F)\times\dim(F)}\right) R_{0i}Q_i,$$

but clearly

$$\sum_{n=1}^{\infty} R_{00}^n = \sum_{n=0}^{\infty} R_{00}^n - I_{\dim(F)\times\dim(F)},$$

which verifies the guess. One can obtain the same result for w_i by calculating Π^n and then using induction.

For the case when the transient set is a singleton, this implies that

$$w_i = \frac{1}{1 + R_{00}} R_{0i},$$

since $R_{00} < 1$.

We will also show that

$$\sum_{k=1}^{M} \sum_{i=1}^{\dim(E_k)} w_{k,ji} = 1, \quad j = 1, \ldots, \dim(F).$$

For this notice that since Q is a stochastic matrix,

$$\sum_{k=1}^{M} \sum_{\ell=1}^{\dim(E_k)} \sum_{i=1}^{\dim(E_k)} w_{k,ji} q_{k,i\ell} = 1,$$

and that since all the columns of Q_k are the same, $q_{k,i\ell}$ does not depend on i. Hence, since Q_k is a stochastic matrix,

$$\sum_{\ell=1}^{\dim(E_k)} q_{k,i\ell} = 1,$$

which yields the result.

Notice that the elements of $R_{00}^n R_{0i}$ give the probability of going from one of the transient states in F to a state in E_i in n periods. Hence each element in w_i gives the probability of a transition, in any period (summing the probability in all periods), from a specific state in F to a specific state in E_i. Hence the sum of the rows in w_i gives the probability of an eventual transition from a specific state in F to any set in E_i.

Exercise 11.2

By Theorem 7.5 for any bounded and measurable function $f : S \to \mathbf{R}$, there exists a sequence of simple functions f_n such that

$$\lim_{n\to\infty} f_n(x) = f(x) \text{ for all } x \in S.$$

Without loss of generality assume also that $f \geq 0$ (f can be expressed as the substraction of two positive valued functions), then f_n can be chosen such that $0 \leq f_n \leq f_{n+1} \leq f$, all n. Also notice that for any n, f_n can be expressed as a sum of indicator functions. Let $x_i^n \in A_i^n$, where $\{A_i^n\}$ is a partition of S in n sets, be such that

$$f_n(x) \equiv \sum_{i=1}^{n} f(x_i^n)\chi_{A_i^n}, \; A_i^n \in \mathcal{S} \text{ all } i = 1, \ldots, n.$$

Hence,

$$\lim_{n\to\infty}\int f d\lambda_n = \lim_{n\to\infty}\int \lim_{i\to\infty} f_i d\lambda_n$$

$$= \lim_{n\to\infty}\int \lim_{i\to\infty}\sum_{j=1}^{i} f(x_j^i)\chi_{A_j^i} d\lambda_n$$

$$= \lim_{n\to\infty}\lim_{i\to\infty}\sum_{j=1}^{i} f(x_j^i)\lambda_n(A_j^i)$$

$$= \lim_{i\to\infty}\sum_{j=1}^{i} f(x_j^i)\lambda(A_j^i)$$

$$= \int f d\lambda,$$

where the third line uses Theorem 7.10 (Lebesgue Dominated Convergence Theorem) and the fourth line uses equation (1).

Exercise 11.3

The definition of a vector space is given in Section 3.1. Since a signed measure is a real-valued function, properties a. through e. are trivially satisfied for addition and scalar multiplication. To see this, notice that if ν, $\bar{\nu} \in \Phi(S, \mathcal{S})$, there exist a four-tuple of finite measures such that

$$v(C) = \lambda_1(C) - \lambda_2(C), \text{ all } C \in \mathcal{S},$$

and

$$\bar{v}(C) = \bar{\lambda}_1(C) - \bar{\lambda}_2(C), \text{ all } C \in \mathcal{S},$$

hence

$$v(C) + \bar{v}(C) = \left[\lambda_1(C) + \bar{\lambda}_1(C)\right] - \left[\lambda_2(C) + \bar{\lambda}_2(C)\right], \text{ all } C \in \mathcal{S},$$

and since $\lambda_i + \bar{\lambda}_i$, $i = 1, 2$, are finite measures, $v + \bar{v} \in \Phi(S, \mathcal{S})$. Also notice that for any finite real number α, $|\alpha|\,\lambda_1$ and $|\alpha|\,\lambda_2$ are finite measures. So for all $\alpha \in \mathbf{R}$,

$$\alpha v(C) = |\alpha|\,\lambda_1(C) - |\alpha|\,\lambda_2(C), \text{ all } C \in \mathcal{S} \text{ if } \alpha \geq 0$$

or

$$\alpha v(C) = |\alpha| \, \lambda_2(C) - |\alpha| \, \lambda_1(C), \quad \text{all } C \in \mathcal{S} \text{ if } \alpha < 0.$$

Hence, $\alpha v(C) \in \Phi(S, \mathcal{S})$ and so $\alpha v(C)$ is closed under scalar multiplication.

For f. notice that $v \in \Phi(S, \mathcal{S})$ can be defined as

$$v(C) = \lambda(C) - \lambda(C) = 0, \quad \text{all } C \in \mathcal{S},$$

where λ is a finite measure. Hence for any other signed measure $\bar{v} \in \Phi(S, \mathcal{S})$,

$$v(C) + \bar{v}(C) = \bar{v}(C),$$

all $C \in \mathcal{S}$. For g. notice also that

$$0\bar{v}(C) = v(C), \quad \text{all } C \in \mathcal{S}.$$

For part h. let λ_1 and λ_2 be two finite measures so

$$1\lambda_i(C) = \lambda_i(C), \quad \text{all } C \in \mathcal{S}, \; i = 1, 2.$$

Then

$$1v(C) = 1\lambda_1(C) - 1\lambda_2(C) = v(C), \quad \text{all } C \in \mathcal{S}.$$

To show that (1) defines a norm, notice that $\|\lambda\|$ is trivially nonnegative for any $\lambda \in \Phi(S, \mathcal{S})$. Also notice that

$$\|\alpha\lambda\| = \sup \sum_{i=1}^{k} |\alpha\lambda(A_i)| = |\alpha| \sup \sum_{i=1}^{k} |\lambda(A_i)|,$$

since the absolute value is a norm in $\mathbf{R}$. For the triangle inequality, for $\lambda, \mu \in \Phi(S, \mathcal{S})$,

$$\begin{aligned}
\|\lambda + \mu\| &= \sup \sum_{i=1}^{k} |\lambda(A_i) + \mu(A_i)| \\
&\leq \sup \sum_{i=1}^{k} (|\lambda(A_i)| + |\mu(A_i)|) \\
&\leq \sup \sum_{i=1}^{k} |\lambda(A_i)| + \sup \sum_{i=1}^{k} |\mu(A_i)| \\
&= \|\lambda\| + \|\mu\|,
\end{aligned}$$

where we used the properties of the absolute value for the first inequality and the fact that the supremum of the sum is less or equal than the sum of the supremums.

Exercise 11.4

a. Fix $\varepsilon \in (0, 1)$. Since S is a finite set, let $\infty > \phi(s_i) \geq \varepsilon$ for all s_i. Then

$$\sum_{i=1}^{N} \phi(s_i) < \infty,$$

where N is the number of elements in the set. So in this case we can assign enough mass to all states such that the restriction in Condition D never applies.

b. Let M be such that

$$\sup_i \left[1 - \sum_{j=1}^{M} p_{ij} \right] \leq \varepsilon.$$

Notice that the number M exists for all $\varepsilon \in (0, 1)$ since the partial sums $\sum_j p_{ij}$ converge uniformly in i. Let $\phi(s_i) = 2\varepsilon$ for all $i \leq M$ and $\phi(s_i) = 0$ for $i > M$. Then $\phi(S) = 2M\varepsilon$. So if $\phi(A) \leq \varepsilon$,

$$P^N(s_i, A) \leq \sum_{j=M+1}^{\infty} p_{ij} < 1 - \varepsilon,$$

for all $N \geq 1$ and $0 < \varepsilon < 1/2$.

c. Let $\phi(A) \geq \varepsilon$ if $s_0 \in A$ and $\phi(A) = 0$ if $s_0 \notin A$. Then for A such that $s_0 \notin A$,

$$\begin{aligned} P^N(s, A) &\leq P^N(s, S \backslash \{s_0\}) \\ &= 1 - P^N(s, \{s_0\}) \\ &< 1 - \varepsilon, \end{aligned}$$

for some N and $\varepsilon > 0$.

d. If $\phi(A) \leq \varepsilon$, then

$$\begin{aligned} P^N(s, A) &\leq \phi(A) \\ &\leq \varepsilon \\ &< 1 - \varepsilon, \end{aligned}$$

for $0 < \varepsilon < 1/2$.

e. Let $p(s, s') > \delta > 0$ for all $s, s' \in S$ and

$$M \equiv \int_S \mu(ds).$$

Then for all A such that $\mu(A) \leq \varepsilon$,

$$\begin{aligned} P(s, A) &= \int_A p(s, s')\mu(ds') \\ &= 1 - \int_{A^c} p(s, s')\mu(ds') \\ &\leq 1 - \delta \int_{A^c} \mu(ds') \\ &\leq 1 - \delta(1-\varepsilon)M \\ &< 1 - \varepsilon, \end{aligned}$$

for some ε such that

$$\frac{M\delta}{1+M\delta} > \varepsilon.$$

f. Let $p(s, s') < \delta$ for all $s, s' \in S$. Then for all A such that $\mu(A) \leq \varepsilon$,

$$\begin{aligned} P(s, A) &\leq \delta \int_A \mu(ds') \\ &\leq \delta\varepsilon \\ &< 1 - \varepsilon, \end{aligned}$$

for some ε such that $1/(1+\delta) > \varepsilon$.

g. By assumption there exists an ε and an N such that for all A with $\phi(A) \leq \varepsilon$, $P_1^N(s, A) < 1 - \varepsilon$. Define $\hat{\phi}(A) = \alpha\phi(A)$. Then $\phi(S) < \infty$ and $\phi(A) \leq \varepsilon$ implies that $\hat{\phi}(A) \leq \alpha\varepsilon \equiv \hat{\varepsilon}$. Hence for A such that $\phi(A) \leq \varepsilon$,

$$\begin{aligned} P(s, A) &= \alpha P_1(s, A) + (1-\alpha)P_2(s, A) \\ &\leq \alpha P_1(s, A) + (1-\alpha) \\ &\leq 1 - \hat{\varepsilon} = 1 - \alpha\varepsilon. \end{aligned}$$

h. The proof is by contradiction. Suppose there exists a triplet (ϕ, N, ε), such that Condition D is satisfied. Since

$$P^N(s_i, A) = \begin{cases} 1 & \text{if } s_i \in A \\ 0 & \text{otherwise} \end{cases},$$

$P^N(s_i, A) > \varepsilon$ implies that $\phi(s_i) > \epsilon$ and so $\phi(S) = \sum_{i=1}^{\infty} \phi(s_i)$ is not finite.

i. By contradiction. Suppose P satisfies Condition D, then since

$$P^N(s_i, A) = \begin{cases} 1 & \text{if } s_{i+1} \in A \\ 0 & \text{otherwise} \end{cases},$$

$P^N(s_i, A) > \varepsilon$ implies that $\phi(s_{i+1}) > \varepsilon$ and so $\phi(S) = \sum_{i=1}^{\infty} \phi(s_i)$ is not finite.

j. By contradiction. Let $A_i = (1/2^i, 1/2^{i-1}]$, then $P(s_i, A_i) = 1$ if $s_i \in A_{i-1}$ which implies that $\phi(A_i) > \varepsilon$ all i. But then

$$\phi(S) = \phi(\cup_{i=1}^{\infty} A_i) = \sum_{i=1}^{\infty} \phi(A_i)$$

is not finite.

Exercise 11.5

a. Part c.: $P^N(s, \{s_0\}) > \varepsilon$ all $s \in S$. Since for all $A \in \mathcal{S}$ either $s_0 \in A$ or $s_0 \in A^c$, we have that $P^N(s, A) \geq P^N(s, \{s_0\}) \geq \varepsilon$ or $P^N(s, A^c) \geq P^N(s, \{s_0\}) \geq \varepsilon$.

Part e.: Let $P(s, S) \geq \alpha\mu(S)$. Notice that since either $\mu(A) \geq (1/2)\mu(S)$ or $\mu(A^c) \geq (1/2)\mu(S)$, we have that either

$$P^N(s, A) \geq \alpha\mu(A) \geq \varepsilon$$

or

$$P^N(s, A^c) \geq \alpha\mu(A^c) \geq \varepsilon$$

for $\varepsilon < (1/2)\alpha\mu(S)$.

b. Define $\phi(A) = \sup_s P^N(s, A)$, then $\phi(S) = 1$ and $\phi(\emptyset) = 0$. Then $\phi(A) \leq \varepsilon$ implies that $P^N(s, A) \leq \varepsilon$ and by Condition M we have that $P^N(s, A^c) \geq \varepsilon$, and so

$$P^N(s, A) = 1 - P^N(s, A^c) \leq 1 - \varepsilon.$$

c. P satisfies Condition D as a corollary to Exercise 11.4a. To show that Condition M is not satisfied, let $A = \{s_1\}$. Then $P^N(s_2, A) = 0$ for all N, and $P^N(s_1, A^c) = 0$ for all N.

12 Weak Convergence of Markov Processes

Exercise 12.1

a. $S, \emptyset \in \{A \subseteq S : A \in \mathcal{B}^l\}$. If $A \subseteq S$ and $A \in \mathcal{B}^l$, this implies that $S \backslash A \subseteq S$ and since A, $S \in \mathcal{B}^l$, $S \backslash A \in \mathcal{B}^l$. Hence $A \in \{A \subseteq S : A \in \mathcal{B}^l\}$ implies $A^c \in \mathcal{S}$, where the complement is relative to S. Let $A_n \subseteq S$ and $A_n \in \mathcal{B}^l$ for all $n =$ 1, 2 . . . then $U_{n=1}^{\infty} A_n \subseteq S$ and since $A_n \in \mathcal{B}^l$, $U_{n=1}^{\infty} A_n \in \mathcal{B}^l$. Hence $U_{n=1}^{\infty} A_n \in \{A \subseteq S : A \in \mathcal{B}^l\}$.

b. A is open relative to S if for all $x \in A \cap S$ there exists an $\varepsilon > 0$ such that $b(x, \varepsilon) \cap S \subseteq A$. Let $A = A' \cap S$ for $A' \in \mathcal{B}^l$ and A' open relative to $\mathbf{R}^l$. Then $A' \cap S \in \mathcal{B}^l$ and since A' is open, there exist an $\varepsilon > 0$ such that $b(x, \varepsilon) \subseteq A$ for all $x \in A \subset A'$. But then $b(x, \varepsilon) \cap S \subseteq A' \cap S$. So A is open relative to S.

c. The interior of A relative to S is given by

$$int(A) = \{x \in A \cap S : b(x, \varepsilon) \subseteq A \cap S, \text{ for some } \varepsilon > 0\}.$$

We need to show that for all $x \in int(A)$, there exists an ε such that $b(x, \varepsilon) \subseteq int(A) \cap S$. Notice that by definition $int(A) \subset S$ and for all $x \in int(A)$ there exists an ε such that $b(x, \varepsilon) \subseteq A \cap S$. Hence $b(x, \varepsilon/2) \subseteq int(A)$.

d. If A is open relative to x, for all $x \in A \cap S$ there exists an ε such that $b(x, \varepsilon) \subseteq A \cap S$. But this implies that for all $x \in A \cap S$, $x \in int(A)$. Since $int(A) \subseteq A$, we know that $int(A) \cap S \subseteq A \cap S$ and so $int(A) \cap S = A \cap S$. Further notice that if $A \subseteq S$, this implies that $int(A) = A$.

Exercise 12.2

a. First notice that

$$\rho(x, A) = \inf_{z \in A} \rho(x, z) = \rho(x, \bar{x}) \text{ for some } \bar{x} \in A \subseteq S,$$

and

$$\rho(y, A) = \inf_{z \in A} \rho(y, z) = \rho(y, \bar{y}) \text{ for some } \bar{y} \in A \subseteq S.$$

Also notice that by definition

$$\rho(x, \bar{x}) \leq \rho(x, \bar{y}),$$

and

$$\rho(y, \bar{y}) \leq \rho(y, \bar{x}).$$

Hence since ρ is a metric we know that

$$\rho(x, \bar{x}) \leq \rho(x, \bar{y}) \leq \rho(x, y) + \rho(y, \bar{y})$$

and

$$\rho(y, \bar{y}) \leq \rho(y, \bar{x}) \leq \rho(x, y) + \rho(x, \bar{x})$$

which yields the result.

b. Given any $\varepsilon > 0$ and any pair $x, y \in S$ such that

$$\rho(x, y) \leq \varepsilon,$$

by part a.,

$$|\rho(x, A) - \rho(y, A)| \leq \rho(x, y) \leq \varepsilon.$$

Hence $\rho(\cdot, A)$ is uniformly continuous.

c. Suppose $x \in \bar{A}$, then there exists a sequence $\{x_n\}_{n=1}^{\infty}$ such that

$$\lim_{n \to \infty} x_n = x,$$

with $x_n \in A$ for all n. But this implies that

$$\lim_{n \to \infty} \rho(x_n, x) = 0.$$

Since $\rho(\cdot, A)$ is uniformly continuous by part b.,

$$\lim_{n\to\infty} \rho(x_n, A) = \rho(x, A) = 0.$$

For the reverse, suppose x is such that $\rho(x, A) = 0$. Then, for all $\varepsilon > 0$ there exists an $x_\varepsilon \in A$ such that $\rho(x, x_\varepsilon) \le \varepsilon$. Hence, there exists a sequence $\{x_n\}_{n=1}^{\infty} \in A$ such that $\rho(x, x_n) \le 1/n$ all $n = 1, 2, \ldots$ and $\lim_{n\to\infty} x_n = x$. So $x \in \bar{A}$.

Exercise 12.3

F is continuous at x if and only if for any sequence $\{x_n\}_{n=1}^{\infty}$ such that $x_n \to x$,

$$\lim_{n\to\infty} F(x_n) = F(x).$$

Let $\{\varepsilon_n^1\}_{n=1}^{\infty}$ and $\{\varepsilon_n^2\}_{n=1}^{\infty}$ be two sequences of real values such that $\varepsilon_n^1 \uparrow 0$ and $\varepsilon_n^2 \downarrow 0$, and

$$x + \varepsilon_n^1 \underset{\sim}{1} \le x_n \le x + \varepsilon_n^2 \underset{\sim}{1} \text{ for all } n.$$

Then, since F is nondecreasing,

$$F(x + \varepsilon_n^1 \underset{\sim}{1}) \le F(x_n) \le F(x + \varepsilon_n^2 \underset{\sim}{1}) \text{ for all } n.$$

Taking limits this implies that

$$F(x) = \lim_{n\to\infty} F(x + \varepsilon_n^1 \underset{\sim}{1}) \le \lim_{n\to\infty} F(x_n) \le \lim_{n\to\infty} F(x + \varepsilon_n^2 \underset{\sim}{1}) = F(x),$$

where the first and last equalities follow from F continuous from above and below at x. Hence

$$\lim_{n\to\infty} F(x_n) = F(x),$$

and so F is continuous.

Exercise 12.4

Take F closed, then $\hat{\lambda}_n \Rightarrow \hat{\lambda}$ implies by Theorem 12.3 that

$$\limsup_{n\to\infty} \hat{\lambda}_n(F) \le \hat{\lambda}(F).$$

Since F is closed, by Exercise 12.1 b. $F \cap S$ is closed relative to S. By definition

$$\hat{\lambda}_n(F) = \lambda_n(F \cap S),$$

and

$$\hat{\lambda}(F) = \lambda(F \cap S),$$

hence

$$\limsup_{n\to\infty} \lambda_n(F \cap S) \leq \lambda(F \cap S).$$

So by Theorem 12.3 part b., $\lambda_n \Rightarrow \lambda$.

If $\lambda_n \Rightarrow \lambda$ this implies by Theorem 12.3 that

$$\limsup_{n\to\infty} \lambda_n(F) \leq \lambda(F),$$

for some closed set $F \in \mathcal{S}$. Since $\mathcal{S} \subset \mathcal{R}^l$, $F \in \mathcal{B}^l$, which implies that $\hat{\lambda}_n(F) = \lambda_n(F)$ and $\hat{\lambda}(F) = \lambda(F)$. Hence

$$\limsup_{n\to\infty} \hat{\lambda}_n(F) \leq \hat{\lambda}(F),$$

which yields the result.

Exercise 12.5

a. For $x \in \mathcal{S}$, $[a, x] \in \mathcal{A}$ so

$$F_n(x) = \lambda_n\left([a, x]\right).$$

Hence

$$F_n(x) \to F(x) = \lambda\left([a, x]\right).$$

Define $\hat{\lambda}$ as

$$\hat{\lambda}(A) = \lambda(A \cap S), \text{ all } A \in \mathcal{B}^l.$$

Then, since

$$\hat{F}_n(x) \equiv \lambda_n([a, \min(x, b)]) = \hat{\lambda}_n([a, x])$$

and

$$\hat{F}(x) \equiv \lambda([a, \min(x, b)]) = \hat{\lambda}([a, x]),$$

we know that

$$\hat{F}_n(x) \to \hat{F}(x).$$

Theorem 12.8 then implies that $\hat{\lambda}_n \Rightarrow \hat{\lambda}$ and by Exercise 12.4, $\lambda_n \Rightarrow \lambda$.

b. Construct a sequence of monotone and continuous functions as follows. For any $F = [a, c]$, $c \in [a, b]$, let

$$f_n(s) = \begin{cases} 1 - n\rho(s, F) & \text{if } \rho(s, F) \leq \frac{1}{n} \\ 0 & \text{if } \rho(s, F) > \frac{1}{n} \end{cases},$$

where $\rho(s, F)$ is defined in the proof of Lemma 12.1. Then

$$\lambda_n(F) \equiv \int_S f_n d\lambda = \int_S f_n d\mu \equiv \mu_n(F).$$

Notice also that since $f_n(s) \to f(s)$ all $s \in [a, b]$, by the Lebesgue Dominated Convergence Theorem

$$\int_S f_n d\lambda \to \int_S f d\lambda,$$

and so

$$\lim_{n\to\infty} \lambda_n(F) = \lambda(F),$$

and

$$\lim_{n\to\infty} \mu_n(F) = \mu(F).$$

Hence by part a., $\lambda_n \Rightarrow \lambda$ and $\mu_n \Rightarrow \mu$, so $\lambda = \mu$.

Exercise 12.6

a. In the proof of Theorem 12.9 the assumption of support in a common compact set is used to prove that the function G and hence the function F satisfy condition D1 in Theorem 12.7. To see that this is still the case under the weaker assumption proposed in this exercise, first notice that

$$1 \geq F_n\left[\bar{b}(\varepsilon)\right] - F_n\left[\underline{a}(\varepsilon)\right] > 1 - \varepsilon,$$

since F_n is a distribution function for all n. Hence

$$\lim_{\varepsilon\to 0} F_n\left[\bar{b}(\varepsilon)\right] - F_n\left[\underline{a}(\varepsilon)\right] = 1.$$

Now if $\lim_{\varepsilon \to 0} \bar{b}(\varepsilon)$ and $\lim_{\varepsilon \to 0} \underline{a}(\varepsilon)$ are finite, then we are back into the case proven in Theorem 12.9. Hence for this assumption to be weaker, either $\lim_{\varepsilon \to 0} \bar{b}(\varepsilon)$ and or $\lim_{\varepsilon \to 0} \underline{a}(\varepsilon)$ are not finite. Suppose that $\lim_{\varepsilon \to 0} \bar{b}(\varepsilon)$ is not finite but that $\lim_{\varepsilon \to 0} \underline{a}(\varepsilon)$ is, then

$$\lim_{\varepsilon \to 0} F_n \left[\underline{a}(\varepsilon)\right] = 0,$$

and so

$$\lim_{\varepsilon \to 0} F_n \left[\bar{b}(\varepsilon)\right] = 1,$$

all n. This implies that G satisfies condition D1. If $\lim_{\varepsilon \to 0} \bar{b}(\varepsilon)$ is finite but $\lim_{\varepsilon \to 0} \underline{a}(\varepsilon)$ is not, the same type of reasoning applies. If $\lim_{\varepsilon \to 0} \bar{b}(\varepsilon)$ and or $\lim_{\varepsilon \to 0} \underline{a}(\varepsilon)$ are not finite then $\lim_{\varepsilon \to 0} \underline{a}_i(\varepsilon) = -\infty$ for some i, and since F_n is a distribution function for every n,

$$\lim_{\varepsilon \to 0} F_n \left[\underline{a}(\varepsilon)\right] = 0,$$

all n. Hence

$$\lim_{\varepsilon \to 0} F_n \left[\bar{b}(\varepsilon)\right] = 1,$$

and so G satisfies condition D1.

b. Fix ε, then since K is a compact set, there exists a pair of points $\underline{a}(\varepsilon), \bar{b}(\varepsilon) \in \mathbf{R}^l$ such that

$$K \subseteq \left[\underline{a}(\varepsilon), \bar{b}(\varepsilon)\right].$$

For all n define

$$F_n(x) \equiv \lambda_n((-\infty, x]).$$

Then

$$1 - \varepsilon < \lambda_n(K) \leq F_n \left[\bar{b}(\varepsilon)\right] - F_n \left[\underline{a}(\varepsilon)\right].$$

So by part a. we know that there exists a subsequence $\{F_n\}$ and a distribution function F such that $\{F_n\}$ converges weakly to F. Corollary 1 of Theorem 12.9 then yields the desired result.

c. If S is a closed subset of $\mathbf{R}$ there exists a pair $(\underline{s}, \bar{s}) \in S$ such that $S \subseteq [\underline{s}, \bar{s}]$. Notice that $\underline{s}$ and or $\bar{s}$ do not have to be finite. If both $\underline{s}$ and $\bar{s}$ are infinite then we are back to the case in part b. If one of them is not finite, for example $\underline{s}$, then just let $\underline{a}(\varepsilon) = \underline{s}$ for all $\varepsilon > 0$. Since we did not restrict the function $\underline{a}(\varepsilon)$ in part b., this implies that the proof in part b. applies.

Exercise 12.7

$b \Rightarrow a$: Let $s_n \to s$. The continuity of f and $P(s_n, \cdot) \Rightarrow P(s, \cdot)$ imply that

$$\begin{aligned}\lim_{n\to\infty} (Tf)(s_n) &= \lim_{n\to\infty} \int_S f(s')P(s_n, ds') \\ &= \int_S f(s')P(s, ds') \\ &= (Tf)(s).\end{aligned}$$

$a \Rightarrow c$: By Theorem 8.3, $\langle f, T^*\lambda\rangle = \langle Tf, \lambda\rangle$. Part a. implies that $Tf(s)$ is continuous in s, and so

$$\int_S Tf(s)\lambda_n(ds) \to \int_S Tf(s)\lambda(ds),$$

if $\lambda_n \Rightarrow \lambda$. Hence $T^*\lambda_n \Rightarrow T^*\lambda$.

$c \Rightarrow b$: Let

$$\lambda(A) = \begin{cases} 1 & \text{if } s \in A \\ 0 & \text{otherwise} \end{cases},$$

and

$$\lambda_n(A) = \begin{cases} 1 & \text{if } s_n \in A \\ 0 & \text{otherwise} \end{cases}.$$

If $s_n \to s$, for any given continuous function f,

$$\int_S f d\lambda_n = f(s_n),$$

and

$$\int_S f d\lambda = f(s).$$

Hence $\lambda_n \Rightarrow \lambda$. So by c., $P(s_n, A) = T^*\lambda_n(A) \Rightarrow T^*\lambda(A) = P(s, A)$.

Exercise 12.8

a. The transition function is given by

$$P(s, A) = \begin{cases} 1 & \text{if } 1 - s \in A \\ 0 & \text{otherwise} \end{cases}.$$

To show that P has the Feller property notice that

$$Tf(s) = \int_0^1 f(s')P(s, ds') = f(1-s),$$

hence if f is a continuous function Tf is continuous.

b. Applying the operator T^* to δ_s yields

$$T^*\delta_s(A) = \int_0^1 P(s', A)\delta_s(ds') = P(s, A) = \delta_{1-s}(A),$$

and applying the operator again yields

$$T^{*2}\delta_s(A) = T^*(T^*\delta_s)(A) = T^*\delta_{1-s}(A) = P(1-s, A) = \delta_s(A).$$

Hence since the above holds for arbitrary A, $T^{*2n-1}\delta_s = \delta_{1-s}$ all n and $T^{*2n}\delta_s = \delta_s$ all n, which implies that

$$\lim_{n\to\infty} T^{*2n-1}\delta_s = \delta_{1-s},$$

and

$$\lim_{n\to\infty} T^{*2n}\delta_s = \delta_s.$$

Since $s \neq 1/2$, and $\delta_s \neq \delta_{1-s}$, none of the limits is an invariant measure.

c. The invariant measures of the system are given by

$$\lambda_{a,f} = \int_0^1 a(s)\lambda_{f(s)}ds,$$

where

$$\lambda_s = \frac{1}{2}\delta_s + \frac{1}{2}\delta_{1-s},$$

$$\int_0^1 a(s)ds = 1,$$

and $f : [0, 1] \to [0, 1]$. To show this, notice that $\lambda_{a,f}(S) = \lambda_s(S) = 1$ and apply the operator T^* to λ_s to obtain

$$T^*\lambda_s = \frac{1}{2}\delta_{1-s} + \frac{1}{2}\delta_s = \lambda_s.$$

Hence

$$T^*\lambda_a = \int_0^1 a(s) \left[\frac{1}{2}\delta_{1-f(s)} + \frac{1}{2}\delta_{f(s)}\right] ds = \lambda_a.$$

Notice that the invariant measures are symmetric, that is,

$$\lambda_{a,f}(\{s\}) = \lambda_{a,f}(\{1-s\}).$$

Exercise 12.9

a. Note that

$$F_\mu(s) = \mu((-\vec{\infty}, s]) = 1 - \mu([s, \vec{\infty})) = 1 - \int_S \chi_{\{[s,\vec{\infty})\}}(y)\mu(dy).$$

Then the result follows since the indicator function $\chi_{\{[s,\vec{\infty})\}}(y)$ is an increasing function, so

$$\int_S \chi_{\{[s,\vec{\infty})\}}(y)\mu(dy) \geq \int_S \chi_{\{[s,\vec{\infty})\}}(y)\lambda(dy).$$

Here the notation $[s, \vec{\infty})$ allows for s to be a vector and $\vec{\infty}$ is a vector with all its entries equal to ∞.

b. In **R**, $F_\mu(s) \leq F_\lambda(s)$ all $s \in S$ implies that

$$\mu([s, \infty)) \geq \lambda([s, \infty)) \text{ all } s \in S.$$

Let f be an increasing and bounded function and let f_n be a sequence of increasing and bounded step functions such that

$$\lim_{n\to\infty} f_n(s) = f(s) \text{ all } s \in S.$$

Then the inequality above implies that

$$\int_S f_n(s)\mu(ds) \geq \int_S f_n(s)\lambda(ds) \text{ all } n = 1, 2 \ldots.$$

So taking limits, by the Lebesgue Dominated Convergence Theorem,

$$\int_S f(s)\mu(ds) \geq \int_S f(s)\lambda(ds),$$

which yields the intended results since f is an arbitrary increasing and bounded function.

c. Let $s \in \mathbf{R}^2$, then $F_\mu(s) = F_\lambda(s)$ all $s \in S$ implies that

$$\mu([s, \vec{\infty})) = \lambda([s, \vec{\infty})) \text{ all } s \in S.$$

Let $\mu([s, \vec{\infty})) = \mu_x([s_1, \infty))$ and $\lambda([s, \vec{\infty})) = \lambda_y([s_2, \infty))$ where s_i denotes the ith coordinate of vector s. The the equality above implies that

$$\mu_x([s_1, \infty)) = \lambda_y([s_2, \infty)).$$

Let $f(x, y) = 1$ for $x \leq \bar{s}_1$ and $y \leq \bar{s}_2$, $\bar{s}_2 > 1$, and $f(x, y) = y$ otherwise. Notice that $f(x, y)$ is a weakly increasing function in both arguments. Then since $\mu_x[(-\infty, \infty)] = \lambda_y[(-\infty, \infty)] = 1$,

$$\begin{aligned}\int_{-\infty}^{\bar{s}_1}\int_{-\infty}^{\bar{s}_2} f(x, y)\mu(dx, dy) &= \mu_x[(-\infty, \bar{s}_1]] \\ &= \lambda_y[(-\infty, \bar{s}_2]] \\ &= \int_{-\infty}^{\bar{s}_1}\int_{-\infty}^{\bar{s}_2} f(x, y)\lambda(dx, dy).\end{aligned}$$

Notice that

$$\int_{-\infty}^{\bar{s}_1}\int_{-\infty}^{\bar{s}_2} y\mu(dx, dy) = \bar{s}_2\mu_x([\bar{s}_1, \infty)),$$

and that

$$\int_{-\infty}^{\bar{s}_1}\int_{-\infty}^{\bar{s}_2} y\lambda(dx, dy) = \int_{\bar{s}_2}^{\infty} y\lambda_y\,(dy) > \bar{s}_2\lambda_y([\bar{s}_2, \infty)).$$

So

$$\int_S f(x, y)\mu(dx, dy) < \int_S f(x, y)\lambda(dx, dy),$$

which violates $\mu \geq \lambda$.

Exercise 12.10

Let $\{F_{1n}\}$, $\{F_{2n}\}$, F and $\{G_n\}$ be the cdf's of μ_{1n}, μ_{2n}, μ and λ_n. If $\mu_{in} \Rightarrow \mu$, $F_{in} \Rightarrow F$ pointwise at all continuity points of F (by Theorem 12.8). If $\mu_{1n} \leq \lambda_n \leq \mu_{2n}$ by Exercise 12.9a.,

$$F_{1n}(s) \leq G_n(s) \leq F_{2n}(s).$$

Hence $G_n \to F$ at all continuity points of F, and so by Theorem 12.8 $\lambda_n \Rightarrow \mu$.

Exercise 12.11

$a \Rightarrow b : \mu \geq \lambda$ implies, for all f increasing, that $\langle Tf, \mu\rangle \geq \langle Tf, \lambda\rangle$, and so $\langle f, T^*\mu\rangle \geq \langle f, T^*\lambda\rangle$.

$b \Rightarrow c$: Let $\mu(A) = 1$ if $s \in A$, and 0 otherwise, and let $\lambda(A) = 1$ if $s' \in A$ and 0 otherwise. If $s > s'$, for all increasing function f, $f(s) \geq f(s')$. So

$$\int f d\mu = f(s) \geq f(s') = \int f d\lambda,$$

and $T^*\mu(A) \geq T^*\lambda(A)$ and so $P(s, A) \geq P(s', A)$.

$c \Rightarrow a$: Let $s > s'$ so that $P(s, \cdot) > P(s', \cdot)$. Then for f increasing

$$\begin{aligned} Tf(s) &= \int f(x)P(s, dx) \\ &\geq \int f(x)P(s', dx) \\ &= Tf(s'). \end{aligned}$$

Exercise 12.12

In the solution of Exercise 12.8 we showed that

$$T^*\delta_a(A) = P(a, A)$$

for any Borel set $A \subseteq [a, b]$. First we will show by induction that $T^{*n}\delta_a$ is a monotone increasing sequence. For $n = 1$, notice that for any increasing function $f, \langle f, \delta_a\rangle = f(a)$ and since P is monotone

$$\langle f, T^*\delta_a\rangle = \int_a^b f(s)P(a, ds) \geq \int_a^b f(a)P(a, ds) = f(a),$$

hence since f is an arbitrary increasing function $\delta_a \leq T^*\delta_a$. For $n + 1$ assume that for any increasing function f,

$$\langle f, T^{*n}\delta_a\rangle \geq \langle f, T^{*n-1}\delta_a\rangle .$$

Notice that since P is monotone T, f is also an increasing function. Hence using Theorem 8.3,

$$\left\langle f, T^{*n+1}\delta_a\right\rangle = \langle Tf, T^{*n}\delta_a\rangle \geq \left\langle Tf, T^{*n-1}\delta_a\right\rangle = \langle f, T^{*n}\delta_a\rangle,$$

and so $T^{*n+1}\delta_a \geq T^{*n}\delta_a$.

The proof that $T^{*n}\delta_b$ is a decreasing sequence is analogous. Then Corollary 1 and 2 of Theorem 12.9 (Helly's Theorem) guarantee that each sequence converges weakly. To show that each sequence converges to an invariant measure notice that since $T^{*n}\delta_a$ converges,

$$\lim_{n\to\infty} T^{*n}\delta_a = \lim_{N\to\infty} \frac{1}{N}\sum_{n=0}^{N-1} T^{*n}\delta_a.$$

Hence since P has the Feller property, we can use the proof of Theorem 12.10 to show that each sequence converges to an invariant distribution.

Exercise 12.13

a. We first prove that P is monotone. For all $s \geq s'$ and f increasing, $h(s) > h(s')$ and $H(s) > H(s')$ implies that

$$\int f(x)P(s, dx) \geq \int f(x)P(s', dx),$$

and so $P(s, \cdot) \geq P(s', \cdot)$ by Exercise 12.11.

To prove that P satisfies the Feller property, let f be a continuous function. Then

$$\begin{aligned} Tf(s) &= \frac{1}{\mu(h(s), H(s))}\int_{h(s)}^{H(s)} f\,d\mu \\ &= \frac{1}{c}\int_{h(s)}^{H(s)} f\,d\mu \end{aligned}$$

where

$$c = \mu(h(s), H(s)).$$

Take a sequence $s_n \uparrow s$. Then

$$\left|Tf(s_n) - Tf(s)\right| \leq \frac{1}{c}\left|\int_{h(s_n)}^{h(s)} f\,d\mu\right| + \frac{1}{c}\left|\int_{H(s)}^{H(s_n)} f\,d\mu\right|,$$

and the first and second term converge to 0 by the continuity of h and H.

b. First we will show that E_1 is an ergodic set. Let s_1 be such that for all $s \in E_1$, $s_1 \leq s$, and let s_2 be such that for all $s \in E_1$, $s_2 \geq s$. Since $h(s_1) = s_1$, $H(s_2) = s_2$, $H(s) > h(s)$ all $s \in [a, b]$, and from the figure $s_2 - s_1 > H(s_1) - h(s_1)$ and $s_2 - s_1 > H(s_2) - h(s_2)$. We know that

$$[h(s_1), H(s_1)] \subset E_1$$

and

$$[h(s_2), H(s_2)] \subset E_1.$$

So

$$\mu\left(E_1 \cap [h(s_1), H(s_1)]\right) = \mu\left([h(s_1), H(s_1)]\right)$$

and

$$\mu\left(E_1 \cap [h(s_2), H(s_2)]\right) = \mu\left([h(s_2), H(s_2)]\right),$$

which implies that $P(s_1, E_1) = P(s_2, E_1) = 1$. In part a. we showed that P was monotone and so by Exercise 12.11 for all $s \in E_1$

$$P(s_1, E_1) \leq P(s, E_1) \leq P(s_2, E_1).$$

The proof that E_2 is also an ergodic set is analogous. To show that F is a transient set, notice that for all s such that

$$s_2 < s < s_2 + (H(s_2) - h(s_2)),$$

$P(s, F) < 1$ since

$$\mu(F \cap [h(s), H(s)]) < \mu([h(s), H(s)]).$$

Let s_3 be such that for all $s \in E_2$, $s_3 < s$. Then, for all s such that

$$s_3 - (H(s_3) - h(s_3)) < s < s_3,$$

$P(s, F) < 1$. For all s such that

$$s_2 + (H(s_2) - h(s_2)) < s < s_3 - (H(s_3) - h(s_3)),$$

notice that

$$P^n\left(s, [s_2, s_2 + (H(s_2) - h(s_2))] \cup [s_3 - (H(s_3) - h(s_3)), s_3]\right) > 0,$$

for n sufficiently large, since either $H(s) \neq s$ or $h(s) \neq s$ or both. Hence $P^{n'}(s, F) < 1$ for $s \in F$ and $n' > n$, which implies that F is transient.

c. It is not clear from the graph which points are a and b. We will solve the question by letting $a = s_1$ and $b = s_4$ where s_1 is defined as in part b. and s_4 is given by the number such that for all $s \in E_2$, $s_4 \geq s$. Then $a \in E_1$, which implies that for all n

$$T^{*n}\delta_a(A) > 0 \text{ if } A \cap E_1 \neq \emptyset$$

and

$$T^{*n}\delta_a(A) = 0 \text{ if } A \cap E_1 = \emptyset.$$

Symmetrically $b \in E_2$ implies that for all n

$$T^{*n}\delta_b(A) > 0 \text{ if } A \cap E_2 \neq \emptyset$$

and

$$T^{*n}\delta_b(A) = 0 \text{ if } A \cap E_2 = \emptyset.$$

So the limit of $\{T^{*n}\delta_a\}$ assigns mass only to E_1 and the limit of $\{T^{*n}\delta_a\}$ assigns mass only to E_2. This implies that both limits are different since $E_1 \cap E_2 = \emptyset$.

Exercise 12.14

Since P is monotone and satisfies Assumption 12.1,

$$P^N(s, [c, b]) \geq P^N(a, [c, b]) \geq \varepsilon$$

for all $s \in S$, and

$$\begin{aligned} P^N(s, [a, c]) &= 1 - P^N(s, [c, b]) \\ &\geq 1 - P^N(b, [c, b]) \\ &= P^N(b, [a, c]) \\ &\geq \varepsilon, \end{aligned}$$

for all $s \in S$.

13 *Applications of Convergence Results for Markov Processes*

Exercise 13.1

a. From equation (1), we obtain that

$$v(x) = B_1\,[p + \beta v(x-1)], \quad x = 1, 2, \ldots,$$

where

$$B_1 = \frac{\theta}{1-(1-\theta)\beta} < 1.$$

Hence

$$\begin{aligned} v(x) &= B_1 p\left[1 + \beta B_1 + \beta^2 B_1^2 + \ldots + \beta^{x-1} B_1^{x-1}\right] + \beta^x B_1^x v(0) \\ &= \frac{B_1 p}{1-\beta B_1} + \left[v(0) - \frac{B_1 p}{1-\beta B_1}\right](\beta B_1)^x. \end{aligned}$$

Let

$$B_2 = \frac{B_1 p}{1-\beta B_1} > 0,$$

then

$$\begin{aligned} v(0) &= \max_y \left\{-c_0 - c_1 y + v(y)\right\} \\ &= \max_y \left\{ - c_0 - c_1 y + B_2 + \left(v(0) - B_2\right)(\beta B_1)^y \right\}. \end{aligned}$$

Notice from the expression for $v(x)$ that we need $v(0) - B_2 < 0$ for $v(x)$ to be a decreasing function of x.

The gain from increasing the order size by one unit is given by

$$-c_1(y+1) + \left(v(0) - B_2\right)(\beta B_1)^{y+1} - \left(-c_1 y + \left(v(0) - B_2\right)(\beta B_1)^y\right),$$

which can be rearranged to give

$$-c_1 + \left(B_2 - v(0)\right)(1 - \beta B_1)\left(\beta B_1\right)^y .$$

Clearly $1 - \beta B_1 > 0$. We proceed under the guess that $B_2 - v(0) > 0$; this will be verified below. Since $\beta B_1 < 1$, the gain is decreasing in y and the gain converges to $-c_1$ as y goes to infinity. Hence, there exists a finite optimal order size. It is given by the smallest S that satisfies

$$\left(B_2 - v(0)\right)\left(1 - \beta B_1\right)\left(\beta B_1\right)^{S+1} \leq c_1.$$

So $v(0)$ is implicitly defined by

$$v(0) = -c_0 - c_1 S + B_2 + \left[v(0) - B_2\right]\left(\beta B_1\right)^S ,$$

and we have found the value function and the optimal level of the order S. We can rewrite this expression to get

$$B_2 - v(0) = \frac{c_0 + c_1 S}{1 - \left(\beta B_1\right)^S} > 0,$$

which verifies the guess that $B_2 - v(0) > 0$. Also notice that we can substitute this expression in the condition that determines the optimal order size, to get an expression that depends only on the parameters of the model. The optimal order size is the smallest S such that

$$\frac{\left(c_0 + c_1 S\right)\left(\beta B_1\right)^{S+1}}{1 - \left(\beta B_1\right)^S} \leq \frac{c_1}{1 - \left(\beta B_1\right)}.$$

b. The transition matrix is infinite, but the transition function is given by

$$\begin{aligned} P(i, i-1) &= \theta, && \text{for } i \geq 1, \\ P(i, i) &= 1 - \theta, && \text{for } i \geq 1, \\ P(0, S-1) &= \theta, \\ P(0, S) &= 1 - \theta, \end{aligned}$$

and 0 otherwise. An ergodic set is $\{0, 1, 2, 3, \ldots, S\}$ since once we are in one of these states the probability of leaving the set is zero. All other states are transient, and there are no cyclically moving subsets.

c. To guarantee that this process has a unique invariant distribution we will show that Condition M is satisfied. Define the state space $\mathcal{S}$ as $\{0, 1, 2, 3, \ldots, S\}$. Since this is the ergodic set we know that an invariant distribution will only assign positive probability to these states. Since $P^N(s, S) > \theta^{s+1} > \theta^{S+1} > \varepsilon$, for all $s \in \{0, 1, 2, 3, \ldots, S\}$ and some $\varepsilon > 0$, the result in Exercise 11.5.a. holds and Condition M is satisfied. Theorem 11.12 then yields the results. To characterize the invariant distribution, use the transition matrix for the reduced state space S.

$$P_{S\times S} = \begin{pmatrix} 0 & 0 & 0 & 0 & \ldots & 0 & \theta & 1-\theta \\ \theta & 1-\theta & 0 & 0 & \ldots & 0 & 0 & 0 \\ 0 & \theta & 1-\theta & 0 & \ldots & 0 & 0 & 0 \\ 0 & 0 & \theta & 1-\theta & \ldots & 0 & 0 & 0 \\ \cdot & \cdot & \cdot & \cdot & \ldots & \cdot & \cdot & \cdot \\ \cdot & \cdot & \cdot & \cdot & \ldots & \cdot & \cdot & \cdot \\ \cdot & \cdot & \cdot & \cdot & \ldots & \cdot & \cdot & \cdot \\ 0 & 0 & 0 & 0 & \ldots & 1-\theta & 0 & 0 \\ 0 & 0 & 0 & 0 & \ldots & \theta & 1-\theta & 0 \\ 0 & 0 & 0 & 0 & \ldots & 0 & \theta & 1-\theta \end{pmatrix}.$$

Then the unique invariant distribution is given by the rows of

$$\bar{P} = P\bar{P}',$$

where $\sum_{i=0}^{S} \bar{p}_i = 1$. Hence we need to solve a system of S linearly independent equations in S unknowns. That is, we need to solve

$$\bar{p}_0 = \theta\bar{p}_{S-1} + (1-\theta)\bar{p}_S$$
$$\bar{p}_i = \theta\bar{p}_{i-1} + (1-\theta)\bar{p}_i \text{ for } i = 1, \ldots, S.$$

Which implies that $\bar{p}_0 = \bar{p}_i = \bar{p}_{i-1}$ for $i = 1, \ldots, S$. Hence $\bar{p}_0 S = 1$. Therefore,

$$\bar{p}_i = \frac{1}{S} \text{ for } i = 1, \ldots, S.$$

Exercise 13.2

a. Let $A = [a, a']$, where $a \geq s > 0$, then the transition function satisfies

$$\begin{aligned} P(x, A) &= \mu\left([x-a', x-a]\right) && \text{for } x > s, \\ P(x, A) &= \mu\left([S-a', S-a]\right) && \text{for } x \leq s, \\ P(x, \{0\}) &= \mu([x, \bar{z}]) && \text{for } x > s, \\ P(x, \{0\}) &= \mu([S, \bar{z}]) && \text{for } x \leq s. \end{aligned}$$

This defines a transition function, since $P(x, X) = 1$, and using the closed intervals, unions and complements we can calculate $P(x, A)$ for all $A \in \mathcal{X}$.

Define $F(y; x) \equiv P(x, [y, \max[0, x - \bar{z}])$, then

$$F(y; x) = \int_{x-y}^{x} \mu(dz) + \int_{x}^{\bar{z}} \mu(dz) = \int_{x-y}^{\bar{z}} \mu(dz) = 1 - G(x - y)$$

for $x > s$,

$$F(y; x) = \int_{S-y}^{\bar{z}} \mu(dz) = 1 - G(S - y)$$

for $x \leq s$,

where $G(x) = \int_0^x \mu(dz)$. And notice that if $\{x_n\}_{n=1}^{\infty}$ is an increasing sequence with $x_n \uparrow s$, and $\{\bar{x}_n\}_{n=1}^{\infty}$ is a decreasing sequence with $\bar{x}_n \downarrow s$,

$$F(y, x_n) = 1 - G(S - y) \neq 1 - G(s - y) \leftarrow 1 - G(\bar{x}_n - y) = F(y, \bar{x}_n),$$

hence P does not have the Feller property by Exercise 12.7b.

b. Since

$$P(x, \{0\}) = \mu([x, \bar{z}]) \text{ for } S \geq x > s \text{ and}$$
$$P(x, \{0\}) = \mu([S, \bar{z}]) \text{ for } x \leq s,$$

if $S < \bar{z}$, then $\mu([S, \bar{z}]) > \varepsilon > 0$ for some $\varepsilon > 0$. Hence $P^N(x, \{0\}) > \varepsilon$ all $x \in [0, S]$ and all $N = 1, 2, \ldots$. If $S \geq \bar{z}$ there exists an x^* such that $x^* < \bar{z}$ and $\mu\left([x^*, \bar{z}]\right) > 1 - \alpha$ and $\mu\left([0, S - x^*]\right) > \alpha$. Then

$$P^N(S, [0, S - x^*]) = \left(\mu([x^*, S])\right)^N = (1 - \alpha)^N$$

and so

$$P^{N+1}(S, \{0\}) > \alpha P^N(S, [0, S - x^*]) = \alpha\,(1 - \alpha)^N.$$

For any $N > 2$, let $\varepsilon < \alpha\,(1 - \alpha)^N$. Then $P^{N+1}(S, \{0\}) > \varepsilon$, which yields the result.

Exercise 13.3

a.–c. The arguments to prove the first part of results in this exercise are standard and very similar to the ones described in Section 10.1, so we will not present them here. We will focus on parts d. and e., which guarantee the weak convergence to a unique invariant distribution using Theorem 12.12.

d. Define P by

$$P(x, A) = \mu\left(z : f\,[g(x)]\,z \in A\right).$$

Let $h(x)$ be an increasing function of x, then

$$\int h(x')P(x, dx') = \int h(f\,[g(x)]\,z')\mu(dz')$$

and if $x \geq \bar{x}$ since $g(x)$ is strictly increasing

$$h(f\,[g(x)]\,z') > h(f\,[g(\bar{x})]\,z') \text{ all } z' \in Z,$$

hence P is monotone.

e. We need to show that for some $N \geq 1$ and $\delta > 0$,

$$P^N(\bar{x}, (0, x^*)) \geq P^N(\bar{x}, [\phi_N(x, 1), \phi_N(\bar{x}, 1+\delta)]),$$

the result is then implied by equation (3b). Consider the sequence

$$\phi_0(\bar{x}, 1) = \bar{x} > f(\bar{x}) = f\,[g(x)] = \phi_1(\bar{x}, 1).$$

It follows by induction from the fact that f and g are nondecreasing that this sequence is nonincreasing. Since it is bounded from below by 0, it converges to a value $\vartheta \in X$. The continuity of f and g then implies that $\vartheta = f\,[g(\vartheta)]$. Hence

$$\begin{aligned} U'[c(\vartheta)] &= \beta \int U'[c(f[g(\vartheta)]z)]f'[g(\vartheta)]z'\mu(dz') \\ &= \beta f'[g(\vartheta)] \int U'[c(\vartheta z)]z'\mu(dz') \\ &< \beta f'[g(\vartheta)]U'[c(\vartheta)] \int z'\mu(dz') \\ &= \beta f'[g(\vartheta)]U'[c(\vartheta)]z^* \end{aligned}$$

where the inequality follows from the fact that $z \in [1, \bar{z}]$ and the strict concavity of U. Hence $1 < \beta f'[g(\vartheta)]z^*$, which implies that $\vartheta < x^*$. Choose $N \geq 1$ such that $\phi_N(\bar{x}, 1) < x^*$ and $\delta > 0$ such that $\phi_N(\bar{x}, 1+\delta) < x^*$. Then $x^* > \phi_N(\bar{x}, 1+\delta) > \phi_N(\bar{x}, 1) > 0$, which yields the result.

Exercise 13.5

a. Define

$$F(m, m') = U(m + y - m'),$$

and

$$\Gamma(m) = [y, m + y].$$

Assumptions 9.4 and Assumption 9.5 are trivially satisfied, since $X = \mathbf{R}_+$, and the shock to preferences is i.i.d. Assumption 9.6 and 9.7 are satisfied since $y \in \Gamma(m)$ for all $m \in X$, $\Gamma(m)$ is a closed interval defined by continuous functions of m, and U is bounded and continuous so F is too. Hence Theorem 9.6 yields the result.

b. Assumption 9.8 is satisfied since U is strictly increasing and Assumption 9.9 too, since the upper bound of $\Gamma(m)$ is increasing in m. Hence Theorem 9.7 implies that $v(\cdot, z)$ is strictly increasing. To show that $v(\cdot, z)$ is strictly concave, notice that we cannot use Theorem 9.8 since Assumption 9.10 is not satisfied. The linearity of the resource constraint with respect to both today's and tomorrow's real balances creates this problem. We can, however, prove strict concavity of $v(\cdot, z)$ using the sequential problem and the principle of optimality. Notice that since Assumptions 9.4–9.7 hold by part a., the conditions of Theorems 9.2 and 9.4 are satisfied.

The resource constraint in present value for the sequential problem is given by

$$\sum_{t=0}^{\infty} y + m_0 \geq \sum_{t=0}^{\infty} c_t,$$

hence if $m_0 > \bar{m}_0$ and $\{c_t\}_{t=0}^{\infty}$ and $\{\bar{c}_t\}_{t=0}^{\infty}$ are the corresponding optimal consumption sequences, as the constraint binds it must be the case that $c_t \neq \bar{c}_t$

for some t. Hence, if $\{c_t^\theta\}_{t=0}^\infty$ is the optimal consumption sequence associated with initial real money balances $\theta m_0 + (1-\theta)\bar{m}_0$,

$$\begin{aligned}
&v(\theta m_0 + (1-\theta)\bar{m}_0) \\
&= E\left[\sum_{t=0}^{\infty} \beta^t U(c_t^\theta, z_t)\right] \\
&\geq E\left[\sum_{t=0}^{\infty} \beta^t U(\theta c_t + (1-\theta)\bar{c}_t, z_t)\right] \\
&> E\left[\sum_{t=0}^{\infty} \beta^t \left[\theta U(c_t, z_t) + (1-\theta)U(\bar{c}_t, z_t)\right]\right], \\
&= \theta E\left[\sum_{t=0}^{\infty} \beta^t U(c_t, z_t)\right] + (1-\theta)E\left[\sum_{t=0}^{\infty} \beta^t U(\bar{c}_t, z_t)\right] \\
&= \theta v(m_0, z) + (1-\theta)v(\bar{m}_0, z),
\end{aligned}$$

where the weak inequality comes from the fact that $\theta c_t + (1-\theta)\bar{c}_t$ may not be an optimal consumption sequence for $\theta m_0 + (1-\theta)\bar{m}_0$, the strict inequality from the strict concavity of U and the fact that the consumption sequences cannot be identical, and the second equality from the linearity of the expectation.

Assumption 9.12 holds because of the differentiability of U, hence since we showed above that $v(\cdot, z)$ is strictly concave, we can use Theorem 9.10 to prove the differentiability of $v(\cdot, z)$ in the interior of X. Hence for $m \in \text{int} X$ and $m' \in \text{int}\Gamma(m)$,

$$v_1(m, z) = U_1(m + y - m').$$

Now suppose $m' = y$. Then

$$v(m, z) = U(m, z) + \beta \int v(y, z')\mu(dz'),$$

so

$$v_1(m, z) = U_1(m, z).$$

Hence since both derivatives coincide, $v(\cdot, z)$ is differentiable.

c. Since we have shown that $v(\cdot, z)$ is strictly concave, and since $\Gamma(m)$ is convex, the Theorem of the Maximum implies that $g(m, z)$ is single valued and continuous.

d. The first-order condition is given by

$$U_1(m + y - g(m, z), z) \geq \int v_1(y, z')\mu(dz') \text{ with equality if } m' > y.$$

Consider the problem without the cash-in-advance constraint,

$$\bar{v}(m, z) = \max_{0 \leq m' \leq m+y} \left\{ U(m + y - m') + \beta \int \bar{v}(y, z')\mu(dz') \right\}.$$

Using exactly the same arguments as in parts a.–c., there exists a unique, continuous, increasing in x and differentiable function $\bar{v}$ that solves the problem above. Furthermore, the corresponding policy function $\bar{g}(m, z)$ is single valued and continuous. We will show next that $\bar{g}(m, z)$ is strictly increasing in m. The first-order condition of the unconstrained problem is given by

$$U_1(m + y - \bar{g}(m, z), z) = \beta \int \bar{v}_1(\bar{g}(m, z), z')\mu(dz').$$

Suppose that $\bar{g}(m, z)$ is nonincreasing in m, then for $m > \hat{m}$,

$$\bar{g}(m, z) \leq \bar{g}(\hat{m}, z),$$

and so by the concavity of $\bar{v}$,

$$\bar{v}_1(\bar{g}(m, z), z') > \bar{v}_1(\bar{g}(\hat{m}, z), z').$$

Hence by the first-order condition and the concavity of U,

$$m + y - \bar{g}(m, z) < \hat{m} + y - \bar{g}(\hat{m}, z),$$

which implies that $\bar{g}(m, z) > \bar{g}(\hat{m}, z)$, a contradiction. Hence $\bar{g}$ is strictly increasing in m.

So

$$g(m, z) = \max \{\bar{g}(m, z), y\}.$$

Let $\phi(z)$ be implicitly defined by

$$\bar{g}(\phi(z), z) = y.$$

$\phi(z)$ is well defined since $\bar{g}$ is a strictly increasing function in m, and for some z^H

$$\bar{g}(0, z) < y \text{ for all } z \in \left[z^H, \bar{z}\right] \text{ and } \lim_{m \to \infty} \bar{g}(m, z) > y \text{ for all } z \in Z.$$

Notice that if we want $z^H = \underline{z}$, we need to assume that

$$\lim_{m \to 0} U'(m, z) = \infty;$$

that is an Inada condition so that

$$U'(0, z) > \beta \int U'(y, z')\mu(dz').$$

e. By contradiction. Suppose $m > \hat{m}$ and $c(m, z) \leq c(\hat{m}, z)$. Then by the strict concavity of U,

$$U_1(c(m, z), z) \geq U_1(c(\hat{m}, z), z) \text{ all } z \in Z,$$

and so by the first-order condition,

$$\int v_1(g(m, z), z')\mu(dz') \geq \int v_1(g(\hat{m}, z), z')\mu(dz'),$$

a contradiction with $g(m, z)$ increasing in m and v concave.

This implies that for $m_1 < m_2$,

$$m_1 + y - \bar{g}(m_1, z) < m_2 + y - \bar{g}(m_2, z)$$

and so

$$\bar{g}(m_2, z) - \bar{g}(m_2, z) < m_2 - m_1.$$

f. We need to show that there exists an $\bar{m}$ such that

$$U_1(y, \underline{z}) = \beta \int v_1(\bar{m}, z')\mu(dz').$$

Notice that by the concavity of v the right-hand side is a decreasing function of $\bar{m}$, and that the left-hand side does not depend on $\bar{m}$. Also by concavity of v and since $v \leq B$ for all $m \in X$ and $z \in Z$, for some B big enough,

$$v(0, z) \leq v(m, z) - v_1(m, z)m.$$

Hence

$$0 \leq v_1(m, z)m \leq v(m, z) - v(0, z) \leq B - v(0, z),$$

and so

$$\lim_{m \uparrow \infty} v_1(m, z) = 0.$$

Notice also that

$$U_1(y, \underline{z}) < \beta \int v_1(y, z')\mu(dz')$$

since if not, $g(m, z) = y$ all $m \in X$ and $z \in Z$. Hence $\bar{m}$ is well defined and it exists.

g. By the first-order condition, since U is an increasing function of z we know that by the envelope condition

$$U_1(y, \bar{z}) > \beta \int v_1(y, z')\mu(dz') = \beta \int U_1(y, z')\mu(dz'),$$

hence for $m \leq y$, $g(m, \bar{z}) = y$.

h. By contradiction. Suppose c is decreasing in z. Then for $z > \bar{z}$, $c(m, z) < c(m, \bar{z}) \leq m$ and so $g(m, z) > g(m, \bar{z})$. Then since U is concave,

$$\begin{aligned} U_1(c(m, z), z) &> U_1(c(m, \bar{z}), \bar{z}) \\ &\geq \beta \int v_1(g(m, \bar{z}), z')\mu(dz') \\ &> \beta \int v_1(g(m, z), z')\mu(dz') \\ &= U_1(c(m, z)). \end{aligned}$$

Hence c is weakly increasing in z and so g is weakly decreasing.

i. The transition function P is given by

$$\begin{aligned} P(m, A) &= \int \mathbf{1}_{\{g^{-1}(m, A)\}}\mu(dz') \\ &= \mu\,[\{z : g(m, z) \in A\}] \end{aligned}$$

for all $A \in \mathcal{X}$.

First we will prove that P has the Feller property. Since $g(m, z)$ is continuous, for any bounded and continuous function f,

$$Tf(m) = \int_X f(m')P(m, dm') = \int_Z f(g(m, z'))\mu(dz'),$$

which is continuous by the Lebesgue Dominated Convergence Theorem (see the proof of Theorem 9.14 for an alternative proof).

Take f to be increasing, then since g is increasing in m, for $m > \hat{m}$,

$$\int_Z f(g(m, z'))\mu(dz') > \int_Z f(g(\hat{m}, z'))\mu(dz').$$

So the transition function P is monotone since $Tf(m) > Tf(\hat{m})$.

Before showing that Assumption 12.1 holds, we will show that if $\hat{z} = \phi^{-1}(y) < \bar{z}$, Condition M in Section 11.4 is satisfied. For $m < \phi(\bar{z})$,

$$\begin{aligned} P(m, \{y\}) &= \mu\,[\{z : g(m, z) = y\}] \\ &= \mu\,[\{z : \phi(z) > m\}] \\ &\geq \alpha(\bar{z} - \hat{z}). \end{aligned}$$

For $m \geq \phi(\bar{z})$, notice that there exists an $N \geq 1$ sufficiently large and an $\varepsilon > 0$ sufficiently small such that

$$\begin{aligned} P^N(m, [y, \phi(\bar{z}))) &> [\mu((\hat{z}, \bar{z}))]^N \\ &\geq [\alpha(\bar{z} - \hat{z})]^N > \varepsilon. \end{aligned}$$

Hence Condition M is satisfied by Exercise 11.5a, so we can use Theorem 11.12 to guarantee the strong convergence to a unique invariant distribution.

To prove that Assumption 12.1 is satisfied, let $\bar{m} > c > \phi(\bar{z})$ and $\tilde{z} = \{z : g(c, z) = z\}$. Then there exists an $N^1 \geq 1$ large enough such that

$$\begin{aligned} P^N(y, [c, \bar{m}]) &> [\mu((\underline{z}, \tilde{z}))]^{N^1} \\ &\geq [\alpha(\tilde{z} - \underline{z})]^{N^1}. \end{aligned}$$

Similarly, there exists an $N^2 \geq 1$ sufficiently large such that

$$\begin{aligned} P(\bar{m}, [y, c]) &> [\mu((\tilde{z}, \bar{z}))]^{N^2} \\ &\geq [\alpha(\bar{z} - \tilde{z})]^{N^2}. \end{aligned}$$

Hence we can define $N = \max[N^1, N^2]$ and $\varepsilon = \min\left\{[\alpha(\tilde{z} - \underline{z})]^N, [\alpha(\bar{z} - \tilde{z})]^N\right\} > 0$, which yields Assumption 12.1 with c as the middle point.

j. Define f by $f(m) = m$. Then

$$\begin{aligned}\int\int g(m, z)\mu(dz)\lambda^*(dm) &= \int\int f(m')P(m, dm')\lambda^*(dm) \\ &= \langle Tf, \lambda^*\rangle \\ &= \langle f, T^*\lambda^*\rangle \\ &= \langle f, \lambda^*\rangle = \frac{M}{p}.\end{aligned}$$

Exercise 13.7

a. The first-order condition of the problem is given by

$$-qz + \beta\int v_1(w', z')\mu(dz') + \theta - \lambda = 0,$$

where $\theta \geq 0$ is the Lagrange multiplier associated with the constraint $0 \leq w'$ so $\theta w' = 0$ and $\lambda \geq 0$ is the multiplier corresponding to the constraint

$$w' \leq (1 + \frac{y}{q})w,$$

so

$$\lambda((1 + \frac{y}{q})w - w') = 0.$$

The envelope condition (for an interior solution) is given by

$$v_1(w, z) = (y + q).$$

Notice that $\theta > 0$ and $\lambda > 0$ is not a possible case, hence we need to take into consideration only the cases $\theta > 0$, $\lambda = 0$ and $\theta = 0$, $\lambda > 0$, plus $\theta = \lambda = 0$.

Suppose the first case, $\theta > 0$, $\lambda = 0$, then

$$\beta\int v_1(w', z')\mu(dz') < qz,$$

and therefore substituting the envelope and letting $A \equiv \int \mu(dz')$, we obtain that

$$\zeta \equiv \frac{\beta A(y + q)}{q} < z.$$

Hence, if z satisfies the condition above, $w' = 0$.

In the second case, $\theta = 0$, $\lambda > 0$, we obtain that

$$\beta \int v_1(w', z')\mu(dz') > qz,$$

then

$$\zeta = \frac{\beta A(y+q)}{q} > z,$$

and $w' = (1 + \frac{y}{q})w$.

If $\theta = \lambda = 0$ we have that $\zeta = z$, and w' can take any value. For example, we can let $w' = 0$ to obtain the result in the book.

b. The transition function for this problem is given by

$$P(w, w') = \mu\left(\{z : g(w, z) = w'\}\right)$$
$$= \begin{cases} \mu([\zeta, 1]) & \text{if } w' = 0 \\ \mu([0, \zeta]) & \text{if } w' = (1 + \frac{y}{q})w \\ 0 & \text{otherwise.} \end{cases}$$

We will first show that one of the assumptions in Theorem 12.12 is not satisfied. This, of course, only proves that the sufficient conditions in the theorem are not satisfied. However there could still exist an invariant distribution.

Let $w_n \downarrow 0$, and let $w' = 0$, then

$$P(w_n, w') = \mu([\zeta, 1]) \text{ all } n = 1, 2, \ldots$$

so

$$\lim_{n \to \infty} P((w_n, w') = \mu([\zeta, 1]),$$

but

$$P(0, 0) = 1.$$

Hence by Exercise 12.7 P does not have the Feller property.

Define $\delta \equiv \mu\left([\zeta, 1]\right)$. The evolution of the distribution is given by

$$\Psi_t(0) = \Psi_0(0) + \left(1 - \Psi_0(0)\right)\left[\delta + (1-\delta)\,\delta + \ldots + (1-\delta)^t\,\delta\right]$$

and

$$\Psi_t\left((0, w]\right) = (1-\delta)^t\,\Psi_0\left((0, \frac{w}{1 + yq^{-1}}]\right).$$

In particular, $\lim_{t\to\infty} \Psi_t(0) = 1$ and $\lim_{t\to\infty} \Psi_t((0, w]) = 0$ all w. The obvious candidate for the stationary distribution is a distribution with all the mass concentrated at 0, $\Psi^*(\{0\}) = 1$, zero for any set not containing 0. To see that this is a limiting distribution, we are going to check condition a. in Theorem 12.3 (i.e., $\lim_{n\to\infty} \int f d\lambda_n = \int f d\lambda$, all $f \in C(S)$).

$$\begin{aligned}\int f(w)\Psi_t(dw) &= f(0)\,\Psi_t(0) + \int_{w\in(0,\infty)} f(w)\,\Psi_t(dw)\\ &\leq f(0)\,\Psi_t(0) + \|f\| \int_{w\in(0,\infty)} \Psi_t(dw)\\ &= f(0)\,\Psi_t(0) + \|f\|\,\Psi_t((0,\infty))\end{aligned}$$

So,

$$\lim_{t\to\infty} \int f(w)\Psi_t(dw) \leq f(0) = \int f(w)\Psi^*(dw).$$

We get the other inequality if we use $-\|f\|$ instead of $\|f\|$.

So the Markov process defined by the policy function g together with μ has an invariant measure (i.e., the sequence $\{T^{*t}\Psi_0\}$ converge weakly to an invariant measure). But notice that the sequence converges weakly to an invariant measure Ψ^* that does not satisfy (1).

c. By induction, (you can check that it works for $t = 1$) if

$$\int w\Psi_{t-1}(dw) = 1,$$

then

$$\begin{aligned}\int w'\Psi_t(dw') &= \int (1 + yq^{-1}) w\mu([0,\zeta])\,\Psi_{t-1}(dw)\\ &= (1 + yq^{-1})\mu([0,\zeta]) \underbrace{\int w\Psi_{t-1}(dw)}_{=1}\\ &= (1 + yq^{-1})\mu([0,\zeta]).\end{aligned}$$

So a necessary condition for an equilibrium is

$$(1 + yq^{-1})\mu([0,\zeta]) = 1.$$

In addition, we can use the constant returns to scale results developed in Section 9.3 to write

$$v(w, z) = w\hat{v}(z).$$

The two equations above, together with the equation that determines ζ, imply that

$$q\zeta = \beta \int \bar{v}_1 (z') \mu (dz').$$

This expression characterizes the equilibrium price. The implicit function theorem can be used to analyze how q depends on β, etc.

Exercise 13.8

a. Let $\theta > 0$ and define the operator T by

$$Tv(x, z) = \max \left\{\theta,\ f(x, z) + \min \left\{\theta, \beta \int v(x, z')Q(z, dz')\right\}\right\}.$$

First we will prove that $T : C(X \times Z) \to C(X \times Z)$. For this notice that $f(x, z) \leq f(0, z)$ for all $x \in X$ and $z \in Z$. Hence for $v \in C(X \times Z)$,

$$Tv(x, z) \leq \max \left\{\theta,\ f(0, \bar{z}) + \min \{\theta, \beta B\}\right\},$$

where B satisfies $v(x, z) \leq B$ for all $x \in X$ and $z \in Z$. Hence $Tv(x, z)$ is bounded. And since Q has the Feller property, if v is continuous, then so is Tv by Theorem 12.14.

Next we will show that T is a contraction; for this we will use Blackwell sufficient conditions. For monotonicity notice that if

$$\eta(x, z) \geq v(x, z)$$

for all $x \in X$ and $z \in Z$,

$$\beta \int \eta(x, z')Q(z, dz') \geq \beta \int v(x, z')Q(z, dz') \text{ for all } x \in X \text{ and } z \in Z,$$

which implies that

$$T\eta(x, z) \geq Tv(x, z).$$

For discounting notice that

$$
\begin{aligned}
&T(\upsilon(x, z) + a) \\
&= \max\left\{\theta,\ f(x, z) + \min\left\{\theta, \beta \int (\upsilon(x, z') + a) Q(z, dz')\right\}\right\} \\
&\leq \max\left\{\theta,\ f(x, z) + \min\left\{\theta, \beta \int \upsilon(x, z') Q(z, dz')\right\}\right\} + \beta a.
\end{aligned}
$$

Hence by the Contraction Mapping Theorem there exists a unique continuous and bounded function υ such that

$$
\upsilon(x, z) = \max\left\{\theta,\ f(x, z) + \min\left\{\theta, \beta \int \upsilon(x, z') Q(z, dz')\right\}\right\}.
$$

By the argument above, we know that

$$
\begin{aligned}
\upsilon(x, z) &\leq \max\left\{\theta,\ f(0, \bar{z}) + \min\left\{\theta, \beta \int \upsilon(x, z') Q(z, dz')\right\}\right\} \\
&\leq \max\left\{\theta,\ f(0, \bar{z}) + \beta \int \upsilon(x, z') Q(z, dz')\right\} \\
&\leq \max\left\{\theta,\ \frac{f(0, \bar{z})}{1 - \beta}\right\}.
\end{aligned}
$$

Since f is decreasing in x, the operator T maps strictly decreasing into nonincreasing functions of x, since only one of the two terms in the maximum decreases if x increases. Hence, by Corollary 2 of the Contraction Mapping Theorem $\upsilon(x, \cdot)$ is nonincreasing in x. Since f is strictly increasing in z and since Q is monotone, by the same argument, T maps strictly increasing functions of z into nondecreasing functions and so υ is nondecreasing in z.

b. First notice that if $g(x, z)$ solves (5a), it does not depend on x. Hence, define $\bar{g}(z) \equiv g(x, z)$, with $\bar{g}(z) = 0$ if there is no positive number such that (5a) is satisfied with equality. Similarly, if $g(x, z)$ solves (5c), let $\underline{g}(z) \equiv g(x, z)$, where again we choose a notation that emphasizes that $g(x, z)$ does not depend on x in this case. Combining (5a) and (5c) we obtain,

$$
\beta \int \upsilon(\underline{g}(z), z') Q(z, dz') \geq f(\bar{g}(z), z) + \beta \int \upsilon(\bar{g}(z), z') Q(z, dz').
$$

By part a., υ is nonincreasing in x as well as f. Hence the above inequality implies that $\underline{g}(z) \geq \underline{g}(z)$. Since the inequalities (2a–c) partition X, for any

$x \in X$, $g(x, z)$ is either constant at $\bar{g}(z)$ or $\underline{g}(z)$, or $g(x, z) = x$. Hence $g(x, z)$ is nondecreasing in x.

To show that $g(x, z)$ in nondecreasing in z, first we will show that $\bar{g}(z)$ and $\underline{g}(z)$ are nondecreasing. Toward a contradiction suppose that $z > \hat{z}$ and $\bar{g}(z) < \bar{g}(\hat{z})$. Then by (5a) and part a. together with the monotonicity assumption on Q,

$$\begin{aligned}\theta &\geq f(\bar{g}(z), z) + \beta \int v(\bar{g}(z), z')Q(z, dz') \\ &> f(\bar{g}(\hat{z}), \hat{z}) + \beta \int v(\bar{g}(\hat{z}), z')Q(\hat{z}, dz') = \theta.\end{aligned}$$

Again toward a contradiction assume that $z > \hat{z}$ and $\underline{g}(z) < \underline{g}(\hat{z})$. Then

$$\begin{aligned}\theta &= \beta \int v(\underline{g}(z), z')Q(z, dz') \\ &> \beta \int v(\underline{g}(\hat{z}), z')Q(\hat{z}, dz') = \theta.\end{aligned}$$

Since either $g(x, z)$ is increasing in z, as shown above, or $g(x, z) = x$, $g(x, z)$ is nondecreasing in z.

Let $x > x'$, then for any $z \in Z$,

$$|g(x, z) - g(x', z)| = \begin{cases} 0 & \text{if } x > x' > \bar{g}(z) > \underline{g}(z) \\ |\bar{g}(z) - x'| & \text{if } x > \bar{g}(z) > x' > \underline{g}(z) \\ |\bar{g}(z) - \underline{g}(z)| & \text{if } x > \bar{g}(z) > \underline{g}(z) > x' \\ |x - x'| & \text{if } \bar{g}(z) > x > x' > \underline{g}(z) \\ |x - \underline{g}(z)| & \text{if } \bar{g}(z) > x > \underline{g}(z) > x' \\ 0 & \text{if } \bar{g}(z) > \underline{g}(z) > x > x' \end{cases},$$

which implies the result.

c. Since by part a., v and f are continuous in $X \times Z$ and Q has the Feller property, both $\bar{g}(z)$ and $\underline{g}(z)$ are continuous in z. Because of the same conditions, the boundaries of the sets in which (2a) and (2c) hold are continuous in $X \times Z$. In addition, if (2b) holds, $g(x, z)$ is continuous. Therefore, $g(x, z)$ is continuous in $X \times Z$.

d. The transition function P is given by

$$P(x, z; A \times B) = \chi_{\{g(x,z) \in A\}} Q(z, B).$$

We need to prove that P is monotone, has the Feller property and satisfies Assumption 12.1. Then we can use Theorem 12.12 to prove the result. Since $g(x, z)$ is monotone in both arguments and Q is monotone by assumption, P is monotone. Since assumptions 9.4 and 9.5 are satisfied, we can use Theorem 9.14 to prove that P has the Feller property.

Proving that P satisfies Assumption 12.1 requires (6). First notice that if we define

$$\bar{\theta} \equiv \frac{f(0, \bar{z})}{1-\beta},$$

$\theta \geq \bar{\theta}$ implies that $v(x, z; \theta) = \theta$ and $g(x, z; \theta) = 0$. Here the first result comes from part a., and the second from the fact that nobody else arrives at the island since

$$\beta \int v(x, z'; \theta) Q(z, dz') = \beta\theta < \theta,$$

and everybody leaves since

$$f(x, z) + \beta \int v(x, z'; \theta) Q(z, dz') < f(0, \bar{z}) + \beta\theta \leq \theta.$$

So if $\theta \geq \bar{\theta}$, $P(x, z; A \times B) = \chi_{\{0 \in A\}}$, which implies that $\lambda(AxB) = 1$ if $0 \in A$ and 0 otherwise.

If $\theta \in (0, \bar{\theta})$, then (6) guarantees that Assumption 12.1 is satisfied. To show this we will first show that (6) implies that $\bar{g}(\underline{z}) < \underline{g}(\bar{z})$. Suppose not. Then there exists an x such that

$$f(x, \bar{z}) + \beta \int v(x, z'; \theta) Q(\bar{z}, dz') \geq \theta \geq \beta \int v(x, z'; \theta) Q(\bar{z}, dz')$$

and

$$f(x, \underline{z}) + \beta \int v(x, z'; \theta) Q(\underline{z}, dz') \geq \theta \geq \beta \int v(x, z'; \theta) Q(\underline{z}, dz').$$

and $g(x, \bar{z}) = g(x, \underline{z}) = x$. Hence by (3b)

$$v(x, \bar{z}; \theta) = f(x, \bar{z}) + \beta \int v(x, z'; \theta) Q(\bar{z}, dz') = w(x, \bar{z})$$

and

$$v(x, \bar{z}; \theta) = f(x, \underline{z}) + \beta \int v(x, z'; \theta) Q(\underline{z}, dz') = w(x, \underline{z}).$$

But then

$$w(x, \underline{z}) \geq \beta \int v(x, z'; \theta) Q(\bar{z}, dz') = \beta \int w(x, z') Q(\bar{z}, dz')$$

which contradicts (6).

The ergodic set of the problem is given by $[\bar{g}(\underline{z}), \underline{g}(\bar{z})]$. Notice that $g(x, z)$ is monotone in x and z. The assumption on Q used in Section 13.4 then guarantees that there exists a triple (ε, N, b) such that

$$P^N[\bar{g}(\underline{z}), z; [b, \underline{g}(\bar{z})] \times B] \geq \varepsilon$$

and

$$P^N[\underline{g}(\bar{z}), z; [\bar{g}(\underline{z}), b] \times B] \geq \varepsilon$$

for any $B = (b_1, b_2]$ with $b_1 < b_2$.

e. In the modified model

$$v(x, z) = \max\left\{\theta,\ f(x, z) + \min\left\{\theta, \beta \int v(x(1-\gamma), z') Q(z, dz')\right\}\right\}.$$

So $g(x, z)$ is defined by

$$f(g(x, z), z) + \beta \int v(g(x, z)(1-\gamma), z') Q(z, dz') \leq \theta$$

with equality if $g(x, z) > 0$, if

$$f(x, z) + \beta \int v(x(1-\gamma), z') Q(z, dz') < \theta;$$

$$g(x, z) = x(1-\gamma)$$

if

$$f(x, z) + \beta \int v(x(1-\gamma), z') Q(z, dz') \leq \theta$$

$$\leq \beta \int v(x(1-\gamma), z') Q(z, dz');$$

and

$$\beta \int v(g(x, z)(1-\gamma), z') Q(z, dz') = \theta$$

if

$$\beta \int v(x(1-\gamma), z')Q(z, dz') > \theta.$$

All of the analysis above holds except that the ergodic set is given by $[g(\underline{z}), g(\bar{z})]$. Notice that in this case we do not need the assumption in (6) to guarantee that Assumption 12.1 is satisfied, since $g(\underline{z}) < g(\bar{z})$ follows from f and v nondecreasing in z, and Q monotone. The monotonicity of $g(x, z)$ in both x and z and assumption (2) in Section 13.4 then guarantee that Assumption 12.1 is satisfied.

f. By (F2) $f(\bar{x}, z) = 0$ for all $z \in Z$. $\theta = 0$ implies that (2c) always holds and so

$$v(x, z) = f(x, z).$$

Hence $g(x, z)$ is given by

$$\beta \int f(g(x, z; \theta), z')Q(z, dz') = 0,$$

which implies that $g(x, z; 0) = \bar{x}$. Hence $\lambda_\theta(A \times B) = 1$ if $\bar{x} \in A$ and 0 otherwise. So $D(0) = \bar{x}$. We proved in part d. that if $\theta \geq \bar{\theta}$, $g(x, z; \theta) = 0$. Hence $\lambda_\theta(A \times B) = 1$ if $0 \in A$ and 0 otherwise. Hence $D(\theta) = 0$.

g. Clearly $[0, \bar{x}] \times [\underline{z}, \bar{z}]$ is compact. Given a continuous function h we need to show that

$$\lim_{(x_n, z_n, \theta_n) \to (x_0, z_0, \theta_0)} \int h(x, z)P_{\theta_n}[(x_n, z_n); dx \times dz]$$
$$= \int h(x, z)P_{\theta_0}((x_0, z_0; dx \times dz),$$

or (see Exercise 9.15a.)

$$\lim_{(x_n, z_n, \theta_n) \to (x_0, z_0, \theta_0)} \int h(g(x_n, z_n; \theta_n), z')Q(z_n, dz')$$
$$= \int h(g(x_0, z_0; \theta_0), z')Q(z_0, dz').$$

The triangle inequality implies that

$$\begin{aligned}
&\left|\int h(g(x_n, z_n; \theta_n), z')Q(z_n; dz') \right.\\
&\qquad \left. - \int h(g(x_0, z_0; \theta_0), z')Q(z_0; dz')\right| \\
&< \left|\int h(g(x_n, z_n; \theta_n), z')Q(z_n; dz') \right.\\
&\qquad \left. - \int h(g(x_0, z_0; \theta_n), z')Q(z_n; dz')\right| \\
&+ \left|\int h(g(x_0, z_0; \theta_n), z')Q(z_n; dz') \right.\\
&\qquad \left. - \int h(g(x_0, z_0; \theta_0), z')Q(z_n; dz')\right| \\
&+ \left|\int h(g(x_0, z_0; \theta_0), z')Q(z_n; dz') \right.\\
&\qquad \left. - \int h(g(x_0, z_0; \theta_0), z')Q(z_0; dz')\right| .
\end{aligned}$$

In the right-hand side, the first term can be made arbitrarily small by the choice of n, since $g(x, z; \theta)$ is continuous in (x, z). The second can also be made arbitrarily small by the choice of n, since f is a continuous function in x and so is υ by part a. Hence, $g(x, z; \theta)$ is continuous in θ. The third term can be made arbitrarily small since Q satisfies the Feller property.

We also proved in part d. that for every $\theta > 0$ there is an invariant distribution. Hence all the assumptions of Theorem 12.13 have been verified, so λ_{θ_n} converges weakly to λ_{θ_0}. This implies that $D(\theta_n) \to D(\theta_0)$ and so D is a continuous function. The result then follows by the Mean Value Theorem.

h. First notice that

$$\begin{aligned}
T_\theta x(x, z) &= \int x' P_\theta(x, z; dx' \times dz') \\
&= \int g(x, z; \theta)Q(z, dz') \\
&= g(x, z; \theta).
\end{aligned}$$

Hence we need to show that $g(x, z; \theta)$ is a nonincreasing function of θ. Toward a contradiction suppose $\theta > \theta'$ and $g(x, z; \theta) > g(x, z; \theta')$. Then if the pair (x, z) is such that for both θ and θ' (2a) holds, $g(x, z; \theta) = \bar{g}(z; \theta)$ and $g(x, z; \theta') = \bar{g}(z; \theta')$. And so

$$\begin{aligned}\theta &= f(\bar{g}(z; \theta), z) + \beta \int v(\bar{g}(z; \theta), z')Q(z, dz') \\ &< f(\bar{g}(z; \theta'), z) + \beta \int v(\bar{g}(z; \theta'), z')Q(z, dz') \leq \theta',\end{aligned}$$

a contradiction. If (x, z) is such that (2c) holds for θ and θ', then $g(x, z; \theta) = \underline{g}(z; \theta)$ and $g(x, z; \theta') = \underline{g}(z; \theta')$. Hence

$$\begin{aligned}\theta &= \beta \int v(\underline{g}(z; \theta), z')Q(z, dz') \\ &< \beta \int v(\underline{g}(z; \theta'), z')Q(z, dz') = \theta',\end{aligned}$$

a contradiction. If (x, z) satisfies (2b) for both θ and θ', then

$$g(x, z; \theta) = g(x, z; \theta') = x,$$

a contradiction. We still have to consider the case in which (x, z) satisfies (2a) for θ but (2b) for θ' and the case in which (x, z) satisfies (2b) for θ and (2c) for θ'. In the first case notice that $g(x, z; \theta) = \bar{g}(z; \theta)$ and $g(x, z; \theta') = x$. But since $\bar{g}(z; \theta) \leq x$, $g(x, z; \theta) \leq g(x, z; \theta')$, a contradiction. The last case can be proven similarly. So $T_\theta x$ is a decreasing function of θ given a pair (x, z) and so D is a nonincreasing function. Notice that in order for the proof above to follow for $g(x, z; \theta)$ decreasing in θ, we need the probability of (2c) holding to be positive. Notice that this is guaranteed by the assumption in (6): see part d.

14 *Laws of Large Numbers*

Exercise 14.1

Let $k \geq 1$ index the sequence $\{f_k\} = \{f_{11}, f_{21}, f_{22}, f_{31}, \ldots\}$.

a. To see that the sequence does not converge at any $\omega \in \Omega$, note that for all $\omega \in \Omega$ and for any $K > 0$, there exists a $k_1 \geq K$ such that $f_{k_1}(\omega) = 1$ and a $k_2 \geq K$ such that $f_{k_2}(\omega) = 0$.

b. For all $k \geq 1$ and for all $\varepsilon > 0$,

$$\mu(\omega \in \Omega : |f_k(\omega)| > \varepsilon) = 1/n,$$

where $f_k = f_{ni}$. But as $k \to \infty$, $n \to \infty$ and so

$$\lim_{k \to \infty} \mu(\omega \in \Omega : |f_k(\omega)| > \varepsilon) = 0.$$

c. Consider the subsequence $\{f_{k_j}\} = \{f_{jj}\}$, so that for $j \geq 1$ we have

$$f_{k_j}(\omega) = \begin{cases} 1 & \text{if } \omega \in [1 - 1/j, 1) \\ 0 & \text{otherwise} \end{cases}.$$

For all $\omega \in \Omega = [0, 1)$ there exists J such that for all $j \geq J$, $\omega < 1 - 1/j$. Hence, $\{f_{k_j}\}$ converges to the random variable that is indentically zero everywhere in Ω. Hence, $\{f_{k_j}\}$ also converges μ-almost everywhere.

Exercise 14.2

a. Let $\{f_n\}$ and f be random variables, and let $\{\varepsilon_n\}$ be a sequence of positive numbers converging to zero. For any $\varepsilon > 0$ define the set

$$A_n(\varepsilon) = \{\omega \in \Omega : |f_n(\omega) - f(\omega)| > \varepsilon\},$$

and for convenience denote by B_n the set $A_n(\varepsilon_n)$. By the results of Lemmas 14.2 and 14.3, it suffices to show that

$$\sum_{n=1}^{\infty} \mu(B_n) < \infty \text{ implies } \sum_{n=1}^{\infty} \mu(A_n(\varepsilon)) < \infty,$$

for all $\varepsilon > 0$. Fix $\varepsilon > 0$ and note that as $\{\varepsilon_n\}$ converges to zero there exists an N such that $\varepsilon_n < \varepsilon$ for all $n \geq N$. But then for all $n \geq N$, $B_n \supset A_n(\varepsilon)$ and hence $\mu(B_n) \geq \mu(A_n(\varepsilon))$. Therefore,

$$\sum_{n=N}^{\infty} \mu(A_n(\varepsilon)) \leq \sum_{n=N}^{\infty} \mu(B_n) \leq \sum_{n=1}^{\infty} \mu(B_n) < \infty.$$

Hence, as μ is a probability measure, $\sum_{n=1}^{\infty} \mu(A_n(\varepsilon)) < \infty$.

b. The proof is constructive and follows the Hint. As f_n converges to f in probability, for all $\varepsilon > 0$ we have

$$\lim_{n\to\infty} \mu(|f_n - f| > \varepsilon) = 0.$$

Hence, for all $\varepsilon > 0$ and all $\delta > 0$ there exists an N such that for all $n \geq N$

$$\mu(|f_n - f| > \varepsilon) < \delta.$$

For example, if we set $\varepsilon = 1$ and $\delta = 1/2$ there exists an n_1 such that for all $n \geq n_1$, $\mu(|f_n - f| > 1) \leq 1/2$. In general, for $k \geq 1$, if we set $\varepsilon = 1/k$ and $\delta = 1/2^k$ there exists an n_k such that for all $n \geq n_k$, $\mu(|f_n - f| > 1/k) \leq 1/2^k$.

Now consider the subsequence $\{f_{n_k}\}$ generated by these n_k. Then

$$\sum_{k=1}^{\infty} \mu(|f_n - f| > 1/k) \leq \sum_{k=1}^{\infty} \frac{1}{2^k} < \infty,$$

and by the result of part a., f_{n_k} converges to f μ-almost everywhere.

Exercise 14.3

a. Let $x, y \in X$ and $\alpha, \beta \in \mathbf{R}$. The proof that T^k is linear for all k, is by induction. Note that

$$T^0(\alpha x + \beta y) = \alpha x + \beta y = \alpha T^0 x + \beta T^0 y,$$

and hence T^0 is linear. Assume that

$$T^{k-1}(\alpha x + \beta y) = \alpha T^{k-1} x + \beta T^{k-1} y.$$

Then

$$\begin{aligned} T^k(\alpha x + \beta y) &= T(T^{k-1}(\alpha x + \beta y)) \\ &= T(\alpha T^{k-1} x + \beta T^{k-1} y) \\ &= \alpha T^k x + \beta T^k y, \end{aligned}$$

since T is linear and by definition of T^k.

The proof that for all k, $\|T^k\| \leq 1$, is by induction. Note that

$$\begin{aligned} \|T^0\| &= \sup_{x \in X, \|x\|_X \leq 1} \|T^0 x\|_X \\ &= \sup_{x \in X, \|x\|_X \leq 1} \|x\|_X \leq 1. \end{aligned}$$

Assume that $\|T^{k-1}\| \leq 1$. Then

$$\begin{aligned} \|T^k\| &= \sup_{x \in X, \|x\|_X \leq 1} \|T^k x\|_X \\ &= \sup_{x \in X, \|x\|_X \leq 1} \|T(T^{k-1} x)\|_X \\ &\leq \|T\| \cdot \sup_{x \in X, \|x\|_X \leq 1} \|T^{k-1} x\|_X \\ &\leq \|T^{k-1}\| \leq 1, \end{aligned}$$

where the third line follows from $\|T\| \leq 1$.

b. Let $x, y \in X$ and $\alpha, \beta \in \mathbf{R}$. The proof that for all n, H_n is linear, is by induction. Note that

$$H_1(\alpha x + \beta y) = T^0(\alpha x + \beta y),$$

and so is linear by part a. Assume that $H_{n-1}(\alpha x + \beta y) = \alpha H_{n-1}x + \beta H_{n-1}y$. Then

$$
\begin{aligned}
H_n(\alpha x + \beta y) &= \frac{1}{n}\sum_{k=1}^{n} T^{k-1}(\alpha x + \beta y) \\
&= \frac{1}{n}T^{n-1}(\alpha x + \beta y) + \frac{n-1}{n}H_{n-1}(\alpha x + \beta y) \\
&= \frac{\alpha}{n}T^{n-1}x + \frac{\beta}{n}T^{n-1}y \\
&\quad + \frac{n-1}{n}\left[\frac{\alpha}{n-1}\sum_{k=1}^{n-1} T^{k-1}x + \frac{\beta}{n-1}\sum_{k=1}^{n-1} T^{k-1}y\right] \\
&= \alpha H_n x + \beta H_n y,
\end{aligned}
$$

where the third line follows by part a.

To see that for all n, $\|H_n\| \leq 1$, note that for all n

$$
\begin{aligned}
\|H_n\| &= \sup_{x\in X, \|x\|_X \leq 1} \left\| \frac{1}{n}\sum_{k=1}^{n} T^{k-1}x \right\|_X \\
&\leq \frac{1}{n} \sup_{x\in X, \|x\|_X \leq 1} \sum_{k=1}^{n} \|T^{k-1}x\|_X \\
&\leq \frac{1}{n}\sum_{k=1}^{n} \sup_{x\in X, \|x\|_X \leq 1} \|T^{k-1}x\|_X \\
&= \frac{1}{n}\sum_{k=1}^{n} \|T^{k-1}\| \leq 1,
\end{aligned}
$$

by the result of part a.

Exercise 14.4

Recall that if P is a transition function on $(S, \mathcal{S})$, and if $f \in C(S)$, under Assumption 14.2 we define the operator $T : C(S) \to C(S)$ by

$$(Tf)(s) = \int f(s')P(s, ds'),$$

for all $s \in S$.

To see that T is a linear operator, let $f,\ g \in C(S)$ and $\alpha,\ \beta \in \mathbf{R}$. Then for all $s \in S$

$$
\begin{aligned}
T\,(\alpha f + \beta g)\,(s) &= \int (\alpha f + \beta g)\, P(s, ds') \\
&= \alpha \int f P(s, ds') + \beta \int g P(s, ds') \\
&= \alpha\,(Tf)\,(s) + \beta\,(Tg)\,(s)\,,
\end{aligned}
$$

where the second equality comes from the linearity of the integral (Exercise 7.26c.). Hence,

$$T\,(\alpha f + \beta g) = \alpha T f + \beta T g.$$

To see that $\|T\|_L = 1$, let $f \in C\,(S)$ with $\|f\| = \sup_{s \in S} |f\,(s)| \leq 1$. Then for all $s \in S$

$$
\begin{aligned}
|(Tf)\,(s)| &= \left| \int f(s') P(s, ds') \right| \\
&\leq \int \left| f(s') \right| P(s, ds') \\
&\leq 1,
\end{aligned}
$$

as $\|f\| \leq 1$. Hence,

$$\|Tf\| = \sup_{s \in S} |(Tf)\,(s)| \leq 1,$$

and

$$\|T\|_L = \sup_{f \in C(S), \|f\| \leq 1} \|Tf\| \leq 1.$$

Next, consider the function g such that for all $s \in S$, $g\,(s) = 1$. Clearly, g is a bounded and continuous function on S, and satisfies $\|g\| \leq 1$. But then

$$
\begin{aligned}
\|T\|_L &= \sup_{f \in C(S), \|f\| \leq 1} \|Tf\| \\
&\geq \|Tg\| \\
&= \sup_{s \in S} |(Tg)\,(s)| = 1.
\end{aligned}
$$

Hence, $\|T\|_L = 1$.

To see that every constant function is a fixed point of T, let $f : S \to \mathbf{R}$ be defined by $f(s) = a$ for all $s \in S$. Then, for all $s \in S$,

$$\begin{aligned}(Tf)(s) &= \int f(s')P(s, ds') \\ &= a \int P(s, ds') \\ &= a,\end{aligned}$$

and hence $(Tf)(s) = f(s) = a$ for all $s \in S$.

15 *Pareto Optima and Competitive Equilibria*

Exercise 15.1

Let $\{\phi_n^*\}$ be a Cauchy sequence in S^*. That is, for all $\varepsilon > 0$ there exists a N_ε such that $\|\phi_n^* - \phi_m^*\|_d < \varepsilon$ for all $m, n \geq N_\varepsilon$. As $\phi_n^* - \phi_m^*$ is a bounded linear functional by Theorem 15.1, for any $s \in S$ the sequence of scalars $\{\phi_n^*(s)\}$ satisfies

$$|\phi_n^*(s) - \phi_m^*(s)| \leq \|\phi_n^* - \phi_m^*\|_d . \|s\|_S,$$

and is hence a Cauchy sequence. Hence, as $\mathbf{R}$ is complete, for each $s \in S$ there exists a scalar $\phi^*(s)$ such that $\phi_n^*(s) \to \phi^*(s)$. The proof will be complete if we can show that the function $\phi^*(s)$ defined in this way for all $s \in S$ is an element of S^*, and that $\phi_n^* \to \phi^*$ in the norm $\|.\|_d$.

That ϕ^* is linear follows from the fact that for $s, t \in S$ and $\alpha, \beta \in \mathbf{R}$ we have

$$\begin{aligned}
\phi^*(\alpha s + \beta t) &= \lim_{n\to\infty} \phi_n^*(\alpha s + \beta t) \\
&= \alpha \lim_{n\to\infty} \phi_n^*(s) + \beta \lim_{n\to\infty} \phi_n^*(t) \\
&= \alpha\phi^*(s) + \beta\phi^*(t),
\end{aligned}$$

from the linearity of the ϕ_n^*.

To see that ϕ^* is bounded, note that as $\{\phi_n^*\}$ is Cauchy, for every $\varepsilon > 0$ there exists an N_ε such that $|\phi_n^*(s) - \phi_m^*(s)| < \|s\|\varepsilon/2$ for all $m, n \geq N_\varepsilon$ and all $s \in S$. But as $\mathbf{R}$ is complete, $\phi_n^*(s) \to \phi^*(s)$, and hence

$$(15.1) \qquad |\phi^*(s) - \phi_m^*(s)| \leq \frac{\varepsilon}{2}\|s\|_S < \varepsilon\|s\|_S,$$

for all $m \geq N_\varepsilon$. Hence

$$\begin{aligned}|\phi^*(s)| &= |\phi^*(s) - \phi_m^*(s) + \phi_m^*(s)| \\ &\leq |\phi^*(s) - \phi_m^*(s)| + |\phi_m^*(s)| \\ &\leq \varepsilon \|s\|_S + \|\phi_m^*\|_d \|s\|_S = (\varepsilon + \|\phi_m^*\|_d)\|s\|_S,\end{aligned}$$

and so ϕ^* is bounded.

Finally, by (15.1) we have that for all $\varepsilon > 0$ there exists an N_ε such that for all $m \geq N_\varepsilon$

$$\|\phi^* - \phi_m^*\|_d = \sup_{\|s\|_S \leq 1} |\phi^*(s) - \phi_m^*(s)| < \varepsilon.$$

Hence, $\phi_m^* \to \phi^*$ in the norm $\|.\|_d$.

Exercise 15.2

a. Let ϕ be a continuous linear functional on l_2, and for all n let e_n denote the sequence that is zero everywhere except for the nth term, which is one. If $x \in l_2$, then

$$\lim_{N\to\infty} \left\| x - \sum_{n=1}^{N} x_n e_n \right\|_2 = 0,$$

and by linearity we can write $\phi(x) = \sum_{i=1}^{\infty} x_i \phi(e_i)$. The sequence defined by $y_i = \phi(e_i)$ is our y; we need to show that $y \in l_2$.

Note that for all N

$$\begin{aligned}\sum_{n=1}^{N} y_n^2 &= \sum_{n=1}^{N} y_n \phi(e_n) = \phi\left(\sum_{n=1}^{N} y_n e_n\right) \\ &\leq \|\phi\| \cdot \left(\sum_{n=1}^{N} y_n^2\right)^{1/2},\end{aligned}$$

where the second equality comes from linearity and the inequality from continuity. Hence

$$\left(\sum_{n=1}^{N} y_n^2\right)^{1/2} \leq \|\phi\| < \infty,$$

for all N. Taking limits as $N \to \infty$ we get $\|y\|_2 \leq \|\phi\|$ and hence $y \in l_2$.

Conversely, let $y \in l_2$. If $x \in l_2$, then $\phi(x) = \sum_{i=1}^{\infty} y_i x_i$ is a continuous linear functional on l_2 since by the Hölder inequality

$$|\phi(x)| \leq \sum_{i=1}^{\infty} |y_i x_i| \leq \|y\|_2 \cdot \|x\|_2 ,$$

and thus $\|\phi\| \leq \|y\|_2$.

b. Let ϕ be a continuous linear functional on l_1, and for all n define e_n as for part a. Note that if $x \in l_1$, then

$$\lim_{N\to\infty} \left\| x - \sum_{n=1}^{N} x_n e_n \right\|_1 = 0,$$

and by linearity we can write $\phi(x) = \sum_{i=1}^{\infty} x_i \phi(e_i)$. The sequence defined by $y_i = \phi(e_i)$ is our y; we need to show that $y \in l_\infty$. But,

$$|y_i| = |\phi(e_i)| \leq \|\phi\|,$$

and hence $\|y\|_\infty \leq \|\phi\| < \infty$.

Conversely, let $y \in l_\infty$. If $x \in l_1$, then $\phi(x) = \sum_{i=1}^{\infty} y_i x_i$ is a continuous linear functional on l_1 since by the Hölder inequality

$$|\phi(x)| \leq \sum_{i=1}^{\infty} |y_i x_i| \leq \|y\|_\infty \cdot \|x\|_1,$$

and thus $\|\phi\| \leq \|y\|_\infty$.

Exercise 15.3

Let $y \in l_1$ and for all $x \in l_\infty$ define

$$\phi(x) = \lim_{N\to\infty} \sum_{n=1}^{N} y_n x_n,$$

which is well defined because $\lim_{N\to\infty} \sum_{n=1}^{N} y_n$ is finite and the x_n are bounded. We need to show that this is a continuous linear functional. To show linearity, let $x, z \in l_\infty$ and $\alpha, \beta \in \mathbf{R}$. Then

$$\begin{aligned}\phi(\alpha x + \beta z) &= \lim_{n\to\infty} \sum_{i=1}^{n} y_i(\alpha x_i + \beta z_i) \\ &= \alpha \lim_{n\to\infty} \sum_{i=1}^{n} y_i x_i + \beta \lim_{n\to\infty} \sum_{i=1}^{n} y_i z_i \\ &= \alpha\phi(x) + \beta\phi(z).\end{aligned}$$

By Theorem 15.1, ϕ is continuous if and only if it is bounded. But for all $x \in l_\infty$

$$|\phi(x)| \le \sum_{i=1}^{\infty} |y_i x_i| \le \|x\|_\infty \cdot \sum_{i=1}^{\infty} |y_i| = \|y\|_1 . \|x\|_\infty < \infty,$$

and hence $\|\phi\| \le \|y\|_1 < \infty$.

Exercise 15.4

Let c_0 be as defined in the text, and for all $x \in c_0$ let

$$\|x\|_{c_0} = \|x\|_\infty = \sup_n |x_n| = \max_n |x_n|.$$

That c_0 is a vector space follows from the fact that if x, $y \in c_0$ and $\alpha \in \mathbf{R}$, we have

$$\lim_{n\to\infty} (x_n + y_n) = \lim_{n\to\infty} x_n + \lim_{n\to\infty} y_n = 0,$$

and

$$\lim_{n\to\infty} \alpha x_n = \alpha \lim_{n\to\infty} x_n = 0.$$

As $c_0 \subset l_\infty$, $\|.\|_\infty$ is obviously a norm on c_0.

Let ϕ be a continuous linear functional on c_0 and for all n define e_n as for Exercise 15.2. If $x \in c_0$, then

$$\lim_{N\to\infty} \left\| x - \sum_{n=1}^{N} x_n e_n \right\|_\infty = 0,$$

because $\lim_{n\to\infty} x_n = 0$ (this would not be the case in general for $x \in l_\infty$). Hence, by linearity we can write $\phi(x) = \sum_{i=1}^{\infty} x_i \phi(e_i)$. The sequence defined by $y_i = \phi(e_i)$ is our y; we need to show that $y \in l_1$.

Define

$$\zeta_n = \begin{cases} 1 & \text{if } \phi(e_n) > 0 \\ -1 & \text{if } \phi(e_n) \le 0, \end{cases}$$

and for all $N \geq 1$, let

$$z^N = (\zeta_1, \zeta_2, \ldots, \zeta_N, 0, 0, \ldots)$$

which is an element of c_0. Then

$$\phi(z^N) = \sum_{n=1}^{\infty} z_n^N \phi(e_n) = \sum_{n=1}^{N} \zeta_n \phi(e_n) = \sum_{n=1}^{N} |\phi(e_n)| = \sum_{n=1}^{N} |y_n|,$$

which for all N satisfies $|\phi(z^N)| \leq \|\phi\| . \|z^N\|_\infty = \|\phi\| < \infty$. Taking limits, we get

$$\sum_{n=1}^{\infty} |y_n| \leq \|\phi\| < \infty,$$

and hence $y \in l_1$.

Conversely, let $y \in l_1$. If $x \in c_0$, then $\phi(x) = \sum_{n=1}^{\infty} y_n x_n$ is well defined because x is bounded and $\sum_{n=1}^{\infty} y_n$ converges. Then ϕ is a continuous linear functional on c_0 since

$$|\phi(x)| \leq \sum_{n=1}^{\infty} |y_n x_n| \leq \|x\|_\infty \sum_{n=1}^{\infty} |y_n| = \|y\|_1 . \|x\|_\infty,$$

and thus $\|\phi\| \leq \|y\|_1$.

Exercise 15.5

a. To see that ϕ is linear, let $x, y \in L_\infty(Z, \mathcal{Z}, \mu)$ and $\alpha, \beta \in \mathbf{R}$. Then

$$\begin{aligned}
\phi(\alpha x + \beta y) &= \int (\alpha x(z) + \beta y(z)) f(z) d\mu(z) \\
&= \alpha \int x(z) f(z) d\mu(z) + \beta \int y(z) f(z) d\mu(z) \\
&= \alpha \phi(x) + \beta \phi(y)
\end{aligned}$$

by the linearity of the Lebesgue integral.

For all $x \in L_\infty(Z, \mathcal{Z}, \mu)$, $|\phi(x)| \leq \|f\|_1 . \|x\|_\infty$ and hence $\|\phi\| \leq \|f\|_1$ so that ϕ is bounded and hence continuous by Theorem 15.1.

b. Let $f \in L_1(Z, \mathcal{Z}, \mu)$. As f^+ and f^- are in $M^+(Z, \mathcal{Z}, \mu)$, by Exercise 7.21 both define finite measures, say ν^+ and ν^-, on $\mathcal{Z}$. But, for any $A \in \mathcal{Z}$ we have

$$\begin{aligned}\nu(A) &= \int_A f(z)d\mu(z) \\ &= \int_A f^+(z)d\mu(z) - \int_A f^-(z)d\mu(z) \\ &= \nu^+(A) - \nu^-(A),\end{aligned}$$

and by definition $\nu = \nu^+ - \nu^-$ is a signed measure.

To see that ν is absolutely continuous with respect to μ, let $A \in \mathcal{Z}$ be such that $\mu(A) = 0$. Then by Exercise 7.20b., $\nu^+(A) = \nu^-(A) = 0$ and hence $\nu(A) = 0$.

Exercise 15.6

Toward a contradiction, assume that $\theta \in int(B)$. Then there exists an open neighborhood of θ, say $N(\theta, \varepsilon)$, that is a subset of B. As $\beta \in (0, 1)$ there exists a T such that $\varepsilon > \beta^{T-1}$, and consider the point $y_T = (0, 0, \ldots, 0, \varepsilon/\beta^{T-1}, 0, \ldots)$ which is zero except at the Tth position. Then

$$\|y_T\| = \sum_{t=0}^{\infty} \beta^t |y_{Tt}| = \beta\varepsilon < \varepsilon,$$

and hence $y_T \in N(\theta, \varepsilon)$. But as $|y_{Tt}| = \varepsilon/\beta^{T-1} > 1$, we also have $y_T \notin B$, a contradiction.

Exercise 15.7

a. Toward a contradiction, assume that x is an interior point of the positive orthant of l_p, which we denote as l_p^+. Then for some $\epsilon > 0$, the open ball $B(x, \epsilon) \subset l_p^+$. We produce a contradiction by exhibiting an element of $B(x, \epsilon)$ that is not in l_p^+.

As $x \in l_p$, there exists an N such that, for all $n \geq N$, $|x_n| < \epsilon/2$. Define $z \in l_p$ such that $z_n = x_n$ for all $n \neq N$ and $z_N = x_N - \epsilon/2$. Then $z \notin l_p^+$ (as $z_N < 0$) but $z \in B(x, \epsilon)$ as

$$\begin{aligned}\|x - z\|_p &= \left(\sum_{n=1}^{\infty} |x_n - z_n|^p\right)^{1/p} \\ &= \epsilon/2.\end{aligned}$$

b. Consider the point $x = (1, 1, \ldots)$ and pick $\varepsilon \in (0, 1)$. Then if $y \in N(x, \varepsilon)$, we have for all $t \geq 1$ that $y_t \in (0, 1 + \varepsilon)$ and hence is an element of the positive orthant of l_∞. Hence x is an interior point of the positive orthant of l_∞.

Exercise 15.8

A15.1: The proof that $X = l_\infty^+$ is convex is straightforward.

A15.2: Let $x, x' \in X$ with

$$u(x) = \inf_t x_t > \inf_t x'_t = u(x'),$$

and let $\theta \in (0, 1)$. Then

$$\theta \inf_t x_t + (1 - \theta) \inf_t x'_t,$$

is a lower bound on the sequence $\{x_t^\theta\} \equiv \{\theta x_t + (1 - \theta) x'_t\}$ and so

$$\inf_t (\theta x_t + (1 - \theta) x'_t) \geq \theta \inf_t x_t + (1 - \theta) \inf_t x'_t > \inf_t x'_t.$$

A15.3: Fix $\varepsilon > 0$ and choose $x, x' \in l_\infty$ such that $\|x - x'\|_\infty < \delta \equiv \varepsilon/2$, where we have, without loss of generality, labelled these elements of l_∞ such that $\inf x' \leq \inf x$. Then, for all $t \geq 1$,

$$\begin{aligned} |u(x) - u(x')| &= \left| \inf_s x_s - \inf_s x'_s \right| \\ &\leq \left| x_t - \inf_s x'_s \right|. \end{aligned}$$

By definition of the infimum, there exists a T such that $x'_T < \inf_s x'_s + \varepsilon/2$. Hence,

$$\begin{aligned} |u(x) - u(x')| &\leq \left| x_T - \inf_s x'_s \right| \\ &= \left| \inf_s x'_s - x'_T + x'_T - x_T \right| \\ &\leq \left| \inf_s x'_s - x'_T \right| + \left| x'_T - x_T \right| \\ &< \frac{\varepsilon}{2} + \frac{\varepsilon}{2} = \varepsilon, \end{aligned}$$

and so u is continuous.

A15.4: As Y is defined by a sequence of linear inequalities, it is convex.

A15.5: To see that Y has an interior point, consider the point y defined by $y_t = 1/2$ for all $t \geq 1$. Then for $\varepsilon \in (0, 1/2)$ we have that the ε-neighborhood $N(y, \varepsilon) \subset Y$ because for all t, $y_t \in (0, 1)$.

Exercise 15.9

To show that u is not continuous if the norm

$$\|x\| = \sum_{t=1}^{\infty} \beta^t |x_t|,$$

is used, it is sufficient to establish that there exists an $\varepsilon > 0$ such that for all $\delta > 0$ there exists $x, x' \in X_i$ with $\|x - x'\| < \delta$ and $|u(x) - u(x')| \geq \varepsilon$. Fix $\varepsilon > 0$ and note that for all $\delta > 0$ we can find a T such that $\beta^T \varepsilon < \delta$. Consider the sequences $x = (1, 1, \ldots)$ and $x' = (1, 1, \ldots, 1, 1 - \varepsilon, 1, \ldots)$, where the $1 - \varepsilon$ appears at the Tth position, which are both bounded in $\|.\|$. Then we have

$$\begin{aligned} \|x - x'\| &= \sum_{t=1}^{\infty} \beta^t |x_t - x'_t| \\ &= \beta^T \varepsilon < \delta, \end{aligned}$$

but also

$$|u(x) - u(x')| = \left|\inf_t x_t - \inf_t x'_t\right| = \varepsilon.$$

Exercise 15.10

a. To see that A15.1 holds, note that as C is convex, then X_i is convex. To see that A15.6 holds, let $x \in X_i$. Then for all $t \geq 1$, $x_t \in C$. But by assumption, $\theta \in C$ and hence for all T,

$$x^T = (x_1, x_2, \ldots, x_T, \theta, \theta, \ldots) \in X_i.$$

b. First, note that the assumptions of the problem are not sufficient to show that u_i satisfies A15.2. As a counterexample, let $X = \mathbf{R}$, $C = [0, 1]$ and define $U_i : C \to \mathbf{R}$ by $U_i(x) = x^2$. As C is compact, and U_i is continuous, it is bounded on C. Further, as U_i is monotone on C, then if $x, x' \in C$ we have $x > x'$ if and only if $U_i(x) > U_i(x')$. Hence, for $\theta \in (0, 1)$, we have $\theta x + (1 - \theta)x' > x'$ and hence $U_i(\theta x + (1 - \theta)x') > U_i(x')$ so that U_i satisfies A15.2. To see that

u_i need not satisfy A15.2, consider the points $y = (1, 0, 0, \ldots) \in X_i$ and $y' = (0, 1, 0, 0, \ldots) \in X_i$. Then

$$u_i(y) = 1 > \beta = u_i(y').$$

But if $\theta \in (0, 1)$, we have that $u_i(\theta y + (1-\theta)y') = \theta^2 + \beta(1-\theta)^2$ which is less than $u_i(y') = \beta$ for combinations of θ and β satisfying $\theta^2(1+\beta) - 2\beta\theta < 0$. Given β, this is true for

$$\theta \in \left(0, \frac{2\beta}{1+\beta}\right).$$

For example, if $\beta = 1/2$, this holds for $0 < \theta < 2/3$. To recover the result, we place the following stronger restriction on U_i.

To recover the result, we place the following stronger restriction on U_i.

ASSUMPTION 15.2′: *(Concavity) For each i, if $x, x' \in C$, and $\theta \in (0, 1)$, then $U_i(\theta x + (1-\theta)x') \geq \theta U_i(x) + (1-\theta)U_i(x')$.*

To see that u_i satisfies A15.2, under A15.2′ on U_i, let $x, x' \in X_i$ with $u_i(x) > u_i(x')$, and let $\theta \in (0, 1)$. Then for all T

$$\sum_{t=0}^{T} \beta^t U_i(\theta x_t + (1-\theta)x_t') \geq \theta \sum_{t=0}^{T} \beta^t U_i(x_t) + (1-\theta) \sum_{t=0}^{T} \beta^t U_i(x_t').$$

Taking limits as $T \to \infty$, which exist because U_i is bounded, gives

$$u_i(\theta x + (1-\theta)x') \geq \theta u_i(x) + (1-\theta)u_i(x') > u_i(x').$$

To see that u_i satisfies A15.3, let $\varepsilon > 0$ be given. As U_i is continuous, we can choose $\delta > 0$ such that $\|x_t - x_t'\|_X < \delta$ implies that $|U_i(x_t) - U_i(x_t')| < \varepsilon(1-\beta)$. Now if $x, x' \in X_i$ such that $\|x - x'\|_{X_i} < \delta$, this implies that $\|x_t - x_t'\|_X < \delta$ for all $t \geq 0$. Hence

$$\begin{aligned} \left|u_i(x) - u_i(x')\right| &\leq \sum_{t=0}^{\infty} \beta^t \left|U_i(x_t) - U_i(x_t')\right| \\ &< \varepsilon(1-\beta) \sum_{t=0}^{\infty} \beta^t = \varepsilon, \end{aligned}$$

and so u_i is continuous (in the norm topology).

To see that u_i satisfies A15.7, let $x, x' \in X_i$ with $u_i(x) > u_i(x')$. As U_i is bounded, there exists an $M \in \mathbf{R}$ such that $|U_i| \leq M$. Fix $\varepsilon \in (0, u_i(x) - u_i(x'))$ and choose T^* such that

$$\beta^{T+1}\frac{M}{1-\beta} < \frac{\varepsilon}{2},$$

for all $T \geq T^*$. Then for all such T,

$$\begin{aligned} u(x^T) &= \sum_{t=0}^{T}\beta^t U(x_t) + \sum_{t=T+1}^{\infty}\beta^t U(0) \\ &= u_i(x) - \sum_{t=T+1}^{\infty}\beta^t(U(x_t) - U(0)) \\ &\geq u_i(x) - 2\beta^{T+1}\frac{M}{1-\beta} \\ &> u_i(x) - \varepsilon \\ &> u_i(x'). \end{aligned}$$

c. By Exercise 5.11d. u_W is concave. But all concave functions are quasi-concave. To see this, note that if $x, x' \in X$ with $u_W(x) > u_W(x')$ and $\theta \in (0, 1)$, then

$$u_W(\theta x + (1-\theta)x') \geq \theta u_W(x) + (1-\theta)u_W(x') > u_W(x').$$

Hence u_W satisfies A15.2. Similarly, by Exercise 5.11d., u_W is continuous in the sup-norm. Hence it satisfies A15.3.

To see that u_W satisfies A15.7, let $x, x' \in X$ with $u_W(x) > u_W(x')$. By Exercise 5.11d., u_W satisfies

$$|u_W(x) - u_W(x^T)| \leq \beta^T \|u_W\|,$$

for all T, all $x \in X$ and some $\beta \in (0, 1)$. Fix $\varepsilon \in (0, u_W(x) - u_W(x'))$ and choose T^* such that $\beta^{T^*}\|u_W\| < \varepsilon$. Then for all $T \geq T^*$, we have $|u_W(x) - u_W(x^T)| < \varepsilon$ and hence $u_W(x^T) > u_W(x')$.

Exercise 15.11

a. To see this, let $X = \{x \in l_\infty : 0 \leq x_t \leq 1\}$. Then the points x defined by $x_t = 1$ for all $t \geq 1$, and x' defined by $x'_t = 1/2$ for all $t \geq 1$ are in X and satisfy

$$u(x) = \inf_t x_t = 1 > \frac{1}{2} = \inf_t x'_t = u(x').$$

But then for all T,

$$u(x^T) = 0 < \frac{1}{2} = u(x').$$

b. To simplify the notation, drop the index i. First, assume that for all $x \in X$, $u(x) = \lim_{T\to\infty} u(x^T)$. To show that A15.7 holds, let $x, x' \in X$ with $u(x) > u(x')$. Fix $\varepsilon \in (0, u(x) - u(x'))$. Then there exists a T^* such that for all $T \geq T^*$,

$$|u(x) - u(x^T)| < \varepsilon.$$

Hence, for all $T \geq T^*$, $u(x^T) > u(x')$.

One can prove a partial converse: A15.7 implies that

$$\lim_{T\to\infty} u(x^T) \geq u(x),$$

all $x \in X$. To establish this, we must show that the limit on the LHS exists and that the inequality holds. To show the former, note that for any $x \in X$, the relevant limit exists if and only if

$$\lim_{T\to\infty} \sup u(x^T) = \lim_{T\to\infty} \inf u(x^T).$$

Suppose to the contrary that for some x the LHS is strictly bigger. Choose $\hat{x}$ such that

$$\lim_{T\to\infty} \sup u(x^T) > u(\hat{x}) > \lim_{T\to\infty} \inf u(x^T).$$

A15.1–A15.3 ensure that this is possible. Choose some $\hat{T}$ with

$$u(x^{\hat{T}}) > u(\hat{x}).$$

Then A15.7 implies that

$$u(x^T) > u(\hat{x}),$$

for *all* $T > \hat{T}$ sufficiently large, a contradiction. Hence $\lim_{T\to\infty} u(x^T)$ is well defined for all x.

To show that the inequality holds, suppose to the contrary that for some x,

$$\lim_{T\to\infty} u(x^T) < u(x).$$

Then A15.7 immediately gives a contradiction.

Notice that this inequality is sufficient, in combination with Assumptions 15.1–15.6, to establish Theorem 15.6. It implies that "tail" pieces cannot increase utility, although they can reduce it. Thus, if the "tail" piece has a positive price, the consumer will choose the (cheaper and better) truncated sequence instead. If the "tail" piece had a negative price, the consumer might want to buy it, since it would ease his budget constraint. But firms would not want to produce it: if Assumption 15.6 holds, they will choose to produce the (feasible and more valuable) truncated sequence instead.

Exercise 15.12

A15.2: As in Exercise 15.10b., this need not be true. Instead, assume that U_i satisfies Assumption 15.2′. Let $x, x' \in X_i$ with $u_i(x) > u_i(x')$, and let $\theta \in (0, 1)$. Then

$$\begin{aligned}
&u_i(\theta x + (1-\theta)x') \\
&= \int U_i(\theta x(z) + (1-\theta)x'(z))\, d\mu_i(z) \\
&\geq \theta \int U_i(x(z))\, d\mu_i(z) + (1-\theta)\int U_i(x'(z))\, d\mu_i(z) \\
&= \theta u_i(x) + (1-\theta)u_i(x') \\
&> u_i(x').
\end{aligned}$$

A15.3: To see that u_i satisfies A15.3, let $\varepsilon > 0$ be given. As U_i is continuous, we can choose $\delta > 0$ such that $|x(z) - x'(z)| < \delta$ implies that $|U_i(x(z)) - U_i(x'(z))| < \varepsilon$ for each $z \in Z$. Now if $x, x' \in X_i$ such that $\|x - x'\|_\infty < \delta$, this implies that $|x(z) - x'(z)| < \delta$ for all $z \in B$ for some set $B \in \mathcal{Z}$ with $\mu(B^c) = 0$. Hence

$$\begin{aligned}
\left|u_i(x) - u_i(x')\right| &\leq \int \left|U_i(x(z)) - U_i(x'(z))\right| d\mu_i(z) \\
&< \varepsilon,
\end{aligned}$$

and u_i is continuous (in the norm topology).

A15.9: Let $x, x' \in X_i$, such that $u_i(x) > u_i(x')$, and $A_n \downarrow 0$. Then for all n,

$$\begin{aligned} u_i(x^{A_n}) &= \int U_i(x^{A_n}(z))\, d\mu_i(z) \\ &= \int_{(A_n)^c} U_i(x(z))\, d\mu_i(z) + \int_{A_n} U_i(0)\, d\mu_i(z) \\ &= \int U_i(x(z))\, d\mu_i(z) - \int_{A_n} (U_i(x(z)) - U_i(0))\, d\mu_i(z). \end{aligned}$$

As $x \in L_\infty(Z, \mathcal{Z}, \mu)$, it is bounded except possibly on a set of measure zero. Hence, as U_i is continuous, there exists a $B \in \mathcal{Z}$ with $\mu(B) = 0$ such that $\sup_{z \in B^c} |U_i(z)| \leq M$ for some scalar M. Hence for all n,

$$\begin{aligned} \int_{A^n} (U_i(x(z)) - U_i(0))\, d\mu_i(z) &\leq \int_{A^n} \left|U_i(x(z)) - U_i(0)\right|\, d\mu_i(z) \\ &\leq 2M\mu_i(A_n). \end{aligned}$$

As μ_i is absolutely continuous with respect to μ, we have

$$\lim_{n\to\infty} \mu_i(A_n) = \mu_i(\cap_{n=1}^{\infty} A_n) = \mu(\cap_{n=1}^{\infty} A_n) = 0.$$

Then for all $\varepsilon > 0$ there exists an N_ε such that for all $n \geq N_e$, $\mu_i(A_n) < \varepsilon$. Pick

$$\varepsilon \in \left(0, \frac{u_i(x) - u_i(x')}{2M}\right).$$

Then, for all $n \geq N_\varepsilon$ we have

$$\begin{aligned} u_i(x^{A_n}) &= \int U_i(x(z))\, d\mu_i(z) - \int_{A^n} (U_i(x(z)) - U_i(0))\, d\mu_i(z) \\ &\geq \int U_i(x(z))\, d\mu_i(z) - 2M\mu_i(A_n) \\ &> u_i(x) - 2M\varepsilon \\ &> u_i(x'). \end{aligned}$$

16 *Applications of Equilibrium Theory*

Exercise 16.1

a. As the results of Exercise 5.1 apply, there exists a unique symmetric Pareto efficient allocation. By the First Welfare Theorem (Theorem 15.3) (the nonsatiation requirement follows from the definition of X and U strictly increasing), every competitive equilibrium allocation is Pareto efficient. But since there is only one symmetric Pareto efficient allocation, there can be at most one symmetric competitive equilibrium.

b. We need to verify that assumptions A15.1 through A15.5 hold. A15.1 is obvious; we verify the rest in turn.

A15.2: Let $x, x' \in X$ be such that $u(x) > u(x')$. Let $\theta \in (0, 1)$ and define $x^\theta = \{\theta x_t + (1-\theta) x'_t\}_{t=0}^{\infty}$. By the strict concavity of U, we have for all t that

$$U(x_t^\theta) \geq \theta U(x_t) + (1-\theta) U(x'_t).$$

Hence,

$$\begin{aligned}
u(x^\theta) &= \lim_{T\to\infty} \sum_{t=0}^{T} \beta^t U(x_t^\theta) \\
&\geq \theta \lim_{T\to\infty} \sum_{t=0}^{T} \beta^t U(x_t) + (1-\theta) \lim_{T\to\infty} \sum_{t=0}^{T} \beta^t U(x'_t) \\
&= \theta u(x) + (1-\theta) u(x') > u(x'),
\end{aligned}$$

where the limits are well defined by $\beta \in (0, 1)$ and U bounded.

A15.3: Let $\varepsilon > 0$ be given. Then as U is continuous there exist a $\delta > 0$ such that $|x_t - x'_t| < \delta$ implies $|U(x_t) - U(x'_t)| < \varepsilon(1-\beta)$. Let $x, x' \in X$ be such that $\|x - x'\|_\infty < \delta$. Then for all t, $|x_t - x'_t| < \delta$, and hence

$$|u(x) - u(x')| = \left|\sum_{t=0}^{\infty} \beta^t U(x_t) - \sum_{t=0}^{\infty} \beta^t U(x'_t)\right|$$

$$\leq \sum_{t=0}^{\infty} \beta^t |U(x_t) - U(x'_t)| < \varepsilon.$$

A15.4: Let $y, y' \in Y$. Then there exists $k, k' \in l_\infty$ such that $k_0 = k'_0 = \hat{k}$, $k_{t+1} + y_t \leq f(k_t)$ and $k'_{t+1} + y'_t \leq f(k'_t)$, for all t. Let $\theta \in (0, 1)$ and define

$$y^\theta = \{\theta y_t + (1-\theta) y'_t\}_{t=0}^{\infty},$$

$$k^\theta = \{\theta k_t + (1-\theta) k'_t\}_{t=0}^{\infty}.$$

Obviously, $k_0^\theta = \hat{k}$ and

$$k_{t+1}^\theta + y_t^\theta = \theta(k_{t+1} + y_t) + (1-\theta)(k'_{t+1} + y'_t)$$

$$\leq \theta f(k_t) + (1-\theta) f(k'_t) \leq f(k_t^\theta),$$

for all t by the concavity of f. Hence, $y^\theta \in Y$ for all $\theta \in (0, 1)$.

A15.5: We construct an interior point of Y. Let $\hat{k} \in (0, \bar{k})$ and define the point y such that

$$y_t = (1/2)\left[f(\hat{k}) - \hat{k}\right],$$

for all t. This is in Y as the sequence k defined by $k_t = \hat{k}$ for all t satisfies $y_t < f(\hat{k}) - \hat{k}$ for all t. We need to show that there exists an $\varepsilon > 0$ such that the ε-ball $B(y, \varepsilon) \subset Y$. Choose ε such that

$$0 < \varepsilon < (1/3)\left[f(\hat{k}) - \hat{k}\right].$$

Then if $y' \in B(y, \varepsilon)$, we have $0 < y'_t < f(\hat{k}) - \hat{k}$ for all t and hence $B(y, \varepsilon) \subset Y$.

The definition of X and the assumption that U is strictly increasing imply that the nonsatiation requirement is satisfied. Hence the Second Welfare Theorem (Theorem 15.4) applies. To show that the Pareto-efficient allocation (x^0, y^0) is a competitive equilibrium, we need to establish the existence of a "cheaper point" in X.

By construction of X, either $\phi(x^0)$ is strictly positive, or it is equal to zero. If $\phi(x^0) > 0$, the existence of a cheaper point follows from the fact that $\theta = \{0, 0, \ldots\} \in X$ with $\phi(\theta) = 0$. Suppose $\phi(x^0) = 0$. Then either $x^0 = \theta$, or ϕ is identically zero. The second is ruled out by the Second Welfare Theorem (Theorem 15.4). To show that x^0 cannot equal θ, note that by the result that A15.5 applies above, we have the existence of a point $x \in X \cap Y$, with $x \neq \theta$ satisfying $u(x) > u(\theta)$ by the fact that U is strictly increasing. But this contradicts $[x^0, y^0]$ being Pareto efficient.

By Exercise 5.1 we know that a symmetric Pareto efficient allocation exists. Hence, we have the existence of a symmetric competitive equilibrium.

c. We establish each of these in turn.

A15.6: This is obviously true for X. Let $y \in Y$. Then there exists a $k \in l_\infty^+$ such that $k_{t+1} + y_t \leq f(k_t)$ for all t. But then, as $k_{t+1} \leq f(k_t)$, we have that $y^T \in Y$.

A15.7: Let $x, x' \in X$ such that $u(x) > u(x')$ and let $\varepsilon = u(x) - u(x')$. As U is bounded and $\beta \in (0, 1)$ there exists a T^* such that for all $T \geq T^*$,

$$\sum_{t=T+1}^{\infty} \beta^t \left|U(x_t) - U(x_t^*)\right| < \varepsilon,$$

for all $x^* \in X$. Then, for all $T \geq T^*$

$$\begin{aligned} u(x) - u(x') &= u(x) - u(x^T) + u(x^T) - u(x') \\ &\leq \sum_{t=T+1}^{\infty} \beta^t \left|U(x_t) - U(0)\right| + u(x^T) - u(x') \\ &< u(x^T) - u(x') + \varepsilon. \end{aligned}$$

and hence $u(x^T) > u(x')$.

The nonsatiation condition in Theorem 15.6 follows from the definition of X and U strictly increasing. Hence the price system has an inner product representation.

d. We assume an interior solution: Exercise 5.1d. gives sufficient conditions for this to be true. Using standard Lagrange multiplier methods, the first-order conditions for an optimum in the profit maximization problem include

$$\prod_{s=0}^{t-1} \frac{1}{1+r_s} = \lambda_t,$$

and

$$\lambda_t f'(k_t) = \lambda_{t-1},$$

for all $t \geq 1$, where, for each $t \geq 1$, λ_t is the Lagrange multiplier on $y_t + k_{t+1} \leq f(k_t)$ and $\lambda_0 = 1$. Hence we have

$$1 + r_t = f'(k_{t+1}).$$

Similarly, using standard Lagrange multiplier methods, the first-order conditions for an optimum in the consumers problem include

$$\beta^t U'(x_t) = \mu \prod_{s=0}^{t-1} \frac{1}{1+r_s},$$

where μ is the Lagrange multiplier on the consumers' lifetime budget constraint. Hence

$$\beta \frac{U'(x_{t+1})}{U'(x_t)} = \frac{1}{1+r_t}$$

As the capital stock sequence corresponding to this competitive equilibrium is unique (from the uniqueness of the Pareto efficient capital stock sequence), the set of equilibrium real interest rates $\{r_t\}$ is unique, and hence so is the sequence of relative prices $\{p_{t+1}/p_t\}$.

e. Under our assumptions on f and U, the function $q(k)$ defined by

$$q(k) = \beta \frac{U'(c[g(k)])}{U'[c(k)]}$$

is continuous. Further, under our assumptions the space of attainable capital stock choices is bounded; denote it by K. Let $C(K \times K)$ be the space of continuous functions on $K \times K$ bounded in the sup norm, and define the operator T on $C(K \times K)$ by

$$(T\psi)(k, z) = \max_{z', k'} \{f(z) - z' + q(k)\psi[k', z']\},$$

subject to

$$0 \leq z' \leq f(z),$$

and $k' = g(k)$. Given the restriction on the choice of k', this functional equation corresponds to the one defined in (1) in the text.

To see that T maps bounded functions into bounded functions, note that f is bounded above, q is continuous on the bounded set K, and ψ is bounded by assumption. That T preserves continuity follows from the Theorem of the Maximum noting that the constraint correspondence is continuous by the result of Exercise 3.13b.

The existence of a unique fixed point of T will then be established if we can show that T is a contraction mapping. The proof of this result is complicated slightly by the fact there exist $k \in K$ such that $q(k) > 1$. To see this, note that substituting from the Euler equation from the social planners problem, we get

$$q(k) = \frac{1}{f'[g(k)]}.$$

Denoting k^* as in Exercise 6.1, for $k \leq k^*$, we have $g(k) \leq g(k^*)$, and hence

$$f'[g(k)] \geq f'[g(k^*)] = f'(k^*) = 1/\beta.$$

This implies that for $k \leq k^*$, we have $q(k) \leq \beta < 1$. However, for $k > k^*$ it is possible that $q(k) > 1$.

Define $\hat{k}$ such that

$$f'(\hat{k}) = 1.$$

Note that if $k_0 < \hat{k}$, by the properties of $g(k)$ established in Exercise 6.1, we have $q(k_t) < 1$ for all $k_t = g(k_{t-1})$. The interesting case is when $k_0 \geq \hat{k}$. Starting with such a k_0, by the properties of $g(k)$ established in Exercise 6.1, we have $g(k_t) < k_t$ for all t, and further there exists an N such that $k_t = g(k_{t-1}) < \hat{k}$ for all $t \geq N$. Hence, there exists an $M \geq N$ such that

$$q(k)\, q(g(k)) \ldots q(g^n(k)) < 1,$$

for all $n \geq M$.

Our strategy will be to show that the operator T^M, defined by iterating on T a total of M times, satisfies Blackwell's sufficient conditions for a contraction.

Monotonicity of T^M follows from the fact that T itself is monotone. To see that T is monotone, note that if $\psi_1 \geq \psi_2$, then we have

$$\begin{aligned}(T\psi_1)(k, z) &= \{f(z) - z_1' + q(k)\,\psi_1[g(k), z_1']\} \\ &\geq \{f(z) - z_2' + q(k)\,\psi_1[g(k), z_2']\} \\ &\geq \{f(z) - z_2' + q(k)\,\psi_2[g(k), z_2']\} \\ &= (T\psi_2)(k, z),\end{aligned}$$

where z_1' and z_2' are the optimal choices corresponding to ψ_1 and ψ_2 respectively, the second line follows from the fact that z_2' is feasible and not chosen for the problem with ψ_1, and the last line is by assumption that $\psi_1 \geq \psi_2$ pointwise.

To see discounting, note that for any $a > 0$ we have

$$T(\psi + a)(k, z) = (T\psi)(k, z) + q(k)\,a,$$

so that

$$T^M(\psi + a)(k, z) = (T^M\psi)(k, z) + q(k)\,q(g(k))\ldots q(g^M(k))a,$$

with

$$Q \equiv q(k)\,q(g(k))\ldots q(g^M(k)) < 1.$$

Hence, T^M is a contraction of modulus Q.

The Theorem of the Maximum implies that h is upper hemi-continuous. To show that it is continuous, it is sufficient to show that it is single valued. This will be true if, for a given (k, z), the problem in z' is strictly concave, which in turn will be true if the function ψ is strictly concave in z.

The usual proof of strict concavity does not apply because the return function is only concave in z' for a given z. However, exploiting the fact that ψ also solves the sequence problem, strict concavity can be proven directly. Let z_0^1 and z_0^2 be two distinct levels of initial capital with associated optimal sequences z^1 and z^2, and let $\lambda \in (0, 1)$. For all t define $z_t^\lambda = \lambda z_t^1 + (1 - \lambda)\,z_t^2$. Then

$$\begin{aligned}\psi(k, z_0^\lambda) &\geq f(z_0^\lambda) - z_1^\lambda + q(k)\,[f(z_1^\lambda) - z_2^\lambda \\ &\quad + q(g(k))\,[f(z_2^\lambda) - z_3^\lambda \\ &\quad + q(g^2(k))[f(z_3^\lambda) - z_4^\lambda + \ldots]]] \\ &> \lambda\psi(k_0, z_0^1) + (1 - \lambda)\,\psi(k_0, z_0^2),\end{aligned}$$

where the first inequality follows from the fact that for all t

$$f(z_t^\lambda) \geq \lambda f(z_t^1) + (1-\lambda) f(z_t^2)$$
$$\geq \lambda z_{t+1}^1 + (1-\lambda) z_{t+1}^2 = z_{t+1}^\lambda,$$

so that z^λ is feasible from z_0^λ, and the second from the fact that f is strictly concave and the sequences are distinct. Hence ψ is strictly concave in z.

To show that Ω is the unique continuous and bounded, function satisfying (2), define the operator T on $C(K \times K)$ by

$$(T\Omega)(k, a) = \max_{a',k'} \left\{ U\left[a - q(k)\, a'\right] + \beta\Omega\left(k', a'\right) \right\},$$

subject to

$$0 \leq a' \leq \frac{a}{q(k)},$$

and $k' = g(k)$. The continuity of g and q on the bounded set K, combined with U and Ω bounded, ensures that $T\Omega$ is bounded. That T preserves continuity comes from q continuous and the Theorem of the Maximum. That T is a contraction mapping comes from verifying that Blackwell's sufficient conditions for a contraction hold.

The Theorem of the Maximum implies that ω is upper hemi-continuous. To show that ω is single valued, it is sufficient to show that, for each k fixed, $\Omega(k, a)$ is concave in a. Once again we exploit the fact that Ω also solves the sequence problem. Let a_0^1 and a_0^2 be two distinct levels of a and let a^1 and a^2 be the associated optimal sequences. Let $\lambda \in (0, 1)$ and define, for each t, $a_t^\lambda = \lambda a_t^1 + (1-\lambda)\, a_t^2$. As the constraint on the choice of a' is linear, a_{t+1}^λ is feasible from a_t^λ. Then

$$\Omega(k, a_0^\lambda) \geq U\left[a_0^\lambda - q(k)\, a_1^\lambda\right] + \beta\left[U\left[a_1^\lambda - q(g(k))a_2^\lambda\right]\right.$$
$$\left.+ \beta\left[U\left[a_2^\lambda - q(g^2(k))a_3^\lambda\right] + \ldots\right]\right]$$
$$\geq \lambda\Omega(k, a_0^1) + (1-\lambda)\Omega(k, a_0^2),$$

where the first line follows from feasibility and the second from the fact that U is concave (the inequality is not necessarily strict because, although a_0^1 and a_0^2 are distinct, $a_0^1 - q(k)\, a_1^1$ and $a_0^2 - q(k)\, a_1^2$ need not be distinct).

f. The first-order conditions of the firms problem gives

$$1 = q(k)\, f'\left[h(k, k)\right],$$

which, combined with the definition of $q(k)$, gives

$$U'[f(k) - g(k)] = \beta f'[h(k, k)] U'\left(f[g(k)] - g[g(k)]\right).$$

But by definition, $g(k)$ solves

$$U'[f(k) - g(k)] = \beta f'[g(k)] U'\left(f[g(k)] - g[g(k)]\right).$$

Hence $g(k) = h(k, k)$, all k.

By definition of the firms problem we have

$$\psi(k, k) = f(k) - h(k, k) + q(k)\psi(g(k), h(k, k)),$$

which, using the result above, implies

$$f(k) - g(k) = \psi(k, k) - q(k)\psi(g(k), g(k)).$$

Substituting this into the Euler equation that defines $g(k)$ and using the definition of $q(k)$ we get

$$\begin{aligned} &q(k) U'[\psi(k, k) - q(k)\psi(g(k), g(k))] \\ &= \beta U'\left(\psi[g(k), g(k)] - q[g(k)]\psi\left[g^2(k), g^2(k)\right]\right). \end{aligned}$$

But the first-order conditions of the consumers problem imply

$$\begin{aligned} &q(k) U'[a - q(k)\omega(k, a)] \\ &= \beta U'\left(\omega(k, a) - q[g(k)]\omega[g(k), \omega(k, a)]\right), \end{aligned}$$

so that if $\psi(k, k) = a$ we get

$$\omega(k, \psi(k, k)) = \psi(g(k), g(k)).$$

g. Given the function $g(k)$ defined in (3) and the price $q(k)$ defined in (4), part e. of this question exhibits the functions $\psi(k, z)$ and $h(k, z)$ which satisfy (R1) and govern the behavior of the firm, as well as the functions $\Omega(k, a)$ and $\omega(k, a)$ which satisfy (R2) and govern the behavior of the consumer. Part f. then establishes that individual and aggregate behavior are compatible (R3), and that market clearing (R4) holds. Hence, all the elements of a recursive competitive equilibrium are present, and all that remains is to establish that they deliver the allocation (x_0, y_0).

Given a value for the firm's initial capital stock $z_0 = k_0$, we can construct the sequence of firm capital stocks from

$$z_{t+1} = h(k_t, z_t) = h(k_t, k_t) = g(k_t) = k_{t+1}.$$

Then we have from the firms problem that

$$\begin{aligned} y_t &= f(k_t) - h(k_t, k_t) \\ &= f(k_t) - g(k_t), \end{aligned}$$

where the second line comes from (R3), for all t, which delivers the sequence y_0 by the results of Exercise 5.1.

Given an initial value of assets $a = \psi(k_0, k_0)$, we can construct the consumers asset sequence from

$$a_{t+1} = \omega(k_t, a_t) = \omega(k_t, \psi(k_t, k_t)) = \psi(k_{t+1}, k_{t+1}).$$

Then we have from the consumers problem that

$$\begin{aligned} x_t &= a_t - q(k_t)\,\omega(k_t, a_t) \\ &= \psi(k_t, k_t) - q(k_t)\,\psi(k_{t+1}, k_{t+1}) \\ &= f(k_t) - g(k_t), \end{aligned}$$

for all t, where the third line comes from the definition of the firms problem and the result above. But this delivers the sequence x_0 by the results of Exercise 5.1.

Exercise 16.3

a. Define $\hat{\theta} = \gamma^{1/(1-\alpha)}$ and let $\hat{k}_{t+1} = k_{t+1}/\hat{\theta}^t$, and $\hat{y}_t = y_t/\hat{\theta}^t$. We also require that $y_t \geq 0$. Then (1) can be rewritten as

$$\hat{k}_{t+1} + \hat{y}_t \leq \hat{k}_t^{\alpha}.$$

Written this way, familiar results imply that $\hat{y}_t$ and $\hat{k}_t$ are bounded above by some number, say M, which implies $|\hat{y}_t| \leq M$ for all t. Hence, we have

$$|y_t| \leq M\hat{\theta}^t,$$

for all t. Then, for all $\theta \geq \hat{\theta}$, we have for all $y \in Y$ and all t that

$$|\theta^{-t} y_t| \leq M\left(\frac{\hat{\theta}}{\theta}\right)^t \leq M.$$

That is, for all $\theta \geq \hat{\theta}$, we have $Y \subset S_\theta$.

b. We will establish that, for $\theta \leq \hat{\theta} = \gamma^{1/(1-\alpha)}$, and only for such θ, Y has an interior point when viewed as a subset of S_θ.

First, let $\theta > \hat{\theta}$, and toward a contradiction assume that y is an interior point of Y. Then there exists an $\epsilon > 0$ such that

$$B(y, \epsilon) = \left\{ y' \in S_\theta : \|y' - y\|_\theta < \epsilon \right\} \subset Y.$$

Consider the bundle y' defined for all t as $y_t + \delta\theta^t$ for some $\delta \in (0, \epsilon)$. Then for all t,

$$\left|\theta^{-t}\left(y_t' - y_t\right)\right| = \delta < \epsilon,$$

and hence $y' \in B(y, \epsilon)$. However, as $\theta > \hat{\theta} > 1$, and $|y_t| \leq M\hat{\theta}^t$, there exists a T such that

$$\hat{\theta}^{-T} y_T + \delta \left(\frac{\theta}{\hat{\theta}}\right)^T > M,$$

for all $t \geq T$, where M was defined in part a. above. Hence

$$y_t' = \left(\hat{\theta}^{-t} y_t + \delta \left(\frac{\theta}{\hat{\theta}}\right)^t\right) \hat{\theta}^t,$$

is not in Y for all $t \geq T$, a contradiction.

Second, let $\theta \leq \hat{\theta}$. We must find a bundle y and an $\epsilon > 0$ such that $B(y, \epsilon) \subset Y$. From any k_0, construct a sequence k according to

$$k_{t+1} = \frac{1}{2}\gamma^t k_t^\alpha,$$

and a sequence y by

$$y_t = \frac{1}{4}\gamma^t k_t^\alpha.$$

By construction

$$L \equiv \inf_t \hat{\theta}^{-t}\gamma^t k_t^\alpha,$$

is finite and strictly positive so that we can pick ϵ such that

$$0 < \epsilon < \frac{1}{4}L.$$

Then for any $y' \in B(y, \epsilon)$, we have that

$$|y_t - y_t'| < \epsilon\theta^t \leq \epsilon\hat{\theta}^t,$$

as $\theta \leq \hat{\theta}$, and hence,

$$y_t - \epsilon\hat{\theta}^t \leq y_t' \leq y_t + \epsilon\hat{\theta}^t.$$

But

$$\begin{aligned}\epsilon\hat{\theta}^t &< \frac{1}{4}\hat{\theta}^t L \\ &\leq \frac{1}{4}\gamma^t k_t^\alpha.\end{aligned}$$

for all t, so that

$$0 \leq y_t' \leq \gamma^t k_t^\alpha - k_{t+1}$$

and hence $y' \in Y$ (using the same sequence k as for y).

c. In what follows, let $\theta = \hat{\theta}$. Let $\varepsilon > 0$ be given, let D be the bound on U, and pick T such that

$$\beta^T \frac{2D}{1-\beta} < \frac{\varepsilon}{2}.$$

As U is continuous, we can find a $\delta_1 > 0$ such that $|x_t - x_t'| < \delta_1$ implies that

$$|U(x_t) - U(x_t')| < \frac{\varepsilon}{2}\frac{1-\beta}{1-\beta^T}.$$

Then, if $x, x' \in X$ such that

$$\|x - x'\|_\theta < \delta_2 = \theta^{-T}\delta_1,$$

we have that

$$|x_t - x_t'| < \theta^t\delta_2 = \theta^t\theta^{-T}\delta_1,$$

for all $t \geq 0$. Hence, for such x, x', we have

$$\begin{aligned}|u(x) - u(x')| &\leq \sum_{t=0}^{\infty} \beta^t |U(x_t) - U(x_t')| \\ &\leq \sum_{t=0}^{T-1} \beta^t |U(x_t) - U(x_t')| + \beta^T \frac{2D}{1-\beta} \\ &\leq \sum_{t=0}^{T-1} \beta^t \frac{\varepsilon}{2}\frac{1-\beta}{1-\beta^T} + \frac{\varepsilon}{2} = \varepsilon,\end{aligned}$$

where the third inequality comes from the fact that for $t \leq T$, we have $|x_t - x_t'| < \delta_1$. Hence, u is continuous in the norm topology.

d. To show boundedness, first note that, for all $x \in X$, where X is defined as

$$X = \left\{ x \in S_\theta^+ : \inf_t |\theta^{-t} x_t| \geq a \right\},$$

we have that there exists a b such that $|x_t| \leq \theta^t b$ for all t. Then

$$\begin{aligned}
\sum_{t=0}^{\infty} \beta^t U(x_t) &\leq \sum_{t=0}^{\infty} \beta^t U(\theta^t b) \\
&= \sum_{t=0}^{\infty} \beta^t \frac{(\theta^t b)^{1-\sigma} - 1}{1-\sigma} \\
&= \frac{b^{1-\sigma}}{1-\sigma} \sum_{t=0}^{\infty} \left(\beta\theta^{1-\sigma}\right)^t - \frac{1}{(1-\beta)(1-\sigma)} \\
&\equiv \overline{M}.
\end{aligned}$$

This is finite, by the assumption that $\beta\theta^{1-\sigma} < 1$, and hence u is bounded above on X.

To see that u is bounded below, note that for all $x \in X$ we have

$$\begin{aligned}
\sum_{t=0}^{\infty} \beta^t U(x_t) &\geq \sum_{t=0}^{\infty} \beta^t U(\theta^t a) \\
&= \frac{a^{1-\sigma}}{1-\sigma} \sum_{t=0}^{\infty} \left(\beta\theta^{1-\sigma}\right)^t - \frac{1}{(1-\beta)(1-\sigma)} \\
&\equiv \underline{M},
\end{aligned}$$

which is finite. Hence, u is bounded. Note that these assumptions are sufficient, but overly strong. For example, for the case of $\sigma \in (0, 1)$, U is bounded below, and the extra restriction on consumption bundles is not necessary.

To see that u is also continuous, let $\varepsilon > 0$ be given and pick T such that

$$\left(\beta\theta^{1-\sigma}\right)^T (\overline{M} - \underline{M}) < \frac{\varepsilon}{2},$$

where $\overline{M}$ and $\underline{M}$ were defined immediately above. As U is continuous, we can find a $\delta_1 > 0$ such that $|x_t - x_t'| < \delta_1$ implies that

$$|U(x_t) - U(x_t')| < \frac{\varepsilon}{2} \frac{1-\beta}{1-\beta^T}.$$

Then, if $x, x' \in X$ such that

$$\|x - x'\|_\theta < \delta_2 = \theta^{-T}\delta_1,$$

we have

$$|x_t - x_t'| < \theta^t \delta_2 = \theta^t \theta^{-T} \delta_1.$$

for all $t \geq 0$. Hence, for such x, x', we have

$$\begin{aligned}
&|u(x) - u(x')| \\
&\leq \left|\sum_{t=0}^{T-1} \beta^t \left[U(x_t) - U(x_t')\right]\right| + \left|\sum_{t=T}^{\infty} \beta^t \left[U(x_t) - U(x_t')\right]\right| \\
&\leq \sum_{t=0}^{T-1} \beta^t \left|U(x_t) - U(x_t')\right| \\
&\quad + \left(\beta\theta^{1-\sigma}\right)^T \left|\sum_{s=0}^{\infty} \beta^s \left[U\left(\theta^{-T} x_{T+s}\right) - U\left(\theta^{-T} x_{T+s}'\right)\right]\right| \\
&\leq \sum_{t=0}^{T} \beta^t \frac{\varepsilon}{2} \frac{1-\beta}{1-\beta^T} + \left(\beta\theta^{1-\sigma}\right)^T \left(\overline{M} - \underline{M}\right) \\
&< \varepsilon,
\end{aligned}$$

where the third inequality comes from the fact that for $t \leq T$, we have $|x_t - x_t'| < \delta_1$, and the fact that for all t, we have

$$a\theta^t < x_t < b\theta^t,$$

so that

$$a\theta^s < \theta^T x_{T+s} < b\theta^s,$$

and we can use the same bounds constructed above. Hence, u is continuous in the norm topology.

Exercise 16.6

a. We establish each of the assumptions in turn.

A15.1: $X = l_\infty^+$ is obviously convex.

A15.2: This follows from the fact that

$$1 - \exp\left(-x_t 2^t\right),$$

is strictly concave. To see this, let x, $x' \in X$ with $u(x) > u(x')$, and let $\theta \in (0, 1)$. Then

$$\begin{aligned} u\left[\theta x + (1-\theta) x'\right] &= \sum_{t=1}^{\infty} 2^{-t} \left[1 - \exp\left(-\left[\theta x_t + (1-\theta) x_t'\right] 2^t\right)\right] \\ &\geq \sum_{t=1}^{\infty} 2^{-t} \left\{\theta \left[1 - \exp\left(-x_t 2^t\right)\right]\right. \\ &\quad \left. + (1-\theta) \left[1 - \exp\left(-x_t' 2^t\right)\right]\right\} \\ &= \theta u(x) + (1-\theta) u(x') \\ &> u(x'). \end{aligned}$$

A15.3: Let $\varepsilon > 0$ be given. As $1 - \exp\left(-x_t 2^t\right)$ is continuous, we can choose $\delta > 0$ such that $\left|x_t - x_t'\right| < \delta$ implies that

$$\begin{aligned} &\left|\exp\left(-x_t' 2^t\right) - \exp\left(-x_t 2^t\right)\right| \\ &= \left|1 - \exp\left(-x_t 2^t\right) - 1 + \exp\left(-x_t' 2^t\right)\right| < \varepsilon. \end{aligned}$$

Now if x, $x' \in X$ such that $\left\|x - x'\right\|_{\infty} < \delta$, then $\left|x_t - x_t'\right| < \delta$ for all $t \geq 1$. Hence

$$\begin{aligned} \left|u_i(x) - u_i(x')\right| &\leq \sum_{t=1}^{\infty} 2^{-t} \left|\exp\left(-x_t' 2^t\right) - \exp\left(-x_t 2^t\right)\right| \\ &< \varepsilon \sum_{t=1}^{\infty} 2^{-t} = \varepsilon, \end{aligned}$$

and so u_i is continuous.

A15.4: Y is obviously convex, being defined by a sequence of linear inequalities.

A15.5: As $l_{\infty}^{-} \subset Y$, and as l_{∞}^{-} contains an interior point (see Exercise 15.7), therefore Y contains an interior point.

A15.6: This is obviously true of $X = l_{\infty}^{+}$. That it is true of Y follows from the fact that, for all t, $2^{-t} > 0$.

A15.7: Let $x,\ x' \in X$ with $u(x) > u(x')$, and pick $\varepsilon \in (0, u(x) - u(x'))$. Choose T^* such that

$$2^{-(T^*+1)} < \varepsilon.$$

Then for all $T \geq T^*$, we have

$$\begin{aligned}\left|u(x) - u\left(x^T\right)\right| &= \left|\sum_{t=T+1}^{\infty} 2^{-t}\left[1 - \exp\left(-x_t 2^t\right)\right]\right| \\ &\leq \sum_{t=T+1}^{\infty} 2^{-t}\left|1 - \exp\left(-x_t 2^t\right)\right| \\ &\leq \sum_{t=T+1}^{\infty} 2^{-t} < \varepsilon,\end{aligned}$$

and hence $u\left(x^T\right) > u\left(x'\right)$.

b. By Theorem 15.1, a linear functional on l_∞ is continuous if and only if it is bounded. But

$$\begin{aligned}\|p\| &= \sup_{\|x\|_\infty \leq 1} |p.x| \\ &= \sup_{\|x\|_\infty \leq 1} \left|\sum_{t=1}^{\infty} p_t x_t\right| \\ &\geq \left|\sum_{t=1}^{\infty} p_t\right|,\end{aligned}$$

which is not finite, and where the last line comes from the fact that $x' = (1, 1, \ldots) \in l_\infty$, with $\|x'\|_\infty = 1$.

c. Let ϕ be a continuous linear functional on l_∞ that satisfies (1) and (2), and let ψ be the continuous linear functional that satisfies (3). By Lemma 15.5, for all $x \in l_\infty$ we can write ψ as

$$\psi(x) = \sum_{t=1}^{\infty} p_t x_t,$$

for $p_t \in \mathbf{R}$ for all t. Note that if, for any t, $p_t < 0$, then $\psi(y^*)$ cannot satisfy (2), for then we could set $y_t = -\infty$ and increase profits. Hence we must have $p_t \geq 0$ for all t. If there exists a t such that $p_t > p_1$, then consider the allocation x'

constructed from x^* by reducing x_t by some small amount, and increasing x_1 by this amount. This is affordable, and increases utility, which contradicts (1). Now suppose that $p_1 > p_t$ for some $t \geq 2$, and consider the allocation x' constructed from x^* by increasing x_t by some small amount and decreasing x_1 by a smaller amount such that $\psi(x') = \psi(x^*)$. This is possible, and as

$$\exp\left[-2^1 x_1^*\right] = \exp\left[-2^t x_t^*\right],$$

for all t, this increases utility, a contradiction of (1). Hence, we must have $p_t = p_1$ for all t. But then ψ is not a continuous linear functional on l_∞ unless $p_t = 0$ for all t.

d. We first establish that, if the commodity space is l_1, then Y has an empty interior. Toward a contradiction, assume that there exists a $y \in int(Y)$. Then there exists an open neighborhood of y, say $B(y, \varepsilon)$, that is a subset of Y. We produce a contradiction by exhibiting an element of $B(y, \epsilon)$ that is not in Y.

As $y \in l_1$, there exists an N_1 such that, for all $n \geq N_1$, $|y_n| < \epsilon/4$. Further, there exists an N_2 such that, for all $n \geq N_2$, $2^{-n} < \epsilon/4$. Set $N = \max\{N_1, N_2\}$, and define $z \in l_1$ such that $z_n = y_n$ for all $n \neq N$ and $z_N = y_N + \epsilon/2$. Then $z \in B(y, \epsilon)$, as

$$\begin{aligned} \|y - z\|_1 &= \sum_{n=1}^{\infty} |y_n - z_n| \\ &= \epsilon/2. \end{aligned}$$

But, $z \notin Y$, as

$$z_N = y_N + \frac{\epsilon}{2} > \frac{\epsilon}{4} > 2^{-N}.$$

To show that (x^*, y^*, p) is a competitive equilibrium, note first that (x^*, y^*) is obviously feasible. Second, note that if $y \in Y$, then $y_t \leq 2^{-t}$ for all $t = 1, 2, \ldots$, and hence

$$\phi(y) = \sum_{t=1}^{\infty} c y_t \leq \sum_{t=1}^{\infty} c 2^{-t} = \sum_{t=1}^{\infty} c y_t^* = \phi(y^*),$$

which establishes (2). Finally, let $x \in X$ such that $u(x) > u(x^*)$. That is,

$$\sum_{t=1}^{\infty} \frac{1 - \exp(-2^t x_t)}{2^t} \geq \sum_{t=1}^{\infty} \frac{1 - \exp(-1)}{2^t}.$$

We will show that this implies that $\phi(x) > \phi(x^*)$. As an input to this result, note that for all $z \in \mathbf{R}$ we have that the function

$$g(z) = z + \exp(1 - z) - 2,$$

is nonnegative. This follows from the fact that

$$g'(z) = 1 - \exp(1 - z),$$

and

$$g''(z) = \exp(1 - z),$$

so that g attains its global minimum at $z = 1$, where $g(1) = 0$. Then

$$\begin{aligned}
p \cdot x &= c \sum_{t=1}^{\infty} x_t = c \sum_{t=1}^{\infty} \frac{2^t x_t}{2^t} \\
&\geq c \sum_{t=1}^{\infty} \frac{2 - \exp\left(1 - 2^t x_t\right)}{2^t} \\
&= c \sum_{t=1}^{\infty} \frac{2 - \exp(1) + \exp(1)\left(1 - \exp\left(-2^t x_t\right)\right)}{2^t} \\
&> c \sum_{t=1}^{\infty} \frac{2 - \exp(1) + \exp(1)\left(1 - \exp(-1)\right)}{2^t} \\
&= c \sum_{t=1}^{\infty} \frac{1}{2^t} = p \cdot x^*,
\end{aligned}$$

where the second line follows the result proven immediately above, and the strict inequality from the fact that $u(x) > u(x^*)$ by assumption.

17 Fixed-Point Arguments

Exercise 17.1

For all $x \in X$, the agent's problem is to choose $n \in [0, L)$ to maximize

$$-H(n) + \int V\left[\frac{xnp(x)}{p(x')}\right]\pi(x, dx').$$

As $n \to L$ this objective goes to $-\infty$, while at $n = 0$ the objective is finite valued and has a positive slope. Further, by the strict convexity of H and the strict concavity of V this objective is strictly concave in n. Hence this problem has a unique solution on $[0, L)$.

The first-order condition for an optimum is

$$-H'(n) + \int \frac{xp(x)}{p(x')}V'\left[\frac{xnp(x)}{p(x')}\right]\pi(x, dx')\begin{cases} > 0 & \text{if } n = L \\ = 0 & \text{if } n \in (0, L) \\ < 0 & \text{if } n = 0. \end{cases}$$

As $H'(L) = +\infty$ and as $V'[xLp(x)/p(x')]$ is finite and positive for all (x, x'), $n = L$ cannot be a solution. As $H'(0) = 0$ and $V'(0) > 0$, $n = 0$ cannot be a solution. Hence the choice of n satisfies the first-order condition with equality, and for all $x \in X$ the optimum choice $n(x)$ is strictly positive.

Exercise 17.2

a. For $f \in F$, as G is continuous and π satisfies the Feller property, Tf is continuous. As G takes values in D and D is convex, $Tf : X \to D$. Therefore, all we have to show is that Tf is bounded. But this follows from the fact that f is bounded, G is continuous and X is bounded.

b. The proof of completeness follows that of Theorem 3.1 closely. The only extra step is involved in the construction of the candidate limit function f. Fix

$x \in X$ and let $\{f_n\}$ by a Cauchy sequence in F. The sequence of real numbers $\{f_n(x)\}$ satisfies

$$|f_n(x) - f_m(x)| \leq \sup_{y \in X} |f_n(y) - f_m(y)| = \|f_n - f_m\|.$$

As the sequence of functions $\{f_n\}$ is Cauchy, the sequence of real numbers $\{f_n(x)\}$ is also a Cauchy sequence in D. As D is a closed subset of $\mathbf{R}$ by the result of Exercise 3.6b., this sequence converges to a point, call it $f(x)$, in D. For all $x \in X$ define $f(x)$ in this fashion as our candidate limit function. The rest of the proof follows that of Theorem 3.1.

Exercise 17.3

Note that in this case with $G(x, x', y) = \phi[x'\varsigma^{-1}(y)]$ we have that

$$G_3(x, x', y) = \frac{\phi'[x'\varsigma^{-1}(y)]x'}{\varsigma'(y)}.$$

Now $\lim_{y \to 0} \varsigma'(y) = 0$ while $\lim_{y \to 0} \varsigma^{-1}(y) = 0$. But $\phi'(0) > 0$ and so there exist (x, x', y) such that $|G_3(x, x', y)| > 1$.

Exercise 17.4

a. As the logarithmic and exponential functions are continuous, π satisfies the Feller property, G is continuous and $g \in \hat{F}$, we have that $\hat{T}g$ is continuous. As G is continuous and X is bounded, $\hat{T}g$ is bounded. Finally, note that $\hat{T}g : X \to \hat{D}$ as G takes on values in D which is convex. Hence, $\hat{T} : \hat{F} \to \hat{F}$.

b. Note that as D is closed and convex, so is $\hat{D}$. The proof then follows part b. of Exercise 17.2 above.

Exercise 17.5

a. We analyze the following problem. Consider the differential equation and boundary condition

$$\frac{dx(t)}{dt} = f[x(t)],$$

for $t \geq 0$ with $x(0) = c$. Show that if f is continuous, then there exists a $t_0 \in (0, 1]$ such that this equation has a solution on $[0, t_0]$.

For some $t_0 > 0$, define the operator $T : C([0, t_0]) \to C([0, t_0])$ by

$$(Tx)(t) = \int_0^t f(x(s))ds + c.$$

We will use Schauder's Theorem to show that this operator has a fixed point in $C([0, t_0])$ for some $t_0 \in (0, 1]$.

As f is continuous, for all $\varepsilon > 0$ there exists a $\delta > 0$ such that $|z - c| \leq \delta$ implies $|f(z)| \leq |f(c)| + \varepsilon$. Choose

$$t_0 = \min\left\{1, \frac{\delta}{|f(c)| + \varepsilon}\right\},$$

so that $t_0\{|f(c)| + \varepsilon\} \leq \delta$. Let D be the closed δ-ball about zero in $C([0, t_0])$. Then clearly D is closed, bounded, and convex, and the result will be proven if we can establish that $T(D) \subset D$, that T is continuous, and that $T(D)$ is equicontinuous.

To see that $T(D) \subset D$, let $x \in D$, so that $|x(t) - c| \leq \delta$ for all $t \in [0, t_0]$. But then

$$\begin{aligned}|(Tx)(t) - c| &= \left|\int_0^t f(x(s))ds\right| \\ &\leq t \sup_{s\in[0,t_0]} |f(x(s))| \\ &\leq t\{|f(c)| + \varepsilon\}.\end{aligned}$$

Hence, we have that

$$\begin{aligned}\|Tx - c\| &= \sup_{t\in[0,t_0]} |(Tx)(t) - c| \\ &\leq t_0\{|f(c)| + \varepsilon\} \\ &\leq \delta,\end{aligned}$$

so that $T(D) \subset D$.

The continuity of T follows from the fact that f is continuous, and that the integral preserves continuity. To see that $T(D)$ is equicontinuous, note that for any $\phi > 0$, we can choose κ such that

$$\kappa < \frac{\phi}{|f(c)| + \varepsilon},$$

where ε was defined above in the construction of D. Then, for any t, $t' \in [0, t_0]$ such that $|t' - t| < \kappa$, and any $Tx \in T(D)$, we have that

$$\begin{aligned}
|(Tx)(t) - (Tx)(t')| &= \left| \int_0^t f[x(s)]\, ds - \int_0^{t'} f[x(s)]\, ds \right| \\
&= \left| \int_t^{t'} f[x(s)]\, ds \right| \\
&\leq |t' - t| \sup_{s \in [t,t']} |f[x(s)]| \\
&\leq |t' - t| \{|f(c)| + \varepsilon\} \\
&\leq \kappa \{|f(c)| + \varepsilon\} \\
&< \phi,
\end{aligned}$$

where the second inequality follows from the construction of D. Hence, $T(D)$ is equicontinuous.

b. Obviously, $x(t) = 0$ is one solution. To find another, if $x \neq 0$ we can write rewrite this equation as

$$x^{-\frac{1}{2}} dx = dt.$$

Integrating both sides and using the initial condition we get that

$$x(t) = \left(\frac{t}{2}\right)^2,$$

is also a solution.

c. Unlike in Exercise 3.10 (not Exercise 3.8), we have that our function does not satisfy the Lipschitz condition. For if $x > 0$ we have that

$$\frac{\left|x^{\frac{1}{2}} - 0\right|}{|x - 0|} = x^{-\frac{1}{2}},$$

which is unbounded as x goes to zero.

Exercise 17.6

Let $\{f_n\}$ be a sequence of functions in F converging to f and fix $\varepsilon > 0$. Then

$$\begin{aligned}
&\|Tf_n - Tf\| \\
&= \sup_{x\in X} |Tf_n(x) - Tf(x)| \\
&= \sup_{x\in X} \left| \int \{G[x, x', f_n(x')] - G[x, x', f(x')]\} \pi(x, dx') \right| \\
&\leq \sup_{x\in X} \int |G[x, x', f_n(x')] - G[x, x', f(x')]| \pi(x, dx').
\end{aligned}$$

But as G is uniformly continuous in its third argument, there exists a $\delta > 0$ such that $|f_n(x') - f(x')| < \delta$ implies that

$$|G[x, x', f_n(x')] - G[x, x', f(x')]| < \varepsilon,$$

for all $x, x' \in X$. Then we have that for all $\varepsilon > 0$ there exists a $\delta > 0$ such that if $\|f_n - f\| < \delta$ we have $\|Tf_n - Tf\| < \varepsilon$ and hence T is continuous.

Exercise 17.7

We will establish that Schauder's Theorem applies to the operator T defined by

$$(Tn)(x) = \zeta^{-1}\left[\int \phi(x'n(x'))\pi(x, dx')\right],$$

for all $x \in X$, for an appropriately defined set of functions F.

Note that the set of continuous and bounded functions on X taking values in $[0, L)$ is not a closed subset of $C(X)$. However, for a given x the function $\phi(xn)$ is nonnegative and is bounded for $n \in [0, L)$. As X is bounded and ζ^{-1} is continuous, there exists a closed set $D \subset [0, L)$ such that we can restrict attention to the set F of continuous and bounded functions on X that take values in D. Let B be a bound on D. This set F is nonempty, closed, bounded and convex. That T is continuous follows from the fact that both ϕ and ζ^{-1} are continuous functions and π satisfies the Feller property.

To show that $T(F)$ is equicontinuous, fix $\varepsilon > 0$. As ζ^{-1} is continuous, for every $\varepsilon > 0$ there exists an $\kappa > 0$ such that for all $z, z' \in \mathbf{R}_+$ with $|z - z'| < \kappa$ we have

$\left|\zeta^{-1}(z) - \zeta^{-1}(z')\right| < \varepsilon$. Further, by the argument of Lemma 17.5, for ever $\kappa > 0$ there exists a $\delta > 0$ such that for any $x, \widetilde{x} \in X$ with $\|x - \widetilde{x}\| < \delta$ we have

$$\left|\int \phi(x'n(x'))\pi(x, dx') - \int \phi(x'n(x'))\pi(\widetilde{x}, dx')\right| < \kappa,$$

for all $n \in F$, where the κ and δ are independent of the function n. Combining these results we get that $T(F)$ is equicontinuous.

Combining all of the above and using Schauder's Theorem gives the desired result.

Exercise 17.8

a. $G(\widetilde{\theta}|\widetilde{z}) = \Pr\left\{\theta \leq \widetilde{\theta}|z = \widetilde{z}\right\}$. But

$$\Pr\left\{\theta \leq \widetilde{\theta}|z = \widetilde{z}\right\} = \frac{\Pr\left\{\theta \leq \widetilde{\theta} \text{ and } z = \widetilde{z}\right\}}{\Pr\left\{z = \widetilde{z}\right\}}$$
$$= \int_{\underline{\theta}}^{\widetilde{\theta}} \frac{g(s)\psi(s\widetilde{z})}{\pi(\widetilde{z})} ds.$$

Hence,

$$g(\tilde{\theta}|\tilde{z}) = G'(\tilde{\theta}|\tilde{z})$$
$$= \frac{g(\tilde{\theta})\psi(\tilde{\theta}\tilde{z})}{\pi(\tilde{z})}.$$

Since ψ and g are continuous, $g(.\,|z)$ is continuous for each $z \in \text{int} Z$.

b. By the result of Exercise 12.7b., it is sufficient to show that if f is continuous and bounded on Θ, then

$$(Tf)(z) = \int f(\theta)G(d\theta|z)$$
$$= \int f(\theta)g(\theta|z)d\theta$$
$$= \int f(\theta)\frac{g(\theta)\psi(\theta z)}{\pi(z)}d\theta,$$

is continuous and bounded on Θ. But this follows from the fact that ψ and π are continuous.

Exercise 17.9

As noted in the text, the proof strategy follows that of Proposition 2 closely. As in that proof, for $k = 1, 2, \ldots$ define

$$\varepsilon_k = \min\left\{\varepsilon > 0 : \zeta^{-1}(\varepsilon) = k\varepsilon\right\},$$

which is a strictly decreasing sequence. Note that

$$\frac{\theta'}{\tilde{\theta}} \in \left[\frac{\underline{\theta}}{\bar{\theta}}, \frac{\bar{\theta}}{\underline{\theta}}\right],$$

and that ζ^{-1} is bounded above by L so that for all $(\theta', \tilde{\theta}, z')$ we have that

$$\frac{\theta'}{\tilde{\theta}} V'\left(\frac{\theta'}{\tilde{\theta}}\zeta^{-1}(f(z))\right) \geq \frac{\underline{\theta}}{\bar{\theta}} V'\left(\frac{\bar{\theta}}{\underline{\theta}} L\right) \equiv C > 0.$$

Pick some $K > 1/C$ and consider functions $f : Z \to [\varepsilon_K, +\infty)$. We have that

$$\begin{aligned}\phi\left(\frac{\theta'}{\tilde{\theta}}\zeta^{-1}(f(z))\right) &= \frac{\theta'}{\tilde{\theta}}\zeta^{-1}(f(z))V'\left(\frac{\theta'}{\tilde{\theta}}\zeta^{-1}(f(z))\right)\\ &\geq \frac{\underline{\theta}}{\bar{\theta}}\zeta^{-1}(\varepsilon_K)V'\left(\frac{\bar{\theta}}{\underline{\theta}}L\right),\end{aligned}$$

as ζ^{-1} is increasing. Hence

$$\begin{aligned}\phi\left(\frac{\theta'}{\tilde{\theta}}\zeta^{-1}(f(z))\right) &\geq \zeta^{-1}(\varepsilon_K)C\\ &= K\varepsilon_K C > \varepsilon_K.\end{aligned}$$

Define the closed, convex set $D = [\varepsilon_K, +\infty) \subset \mathbf{R}_{++}$ and let F be the set of bounded continuous functions $f : Z \to D$. The above argument establishes that $Tf : Z \to D$; the continuity and boundedness of Tf follows as before.

Take logs and define $\hat{T}$ and $\hat{F}$ as in Proposition 2. Fix g and h in $\hat{F}$ and define $w(\theta', \tilde{\theta}, z', z)$ as

$$\frac{\phi\left(\frac{\theta'}{\tilde{\theta}}\zeta^{-1}(\exp h(z'))\right)}{\int_\Theta \int_Z \int_\Theta \phi\left(\frac{\theta'}{\tilde{\theta}}\zeta^{-1}(\exp h(u))\right) G(d\theta'|u)\pi(du)G(d\tilde{\theta}|z)},$$

which is positive and satisfies

$$\int_{\Theta}\int_{Z}\int_{\Theta} w(\theta', \tilde{\theta}, z', z)G(d\theta'|z')\pi(dz')G(d\tilde{\theta}|z) = 1,$$

for all $z \in Z$. Therefore, $(\hat{T}g)(z) - (\hat{T}h)(z)$ equals the difference between

$$\ln\left\{\int_{\Theta}\int_{Z}\int_{\Theta} \phi\left(\frac{\theta'}{\tilde{\theta}}\zeta^{-1}(\exp g(z'))\right) G(d\theta'|z')\pi(dz')G(d\tilde{\theta}|z)\right\},$$

and

$$\ln\left\{\int_{\Theta}\int_{Z}\int_{\Theta} \phi\left(\frac{\theta'}{\tilde{\theta}}\zeta^{-1}(\exp h(z'))\right) G(d\theta'|z')\pi(dz')G(d\tilde{\theta}|z)\right\},$$

which can be rearranged to give

$$\ln\left\{\int_{\Theta}\int_{Z}\int_{\Theta} w(\theta', \tilde{\theta}, z', z) \times \right.$$
$$\left.\frac{\phi\left(\frac{\theta'}{\tilde{\theta}}\zeta^{-1}(\exp g(z'))\right)}{\phi\left(\frac{\theta'}{\tilde{\theta}}\zeta^{-1}(\exp h(z'))\right)} G(d\theta'|z')\pi(dz')G(d\tilde{\theta}|z)\right\},$$

which is no greater than

$$\sup_{\theta',\tilde{\theta},z',z}\left\{\ln\left\{\frac{\phi\left(\frac{\theta'}{\tilde{\theta}}\zeta^{-1}(\exp g(z'))\right)}{\phi\left(\frac{\theta'}{\tilde{\theta}}\zeta^{-1}(\exp h(z'))\right)}\right\}\right\}$$
$$= \sup_{\theta',\tilde{\theta},z',z}\left\{\ln\left\{\phi\left(\frac{\theta'}{\tilde{\theta}}\zeta^{-1}(\exp g(z'))\right)\right\}\right.$$
$$\left. - \ln\left\{\phi\left(\frac{\theta'}{\tilde{\theta}}\zeta^{-1}(\exp h(z'))\right)\right\}\right\}.$$

Note that for all z' fixed, $g(z')$ and $h(z')$ are numbers. Hence, by the Mean Value Theorem there exists a number $\lambda \in (0, 1)$ such that if $\widehat{y} = \lambda g(z') + (1 - \lambda)h(z')$

$$\ln\left\{\phi\left(\frac{\theta'}{\tilde{\theta}}\zeta^{-1}(\exp g(z'))\right)\right\} - \ln\left\{\phi\left(\frac{\theta'}{\tilde{\theta}}\zeta^{-1}(\exp h(z'))\right)\right\}$$
$$= \frac{\frac{\theta'}{\tilde{\theta}}\zeta^{-1\prime}(\exp \widehat{y}) \exp \widehat{y}\phi'\left(\frac{\theta'}{\tilde{\theta}}\zeta^{-1}(\exp \widehat{y})\right)}{\phi\left(\frac{\theta'}{\tilde{\theta}}\zeta^{-1}(\exp \widehat{y})\right)}(g(z') - h(z')),$$

which can be rearranged to give

$$\frac{\frac{\theta'}{\tilde{\theta}}\zeta^{-1}(\exp\widehat{y})\phi'\left(\frac{\theta'}{\tilde{\theta}}\zeta^{-1}(\exp\widehat{y})\right)}{\phi\left(\frac{\theta'}{\tilde{\theta}}\zeta^{-1}(\exp\widehat{y})\right)}\frac{\exp\widehat{y}\zeta^{-1\prime}(\exp\widehat{y})}{\zeta^{-1}(\exp\widehat{y})}(g(z')-h(z')).$$

But from Proposition 2 we know that for all $y = \exp\widehat{y} \in D$,

$$\frac{y\zeta^{-1\prime}(y)}{\zeta^{-1}(y)} \leq 1,$$

while by Assumption 17.2 we have that

$$\left|\frac{\frac{\theta'}{\tilde{\theta}}\zeta^{-1}(y)\phi'\left(\frac{\theta'}{\tilde{\theta}}\zeta^{-1}(y)\right)}{\phi\left(\frac{\theta'}{\tilde{\theta}}\zeta^{-1}(y)\right)}\right| \leq \beta,$$

for any $(\theta', \tilde{\theta}, z')$. Hence

$$\begin{aligned}(\widehat{T}g)(z) - (\widehat{T}h)(z) &\leq \beta \sup_{z'}\{g(z') - h(z')\} \\ &\leq \|g - h\|.\end{aligned}$$

Repeating the analysis with the roles of g and h reversed gives

$$\|\widehat{T}g - \widehat{T}h\| \leq \|g - h\|.$$

Since g and h were arbitrary elements of $\widehat{F}$, it follows that $\widehat{T}$ is a contraction of modulus β on $\widehat{F}$. Hence by the Contraction Mapping Theorem $\widehat{T}$ has a unique fixed point g^* in $\widehat{F}$.

Exercise 17.11

For all $\theta', \tilde{\theta} \in \Theta$ fixed, we saw in Exercise 17.9 above that

$$\phi\left(\frac{\theta'}{\tilde{\theta}}\zeta^{-1}(f(z'))\right),$$

was bounded. As Θ is compact, there exists a compact interval $D \subset R_{++}$ such that for all f and for all $(\theta', \tilde{\theta}, z')$, ϕ takes values in D. Let $F \subset C(Z)$ be the subset of continuous and bounded functions $f : Z \to D$.

Let $f \in F$. Clearly, $Tf : Z \to D$ and is bounded. That it is continuous comes from the continuity of ϕ and ζ^{-1} and the fact that the uniform distribution satisfies the Feller property.

To see that the operator T is continuous, let $\{f_n\}$ be a sequence of functions in F converging to f and fix $\varepsilon > 0$. Then

$$\begin{aligned}
&\|Tf_n - Tf\| \\
&= \sup_{x\in X} |Tf_n(x) - Tf(x)| \\
&= \sup_{x\in X} \left| \int \{G[x, x', f_n(x')] - G[x, x', f(x')]\}\pi(x, dx') \right| \\
&\le \sup_{x\in X} \int \left|G[x, x', f_n(x')] - G[x, x', f(x')]\right| \pi(x, dx').
\end{aligned}$$

But as G is uniformly continuous in its third argument, there exists a $\delta > 0$ such that $|f_n(x') - f(x')| < \delta$ implies that

$$\left|G[x, x', f_n(x')] - G[x, x', f(x')]\right| < \varepsilon,$$

for all $x, x' \in X$. Then we have that for all $\varepsilon > 0$ there exists a $\delta > 0$ such that if $\|f_n - f\| < \delta$ we have $\|Tf_n - Tf\| < \varepsilon$ and hence T is continuous.

Exercise 17.12

There are four cases to consider. First, consider the case where $z \ge \underline{x}/\underline{\theta}$, and $z \ge \overline{x}/\overline{\theta}$. Then we have that $\theta \le \overline{x}/z \equiv b(z) \le \overline{\theta}$, and further that $x \ge z\underline{\theta}$. In this case, we have

$$\begin{aligned}
G(\theta^*|z) &= \Pr\left\{\theta \le \theta^* | \frac{x}{\theta} = z\right\} \\
&= \Pr\left\{\frac{x}{z} \le \theta^* | x \ge z\underline{\theta}\right\} \\
&= \frac{\theta^* z - \underline{\theta} z}{\overline{x} - \underline{\theta} z} \\
&= \frac{\theta^* - \underline{\theta}}{\overline{x}/z - \underline{\theta}} \\
&= \frac{\theta^* - a(z)}{b(z) - a(z)}.
\end{aligned}$$

Next consider the case where $z \leq \underline{x}/\overline{\theta}$, and $z \leq \overline{x}/\overline{\theta}$. Then we have that $\theta \geq \underline{x}/z \equiv a(z) \geq \overline{\theta}$, and further that $x \leq z\overline{\theta}$. In this case, we have

$$\begin{aligned} G(\theta^*|z) &= \Pr\left\{\theta \leq \theta^* | \frac{x}{\theta} = z\right\} \\ &= \Pr\left\{\frac{x}{z} \leq \theta^* | x \leq z\overline{\theta}\right\} \\ &= \frac{\theta^* z - \underline{x}}{\overline{\theta} z - \underline{x}} \\ &= \frac{\theta^* - \underline{x}/z}{\overline{\theta} - \underline{x}/z} \\ &= \frac{\theta^* - a(z)}{b(z) - a(z)}. \end{aligned}$$

The remaining cases, that $\underline{x}/\overline{\theta} \leq z \leq \overline{x}/\overline{\theta}$ and that $\overline{x}/\overline{\theta} \leq z \leq \underline{x}/\overline{\theta}$, are proven analogously.

Exercise 17.13

By Assumption 17.1, V is twice continuously differentiable, so that ϕ' is continuous. The function ζ^{-1} is bounded and by Assumption 17.5, Θ is compact. Hence, for all $f \in F$ there exists a $B_\theta < +\infty$ that is independent of f such that

$$\begin{aligned} &\left|\phi'_f(\tilde{\theta})\right| \\ &= \left|\int_Z \int_\Theta \phi'\left(\frac{\theta'}{\tilde{\theta}}\zeta^{-1}[f(z')]\right)\frac{\theta'}{\tilde{\theta}^2}\zeta^{-1}[f(z')]G(d\theta'|z')\pi(dz')\right| \\ &< B_\theta. \end{aligned}$$

But $\phi'_f(\tilde{\theta})$ continuous in $\tilde{\theta}$ and Θ compact, implies that there exists a $B < +\infty$ such that

$$\left|\phi'_f(\tilde{\theta})\right| < B,$$

for all $f \in F$ and all $\tilde{\theta}$.

Exercise 17.14

a. As $\rho(z) = z/\eta(z)$, we have

$$\rho'(z) = \frac{1}{\eta(z)}\left[1 - \frac{z\eta'(z)}{\eta(z)}\right].$$

Therefore, $\rho'(z) > 0$ if and only if $z\eta'(z)/\eta(z) < 1$.

b. As $\eta'[H' + \eta H''] = J'$ we have

$$\frac{zJ'(z)}{J(z)} = \frac{z\eta'(z)}{\eta(z)} \frac{[H'(\eta(z)) + \eta(z)H''(\eta(z))]}{H'(\eta(z))}.$$

Note that

$$\frac{[H'(\eta(z)) + \eta(z)H''(\eta(z))]}{H'(\eta(z))} > 1,$$

and so $z\eta'(z)/\eta(z) < 1$ if $zJ'(z)/J(z) < 1$.

c. As $\phi(y) = yV'(y)$ we have

$$\begin{aligned}\frac{y\phi'(y)}{\phi(y)} &= \frac{V'(y) + yV''(y)}{V'(y)} \\ &= 1 + \frac{yV''(y)}{V'(y)}.\end{aligned}$$

By Assumptions 17.1 and 17.4, $0 \geq yV''/V' \geq -1$, so

$$0 \leq \frac{y\phi('y)}{\phi(y)} \leq 1.$$

Now

$$\xi'(\theta) = -E\left[\frac{\theta'}{\theta}\eta(z')\phi'\left(\frac{\theta'}{\theta}\eta(z')\right)\right],$$

so that

$$\frac{\theta\xi'(\theta)}{\xi(\theta)} = \frac{-E\left[\frac{\theta'}{\theta}\eta(z')\phi'\left(\frac{\theta'}{\theta}\eta(z')\right)\right]}{E\left[\phi\left(\frac{\theta'}{\theta}\eta(z')\right)\right]},$$

and hence

$$-1 \leq \frac{\theta\xi'(\theta)}{\xi(\theta)} \leq 0.$$

d. Note that

$$J'(z) = \frac{-[b'(z) - a'(z)]}{b(z) - a(z)} J(z) + \frac{\xi(b(z))b'(z) - \xi(a(z))a'(z)}{b(z) - a(z)},$$

so that

$$\frac{zJ'(z)}{J(z)} = \frac{-[b'(z)z - a'(z)z]}{b(z) - a(z)} + \frac{\xi(b(z))b'(z)z - \xi(a(z))a'(z)z}{\int_{a(z)}^{b(z)} \xi(\theta)d\theta}.$$

There are four cases to consider. One, if $a'(z) = b'(z) = 0$ then we have $J'(z) = 0$. Two, if $a'(z)z = -a(z)$ and $b'(z)z = -b(z)$, then we need to show that

$$\frac{zJ'(z)}{J(z)} = 1 - \frac{\xi(b(z))b(z) - \xi(a(z))a(z)}{\int_{a(z)}^{b(z)} \xi(\theta)d\theta} \leq 1.$$

The result in part c. implies that

$$\frac{d}{d\theta}(\theta\xi(\theta)) = \xi(\theta)\left[1 + \frac{\theta\xi'(\theta)}{\xi(\theta)}\right] \geq 0,$$

and so $\theta\xi(\theta)$ is an increasing function. Hence, the second term above is positive and the desired result holds.

Three, if $a'(z)z = -a(z)$ and $b'(z) = 0$, we have to show that

$$\frac{zJ'(z)}{J(z)} = \frac{-a(z)}{b(z) - a(z)} + \frac{\xi(a(z))a(z)}{\int_{a(z)}^{b(z)} \xi(\theta)d\theta} \leq 1,$$

or

$$\frac{\xi(a(z))a(z)}{\int_{a(z)}^{b(z)} \xi(\theta)d\theta} \leq \frac{b(z)}{b(z) - a(z)}.$$

But note that

$$\xi(a(z))a(z) \leq \frac{1}{b(z) - a(z)} \int_{a(z)}^{b(z)} \theta\xi(\theta)d\theta$$

$$\leq \frac{b(z)}{b(z) - a(z)} \int_{a(z)}^{b(z)} \xi(\theta)d\theta,$$

which holds since $\theta\xi(\theta)$ is an increasing function.

Four, if $a'(z) = 0$ and $b'(z)z = -b(z)$, we have to show that

$$\frac{zJ'(z)}{J(z)} = \frac{b(z)}{b(z) - a(z)} - \frac{\xi(b(z))b(z)}{\int_{a(z)}^{b(z)} \xi(\theta)d\theta} \leq 1,$$

or

$$\frac{\xi(b(z))b(z)}{\int_{a(z)}^{b(z)} \xi(\theta)d\theta} \geq \frac{a(z)}{b(z) - a(z)}.$$

But note that

$$\begin{aligned}\xi(b(z))b(z) &\geq \frac{1}{b(z) - a(z)} \int_{a(z)}^{b(z)} \theta\xi(\theta)d\theta \\ &\geq \frac{a(z)}{b(z) - a(z)} \int_{a(z)}^{b(z)} \xi(\theta)d\theta,\end{aligned}$$

which holds since $\theta\xi(\theta)$ is an increasing function.

18 Equilibria in Systems with Distortions

Exercise 18.1

We impose the assumptions of Exercise 6.1 on the production and utility functions. These are sufficient to ensure interiority of solutions. Given a k_0, define the sequence $\{k_t\}$ recursively by $k_{t+1} = g(k_t)$. Necessary and sufficient conditions for the optimality of solutions to the planning problem are then given by the Euler equation

$$U'[f(k_t) - k_{t+1}] = \beta U'[f'(k_{t+1}) - k_{t+2}]f'(k_{t+1}),$$

and transversality condition

$$\lim_{t\to\infty} \beta^t U'[f(k_t) - k_{t+1}]f'(k_t)k_t = 0.$$

The result will be proven if we can establish that the solution to the individual consumers problem, evaluated at the market clearing conditions, $x_t = k_t$, implies these equations.

Given x_0, define the sequence $\{x_t\}$ recursively by

$$x_{t+1} = G(x_t, k_t; g).$$

The Euler equation for a consumer is

$$\begin{aligned} &U'[f(k_t) - f'(k_t)k_t + x_t f'(k_t) - x_{t+1}] \\ &= \beta U'[f(k_{t+1}) - f'(k_{t+1})k_{t+1} + x_{t+1} f'(k_{t+1}) - x_{t+2}]f'(k_{t+1}), \end{aligned}$$

while the transversality condition is

$$\lim_{t\to\infty} \beta^t U'[f(k_t) - f'(k_t)k_t + x_t f'(k_t) - x_{t+1}]f'(k_t)x_t = 0.$$

Imposing that $x_t = k_t$ for all t, it is easily seen that this reduces to the Euler equation and transversality condition of the social planner. This implies that $G(k, k; g) = g(k)$ and $V(k, k; g) = v(k)$.

Exercise 18.2

Note that transfer income is not taxed. Given aggregate capital holdings k, the after tax (and transfer) income of an agent with capital x is the sum of wages, rents and transfers, or

$$\begin{aligned}&(1-\alpha)[f(k) - kf'(k)] + (1-\alpha-\theta)xf'(k) + \theta kf'(k)\\ &= (1-\alpha)f(k) + (1-\alpha-\theta)(x-k)f'(k).\end{aligned}$$

Assume that the aggregate savings function h is continuous and denote by $H(x, k; h)$ the optimal policy function of an individual. The functional equation for the individuals problem is then

$$\begin{aligned}W(x, k; h) = \max_y\{&U[(1-\alpha)f(k)+\\ &(1-\alpha-\theta)(x-k)f'(k) - y] + \beta W(y, h(k); h)\},\end{aligned}$$

which has first-order condition

$$\begin{aligned}&U'[(1-\alpha)f(k) + (1-\alpha-\theta)(x-k)f'(k) - H(x, k; h)]\\ &= \beta W_1(H(x, k; h), h(k); h),\end{aligned}$$

and envelope condition

$$\begin{aligned}W_1(x, k; h) = (1-\alpha-\theta)f'(k)U'[&(1-\alpha)f(k)+\\ &(1-\alpha-\theta)(x-k)f'(k) - H(x, k; h)].\end{aligned}$$

In equilibrium, $x = k$ and $H(k, k; h) = h(k)$, and writing $\phi(k) = W_1(k, k; h)$ we get

$$\begin{aligned}&U'[(1-\alpha)f(k) - h(k)] = \beta\phi(h(k))\\ &\phi(k) = (1-\alpha-\theta)f'(k)U'[(1-\alpha)f(k) - h(k)].\end{aligned}$$

To see the equivalence with equations (9) and (10), write $\phi(k) = [(1-\alpha-\theta)/(1-\alpha)]w'(k)$ and substitute $\hat{\beta} = (1-\alpha-\theta)/(1-\alpha)$ and we have exactly equations (9) and (10) for a production function equal to $(1-\alpha)f(k)$.

With the envelope and first-order conditions equivalent, the Euler equations implied by the two problems are the same. It is easily verified that transversality conditions are the same also. Hence the solutions to both problems are the same.

Exercise 18.3

Let h_n be a sequence of functions in $D_\lambda(I_\varepsilon)$ converging to h, and fix $\gamma > 0$. By the argument of Proposition 2, for all k, z and z' in I_ε, there exists an m_2 such that

$$|H(k, z) - H(k, z')| \leq m_2|z - z'|,$$

so that

$$\begin{aligned} |H(k, h_n^2(k)) - H(k, h^2(k))| &\leq m_2|h_n^2(k) - h^2(k)| \\ &\leq m_2\lambda|h_n(k) - h(k)|. \end{aligned}$$

Then setting $\delta < \gamma/(m_2\lambda)$, we have that if $\|h_n - h\| < \delta$, then

$$\begin{aligned} \|Th_n - Th\| &= \sup_{k\in I_\varepsilon} |H(k, h_n^2(k)) - H(k, h^2(k))| \\ &\leq m_2\lambda|h_n(k) - h(k)| \\ &\leq m_2\lambda\delta \\ &< \gamma, \end{aligned}$$

and hence T is continuous.

Exercise 18.4

a. Denote by $D_\lambda^{ND}(I_\varepsilon)$ the space of nondecreasing functions that are also in $D_\lambda(I_\varepsilon)$. Let h and h' be elements of $D_\lambda^{ND}(I_\varepsilon)$ such that $h' \geq h$. We aim to show that $Th' \geq Th$. For any $k \in I_\varepsilon$, we have

$$\begin{aligned} (Th')(k) &= H(k, h'^2(k)) \\ &\geq H(k, h(h'(k))), \end{aligned}$$

from the fact that $H_2 > 0$ on $I_\varepsilon \times I_\varepsilon$, and $h'^2(k) \geq h(h'(k))$. As h is nondecreasing, we have $h(h'(k)) \geq h^2(k)$ so that

$$\begin{aligned} (Th')(k) &\geq H(k, h(h'(k))) \\ &\geq H(k, h^2(k)) \\ &= (Th)(k), \end{aligned}$$

or T is monotone on $D_\lambda^{ND}(I_\varepsilon)$.

Note that in order to apply the above results, we also need to show that $T : D_\lambda^{ND}(I_\varepsilon) \to D_\lambda^{ND}(I_\varepsilon)$. Let $h \in D_\lambda^{ND}(I_\varepsilon)$ and consider $k' \geq k$. Then we have

$$\begin{aligned}(Th)(k') &= H(k', h^2(k')) \\ &\geq H(k, h^2(k)) \\ &= (Th)(k),\end{aligned}$$

where the inequality follows from the fact that h is nondecreasing, and both H_1 and H_2 are strictly positive on $I_\varepsilon \times I_\varepsilon$.

b. By construction, if $h \in D_\lambda^{ND}(I_\varepsilon)$, then $\bar{h} \geq h \geq \underline{h}$. Hence, as $T : D_\lambda^{ND}(I_\varepsilon) \to D_\lambda^{ND}(I_\varepsilon)$, we have $\bar{h} \geq T\bar{h}$ and $T\underline{h} \geq \underline{h}$. Then Theorem 17.7 applies (note that $D_\lambda^{ND}(I_\varepsilon)$ is a closed subset of $D_\lambda(I_\varepsilon)$), and hence $\lim T^n\bar{h}$ and $\lim T^n\underline{h}$ are in $D_\lambda(I_\varepsilon)$ and are fixed points of T.

Exercise 18.5

To see that T is well defined, note that if $h \in F$, then by (2) and (6), there exists a $\widetilde{k} > 0$ (possibly with $\widetilde{k} \geq k^*$), such that $\psi(k) - h(k) > 0$. Hence, by (3), for $y \geq \widetilde{k}$,

$$\beta(1-\theta)f'(y)U'[\psi(y) - h(y)],$$

is finite and decreasing in y. For y approaching zero, we have

$$\begin{aligned}\beta(1-\theta)f'(y)U'[\psi(y) - h(y)] &\geq \beta(1-\theta)AU'[\psi(0)] \\ &> U'[\psi(0)],\end{aligned}$$

where the first inequality comes from Assumption 18.2 and the last inequality comes from Assumption 18.1d.

Note that, for any k

$$U'[\psi(k) - y],$$

is strictly increasing in y with limit, as y approaches $\psi(k)$, of $+\infty$, and limit, as y approaches zero, of $U'[\psi(k)]$. As $\psi(k)$ is nondecreasing in k, and U is strictly concave, we have

$$U'[\psi(k)] \leq U'(0).$$

Hence, for any k, $(Th)(k)$ exists, and the operator T is well defined.

To see that $T: F \to F$, we will verify that each of the properties of F are inherited. If $h \in F$, then Th is continuous by the Implicit Function Theorem, using the continuity of U', f', and f (and hence ψ). The rest are verified in turn.

$0 \le (Th)(k) \le \psi(k)$ for all $k \in K$: fix $k \in K$ and note that for $h \in F$, $U'[\psi(k) - y]$ is continuous in y with

$$\lim_{y \to \psi(k)} U'[\psi(k) - y] = \infty,$$

and $U'[\psi(k)]$ is finite. Similarly, $\beta(1-\theta) f'(y) U'[\psi(y) - h(y)]$ is continuous in y with

$$\lim_{y \to \psi(k)} \beta(1-\theta) f'(y) U'[\psi(y) - h(y)],$$

finite and

$$\lim_{y \to 0} \beta(1-\theta) f'(y) U'[\psi(y) - h(y)] = \infty.$$

Hence, $(Th)(k) \in [0, \psi(k)]$.

Th and $\psi - Th$ nondecreasing: Let $k_1, k_2 \in K$ with $k_2 > k_1$ and $h \in F$. Note that for a given y, the right-hand side of (7) is independent of k while left-hand side is decreasing. Using Figure 18.2, it is clear that the y that solves these equations is nondecreasing. Also, from Figure 18.2, the increase in y is no more than the increase in $\psi(k)$ so that $\psi - Th$ is nondecreasing.

$(Th)(k) \ge k$, all $k \le k^*$: Assume not. Then for some $h \in F$ there exists a $k \le k^*$ such that $(Th)(k) < k \le h(k) \le k^*$. Then

$$\begin{aligned} U'[\psi(k) - h(k)] &> U'[\psi(k) - (Th)(k)] \\ &= \beta(1-\theta) f'((Th)(k)) \\ &\quad \times U'[\psi((Th)(k)) - h((Th)(k))] \\ &> \beta(1-\theta) f'(h(k)) U'[\psi(k) - h(k)], \end{aligned}$$

where the last inequality comes from the fact that f and U are strictly concave, and that $\psi - h$ is nondecreasing. But, as $h(k) \le k^*$, $\beta(1-\theta) f'(h(k)) \ge 1$, which is a contradiction.

$(Th)(k^*) = k^*$: Toward a contradiction, assume first that $(Th)(k^*) > k^*$. Then

$$\begin{aligned}
&U'[\psi(k^*) - k^*] \\
&< U'[\psi(k^*) - (Th)(k^*)] \\
&= \beta(1-\theta) f'((Th)(k^*))U'[\psi((Th)(k^*)) - h((Th)(k^*))] \\
&< \beta(1-\theta) f'(k^*)U'[\psi(k^*) - h(k^*)] \\
&= U'[\psi(k^*) - k^*],
\end{aligned}$$

where the first and last inequalities come from the fact that f and U are strictly concave, and that $\psi - h$ is nondecreasing. A contradiction for the case where $(Th)(k^*) < k^*$ can be derived analogously.

$(Th)(k) \leq k$, all $k \geq k^*$: Assume not. Then for some $h \in F$ there exists a $k \geq k^*$ such that $(Th)(k) > k \geq h(k) \geq k^*$. Then

$$\begin{aligned}
&U'[\psi(k) - h(k)] \\
&< U'[\psi(k) - (Th)(k)] \\
&= \beta(1-\theta) f'((Th)(k))U'[\psi((Th)(k)) - h((Th)(k))] \\
&< \beta(1-\theta) f'(h(k))U'[\psi(k) - h(k)],
\end{aligned}$$

where the last inequality comes from the fact that f and U are strictly concave, and that $\psi - h$ is nondecreasing. But, as $h(k) \geq k^*$, $\beta(1-\theta) f'(h(k)) \leq 1$, which is a contradiction.

Exercise 18.6

To see pointwise convergence, fix $k \in K$ and let $\{g_n\}$ be a sequence of functions converging uniformly to g. For each n, let y_n be the solution (which by Exercise 18.5 is unique) to

$$U'[\psi(k) - y_n] = \beta(1-\theta) f'(y_n)U'[\psi(y_n) - g_n(y_n)],$$

with y denoting the equivalent solution for the function g. If we can show that for all $\varepsilon > 0$ there exists an N such that

$$|y_n - y| < \varepsilon,$$

all $n \geq N$, the proof will be complete.

Fix $\varepsilon > 0$. By the Implicit Function Theorem, the equation

$$U'[\psi(k) - y] = \beta(1-\theta)f'(y)U'[\psi(y) - x],$$

defines a continuous function, call it q, mapping values of x into values for y. If we let $\hat{x} = g(k)$, we then have $\hat{y} = q(\hat{x})$. As q is continuous, there exists a $\delta > 0$ such that if $x' \in B(\hat{x}, \delta)$ we have $q(x') \in B(\hat{y}, \varepsilon)$. But as g_n converges to g in the sup norm, there exists an N such that $\|g_n - g\| < \delta$ for all $n \geq N$. Combining these, we have our result.

To show uniform convergence, fix $\varepsilon > 0$. Equicontinuity of F implies that for each $k \in K$ there exists an open set $V_k \subset K$ such that for all $k' \in V_k$ and for all n

$$|(Tg_n)(k) - (Tg_n)(k')| < \varepsilon/3.$$

As this is true for all n we have

$$|(Tg)(k) - (Tg)(k')| \leq \varepsilon/3,$$

for all $k' \in V_k$.

The compactness of K implies that there exists a finite collection $\{V_{k_1}, \ldots, V_{k_N}\}$ of these sets that covers K. Exploiting pointwise convergence, we can choose M_i for $i = 1, \ldots, N$ such that for all $n \geq M_i$,

$$|(Tg_n)(k_i) - (Tg)(k_i)| < \varepsilon/3,$$

and set $M = \max\{M_i, \ldots, M_N\}$. Then for any $k' \in K$, there exists an $i \leq N$ such that

$$\begin{aligned}
&|(Tg_n)(k') - (Tg)(k')| \\
&\leq |(Tg_n)(k') - (Tg_n)(k_i)| \\
&\quad + |(Tg_n)(k_i) - (Tg)(k_i)| + |(Tg)(k_i) - (Tg)(k')| \\
&< \varepsilon
\end{aligned}$$

for all $n \geq M$. As this ε is independent of k', $\{Tg_n\}$ converges uniformly to Tg on K.

Exercise 18.7

Let $h, \hat{h} \in F$ with $\hat{h} \geq h$. Fix $k \in K$. Then for all $y \in K$,

$$\psi(y) - h(y) \geq \psi(y) - \hat{h}(y)$$

and so

$$U'(\psi(y) - h(y)) \leq U'\big(\psi(y) - \hat{h}(y)\big).$$

Using Figure 18.2 for k fixed, we have that

$$\big(T\hat{h}\big)(k) \geq (Th)(k).$$

As k was arbitrary, the result follows.